THE DRAMA OF CELEBRITY

THE
DRAMA
OF
CELEBRITY

———

SHARON MARCUS

PRINCETON UNIVERSITY PRESS
PRINCETON AND OXFORD

Requests for permission to reproduce material from this work
should be sent to permissions@press.princeton.edu

Published by Princeton University Press
41 William Street, Princeton, New Jersey 08540
6 Oxford Street, Woodstock, Oxfordshire OX20 1TR

press.princeton.edu

Library of Congress Control Number: 2018950975
ISBN: 9780691177595

British Library Cataloging-in-Publication Data is available

Editorial: Anne Savarese and Thalia Leaf
Production Editorial: Ellen Foos
Production: Jacqueline Poirier
Publicity: Jodi Price and Katie Lewis
Copyeditor: Stephen Twilley

This book has been composed in Adobe Text Pro and Futura

Printed on acid-free paper. ∞

Printed in the United States of America

10 9 8 7 6 5 4 3 2 1

CONTENTS

INTRODUCTION

On January 28, 1966, *Life* magazine put a French-born actress named Catherine on its cover. Her long, straight hair cascaded down the page, framing the charming face selected to represent a group of ten "lovely young film stars of Europe." Calling the young women "stars" was something of a misnomer, since all were relative newcomers. But given that *Life* was then enjoying a peak circulation of 8.5 million copies, chances were good that at least some of the featured starlets would soon develop into true celebrities.[1] Each had been handed an express ticket to fame, none more so than the woman showcased on the cover.

What would it take for Catherine's big break to result in true celebrity? If stars achieve their status primarily because they are uniquely gifted, attractive, and interesting people, then the answer would depend on the aspiring performer herself. If the public plays the chief role in determining who becomes a celebrity, then Catherine's success would depend on how well she realized its collective ideals and desires. And if the power to confer stardom resides first and foremost with the media, then publicity alone would do the trick.

Each of these three explanations of how celebrity works has received considerable support among both scholars and the general public. The notion that the media determines celebrity has been especially popular since 1961, when cultural historian Daniel Boorstin declared, "The hero created himself; the celebrity is created by the media." For Boorstin, the celebrity was merely a chimera, "a person who is known for his well-knownness."[2] The idea of being famous only for being famous caught on, as did Boorstin's dire view of celebrity as at best an empty tautology, at worst a mirage imposed on hapless citizens unable to distinguish illusions from reality.[3]

Although the occasional economist has since argued that celebrity culture efficiently sorts for quality, many people still cast stars as deceptive effects of a sinister, monolithic, and all-powerful cause: the media.[4] This account presents celebrities as victims who, despite their prestige, wealth, and apparent success, are nothing but commodities used to sell other commodities: movie tickets, clothes, cars. At the same time, this critique also charges celebrities with victimizing the public by putting a glamorous face on the status quo and propping up the myth that anyone who works hard and has talent can succeed.[5] As inauthentic beings themselves, celebrities allegedly excel at peddling the false dreams manufactured by what Frankfurt School critic Theodor Adorno termed "the culture industry," which he accused of promoting "mass deception" and of impeding "the development of autonomous, independent individuals who judge and decide consciously for themselves."[6] By these lights, fans are passive fools, celebrities are deceptively alluring pawns, media companies are evil puppeteers, and celebrity culture is a hoax that critical thinkers must expose.

The notion that celebrities are famous merely for being famous persists to this day, appealing to laudable desires to resist authority and unmask falsehood. Some dissenters have countered this pessimistic view. Film scholars writing case studies of individual stars have pointed out that many celebrities actively mold their own personae and should be given credit for their spectacular successes. Researchers studying fans who create their own materials and organize their own communities have argued that publics play the key role in sustaining celebrity culture.[7] These three approaches disagree over who wields power. But each concludes that celebrity results when one and only one entity exercises overwhelming force over the others. For some, it is celebrities themselves who charm the media and wow the public. Others believe that the public decides who will be a star. And many still contend that producers, publicists, and journalists determine who will be a celebrity.

There is only one problem with these accounts: this is not how celebrity works. No one entity has the power to determine who becomes a celebrity, not even the media. Consider the woman who landed the prime spot on the cover of *Life* magazine, Catherine Spaak (figure I.1). Catherine who? Exactly. Talented and hardworking, Spaak enjoyed a credible career as a minor singer and actor, but she never became a star. By contrast, another Catherine, accorded a mere third of a page toward the article's end, soon became an international sensation and an icon for the ages: Catherine Deneuve (figure I.2). Known both for her starring roles in critically and commercially successful films and for the famous men with whom she had children, Deneuve became the face of Chanel No. 5 perfume in the

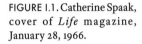

FIGURE I.1. Catherine Spaak, cover of *Life* magazine, January 28, 1966.

FIGURE I.2. "The New Beauties," *Life* magazine, January 28, 1966, pages 46–47.

1970s, starred opposite rock star David Bowie in a 1983 vampire movie, and launched her own perfume and fashion lines. In 1971, she was one of 343 famous French women who publicly acknowledged having had illegal abortions. In 2018, she lumbered into #MeToo territory when she signed an open letter that denounced women protesting harassment as waging war on sexual freedom, then quickly apologized to the many whom her stance offended.

Being showcased on the cover of *Life* in 1966 did not confer stardom on the one Catherine any more than being buried in the story's back pages prevented the other from becoming world famous. No one can become a celebrity without media attention, but media coverage alone does not a celebrity make. Publicists, marketers, and entertainment industries are not omnipotent kingmakers. Stalled campaigns abound.[8] If relentless publicity alone created celebrity, then every one of the many songs that ever benefited from payola would have become a major hit, and every heavily promoted actor would be a star.

A NEW THEORY OF CELEBRITY CULTURE

Celebrity culture is a drama involving three equally powerful groups: media producers, members of the public, and celebrities themselves. Media, star power, and public opinion alone cannot create celebrity, but their interactions can and do. Media producers include journalists, photographers, editors, publishers, directors, producers, and publicists, as well as fans who create original material about their idols and stars who take charge of their own images. Members of the public are so diverse that many scholars (I'm one of them) consider it more accurate to use the plural "publics."[9] Celebrities can range from microstars with 50,000 Instagram followers to superstars like Rihanna, who in 2018 had over 87 million followers on Twitter.

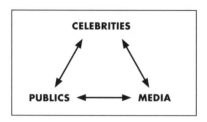

In the drama of celebrity, all three entities—publics, media producers, and stars themselves—have power, and all three compete *and* cooperate to assign value and meaning to celebrities and to those who take an interest in them. Each of the three groups can create, spread, and interpret artful representations of famous people and their followers. Each requires the others in order to play; each can resist and undermine the others or collaborate with and cater to them; and each can, at least temporarily, influence, succumb to, or dominate the other two groups. Sometimes these interactions reinforce dominant values, and figures such as Queen Victoria, Shirley Temple, and Pat Boone come to prominence. Just as often, the drama of celebrity enables its participants to elude social constraints and defy social norms, and outliers such as Oscar Wilde, Muhammad Ali, and Lady Gaga become stars. All three players in the drama of celebrity can form and execute intentions, express preferences, pass judgments, exercise intelligence, and demonstrate initiative. None has perfect power; none is perfectly powerless.

Consider Princess Diana and those who took an interest in her. In 1997, when thousands of people gathered outside Kensington Palace to mourn Diana's sudden death in a car crash (figure I.3), they participated in an event that was not simply staged for the public but created by it.[10] The spontaneous gathering attracted the media, whose coverage then gave voice to the mourners, ordinary people seeking to influence the actions of the royal family. The contest to define the meaning of Diana's death followed a decades-long tussle over who would define her life—itself a

FIGURE I.3. Flowers and mourners at Kensington Palace after Diana's death, September 1997.

proxy for debates about what it meant to be a woman, a mother, a wife, a member of the elite, and, most fundamentally, a human being worthy of admiration. The participants in those debates included the other celebrities in Diana's orbit; the journalists reporting on Diana, often competing with one another for access to her and for the public's interest and attention; and the many people who identified, for diverse reasons, with a privileged person who nonetheless faced challenges similar to their own.

At the center of the struggle to define the princess stood Diana herself. Whether using a photo opportunity to demonstrate that it was safe to touch people with AIDS (figure I.4), leaking information to a biographer, or revealing in television interviews that her husband's infidelities had long preceded hers, Diana knew how to work with the press to reach the public. At her funeral, Diana's brother spoke for many when he accused the media of killing her, but few saw Diana as *simply* the press's victim. Many plausibly considered her a savvy self-presenter who understood contemporary media relations far better than did other members of the royal family. Nor was Diana a villainous mastermind; as biographer Tina Brown observed, one reason that Diana interacted so effectively with the tabloid press was that she herself avidly consumed it.[11]

FIGURE 1.4. Diana, Princess of Wales, and Martin, Mildmay Mission Hospital, February 24, 1989.

Because publics, members of the media, and celebrities themselves all actively shape what it means to be a celebrity and to be interested in celebrities, their contests are too evenly matched for their outcomes to be easily predicted. That unpredictability makes celebrity culture a suspenseful, interactive, serial drama. Though the drama of celebrity has momentary winners and losers, its contests never definitively end; the resulting suspense keeps millions engaged.[12] All three entities in the drama of celebrity have many moves at their disposal. Publics influence media coverage by deciding which stars to follow and which media to consume. They can send letters to editors, post online comments, or, in live settings, choose between boos and applause. Some fans create their own celebrity materials, but most content themselves with collecting and arranging materials produced by others. A few actively seek contact with stars or try to influence them by offering criticism, praise, and advice. Many prefer to idolize celebrities from afar and to experience them as transcendent and overpowering. Celebrities, too, vary in the degree of say they have over their self-presentation and careers. Some cede or lose control to photographers and journalists, while others obsessively craft their own personae and find ways to connect directly with publics. Journalists in turn can position themselves as fans, critics, or influencers, and, in addition to framing how the public views celebrities, also shape how the public views fans. Media producers can even become celebrities themselves: think of gossip columnists Hedda Hopper and Walter Winchell, or photographers Richard Avedon and Annie Leibovitz.

Media companies and platforms do not simply create celebrities; they have to work with them. Well into the twenty-first century, heritage newspapers and magazines seeking to remain iconic brands ally themselves with celebrities in order to attract large followings, as when the *New York Times* and the *New Yorker* sponsor festivals that include television, film, and pop music stars. New media formats have long marketed themselves through celebrities already established in older ones.[13] In the 1890s, the manufacturers of Edison phonographic cylinders recorded dozens of celebrity voices in order to interest people in their new medium, and made sure that the packaging for their new product featured a photograph of renowned inventor Thomas Edison. Early short films attracted audiences by portraying famous royals, politicians, and stage actors.[14] Television, at its inception, featured stars already established in radio and film.[15] And twenty-first-century digital platforms such as Facebook, Twitter, Instagram, Tumblr, and YouTube expanded astronomically after pop stars Lady Gaga, Katy Perry, Beyoncé, Adele, Rihanna, and Taylor Swift began to use them.[16] Sites where the famous rubbed shoulders with the obscure combined the celebrity gala with amateur hour. Some B-list celebrities, such as Ashton Kutcher and Donald Trump, were drawn to Twitter because the relatively new platform helped them to bypass those standing guard at older ones. During the 2016 presidential primaries, many rightfully decried the free publicity that television and the press gave Trump. But the game of celebrity is not that simple, with established gatekeepers exercising top-down control over whom and what they cover. Faced with declining circulations, the press took advantage of Trump's savvy for galvanizing public attention.[17] In advertising Trump, news outlets also advertised themselves.

Journalists and editors make influential decisions about who gets free publicity and what kind of publicity that will be, but the biggest celebrities can break the most formidable company's stride. That is what Taylor Swift did in 2015, when with one Tumblr post—"We don't ask you for free iPhones"—she forced Apple to pay royalties to artists featured on its new music platform.[18] In 2018, singer Rihanna caused the shares of social media platform Snapchat to lose $800 million in a single day when she used

Instagram, where she had over 60 million followers, to criticize a Snap-chat game that had mocked her as a victim of intimate partner violence.[19]

Other celebrities outwit the media and their publics by concealing or spinning the facts. Joan Crawford successfully posed as a doting mother for decades; Prince hid his opioid addiction for years. This does not make those who take an interest in celebrity uniformly gullible or passive con-sumers. Some are skeptical of celebrities, while others push back against the press, as did the armies of "Beliebers" who stood ready in 2016 to defend pop singer Justin Bieber against the mildest criticism, only to turn against Bieber himself soon after.[20] Even the youngest fans enjoy influenc-ing their idols. At age eleven, Grace Bedell wrote to President Abraham Lincoln, successfully suggesting that he grow a beard; child theatergoers convinced J. M. Barrie to change the stage version of *Peter Pan*.[21] Publics enjoy celebrity culture not as mere onlookers but as participants who care about outcomes that they help to determine but cannot fully control.

Adding to the drama of celebrity is the fact that each of its three play-ers constitutes a diverse and internally fractious group. Media proliferate and borrow from one another, vie for influence and market share. Some celebrities join forces, as film stars Charlie Chaplin, Mary Pickford, and Douglas Fairbanks did when, in 1919, they formed United Artists with director D. W. Griffith. Others alternately compete and cooperate, as when great athletes face off against one another in regular-season matches but then join forces on All Star or national teams. Still others cooperate in ways that invite the public to compare them and assess who is best, as when different actors play the same roles on alternating nights. Stars can change direction and find their meanings altered, as when America's beloved First Lady Jackie Kennedy morphed into America's scarlet woman Jackie O. Publics are dynamic and heterogeneous; they do not think or act as one for very long. Fans can be fickle. Someone might gush about a celebrity in one breath and belittle them in the next. Subcultures resist being subsumed by the mainstream and abandon favorites when they become too popular. Niche markets form. Diehard fans argue among themselves, often fiercely, about the best Billy Joel song, whether Jennifer Aniston was better off with Justin Theroux or Brad Pitt, and who was the cutest Beatle. (In 1964, US teenagers voted for Ringo.)[22]

Individuals are also genuinely free to ignore celebrity culture, which makes the drama of who will receive our attention even more volatile and suspenseful. Some of us may feel like captive members of an involuntary public, flooded with celebrity factoids we'd prefer to ignore. But we can opt out. Celebrities do not exist without publics, but publics can and do exist without celebrities. Usually, the most serious consequence for not recognizing a pop star or beloved athlete is a teenager's eye roll or a co-worker's incredulity. No one ever did time for ignoring One Direction or not liking Miley Cyrus. My seven-year-old nephew, on learning that I had never heard of his favorite college basketball player, exclaimed, "What? You've never heard of him? He's only, like, the best college player *in the world.*" Seconds later, I had already forgotten the guy's name. My nephew is still talking to me.

A BRIEF HISTORY OF MODERN CELEBRITY CULTURE

Modern celebrity culture began not with Hollywood, nor with the Internet, but in the eighteenth century, when the modern meanings of the words "celebrity" and "star" first became widespread. Famous people have existed for millennia, but the heroes of ancient Greece and Rome sought eternal renown, while medieval saints attained their canonical status only after death.[23] Celebrities are people known *during their lifetimes* to more people than could possibly know one another. For many centuries, rulers and conquerors were the primary celebrities. Only in the eighteenth century did publics begin to take a strong interest in a large number of living authors, artists, performers, scientists, and politicians.[24] In 1782, philosopher Jean-Jacques Rousseau published an autobiography in which he confessed to spanking fantasies, then complained that everyone was gossiping about him. After basing an 1812 poem on his own life, Lord Byron woke up to find himself famous. By the eighteenth century, a host of performers and authors had stalkers and groupies; by the nineteenth, many received hundreds of letters yearly requesting autographs. Nineteenth-century celebrity chef Alexis Soyer, a French cook based in London, sold his own brand of bottled sauces and put pictures of himself wearing his trademark red beret on the labels (figure I.5).[25] A century before the rise of radio and television commercials, celebrities endorsed wigs, face creams, powders, pianos, and bottled water. Well in advance of charity telethons and stadium concerts such as Live Aid, celebrities held benefits for victims of fires, earthquakes, and yellow fever.[26]

FIGURE I.5. Nineteenth-century advertisement for Soyer's Sauce.

Why did modern celebrity culture emerge when it did? As literacy expanded dramatically among all classes in North America and Europe, so too did the number of those able to read about celebrities. As leisure time increased, more people had more time to visit the theaters, opera houses, and lecture halls where they saw celebrities in person.[27] Even more fundamentally, democratic movements in England, France, and the United States gave rise to a new emphasis on individuality. The Romantic cult of genius that ushered in the nineteenth century led to the fin de siècle worship of personality exemplified by Oscar Wilde. In 1911, a theater producer explicitly speculated that the star system loomed so large in the United States because Americans were what he called "an individual-loving people."[28] New visual media catered to that affection. In the 1860s, affordable, compact photographs of celebrities became widely available in shops and via mail order. In the 1890s, heavily illustrated niche magazines devoted to stage stars began to flourish, anticipating the movie magazines that became popular in the 1910s.[29]

Most importantly, democratization made people eager to track current events that they saw themselves as shaping.[30] Celebrity culture would not have taken off without newspapers, but far from imposing curiosity about famous individuals on the public, newspapers used an already existing fascination with celebrities to attract more readers. Until the 1830s, newspapers in England, France, and the United States were costly publications, sponsored by wealthy patrons and read by a small, select group of subscribers who received their papers by mail. In the 1830s, the news became more commercial. To increase circulation, publishers began to charge readers only a penny instead of the traditional six cents, and began to rely on advertisements, subscriptions, and daily sales, including street sales, to turn a profit. Instead of targeting a select group of insiders willing to pay handsomely for exclusive, specialized information, the new penny press appealed to general interests in an effort to reach the largest number of readers possible.[31] Newspapers were so identified with celebrities that in 1841, when one of the most successful new penny papers purchased its own steamship in order to deliver news from across the Atlantic at record speeds, the publisher named it the *Fanny Elssler*, after a world-famous Austrian ballet dancer who had just toured the United States.[32] Steamships and newspapers helped celebrities to expand their fame; in turn, celebrities helped to attract publics to those novel forms of transport and communication.

As the number of commercial papers grew and competition for readers increased, newspapers found that they could not limit themselves to influencing readers; they also needed to please them.[33] Articles about celebrities, especially when illustrated with lithographs and engravings, were a reliable way to boost circulation.[34] An 1862 issue of the *Illustrated London News* covering the Prince of Wales's marriage sold 930,000 copies, more than three times the magazine's usual circulation rate.[35] Addressing journalism students in 1912, a US newspaperman explained, "In publishing a newspaper you endeavor to print what the people want to read."[36] The people wanted to read about celebrities. In turn, celebrities themselves became aware of the power of the press, even arguing with editors about their coverage. In 1829, for example, two popular actors sent a letter to a London newspaper, addressed "To the Publick," in which they accused the publication of misrepresenting them.[37] The editor published their letter to demonstrate his fairness and to avoid a libel suit, but he also published it because the actors were leading figures in London's theater scene, and celebrity sells.

At the very moment that newspapers first came to depend on publics for their success, technological changes in paper production and printing were making those publics larger than ever before. In the eighteenth century, the most successful newspapers had circulations in the low thousands and information still took weeks to travel between capital cities and the provinces. By 1825, a top-selling Parisian newspaper was reaching 16,000 subscribers; by 1880, the leading Paris daily had more than 500,000 readers.[38] Steamships and railways began to deliver newspapers to readers around the world with unprecedented speed. By the 1860s, transoceanic telegraph cables enabled news to travel around many parts of the world almost instantaneously.[39] By the 1880s, a famous actress could get married in London and have the news published in Paris, Rio de Janeiro, and Chattanooga within a week.

The steamships and railways that delivered the news also delivered celebrities themselves. Many performers, authors, and reformers took advantage of the new mode of travel, crossing the Atlantic to conduct readings and deliver lectures that were nineteenth-century versions of twenty-first-century TED talks. Best-selling British novelist Charles Dickens visited the United States in 1842; in 1845, abolitionist Frederick Douglass traveled to England. Three decades later, extensive railway networks enabled celebrities to easily visit both a nation's major cities and its more obscure nooks and crannies. In the 1880s, star actors Edwin Booth (1833–1893) and Helena Modjeska (1840–1909) could perform in world theater capitals such as Paris, London, Berlin, Warsaw, and New York *and* in small towns ranging from Davenport, Iowa, to Zanesville, Ohio.[40] Performers spent so much time traveling that actor Maude Adams (1872–1953) had sliding scenery installed on her customized train car so that she and her troupe could rehearse between stops.

Cheap postage rates, photography, the penny press, telegraphic news agencies, and steam and train travel all provided channels through which celebrities, publics, journalists, and photographers could interact with one another. They did so long before the rise of the Hollywood studio system.[41] Far from creating modern celebrity culture, movie studios simply adapted one that the theater had invented decades earlier. "Star" was a nineteenth-century term coined in English, along with "étoile" and "vedette" in French, to designate a theatrical troupe's most compelling lead actors. In 1855, a young middle-class woman living in Glasgow announced, "Unless there is some Star in the theatre we do not go."[42] In the twenty-first century, live theater has become a niche form of entertainment, albeit one still able to generate blockbusters such as *Hamilton*. But before the advent of film, millions of people regularly attended the theater each year. In 1865, London shows attracted almost twelve million viewers a year; in 1905, New York City alone had eighteen million theatergoers, with Boston, Philadelphia, and Chicago all competing to host equally vibrant theater scenes. In 1886, the United States had almost three hundred touring theater companies. By 1900, Paris and London each had over a hundred playhouses, many seating around three thousand people.[43] Theatrical networks were global: a hit play might open in London, then travel through the United States; make the rounds of the British Empire; or start out in Paris, then be adapted for performance in Berlin, Stockholm, and New York.[44]

Not surprisingly, given the depth and breadth of the theatrical celebrity system, early film producers used stage stars to lure people to the new medium of cinema. The famous 1896 Thomas Edison film now known as "The Kiss" was originally billed "The May Irwin Kiss," because it featured famous theater performer May Irwin in a popular scene from her hit play *The Widow Jones*. The very term "movie star" existed precisely because stars were presumed to belong to the theater. Many of the most famous early film producers, directors, and performers, including Lillian Gish, D. W. Griffith, Cecil B. DeMille, and Barbara Stanwyck, started on the stage, and some shuttled between Hollywood and Broadway for years.[45]

Though Hollywood did not invent stardom, it did briefly change celebrity culture in one important way. Nineteenth-century theatrical celebrities exercised significant autonomy. They had the power to choose their roles, control their schedules, select supporting casts, design costumes and sets, lease and manage theaters, and craft their public personae. From the 1930s through the 1950s, at the height of the studio system, a few freelance film stars, such as Carole Lombard and James Stewart, retained some of the independence enjoyed by their theatrical predecessors.[46] But most film moguls effectively used restrictive contracts, well-oiled publicity departments, and their influence over the press to control what movie stars could do and what the public could learn about them. During the decades when notoriously dictatorial studio heads Louis B. Mayer, the Warner Brothers, and Harry Cohn reigned supreme, many stars received orders about what roles to play, whom to date, and how to dress.[47] In exchange, they received the support of a powerful, integrated entertainment industry. Stars who balked, such as Bette Davis and Katharine Hepburn, often found themselves subject to retaliation, lawsuits, smear campaigns, and periods of unemployment.

The critics who produced the first serious analyses of celebrity in the 1930s and 1940s had two reference points: the authoritarian Hollywood studio system and the fascist, propaganda-driven personality cults formed around Adolf Hitler and Benito Mussolini. Not surprisingly, given those contexts, those who first theorized celebrity culture had little good to say about it. In 1944, Leo Lowenthal built on Adorno's writings to suggest that nineteenth-century "heroes of production" renowned for their great deeds had devolved into twentieth-century "idols of consumption" best known for the cars they drove and the soaps they bought.[48] Lowenthal got his history wrong—celebrity culture had always included heroes of production *and* idols of consumption—but his audience right. Intellectuals have been decrying the ills of celebrity culture ever since. Although towering figures such as Raymond Williams and Stuart Hall argued for popular culture's utopian, redemptive potential, few have applied those more optimistic frameworks to celebrity culture. In 1977, when Richard Dyer established celebrity studies as an academic field, he took the studio system as paradigmatic of the many other forms of celebrity that preceded, followed, and coexisted alongside it.

Taking 1940s Hollywood as the norm has distorted our understanding of how celebrity culture works by making it seem inevitable that a concentrated power exploits and manipulates both celebrities and publics alike. Not only did Hollywood not invent celebrity, its version of celebrity culture was an aberration. The decline of the film studios in the 1960s, the breakdown of broadcast television that began in the 1980s, and the rise of the Internet since the 1990s have returned celebrity culture to its more anarchic nineteenth-century roots. Today, the fact that no single medium or industry controls stars or stardom has made more visible how strongly publics and celebrities have always influenced the course of celebrity culture and how their moves have been crucial to keeping it alive.

SARAH BERNHARDT, THE GODMOTHER OF MODERN CELEBRITY CULTURE

No one shaped modern celebrity culture more than this book's central figure: actress Sarah Bernhardt, a major star from the 1870s until her death, in 1923. No mere product of modern celebrity culture, Bernhardt also helped to produce it. With her genius for acting matched by a flair for self-promotion, Bernhardt became as well known in her lifetime as Charlie Chaplin, Marilyn Monroe, or Michael Jackson in theirs.[49] Born in Paris, in 1844, to a Dutch Jewish courtesan, she won admission at age sixteen to the prestigious Paris dramatic conservatory, and soon after secured a place in France's revered national theater troupe, the Théâtre-Français. In the late 1860s and 1870s, Bernhardt became a celebrity throughout France, thanks to electrifying stage performances as a young male troubadour, a blind grandmother in ancient Rome, a biracial woman avenging her enslaved mother, and a classic turn as Racine's Phèdre, who falls in love with her own stepson.

Bernhardt's enormous success owed much to the offstage publicity tactics that she devised to capture and hold the attention of the Parisian public. She arranged to be photographed in her own bedroom, sleeping in a coffin (figure I.6), and sat for dozens of other photographs and paintings. After embarking on a hot-air balloon trip in 1878, she wrote a book about it narrated from the perspective of a chair that accompanies her on that adventure. Until Bernhardt established her own acting company, in 1880, she

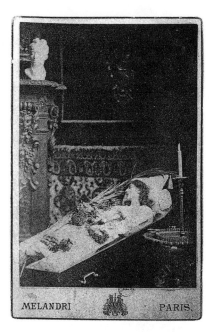

FIGURE I.6. Melandri, photograph of Sarah Bernhardt, circa 1876.

fought constantly with fellow actors and with theater managers; Parisian newspapers reveled in her many battles. By granting interviews and sending frequent letters to editors, Bernhardt sought to influence her press coverage. In 1878, she responded to one newspaper's speculations about her true hair color by dryly observing, "I regret that I cannot prove that I am a natural blonde."[50] In 1879, she considered suing another for claiming that she had not personally executed the paintings she had exhibited at the Paris Salon.[51]

Bernhardt's unusually slender physique, forceful personality, striking fashion sense, transparent ambition, and independence (she had a child without being married, and supported herself financially) ensured that her name, image, and personality attracted press coverage and public attention across France and beyond. Her fame expanded when, in June 1879, she traveled with the Théâtre-Français to London, where thousands—male and female, young and old, aristocratic and middle-class—contracted a major case of Bernhardt mania. Even when performing exclusively in French for audiences who barely understood a word of it, Bernhardt managed to captivate audiences with her exciting presence. Seeking to capitalize on her London success, theatrical agent Henry Edgardo Abbey made Bernhardt a lucrative offer to perform in the United States. The budding international star broke her contract with the Théâtre-Français and embarked on tours of Europe, provincial France, and North America that made her reputation and fortune and established her in a long independent career as a performer, director, and manager.[52] The rest is celebrity history. In 1923, a million mourners witnessed Bernhardt's funeral procession travel from her Paris home to Père Lachaise cemetery, and her name and image dominated international newspaper headlines and magazine covers for weeks after her death.

This book does not tell the story of Bernhardt's life. Instead, it tells the story of her stardom, in order to understand the modern celebrity culture that she helped to invent. Bernhardt appears in each chapter, surrounded not by friends, lovers, and family, as in a conventional biography, but by fans and haters, reporters and reviewers, editors and publishers, photographers and publicists. Each chapter also showcases other influential superstars who preceded and followed her: Lord Byron, Jenny Lind, Oscar Wilde, Marlon Brando, Marilyn Monroe, Elvis Presley, James Brown, the Beatles, Muhammad Ali, Madonna, Lady Gaga, and others. To understand Bernhardt's celebrity, I draw on multiple sources, some familiar, others novel. In charting Bernhardt's life and career, I have benefited greatly from the foundational work of Ernest Pronier, Gerda Taranow, John Stokes, Elaine Aston, Patricia Marks, Noelle Guibert, Carol Ockman, and Kenneth Silver, all authors of superb books on Bernhardt. Their studies make incisive observations about Bernhardt's celebrity. But each focuses on Bernhardt as a singular rather than a representative figure, and none sets out to offer a general theory and history of modern celebrity culture.

Like many before me, I have mined theater archives housed in libraries and museums around the world, from Paris and London to Melbourne and Rio de Janeiro, from New York and San Francisco to Cleveland and Columbus. Archives organized around stars, however, have one significant limitation: people start to collect materials about famous individuals only *after* they have become noteworthy enough to merit documentation. During the many months that I spent in the Bernhardt archives in Paris and London, I encountered almost no material from the years before she rocketed to international stardom, because no archivist would bother to clip articles about someone whose importance had yet to be established. Rich as these archives are, they cannot explain how someone *became* a star.

From the 1860s until the late 1870s, Bernhardt was a respected actress with loyal and enthusiastic followers among Parisians. By 1886, she was a household name on several continents. Her photographs sold by the thousands, her live appearances consistently broke box office records, and her name saturated the news. To understand how Bernhardt became a global celebrity, I tracked down news items published *before* she became the nineteenth century's supreme star, a task facilitated by the recent digitization of many French, British, and US newspapers and magazines. Many of the materials I discuss here are cited for the first time, and allow us to chart how Bernhardt became so famous that for several decades, British newspapers accorded her almost twice the coverage bestowed on Charles Dickens, a native son and best-selling author.[53]

Because celebrity culture is a contest and collaboration among publics, media, and celebrities, newspaper clippings can never be transparent sources of information about a celebrity's personality or achievements. Whether examining how nineteenth-century cartoonists portrayed Oscar Wilde and Sarah Bernhardt or how twentieth-century photographers and reporters wrote about Beatles and Elvis Presley fans, I interpret news items as tactics by journalists, reviewers, and illustrators, approved by editors and publishers, all eager to play a determining role in celebrity's endlessly evolving drama.

Understanding celebrity culture also requires studying the public responses that help to make and break stars, no easy task for the eras before official fan clubs and Internet comments. To learn more about what publics thought about celebrities, I turned to sources rarely used to chart the history of celebrity: scrapbooks, nineteenth-century fan mail, and life writing, a portmanteau genre that includes biographies, diaries, and memoirs. Thanks to the increased literacy and leisure time that characterized the nineteenth century, we have many firsthand accounts written by middle- and upper-class people who dreamed about celebrities and even chased them down streets. Thousands of ordinary theatergoers maintained albums dedicated to recording frequent trips to the theater, and those volumes are an especially precious but overlooked resource for historians of theater and of celebrity (figure I.7).[54]

Scrapbooks perform the invaluable service of placing individual celebrities such as Bernhardt in the context of dozens of other, lesser-known performers. They also offer important information about how audiences interacted with an ever-expanding realm of entertainment and entertainment

FIGURE I.7. Clippings of Julia Marlowe as Lady Macbeth, TRI Scrapbook #111.

journalism. Whenever possible I have cited newspaper articles found in albums, because the fact that an actual theatergoer clipped and preserved them increases their historical significance. Today, the albums preserved in rare book collections often sit neglected, yellowing and crumbling, but these underused sources have a rare capacity to communicate the passionate feelings that celebrities aroused over a century ago. For that reason, scrapbooks play a starring role in many of the chapters to follow.

PREVIEW OF COMING ATTRACTIONS

Unlike most histories of celebrity culture, which focus on change over time, this book highlights continuities, features that have held more or less steady for nearly two centuries, their lease on life renewed with each media revolution. To be sure, much has changed since Bernhardt's heyday. Where her critics lambasted her for being too thin, today's stars find themselves mocked for gaining extra ounces. Most nineteenth-century celebrities were adult men, artists and leaders lauded for their talent and genius, viewed by many as captains of their own fates who deserved their outsized renown. By the twenty-first century, the typical celebrity had become a young female entertainer, often seen as simultaneously exploited and exploitative, and celebrity itself, though still prized, had acquired damningly pejorative connotations. But while many fine points differentiate YouTube celebrities, Hollywood stars, and nineteenth-century theater icons, much has stayed the same since the popular press and commercial photography spawned the first modern celebrities. Now as then, celebrity results from interactions between media producers, publics, and individuals seeking fame or trying to increase it. Sarah Bernhardt, along with those who represented and followed her, invented many of the features of celebrity culture that remain in place to this day. She was one of the first figures to use modern media to achieve truly global celebrity by courting controversy, imitation, and evaluation, as well as one of the first to affect crowds so strongly that many journalists found her supporters alarming. As a pathbreaker who established a template for modern stardom that remains in effect, Sarah Bernhardt was, as celebrities so often are, simultaneously representative and unique.

Each chapter of *The Drama of Celebrity* examines a distinctive configuration of the triangular dramas that define celebrity culture. Chapter 1, "Defiance," asks why large segments of the public so often identify with people who break the rules, even when the press scoffs at the renegades. Chapter 2, "Sensation," explores how journalists and publics alike have long relished the experience of being overpowered by sublimely compelling performers, and asks what celebrities do to have such thrilling effects. Not all journalists approve of the outsized influence that celebrities wield over the public, and chapter 3, "Savagery," shows how media workers eager to challenge star power have long depicted celebrities as unable to control their admirers, whom the press depicts, often in racially charged ways, as violent, unruly outlaws. Chapter 4, "Intimacy," explores how fans seek closeness with celebrities. Some are content to collect, arrange, and bask in materials created by photographers, theater producers, and journalists. Others aim to breach the inherent distance between the anonymous many and the celebrated few by writing letters and bestowing gifts. A rare few contact their favorite stars directly, often to make sexual proposals.

Chapter 5, "Multiplication," explores how celebrity emerges from modern media processes that make replication an engine of singularity. In the 1930s, cultural critic Walter Benjamin argued that the mechanical reproduction of images had destroyed the aura around ancient art objects.

However, his theory also helps us understand the particularly modern halo that surrounds multiples, so that the more copies there are of a person's face or words, the more distinctive he or she appears to be. Chapter 6, "Imitation," focuses on how members of the public seek to emulate celebrities, arguing that the freedom to imitate stars has often been a racial and gender privilege. The final chapters advance what may be this book's most controversial arguments. Chapter 7, "Judgment," shows that publics and journalists often carefully evaluate and rank celebrities' merits, in ways both subjective and objective. Chapter 8, "Merit," demonstrates that many celebrities, far from seeking to hoodwink the media and public, encourage publics and media workers to accurately judge their strengths and weaknesses by comparing them to other celebrated figures.

Celebrity culture is the result of celebrities, publics, and media workers battling and backing one another, uniting and dividing in ways whose outcome can never be foretold with certainty. Agency is everywhere in celebrity culture, and always up for grabs. The resulting mix of familiarity and suspense, reassurance and surprise, is compelling, even addictive. So is the sense that, as members of various publics, our actions—positive, negative, and neutral—help to decide who becomes a celebrity. Whether we love celebrity culture or hate it, follow it avidly or consider it a bore, the drama of celebrity implicates us all. No wonder it keeps so many of us riveted.

CHAPTER 1

DEFIANCE

Why do so many people care so much about celebrities? One common answer to this question is that celebrities embody our cultural ideals.[1] But what of the many celebrities who rise to fame by openly breaking our most cherished rules? Scholar Leo Braudy points to the eighteenth century as the period when people first became celebrated in their lifetimes for displaying nonconformity and indifference to public opinion.[2] Much has changed since then, but defiant celebrity has not gone out of style. Think of John Lennon proclaiming in 1966 that the Beatles were bigger than Jesus; of Madonna announcing in 2015, "I don't follow the rules. I never did, and I'm not going to start"; or of Donald Trump bragging during a nationally televised 2016 presidential debate about the size of his various appendages.[3]

Defiance has its rewards. Although Trump lost the popular vote, he garnered enough electoral votes to become President of the United States. In the 1950s, cult actor James Dean became celebrated for playing noncon-formist characters onscreen and for his eccentric rebelliousness in real life.[4] In 1994, when Madonna broke a record by saying "fuck" fourteen times on a late-night talk show, she only raised its ratings and her own celebrity profile.[5] In 2014, Kim Kardashian defied decorum by posing naked for an online magazine and almost broke the Internet. Others have gained attention by keeping their clothes on. In the 1950s, Marlon Brando became a star thanks to his preference for tight T-shirts and black leather jackets, at a time when most men aspired to gray flannel suits (figure 1.1). Lady Gaga garnered international publicity in 2009 by donning a red-latex creation to meet Queen Elizabeth II. A year later, she topped that statement of sartorial nonconformity by appearing at an award ceremony wearing a garment made of raw beef. (The dress made it to the Rock and Roll Hall of Fame, preserved as a jerky.)

FIGURE 1.1. John
Engstead, photograph
of Marlon Brando, 1951.

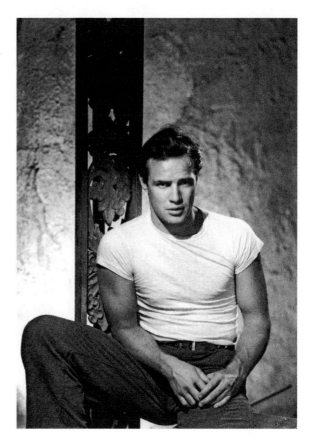

Examples of defiance generating or reinforcing celebrity abound. In the
early 1960s, boxing champion Muhammad Ali became a celebrity not only by
winning major bouts but also by serving as a "symbol of defiance against
an unjust social order."[6] Bragging that he was too fast, too smart, and
too pretty to be defeated, Ali challenged white America's expectations of
deference from African Americans. In a famous declaration of independence the morning after winning his first heavyweight title, Ali told the
press, and the world, "I don't have to be who you want me to be; I'm free to
be who I want."[7] After choosing to be sent to jail rather than be inducted
into an army fighting the Vietnam War, Ali lost some of his best years as
an athlete, but his principled resistance only cemented his celebrity. In
1992, emerging rock star Sinead O'Connor shaved her head, explaining to
a magazine, "I don't conform . . . to an acceptable image of a woman . . .
I just say what I think."[8] O'Connor became even better known after ripping
up a picture of the Pope on *Saturday Night Live* in order to protest child
abuse within the Roman Catholic church. While O'Connor saw her career

suffer as a result, others have found that challenging deeply held proprieties only increased their appeal, at least with some publics. Donald Trump was already a reality TV star when he ran for president in 2016. Early in his campaign, he attracted millions of outraged critics after he slurred Mexicans, mocked a disabled reporter, and boasted about committing sexual assaults. But Trump also garnered millions of admirers, and reporters had no trouble finding many Americans willing to go on record hailing him as an unapologetic maverick willing to defy political correctness.

For better and for worse, celebrities have long attracted interest and even adoration for being unruly. Why?

CELEBRITY AND THE STATE
OF SOCIAL EXCEPTION

One might reasonably expect large numbers of people to condemn, shame, and shun outliers. Why, then, are rampantly defiant celebrities often so popular? Social theorist Erving Goffman offers some answers. When Frenchman Émile Durkheim established sociology as an academic discipline in the 1890s, he focused on how society promoted cohesion by encouraging conformity and by placing checks on individual egotism. Goffman, the most influential sociologist of the twentieth century, saw himself as an heir to Durkheim but devoted much more attention than his predecessor had to the question of how individuals *resist* social rules and demands. In his groundbreaking ethnographic analysis of life inside *Asylums* (1961), for example, Goffman identified the small but significant ways in which inmates defied the rules imposed by total institutions. They might answer questions sullenly, or refuse to answer at all, or place laundry to dry on a radiator. These apparently slight acts each constituted "a movement of liberty" that allowed inmates to refuse "the official view of . . . what sort of self and world they are to accept for themselves."[9] Unlike Durkheim, Goffman saw society as doing more than promoting conformity. In his view, society itself allows individuals to limit the limits placed on them by social claims. A certain amount of socially sanctioned "recalcitrance" becomes essential both to social relations and to securing the self, with individuals emerging as individuals by positioning themselves "*against something.*"[10]

Defiant celebrities speak to a paradoxically social investment in fantasies of anti-social autarky. The public attachment to shameless nonconformity

points to a craving for what critic Roland Barthes called the "distance without which there can be no human society."[11] Celebrities, by boldly making
their shows of defiance *public*, do more than simply display unconventionality. They model an emotional attitude of indifference to nonconformity's
potential consequences. In 1891, a reporter for the *Boston Herald* noted
that actress Sarah Bernhardt's "special boast" was "that she does what she
pleases on all occasions and doesn't hold herself amenable to any law." The
article then quoted her directly: "Whenever I want to do anything I do
it. . . . untrammeled by any consideration of what others may think or what
may happen."[12] At least one journalist explicitly surmised that Bernhardt
could "boast" of doing as she pleased and openly break social rules because
the public gave her bad behavior its "vulgar condonation." Though "vulgar" suggested that he himself disapproved, the celebrity and her mass of
admirers ignored his criticism.[13] Decades later, a *Saturday Review* article
similarly speculated that James Dean "provided a symbolic channel" for
the public's "own rebellions against the pressures of conformity."[14] And
a Beatles fan trying to understand why John Lennon was her favorite attributed her crush to his overt defiance: Lennon "didn't care what anyone
else thought of him," even allegedly announcing, however implausibly,
"I'm not going to change the way I look or the way I feel to conform to
anything."[15] With statements like those, celebrities make themselves into
beacons for everyone who aspires to free-wheeling defiance.

Defiant celebrities perform shamelessness. In another classic work,
Stigma: Notes on the Management of Spoiled Identity (1963), Goffman argues that society does not simply shun or mock those who do not fit a
norm. It exacts a steeper price by requiring the stigmatized to recognize a
society that manifestly does not recognize them in return, and by seeking
to shame the stigmatized into averting their gazes and concealing their
damaged selves. Defiant celebrities reverse this social dynamic in two
ways: they obtain recognition from others without returning the favor,
and they display indifference to rejection in ways that challenge society's
regulatory power. Sometimes this defiance is charming: think Sarah Bernhardt, Marlon Brando, Madonna. At other times, it is appalling: think
Donald Trump.[16] But the appeal is the same. If shame consists of covering
weaknesses and abnormalities and hiding when they are exposed, shameless stars make a show of demanding credit for their obvious indifference
to exposure or censure.

Celebrities who shamelessly display their lack of normalcy are the
bolder equivalent, in the domain of leisure and entertainment, of inmates

drying their clothes on asylum radiators. The widespread affection that many publics feel for openly defiant actions suggests that ordinary people often identify with figures who publicly enact the fantasy of enjoying society's benefits without having to pay its costs. Referring to the common metaphor of "face" for saving or losing one's honor, Goffman reminds readers that no one can confer status on him or herself. Face is an individual's most personal possession, but it is only on loan from society, which will cause anyone who behaves in a disapproved way to lose face.[17] Celebrities dare to show their faces even when behaving badly. They flaunt indifference to the consequences of defying society and appear to deny social debts while claiming boundless social credit. While this may offend us as shareholders in the social collective, it appeals to a common wish to be freeloaders, shirking the obligations created by our dependence on others. Social belonging comes at a cost: society demands conformity, and then asks those who fail to conform to participate in their own exclusion by feeling shame. Who at some point does not dream of reaping the rewards of social belonging without paying the price of social admission?

If celebrity defiance so powerfully symbolizes social dynamics, can it also change them? Sometimes. Helen Keller, Muhammad Ali, Nina Simone, Harry Belafonte, and Lady Gaga are examples of celebrities who used their influence to fight discrimination against racial and sexual minorities; Gaga, for example, made videos encouraging fans to call their elected representatives to protest homophobic government policies. Celebrities as disparate as Charles Dickens, Paul Newman, U2's Bono, and Emma Watson have used their fame to further humanitarian political causes. In 2017, a group of female celebrities, working closely with investigative journalists, sparked a collective outcry when they publicly denounced Harvey Weinstein, a powerful film producer, for having sexually harassed and assaulted them. Their actions inspired close to two million women to participate in a social media campaign, #MeToo, that drew attention to pervasive sexual violence.

Nonetheless, society tolerates defiant celebrities best when they do not seek to have broad social effects. Sarah Bernhardt, despite her own flamboyant independence, never consistently defended women's rights. Stars who suspend or circumvent norms usually do so for themselves alone, not for others. Defiant celebrities occupy what we might call *a state of social exception*, a playpen for the antisocial that creates a highly visible zone of freedom for a few celebrated figures without extending those liberties to anyone else. Although some contended that by defying "all the laws of life,"

Bernhardt "inspire[d] others to do so," Bernhardt herself never claimed that goal.[18] In politics, a state of exception exists when a ruler suspends the law but continues to exercise power. In a state of social exception, an individual suspends adherence to a social norm while still asserting membership in society. If this is experienced as an affront to society, it is, and all the more so when the obstreperous individual does *not* claim to act on behalf of others.

Social exceptions claim the power to rewrite existing social rules for themselves without soliciting the consent of others. Many come from stigmatized groups and showily refuse to acquiesce in society's denigration of them, while still demanding social recognition. What differentiates the state of social exception from a political one is its limited scope. Social exceptions do not enforce their demands with military or police violence. Nor do they often seek to institute new social norms, even when advocating new public policies. Lady Gaga invited her "little monsters" to call their representatives and to relish her outré style, but she never suggested that, like her, they should wear dresses made of meat.

Social exceptions are a paradox: by resisting social demands, they often win the very social awards of wealth and status. Shameless celebrities capture public attention and even elicit adulation by displaying abnormalities rather than hiding them. Complex societies generate fantasies of individual autonomy and omnipotence; celebrity outliers cater to those fantasies. While some outliers plead for tolerance or aspire to assimilation, many dare to presume privilege for themselves alone, and often the public loves them for it. Defiant celebrities appeal not only to the marginal and to the outcast, but to anyone who has ever wanted to bypass conventions, gatekeepers, and experts, or who has savored the prospect of receiving society's benefits without reciprocating them—which is to say, at one point or another, just about all of us.

THE BIRTH OF CELEBRITY DEFIANCE

How long has this been going on? Although we now think of the nineteenth century as an era of extreme conformity, it too had its share of celebrities who attracted popular acclaim by manifesting deliberate indifference to social norms. Even at the time, some commentators voiced their awareness that blatant defiance could garner public admiration on a mass scale.

An 1887 book about *Celebrities of the Century*, for example, singled out Napoleon's "matchless audacity" as the key to his eminence, and novelist and drama critic Henry James identified "unblushing . . . impudence" as the quality most likely to speed the way to celebrity.[19]

Today we tend to remember Oscar Wilde (1854–1900) as an outcast, a gay martyr to English hypocrisy who was sentenced to prison in 1895 for gross indecency, a vague term that criminalized any sexual contact between men. But we should also remember his earlier life as a celebrity rewarded for his overt repudiation of normalcy. In the early 1880s, when most men grew sober beards and wore dark suits, Wilde sported shoulder-length locks and gave lectures while wearing a velvet jacket, knee-length breeches, and shoes trimmed with bows (figure 1.2). A character based on Wilde in an 1894 novel languidly opined, "The art of life is the art of defiance. . . . To know how to be disobedient is to know how to live."[20] At a time when many considered work the path to success and purpose in life, Wilde became famous for what a fashion magazine of the day identified as "paradoxical, audacious" aphorisms such as "hard work is simply the refuge of people who have nothing to do."[21] No one thought any of this was normal, but Wilde's very outrageousness made him a celebrity. Indeed, Wilde advertised himself as liking to annoy the public—because the public "likes to be annoyed."[22] As one observer put it in 1895, "Oscar Wilde has ever been an eccentric man, and by his eccentricity he became popular."[23]

Rising to fame through rebelliousness was not simply a late nineteenth-century phenomenon, nor was it available solely to men. In 1830s and 1840s France, the female novelist Aurore Dupin, born in 1804, who published under the pseudonym George Sand, attracted notoriety by dressing as a man and flaunting the many other ways that she had "shaken herself free from

FIGURE 1.2. Oscar Wilde lecturing in the United States, 1882.

the bonds of custom," as Henry James put it.[24] Sand, who went on to become one of the century's best-known authors, took the first name of her pseudonym, George, from a figure who achieved global notoriety early in the nineteenth century, Romantic poet George Gordon Byron. Born in 1788, Byron was a prototypical celebrity rebel who acquired popularity thanks to his poetic talent, good looks, sexual bravado, and the pleasure he displayed in his own nonconformity.[25] Like many Romantic artists, Byron embraced an aesthetic that valorized liberty over artistic rules and social conventions. Literary critic William Hazlitt, who profiled contemporary authors for periodicals in the 1810s and 1820s, chastised Byron for being a "creature of his own will" who "scorns all things" and "cares little what it is he says, so that he can say it differently from others." In Hazlitt's view, Byron acted this way on purpose, choosing to "shock the public" out of "a conscious sense that this is among the ways and means of procuring admiration."[26] Byron himself might not have disagreed. Commenting knowingly on his success "in the teeth of so many prejudices," the poet speculated, "I almost think people like to be contradicted."[27] Not caring what others thought was as compelling to the public as not doing what others did.

Celebrity culture thrives because many choose to admire a few who defy conventions that most people embrace. The majority of Byron's fans were not rebels themselves, but they keenly enjoyed his open, arrogant disregard for widely accepted social prejudices. Those who adored the bad boy poet ignored experts, such as Hazlitt, who positioned themselves as aesthetic and moral arbiters. Hazlitt was immune to Byron's charms as only a professional journalist could be; after all, he and the poet were competing for the public's attention, and the poet was winning. For Hazlitt to interest readers, he had to write about well-known figures such as Byron. For Byron to wake up and find himself famous (as historian Thomas Macaulay described the poet's overnight success), he had only to hint that his 1812 poem *Childe Harold* was a confessional self-portrait.

Byron, Sand, and Wilde all thrived in notably turbulent times and places: Byron during the Napoleonic wars, Sand during the 1830 and 1848 revolutions in France, Wilde during the fin de siècle. What of celebrities who rose to fame in Europe and the United States during periods marked by placid respectability? Ralph Waldo Emerson, writing in 1841, charged that "the virtue in most request is conformity," while John Stuart Mill warned in his 1859 essay *On Liberty* that the social "tyranny" of "prevailing opinion and feeling" threatened to stifle individual diversity, spontaneity, and freedom.[28] In some respects, nineteenth-century celebrity culture justified Emerson's and Mill's anxieties, since many of its icons did embody highly conventional values. The Duke of Wellington, whose 1852 London funeral drew some of the century's largest crowds, embodied British bravery thanks to his military victories. Queen Victoria cloaked her anomalous power as a female monarch in public displays of wifely deference and maternal domesticity. Impresario P. T. Barnum advertised Swedish opera singer Jenny Lind as a paragon of sweetness, innocence, and altruism, an early embodiment of twentieth-century stars boasting clean-cut images: plucky Shirley Temple, perky Doris Day, and wholesome Pat Boone.[29] Publics across Europe and North America were equally inclined, however, to celebrate individuals brazen enough to flaunt their oddity. Mill's and Emerson's ideas cannot account for the many nineteenth-century figures who became popular not despite but *because* of their unruly individuality.

Consider Sarah Bernhardt, who from her very first interviews in the 1870s presented herself as the quintessential outsider: the least favorite daughter of a neglectful, hostile mother, and an illegitimate child baptized Christian and educated at a convent, but open about her Jewish origins.[30] Anecdotes about Bernhardt's defiance multiplied from the outset of her career. While training at France's elite acting conservatory, she gained a reputation for insubordination that only increased after she joined the Théâtre-Français, the prestigious national theater. So identified was Bernhardt with extreme rebelliousness that when an 1864 newspaper reported on the twenty-year-old actress's refusal to cooperate with a theater manager, they equated her "desire to recover her liberty" and "break her chains" with the ravings of a rabid dog that had escaped its owner's control.[31]

"TOO THIN"

Bernhardt's earliest instance of defiance, when she first rose to fame in the 1860s and 1870s, may surprise us today. In a 1900 interview, Bernhardt recounted how in 1866 a theater manager had refused to hire her, "because he considered me 'too thin'! Yes, it was extraordinary, but that was his objection."[32] So strongly did this quality define the young Bernhardt that when a hack journalist decided to profit from the Bernhardt craze by publishing an 1880 book about her famous peculiarities, he chose as his title: *Too Thin, or Skeleton Sara* (figure 1.3).[33]

Jokes about Bernhardt's weight were rampant during the earliest phase of her celebrity, with many finding her unusual slenderness the most offensive thing about her. Nineteenth-century journalists wrote openly that male theatergoers (evidently the only ones whose opinions mattered) preferred "big dolls" endowed with a "ton of solid flesh" to a "frail and lanky Jewess" like Sarah Bernhardt, whom one journalist described as too small-breasted to need to get anything off her chest.[34] By contrast, a drama critic described Sarah's plump younger sister Jeanne, also a performer, as a "pretty blonde" whose physical charms alone could offset the boredom of the play in which she appeared.[35] Jeanne's lack of talent was deemed less off-putting than Sarah's lack of cleavage. In 1880, an anonymous author published a set of cartoons that claimed to tell the story of how Bernhardt had slept her way to the top.[36] That narrative bore little relationship to any stories about Bernhardt circulating in the global press, and the illustrator could only make his salacious tales plausible by turning the star into a curvy ingenue (figure 1.4) who bore no resemblance to the slender woman portrayed in photographs or lampooned by other cartoonists.

Journalists objected both to Bernhardt's weight, which she could not control, and to her decision to display her unconventional body in public, which she could. When a writer for the *Boston Daily* denounced Bernhardt as a "lawless" woman who did "nothing like other people," his chief example of her nonconformity was her pride in her leanness, which led her to exaggerate her "defect" instead of trying to hide it.[37] Curvy hips and ample bosoms were in such demand in the 1860s and 1870s that journalists responded to Bernhardt's self-display with a venom that resembled, a century later, that of film critics such as John Simon mocking Barbra Streisand for presenting herself as a sex symbol, or of online commenters who insulted aspiring director and performer Lena Dunham for a 2007 video of herself wearing a bikini and splashing in a fountain.[38] In Dunham's case, thousands expressed anger and revulsion that a woman so obviously unskinny would dare to display her nearly nude body by choice.[39] Dunham refused to back down: "People called me fat and hideous, and I lived."[40] She continued to cast herself in graphic sex scenes in her first film and in her HBO series *Girls* and soon became another example of a celebrity whose defiance attracted a huge public following despite mostly unsympathetic press coverage. Bernhardt similarly refused to hide a body

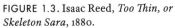

FIGURE 1.3. Isaac Reed, *Too Thin, or Skeleton Sara*, 1880.

FIGURE 1.4. Cartoon from *Sarah Bernhardt: Paris Sketches*, 1880.

that journalists and cartoonists reviled as spectacularly ugly. When posing for photographers and painters, as in an 1876 portrait by Georges Clairin (figure 1.5), she adopted tight-fitting skirts, long gloves, and close bodices that exaggerated what was then considered her deviant skinniness. Instead of demurely turning her head to the side, as most of her fellow actresses did when posing for photographs and paintings (see "Multiplication"), her bold gaze challenged viewers to meet her stare.

Celebrity culture is a contest of wills among the public, media workers, and celebrities themselves over who will become a celebrity and what the celebrity will signify. Male journalists perceived Bernhardt's self-presentation as an affront to their authority as tastemakers and gatekeepers. They were right to do so. Women like Bernhardt challenged fourth-estate judges who sought to prohibit those who did not meet their rigid standards of feminine beauty from appearing in public. She undermined the masculine privilege of evaluating women on the basis of appearance alone and deciding which ones deserved attention and which were to be ignored. And she did so by

FIGURE 1.5. Georges Clairin, *Portrait of Sarah Bernhardt*, 1876.

finding ways to appeal directly to the public, where she found far more admirers than among the press.

To be sure, some of the jokes about Bernhardt's weight were light-hearted attempts at humor designed to capitalize on her celebrity. Commercial newspapers often printed sallies about well-known figures in order to sell more copies in a highly competitive market. As Bernhardt put it, journalists fattened themselves on her skinniness.[41] One wit described her as having "lots of grace but very little grease."[42] When British newspaper *Funny Folks*, circulation 60,000 copies a week, printed a brief article on "Sarah's Future," the main point (as so often in British humor of that era) was to generate puns: "To exhaust the list of her talents she may possibly take a studio in the fashionable vicinity of Lank-aster Gate, and devote herself to skull-pture."[43]

Many of the jokes about Bernhardt's weight in French newspapers, however, had a more hostile edge. Like the *National Enquirer* reporting with lurid glee on the weight gains of Elizabeth Taylor or Oprah Winfrey, Parisian journalists (almost all male) cruelly ridiculed Bernhardt for not conforming to their standards of female beauty. *Le Figaro*, a conservative Parisian daily whose circulation grew from 50,000 in 1872 to 80,000 by 1890, made a particular point of mocking Bernhardt's body.[44] One of the paper's quips suggested that Bernhardt, in one of her sculptures, had based the figure of an aged grandmother on herself, because that was the only way she could ever become a model.[45] Others compared her and her body parts to bones, skulls, and skeletons.[46] A host of French, British, and American newspapers reprinted a bon mot about the Clairin painting of Bernhardt (figure 1.5) lounging on a sofa with a slender greyhound at her feet: "Look, a dog and its bone."[47]

Other jokes expressed a wish to cut the already tiny actress down to size. Several compared her to diminutive objects such as hatpins and toothpicks. One newspaper item jested about a room so crowded that even Sarah Bernhardt could not make her way in, another about an empty carriage driving up to a theater and Sarah Bernhardt descending from it.[48] Some imagined her disappearing altogether. One squib described the "celebrated actress" being challenged to a "contest of thinness" by another "attenuated young lady," only to wonder how a prize could even be awarded to "a veritable 'invisible girl.'"[49] Another imagined a concrete slab falling on the star, who avoids being crushed by pressing herself into a shallow indentation in the sidewalk.[50]

Some jokes implied that by being so slight, Bernhardt was withholding from male spectators what they most craved. One reported that an audience member had thrown a loaf of bread at Bernhardt in the middle of a play, yelling, "I don't like skinny women; I want her to fatten up."[51] An 1870 item imagined someone in front of a Bernhardt portrait commenting on her lack of cleavage by exclaiming, "What a desert!"[52] An 1874 joke similarly imagined Bernhardt failing to satisfy even an insect's appetite: "I just found a flea in Madame Sarah Bernhardt's dressing room. It must be hungry!"[53] In these jokes, hunger is something Bernhardt causes rather than suffers, and journalists attack the slender actress for depriving men (and even fleas) of the female sustenance she so visibly lacked.

FIGURE 1.6. Manuel Luque, caricature of Sarah Bernhardt, *Supplément du Monde Parisien*, circa 1882.

By displaying herself in all her skinniness and ignoring reporters' wishes that she either disappear or change her looks, Bernhardt showed a blatant lack of shame about her lack. She did so as a social exception, never seeking to establish a new style for thinness. By the time Coco Chanel successfully did that, in the 1910s, Bernhardt had long been a comfortably upholstered grandmother. But in the 1870s, when journalists lobbed jokes at Bernhardt to make her pay for showing her anomalous, undesirable body in a public space that they claimed to oversee, they soon found themselves defeated by the "too thin" woman, who charmed the public into liking her precisely for her defiant ways and despite her bad press. As we saw with Hazlitt's profile of Byron, publics had long enjoyed ignoring appointed experts, and theatergoers loved Bernhardt.[54] A cartoon portraying her as a broom sweeping up gold coins mocked her unusual body type but also acknowledged that the scrawny actress was laughing all the way to the bank (figure 1.6).

"LA REVOLTÉE"

In 1878, ever "la revoltée" (the rebellious woman), Bernhardt caused a new scandal by chartering a free-floating hot air balloon that could ascend as high as 2,300 meters and travel well beyond Parisian city limits.[55] Émile Perrin, the director of the theater employing Bernhardt at the time, explicitly forbade her to undertake balloon travel because of the risk of injuries. The "self-willed" actress refused to obey his directives.[56] Defying gravity to launch herself into an aerial realm inaccessible to most travelers, Bernhardt seized what literary critic Margaret Cohen has identified as the "amoral freedom of movement" associated with the protagonists of adventure fiction.[57] The decade before, poet Victor Hugo had hailed balloon travel as "a key to open the cage of tyranny," evoking the bold patriots, enterprising scientists, and daredevil performers then associated with ballooning.[58] Bernhardt responded to the criticism leveled at her by the press and by her theater director by upping the ante and publishing an 1878 book about her aerial travels, *Dans les nuages* (figure 1.7).[59] The book's narrator, a chair that Bernhardt brings aboard the balloon, serves as both model and foil for the female celebrity seeking to exchange objectification

FIGURE 1.7. Sarah Bernhardt, *Dans les nuages: Impressions d'une chaise*, 1878.

for sovereignty. Journalists grumbled and mocked. The public made the book a best seller.

In April 1880, Bernhardt courted further controversy by definitively breaking her contract with the venerable Théâtre-Français, also known as the Comédie-Française, an organization that most actors joined for life, to embark as a free agent on highly successful tours of Europe, provincial French cities, and North America. When visiting London in June 1879 as a member of the Théâtre-Français, Bernhardt had experienced firsthand that the public took far more interest in her than in other company members. Her individual success abroad had sparked negative press back home. Parisian journalists rebuked her for stealing the limelight from other actors, cancelling performances, mixing with British society, exhibiting her sculptures in Piccadilly, allegedly wearing pants in public, and threatening to resign from the Comédie-Française after being forced to perform in Émile Augier's *L'Aventurière*. Always willing to obtain more press by protesting the coverage she was already receiving, Bernhardt sent long exculpatory telegrams to leading Parisian theater critics and requested that French newspapers publish them. More articles resulted, suggesting that Bernhardt was being disloyal to France by seeking fame abroad.

When Bernhardt announced in April 1880 that she would soon under-take a tour of the United States and Canada, the news had an impact in France similar to reports a century later of Soviet ballet dancers defect-ing to the United States. One article about her resignation began: "It is necessary to speak of Mlle Sarah Bernhardt's rupture with the Comédie-Française, because everyone is talking about it."[60] For the next three months, French newspapers presented a curiously divided image of the star: headlines about the "Triumphal Voyage of Mlle Sarah Bernhardt in Holland" and front-page reports about her performances in London ap-peared side by side with lengthy transcripts of the lawsuit underway at the Tribunal Civil de la Seine, where the Théâtre-Français was asking to seize the roughly 40,000 francs in reserve funds that the "fugitive" artist had left invested in the company, while also claiming 300,000 francs in damages.[61] French journalists wrote mockingly of the interest that the British press was taking in the case, but their own detailed attention to the suit belied their professed attempts to distance themselves from it. By the 1890s, French journalists would interpret Bernhardt's break with the Théâtre-Français as expressing her deep "desire for liberty," but at the time of her resigna-tion reporters were more likely to describe her as an outlaw, "in a state of rebellion" against France itself.[62]

A year later, however, Bernhardt won back French reporters with yet another act of defiance, this time directed at a foreign power. In late June 1880, Bernhardt lost the suit brought against her by the Théâtre-Français, though the judge fined her only 100,000 francs instead of the much larger amount requested by the theater's administration. Two months later, she performed in Copenhagen and attended a supper at the Hotel Royal given in her honor by Danish notables, with about three hundred guests present—a sign of the esteem Bernhardt already enjoyed as a European star. Dur-ing the dinner, a Prussian minister, Baron Magnus, gave a toast: "I drink to France, which gives us such great artists, to the beautiful France [*la belle France*], which we all love!" In 1870, Prussia had summarily defeated France in a war that led to the German empire's incorporation of the previ-ously French territories of Alsace and Lorraine. A decade later, that loss still rankled. When the Prussian minister approached his glass to Bernhardt's, she rebuffed him: "Pardon me, Baron, my glass is empty." That empty glass, however, did not stop the star from standing to improvise a toast of her own: "I drink to the Danish people, the royal family of Denmark, from whom I have received such good hospitality, and, like the minister

of Prussia, I drink to France, but to all of France, is that not right, Baron?"
Bernhardt's riposte unleashed a torrent of applause among the Danes, who
had their own reasons to resent Prussian expansionism.[63]

French reporters reveled in the incident. Bernhardt seized control of the
headlines by offering Parisian journalists a chance to hail her as France's
defender. Most reports at the time evoked only the national politics involved, but gender politics were also in play. By pointing out that her glass
was empty and forcing the Baron to drink to her toast instead of consenting
to drink to his, Bernhardt wittily rejected his suggestion that she, like "la
belle France," was there for Prussia's taking. On this metaphorical field of
battle, Bernhardt impudently positioned herself as a warrior rather than
as spoils. Her retort made international headlines, some as much about the
coverage of the event as about the event itself. A US newspaper commented
that the toast had produced "very sensational accounts" in the press, and
British humor magazine *Judy* printed comic verses cheekily saluting the
actress's dual ways of dominating the world stage: "So bless brave Sarah
Bernhardt / Who the Prussian eagle smackt, / And came to Albion's shores
to teach / Our actors how to act!"[64] Even the French reporters who had so
recently hectored Bernhardt for leaving the Théâtre-Français appreciated
her defiance now that she was directing it against France's chief enemy.
The report of the event on the front page of *La Presse* bore the headline
"A New Joan of Arc."[65] When Bernhardt visited Marseille later that fall,
she found herself serenaded not with "La Marseillaise" but with a tune
entitled "Alsace-Lorraine."[66]

Episodes such as these illustrate why one admiring reporter entitled
an article about the actress "Sarah Bernhardt—Superwoman" and why
Bernhardt could plausibly make statements such as this one: "My life has
been a struggle—a struggle to have my own way where I felt I was in the
right."[67] Often, the press resented Bernhardt for being well-known enough
to elude its control, while publics around the world admired her for being
a "rare creature" who sought "independence and freedom of movement."[68]
Indeed, journalists themselves often observed that Bernhardt sparked the
public's curiosity precisely because she did not do as others did.[69] An
article in the US humor magazine *Puck* imagined Walt Whitman, a free-
spirited poet who celebrated the masses, telling the actress: "Blast your
impudence!—I like it."[70] Henry James, less sympathetically, similarly lik-
ened Bernhardt to a "sort of fantastically impertinent *victrix* poised upon
a perfect pyramid of ruins—the ruins of a hundred British prejudices and

SARAH BERNHARDT AS MRS. CLARKSON.
[IN THE FRENCH VERSION OF "THE STRANGER"]

FIGURE 1.8. Sarah Bernhardt as Mrs. Clarkson, circa 1880.

proprieties."[71] Even her harshest critics agreed that Bernhardt succeeded not despite her unconventionality but because of it: she stamped on the world's "prejudices" only to "wring applause from reluctant judgment."[72]

Throughout her career, Bernhardt's choice of stage parts reinforced her aura of intentional difference. One of the early roles in which she made her mark, Mrs. Clarkson in Alexandre Dumas fils's *L'Etrangère*, succeeded because of Bernhardt's ability to personify languid but confrontational insolence (figure 1.8). As soon as the star had the power to choose her own roles, she gravitated to excess and "luxurious criminality," often playing adulterous wives (Phèdre, Frou-Frou); domineering monarchs (Theodora, Cleopatra); and women in love with brigands and nihilists (Fedora).[73] As a disapproving Boston critic put it in 1906, "The divine Sarah never portrays the character of a conventionally chaste and healthy-minded woman."[74] As a more sympathetic reviewer put it in 1895: "Bernhardt would lose half her charm if she obeyed on the stage the ordinary rules of conduct"; the part that suited her best was "that of a woman whose only law lies in her passions."[75] Even after a leg amputation reduced Bernhardt to performing prone, on a litter, she

FIGURE 1.9. Melandri, photograph of Sarah Bernhardt sculpting, circa 1876.

retained her zeal for embodying extravagantly violent women. In 1916, at the age of seventy-two, Bernhardt added to her repertoire a one-act drama whose protagonist kills her unfaithful lover, then herself, with what some critics described as a hatpin, others as a needle—all while reclining on a couch, clad in a kimono.[76]

Bernhardt's offstage persona was equally unusual, and accentuated both her eccentricity and her autonomy. In the 1870s, as her celebrity increased, reports spread that she adopted parrots, tigers, and monkeys as pets; wore a white pantsuit while sculpting (figure 1.9); drank from a skull; kept an actual skeleton in her bedroom; and slept in a satin-lined coffin.[77] Unlike many other actresses of the day, Bernhardt was never publicly linked to a man more powerful than she was. In the United States, female stars were often seen as in thrall to charismatic male impresarios. In England, performers of both sexes attempted to evade their profession's unconventionality by stressing respectable family ties and elite social connections. In France, the most successful female performers were generally also well known as the mistresses of wealthy, influential men. Bernhardt's most formidable predecessor, the tragedian Rachel Félix (1821–1858), no shrinking violet, nonetheless remained closely identified with her father, her male teacher, a male patron, male drama critics, and various male lovers, while her brother served as her manager. One popular caricature of Rachel (usually referred to by her first name only) depicted the diminutive performer between two of the men who had helped create and maintain her stardom.[78]

No equivalent image of male sponsorship existed for Bernhardt, whom the press and public never saw, even in her youth, as the creation of a controlling producer, director, or manager. The conventional roles of dutiful daughter, kept woman, and proper wife and mother were all foreign to Bernhardt's public image.[79] In 1876, a British journalist noted, with somewhat damning neutrality, that "Nothing seems known of the father of the actress."[80] But by 1880, as Bernhardt became a star throughout Europe, journalists began to celebrate her murky origins: "It is the privilege of genius to need no sponsors and no ancestors. As an artist, Sarah Bernhardt was born the day when her histrionic talent first displayed itself."[81] Playwright Edmond Rostand, who worked closely with the actress, idealized her "intelligence, independence, and intrepidity" and described her as her own ancestor: "This heroine has no protecting fairy but herself. Sarah is her own godmother."[82]

Even marital status became irrelevant; one journalist opined, extraordinarily for the era, that an artist of Bernhardt's "rank" had no need for the titles Madame or Mademoiselle. At twenty, the unmarried Bernhardt gave birth to a son, and gave him her own last name. After her celebrity grew, she brought him with her on her travels, flaunting her "peculiar social position" as "a m'mselle and yet a mother."[83] Asked how she would respond to a clergyman who had denounced her for having an illegitimate son, Bernhardt impudently replied, "Had my child been a clergyman's probably he would have been strangled at birth."[84] Her longest relationship was with the female painter Louise Abbéma.[85] Her only marriage, at thirty-eight, to a much younger man, Jacques Damala, ended in separation after a year and did little to domesticate the star even while it lasted. "I retain my independent existence when I choose," Bernhardt declared, telling reporters that she and her husband planned to live in adjoining houses with a communicating door rather than under one roof.[86] Although some tried to depict the star's late embrace of wedlock as a concession to normalcy, Bernhardt did little to encourage that view herself, making it easy for the majority of reporters to describe even her entry into the conventional state of matrimony as yet another item in the long list of her eccentricities.[87]

Americans in particular hailed the star's independence, a trait they identified with as their own and perhaps found easier to appreciate in a foreign woman than in a female compatriot. An 1880 letter to the editor of a London newspaper from a correspondent in New Jersey noted, with some satisfaction, "The lady, in a published interview, 'talks back' to her clerical critics . . . It is quite evident that Sarah Bernhardt is able to take care of herself."[88] Nor did Bernhardt defer to the eminent male playwrights whose works she performed. Newspapers reported that when Alexandre Dumas fils instructed her to give a tragic cast to his line "he'll kill you like a little rabbit," Bernhardt agreed to do so only if he cut the word "rabbit." He refused, and Bernhardt allowed herself "a mischievous smile" at the applause she garnered when she nonetheless read the line her way, *sans* rabbit.[89]

As a theater professional, Bernhardt pursued the same independent path as stars such as Edwin Booth and Henry Irving: from 1880 forward, she chose her own roles, managed her own troupes, supervised the staging of all her productions, and leased her own theaters. Twentieth-century actor John Gielgud observed that combining the functions of actor and manager allowed performers to "make their own rules of conduct and break them if they felt so inclined."[90] In the nineteenth century, actor-managers such as Henry Irving and Sarah Bernhardt had the freedom to spend money on detailed, historically accurate sets and costumes; to rid the theater of ushers who harassed spectators for tips; to determine whether the seats in their theaters would be upholstered in red velvet or gold; and, most importantly, to indulge the personal idiosyncrasies that bestowed on each star an aura of uniqueness.[91] Such practices survived the rise of media conglomerates in the twentieth century. Marilyn Monroe formed her own production company after a dispute with her Hollywood studio; James Brown achieved unprecedented creative control and commercial rewards after he acquired the master tapes for his best-selling 1963 record, *Live at the Apollo*; and Barbra Streisand joined forces with Paul Newman, Sidney Poitier, and Steve McQueen so that each could develop independent projects.[92]

Considered "flagrant in her defiance of public opinion," known not only for her acting talent but also for her refusal to be "commonplace" and her love of doing "unexpected things," Bernhardt, like Byron and Sand before her, made deliberate unconventionality the key to her celebrity persona.[93] An early *New York Times* profile of her suggested that she would do anything "if only it involved a departure from the usages of her sex, the ways of common life. . . . She would live after her own plan, but she sometimes made the mistake of thinking that she could know it for her own only when it was unlike the plan of everybody else."[94] An 1892 article compared the actress to Napoleon and Ulysses S. Grant and singled out, as the traits she shared with those male leaders, her willingness to depart showily from "the ways of common life" and to assert her "superiority to conventional canons of conduct."[95] When Bernhardt died, in 1923, obituaries in French, British, and American newspapers emphasized her distinctiveness as "The Unconventional Sarah," whom the "people loved . . . because she had become a great legend of odd and flavorsome individuality."[96] Journalists underscored her ability to "disregard limitations, and do pretty much as she wished."[97] Emerson and Mill would have been proud to see the actress praised by her nineteenth-century contemporaries for being "sui generis, superbly self-reliant . . . conventionality defied and originality expressed."[98]

Far from being repulsed by Sarah Bernhardt's unusual appearance— her thin body, prominent nose, and unfashionably frizzy hair—audiences seemed to "revel by proxy" in the antics of an anomalously thin young woman who "enjoyed flabbergasting the world."[99] Bernhardt's example demonstrates that although the press, then as now, helped to make celebrities, journalists also had to compete with stars for the public's attention. From the 1830s through the 1890s, newspapers in France, England, and the United States shifted from being organs of political parties bankrolled by rich patrons and wealthy subscribers to commercial business ventures dependent on large circulations and advertising revenues. In the process, newspaper publishers began for the first time to seek the widest possible readerships. To do so, they lowered prices, added illustrations, and reported on a broad range of events, including sports, sensational crimes, entertainment, and entertainers.[100] Like celebrities, newspapers had to publicize themselves and become recognizable brands. In an 1877 article on the Parisian press, novelist Émile Zola commented, "Each journalist strives to make as much noise as possible in order to attract the public's attention to himself," and nineteenth-century French newspapers invested heavily in their own promotion and marketing.[101]

In 1895, newspaper editor Charles A. Dana published a book on *The Art of Newspaper Making.* In it, he described the press as a "powerful agent" wielding great influence but also acknowledged that to succeed, a "newspaper must ... correspond to the wants of the people" and "furnish that sort of information which the people demand" by attending to "everything ... of sufficient importance to arrest and absorb the attention of the public or of any considerable part of it."[102] In order to survive, the press had to give the people what they wanted, and the people wanted Bernhardt. One way for newspapers to assert their autonomy while still attracting readers was to write copiously about celebrities, but in a negative vein. One journalist who published a lengthy article denouncing Bernhardt's balloon trips found himself in the absurd position of arguing that her antics were not fit subjects for reporters—while in the very act of reporting on them. "Mlle Sarah Bernhardt has my full approval for her idea," he wrote (after disapproving of it for many lines), "but why the devil does one have to tell us about it [*nous en fait-on part*] in the newspapers?"[103] The author's odd use of the third person suggests that he had forgotten that *he* was the "one" producing the article in which this plea appears; he even aligns himself with the "us" reading the article instead of the "I" writing it. The article went on to beg the actress to ask her friends to stop "building up her eccentric ascents into exploits" that then became "promotional advertisements in the newspapers." Bernhardt's celebrity had a newspaper writer imploring her to help him stop writing about her.

Although celebrities often cultivate newspaper editors and journalists, they also strive to influence or even evade them. In the twentieth century, for example, Muhammad Ali developed a close relationship with sportscaster Howard Cosell, who kept the star athlete in the public eye during the years that Ali was barred from boxing. But Ali also challenged reporters, yelling at the press, "Eat your words! I shook up the world! I'm king of the world!" after defeating Sonny Liston in a 1964 bout that only a handful of the many journalists covering the event had thought he would win.[104] In 1954, after producer Darryl Zanuck suspended Marilyn Monroe for refusing a role, which her contract did not allow her to do, she defied him by taking a honeymoon trip to Japan with her new husband, celebrity baseball player Joe DiMaggio, during which she stopped in Korea to entertain US troops. Circumventing her punitive Hollywood studio by going straight to the public, Monroe performed in front of 100,000 soldiers. The result was a flood of heartfelt fan mail and positive media attention, effectively neutralizing Zanuck's attempt to weaken her bargaining position.[105] Although in early 1955 he very briefly suspended her again, newspapers at the time awarded the victory to Monroe, who emerged from the conflict with higher pay, a less restrictive contract, and more freedom to choose her roles, along with story and director approval on some films.[106] The public's applause had as much power to create celebrity as newspaper coverage or film studio press releases. Indeed, nineteenth-century theater reviews reported often on how long and heartily audiences clapped for performers and on how much money they paid to see them.[107]

In the 1870s, when Bernhardt first became a major box-office draw and first began to attract reporters' attention, much of it hostile, she often wrote letters to editors protesting how newspapers wrote about her. As late as 1921, two years before her death at age seventy-nine, she served one paper with a writ in order to stop its attacks on how she managed her theater.[108] In commenting to the press about how it wrote about her, Bernhardt took advantage both of her own newsworthiness and of laws that required editors to publish correspondence from subjects challenging the veracity of their press coverage. In 1880, for example, *Le Figaro* published a letter from Bernhardt seeking to set the facts straight about her controversial decision to leave the Théâtre-Français. Bernhardt used the newspaper attacking her as a Trojan horse to communicate her own, very different message. "On one point," her letter stated, "it is important to me to enlighten public opinion from this day forward. . . . Although I have no intention of appearing again very soon on a Parisian stage, I do not want the public, with whom, in exchange for its sympathy, I am connected through deep gratitude, to be able to mistake the motives that made me take such a serious decision." She went on to present her departure from France's national theater as not at all "premeditated" but rather an "explosion," the "spontaneous consequence of a long irritation" at being assigned a role she did not want to play.[109] Portraying herself as simultaneously defiant and cajoling, as highly willful but the victim of her own highly strung nerves, Bernhardt transformed the newspaper that had attacked her into a megaphone for her own speech. But, like other celebrities, Bernhardt also became skilled at making direct appeals to her publics, and it is to those sensational ways of moving millions that the next chapter turns.

CHAPTER 2

SENSATION

Audiences have long relished the experience of being overwhelmed by their favorite stars. In eighteenth-century Edinburgh, one spectator went into "hysterics" and had to be "carried from the theater in a frenzy" during a performance by British actress Sarah Siddons.[1] The nineteenth-century painter Elizabeth Butler described her youthful appreciation for Italian tragedian Adelaide Ristori as a kind of submission: "I . . . became overwhelmed with adoration of that mighty creature." Russian thinker Alexander Herzen used similar language to describe his response to French performer Rachel: "This weak and fragile being dominates you; . . . I cannot imagine that anyone would not abandon himself to her power."[2] Though today we often associate being on display with vulnerability, and spectatorship with aggression, at least one young nineteenth-century woman took the opposite view, fantasizing about being an actress because "Onstage, one dominates, and I need to dominate."[3] Nor was this merely wishful adolescent fantasy. Summing up US actress Charlotte Cushman's gifts after her death, in 1876, theater critic William Winter remarked: "She was incarnate power" and "dominated by intrinsic authority. . . . Of such minds as comprehend authentic leadership she achieved immediate, complete, and permanent conquest." Perhaps most surprisingly to readers today, Winter approved of Cushman's vigor and theatergoers' acquiescence to it: "There was, in her personality, a massive excellence that made admiration natural and entirely justified."[4]

Actors were not the only celebrities to have such hypnotic, imposing effects. Politicians, preachers, and public speakers could similarly mesmerize their auditors. Harriet Beecher Stowe, writing in 1863, compared abolitionist Sojourner Truth to Rachel because both had the "power . . . to move and bear down a whole audience by a few simple words."[5] Nor was rapt, enthralled spectatorship peculiar to the nineteenth century. Upon seeing ballet dancer Anna Pavlova perform in the 1920s, future choreographer Agnes de Mille, not yet an adult, had an intensely physical response: "I sat with the blood beating in my throat. As I walked into the bright glare of the afternoon, my head ached and I could scarcely swallow. I didn't wish to cry. I certainly couldn't speak."[6] In the 1940s, when bobby-soxers went into spasms over Frank Sinatra, a New York City Board of Education commissioner fumed, "We can't tolerate young people making a public display of losing control of their emotions." A photograph in the *Daily News* (figure 2.1) showed a Sinatra audience more rapt than rampaging.[7] A reporter describing a live Elvis Presley performance in 1957 (figure 2.2) observed that the singer "had only to say, 'thank you very much,' and the audience would scream. He'd scratch his nose; another scream. He'd laugh; another scream. At times, the singer seemed to deliberately push the button by dropping his arm or wiggling his shoulder, just to hear his fans react."[8] A 2002 *New Yorker* profile of James Brown, the US recording artist with the most hits after Elvis Presley, called him a "slayer of audiences." Witnessing Brown perform live, profile author Philip Gourevitch elaborated: "He will transport you so totally into the grip of his groove that . . . if he does his job well, he will literally control your breathing."[9] The Beatles and Michael Jackson both exercised similar command, as did rhetorically gifted leaders such as Winston Churchill and Ronald Reagan. When icons like these die, even the most hardened reporters find themselves gushing like groupies about the charismatic politicians, athletes, authors, and performers they have just lost.

What explains any particular celebrity's power to affect others? One often overlooked answer is that people want to be moved, even overcome, and paradoxically use their agency in order to lose it. Writing of Sarah Bernhardt's effect on those who saw her, one journalist remarked: "Her acting thrills as her repose fascinates. She instantly arrests attention. Her influence is irresistible."[10] Another echoed that assessment in even more sensational terms: "I recollect the icy shiver that ran down my vertebrae when I first saw Bernhardt's Theodora, and advise people who have been suffering from grip [sic] to refrain from seeing that performance unless they want to have a relapse!"[11]

A second, equally overlooked explanation of these sensations of pleasurable surrender is that celebrities deliberately and successfully aim to overpower the public. James Brown described his rapport with his public in the starkest terms: "Normally, I just go out there and kill 'em."[12] When

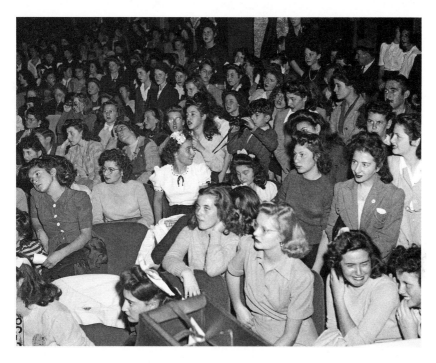

FIGURE 2.1. Audience, Frank Sinatra concert, Paramount Theatre, New York City, 1944.

FIGURE 2.2. Elvis Presley performing circa 1957.

Agnes de Mille sought to describe what Pavlova did to warm her young admirer's blood and make her head ache, she evoked the dancer's "intoxicated rapture, a focus of energy, Dionysian in its physical intensity."[13] Some performers openly admitted a wish to dominate the public. Asked how she handled unsympathetic audiences, Sarah Bernhardt responded: "It is then a battle between me and them, and I always win."[14] To win these battles, stars had to hone skills that enabled them to enact wild emotion without succumbing to it. As one reviewer observed of Bernhardt, "She both is driven by and directs the storm of passion." Praising her "command of the resources of her art," he continued: "Passages that in the hand of another would lapse into frantic incoherence she controls and directs with such certainty that the wild utterance of passion is never blurred by hysteria."[15]

Far from seeing celebrities' sensational effects as the deliberate result of carefully executed techniques, most people view the celebrity's power to move spectators either as duplicitous or as fundamentally mysterious and outside the star's control. Theater historian Joseph Roach, for example, defines celebrity attraction as *It*, an ineffable quality so self-explanatory that his book wittily foregoes a subtitle; you either get "It" or you don't. A mysterious "condition" distinct from talent, "It" lies outside its possessor's command; celebrities are as helpless before It as are those succumbing to its charms.[16] Others see celebrity as a scam that critics have an obligation to unmask, more mystification than mystery. Celebrity as It, celebrity as bunk. These otherwise opposed positions share one assumption: that stars themselves have little or no influence over how they affect others. Even those who view celebrity more positively tend to assign stars themselves little or no part in their own construction, ascribing that power instead to media workers, fans, and publics.[17]

Many consider it especially unlikely that *female* stars would successfully control their destinies or exert power over others. As theater historian Kim Marra has shown, even the most acclaimed actresses of the nineteenth and early twentieth centuries often appeared to be under the sway of domineering male managers.[18] In a debate that continues to this day in opinion pieces about female pop stars, some see even the most successful among them as exploited objects of a controlling, objectifying, and belittling gaze, while others make the case for contemporary female stars as active erotic subjects visibly exercising power in public.[19] A few feminist historians have extended the latter claim to the past, arguing that renowned female performers have long been political trailblazers who made self-determination, self-possession, and self-confidence more acceptable for all women. Scholars Felicity Nussbaum and Susan Glenn have documented how actresses in eighteenth-century England and early twentieth-century America were among the first women to publicize female mastery of skills that included handling the press; traveling large distances; public speaking, often before large, rambunctious audiences; and bargaining for higher salaries and better working conditions. Successful actresses were also among the first women in England, France, and the United States to invent new modes of femininity, such as the brash, athletic style popularized by burlesque performers, or the aggressive sexuality of the vamps and flappers who put nails in the coffin of Victorian decorum. Some female stars, though by no means all, actively supported feminist causes.[20] Extrapolating from these facts, Nussbaum and Glenn have argued (with less compelling evidence) that celebrated actresses inspired women to demand political rights along with professional and economic autonomy.[21]

This particular feminist paradigm views celebrities as role models who readily transmit their capacities for freedom and self-direction to fans who aspire to become equally autonomous. Celebrity can indeed work this way; women have described feeling motivated by pioneer athletes such as Billie Jean King and by erotic mavericks such as Madonna, both of whom explicitly aligned themselves with feminism. The same political capacities extend to celebrities who represent other disempowered groups. When baseball player Jackie Robinson and tennis player Arthur Ashe excelled at sports that had previously been closed to African Americans, they helped to combat discrimination against athletes and to expand civil rights on a larger scale. When lesbian, gay, and trans celebrities publicly embraced identities that for decades were demonized and concealed, they encouraged others to accept queerness.

That said, however, the role model theory of celebrity has its limits. Glenn and Nussbaum offer few concrete examples of ordinary women emulating stars. They assume that past female celebrities sought to share their agency with members of the public and, conversely, that members of the public desired to acquire the powers they admired in their favorite celebrities. In this model, stars seek to transmit their freedom and self-direction to their fans, and fans aspire to become as influential and unconstrained as their idols. This theory of celebrity depends on a particular model of agency as *liberal* agency: orderly, egalitarian, and organized around the conscious intentions of individuals who experience emotions in ways that increase their own autonomy and that of others.[22] The interaction most characteristic of liberal agency is rational argument: logical, nonviolent, evidence-based debate aimed at producing a consensus with which all can more or less agree. The political framework most characteristic of liberalism is formal equality, in which everyone shares the same capacities for reason, self-control, and self-determination. In this model, no tension exists between individual agency and universal equality.

As we saw in the previous chapter, however, celebrities often claimed privileges, such as defiance, for themselves alone. As this chapter will show, many celebrities sought to vanquish their publics, not empower them; critic Jules Lemaître, citing Arsène Houssaye, described Bernhardt as "stronger than all the spectators when she wants to strike them right in the chest with some direct and pointed words."[23] Or, as another journalist put it—in a highly positive review—the audience "literally becomes her plaything, losing volition before the temperamental onslaught."[24] The agency at work in such scenarios is *illiberal*: volatile and tempestuous rather than orderly and harmonious, trafficking in irrational emotions and extreme sensations, prompted by and prompting an explicitly hierarchical relationship. The star, here, willfully exercises agency to dominate publics pleased to experience feelings that they cannot control. When Sarah Bernhardt, the Beatles, or Madonna inspire these reactions, the results can be harmless, even liberating. When celebrities such as Charles Lindbergh and Donald Trump translate media access, name recognition, and influence into bids for political office, the result is often demagoguery.

As this book's chapters on "Judgment" and "Merit" will show, even the most devoted fans can be more rational than we commonly believe. Members of the public as well as professional critics can and do observe, criticize, compare, measure, and evaluate celebrities. But celebrity culture also has a distinctively illiberal streak. Celebrities appeal to hearts and bodies as well as minds; even critics want to feel stirred. While celebrities cannot exist without fans, celebrity culture is nonetheless fundamentally hierarchical, based as it is on the differences between the anonymous many and the celebrated few. The structural inequality between celebrities and publics is hard to erode, though some fans try to lessen the distance separating them from stars (see "Intimacy" and "Imitation"). Nor do publics always aspire to respond to their favorite celebrities rationally. Fandom is often about excess, fantasy, and obsession. Audiences under the spell of celebrity attraction daydream, sigh, weep, faint, shriek, roar, and swarm.

Whether stampeding or swooning, fans treasure the ecstatic experience of feeling their autonomy, reason, and individuality melt away under the influence of the stars.

THE RISE OF OVERPOWERING ACTING

Actors and actresses have always trafficked in expressiveness; but in the eighteenth and early nineteenth centuries, a new, Romantic performance style emerged that encouraged audiences to surrender to strong emotions. Over the course of the eighteenth century, acting treatises began to define performers as conduits of feeling who genuinely experienced the emotions they enacted and aroused similar sentiments in spectators.[25] Trained in a system that correlated fear, joy, love, and anger with specific gestures and vocal qualities, eighteenth-century English and French performers favored a classical, declamatory, almost statuesque acting style that valued elocution over embodiment and words over movement.[26] With the rise of populist democracy in the nineteenth century, acting styles became more physical, more mobile, and more charged, and began to produce even stronger effects on spectators. In his 1835 study of democracy in America, Alexis de Tocqueville observed that theatergoers drawn from the middle and lower strata of society did not anticipate "a work of literature but want to *see* a play." He found American audiences eager to "turn aside from the painting of the soul in order to concentrate on the body; movement and sensation replace the depiction of feelings and ideas."[27] The key word here is "sensation." Though we may now equate sensation with feeling, de Tocqueville tellingly opposed them. Earlier styles of acting had conveyed dignified sentiments through stillness, restraint, and elocution. In the nineteenth century, that technique began to give way to more fluid and asymmetrical movements that signified and provoked abandoned and extreme states.[28]

Compare two images from the late eighteenth century, both depicting British women who acquired global celebrity as performers. Though their poses are in many ways similar, the illustrator depicting Sarah Siddons (1755–1831) makes her seem comparatively static and restrained: intense and full of pathos, but statuesque, studied, controlled, and formal, even when kneeling on the floor, wringing her hands, or flinging open her arms (figure 2.3). The artist who portrayed Emma Hamilton (1765–1815)

FIGURE 2.3. Sarah Siddons in Gilbert Austin, *Chironomia, or, A Treatise on Rhetorical Delivery*, 1806.

FIGURE 2.4. Pietro Novelli, "The Attitudes of Lady Hamilton," circa 1791.

performing her famous "Attitudes" shows the influence of newer tastes. Even when Hamilton adopts postures identical to those of Siddons, and even in a print executed before the one depicting Siddons, the younger performer Hamilton appears far more fluid, spontaneous, and responsive (figure 2.4).

In the first few decades of the nineteenth century, some London and Paris theaters began to stage melodramas, plays that combined the spoken word with dance, music, and song. Those theaters spawned what scholar Jane Moody has dubbed "an aesthetic of illegitimacy" whose hallmarks were "scenic spectacle, mechanical trickery, ... acrobatic virtuosity, ... intensity ... [and] corporeal expressivity."[29] The greatest English exemplar of this aesthetic was the passionate Edmund Kean (1787–1833; figure 2.5), reputed to send female audience members into hysterics and Lord Byron himself into convulsions.[30] Critics compared Kean's explosive acting style to fire, electricity, and lightning, and described his audiences as experiencing "disorder, violence, and pain."[31] By the mid-nineteenth century, the new aesthetic had become so dominant that drama critic George Henry Lewes, who praised Kean's "irresistible power," would fault another performer for lacking "the fervid animation which acts like electricity upon the spectator."[32]

FIGURE 2.5. Philip Massinger, painting of Edmund Kean as Sir Giles Overreach in *A New Way to Pay Old Debts*, 1820.

Kean's influence extended across the Atlantic to US actors such as Edwin Forrest (1806–1872), whose booming voice and muscular calves inspired "idolatry" in the working-class men of the young republic. Forrest, like Kean, broke with the carefully regulated gestures prescribed by British acting manuals, as well as with the prescriptions found in US treatises on oratory. In their place, he substituted "passionate exclamation," extravagant emotion, "frenetic ... action," and what his biographer, in a burst of alliteration, identified as "visceral vitality and vigor."[33] His powerful voice could oscillate quickly between low and high, bass and treble.[34] An enthusiastic biographer described Forrest as belonging to a class of men whose nervous force inspired "common men" to "revere and obey," and opined: "In a country like ours, where all men are free and equal, no aristocracy should be tolerated, save that aristocracy of superior mind, before which none should be ashamed to bow."[35] Like Napoleon, Forrest claimed "the prerogative of breaking from the trammels of common regulation," and he communicated that imperious agency to the "full-sinew'd" male fans whom Walt Whitman praised in the late 1830s for their "electric force and muscle." Though some saw Forrest's audiences as under his control, he is now most famous for the 1849 occasion on which his followers rioted against a rival performer at New York City's Astor Place Theater.[36] By the last decades of the century, critics were praising actors as varied as Italian tragedian Tommaso Salvini (1829–1915), for his "electrical touch of genius," and music hall comedian Jenny Hill, popular from the 1860s to the 1880s, for inspiring "nervous excitement."[37]

In France, melodramatic acting came into its own in 1835, when Marie Dorval (1798–1849), the star of Alfred de Vigny's *Chatterton*, enacted her character's silent distress by slowly collapsing down a curved staircase. The creator of that piece of stage business was Dorval herself, who demanded that the staircase be included when the play was transferred from a boulevard theater to the more staid Théâtre-Français.[38] The demand had to come from Dorval because the French state theater was slow to adopt the new Romantic style. By the 1840s, however, even the theatrical establishment began to incorporate the sensational aesthetic. Rachel became a global star by bringing a new intensity to the French classical tragedies she performed at the Théâtre-Français (figure 2.6). She remained unrivaled until the advent of Sarah Bernhardt, who, like her predecessor, combined classical training with techniques derived from Romantic theater and popular melodrama.[39]

FIGURE 2.6. Rachel Félix as Phèdre.

When Bernhardt first attracted notice in the 1860s and 1870s, critics deemed her even more natural and physical than her most gifted predecessors, Siddons and Rachel.[40] As one reviewer put it, when Siddons played Lady Macbeth, her "power was seated on her brow," the mental temple of reason and contemplation, a dignified and not particularly erotic part of the face that communicates through subtle, finely controlled motions. When Bernhardt played the same role, her "power" was "seated in her arms and lungs," making her force more visible, more audible, and more visceral.[41] Many described how seeing and hearing Bernhardt agitated their nerves, claiming that she "convulsed" audiences, administering jolts, chills, and "electric shocks."[42] Scholars have noted the similarities between Bernhardt's performances and those of Dr. Charcot's hysterics, but more often the hysteria came from her audience.[43] Mary Drew, the daughter of British prime minister William Gladstone, wrote in her journal that Sarah Bernhardt "carried me off my feet." A professional theater critic similarly gushed, "One cannot remain indifferent to those conquering eyes."[44] After seeing Bernhardt in 1880, British diarist Lady Monkswell vowed, "I will not go to be harrowed up again in this most wanton manner. I did not know what beauty of movement was till I saw Sarah, it is overwhelming, bewildering."[45] Like many reporters, Monkswell felt herself to be on a first-name basis with the star and described the sensations Bernhardt inspired as combining pain and pleasure, so strong as to be almost confusing. The diarist's announcement that she could not bear to see Bernhardt again was itself a bit of dramatic hyperbole that testified both to Monkswell's susceptibility to great art and to the actor's power to undo her audiences.

Critics and ordinary theatergoers alike described feeling in Bernhardt's thrall. The actress's "magnetism ... attracts, interests, and finally enslaves," wrote one journalist. Another concurred: "You would not take your eyes off the scene for anything less than a fire or a falling balcony. . . . [I]t is a fascinating, at times even mentally exhausting, seizure of the emotions. You are not simply snared; you are enchained."[46] By the 1890s, Bernhardt's acting also had detractors, including George Bernard Shaw, who in 1895 championed the understated Eleonora Duse and famously dismissed "the whole Bernhardtian range of sensational effects."[47] Shaw charged that, where Duse made "you feel rather than see," Bernhardt's thick stage makeup and "conscious" gestures relied on meretricious spectacle. For Shaw, Bernhardt's skill, such as it was, consisted of "the art of finding out all your weaknesses and practising on them—cajoling you, harrowing you, exciting you—on the whole fooling you."[48] Like Monkswell, Shaw used the unusual word "harrow" to describe Bernhardt's invasive, destructive effects, which seemed almost to flay her spectators.

Shaw's vehement rejection of Bernhardt only confirmed her impact, and few adopted his contrarian dismissal of her gifts. For over four decades, ticket buyers flocked to see Bernhardt in her native Paris and throughout Europe, North and South America, Australia, and New Zealand. Nor was Bernhardt merely a popular success: both during her lifetime and for years after her death, in 1923, a host of professional theater reviewers pronounced her a genius and acclaimed her acting as transcendently moving. Even the coolest critics warmed to her. Lytton Strachey, for example, the Bloomsbury wit best known for his irreverent 1918 profiles of *Eminent Victorians*, lost all detachment in the face of Bernhardt's "extraordinary genius." Paying tribute to the star soon after her death, he wrote that she "could contrive thrill after thrill . . . She could seize and tear the nerves of her audience, she could touch, she could terrify. . . . [I]n Sarah Bernhardt's voice there was more than gold: there was thunder and lightning; there was Heaven and Hell."[49] Strachey sounds almost mesmerized, enacting in words the surrender he had experienced in the theater. Not content with describing Bernhardt's overwhelming force, he performs it in prose more purple than mauve, abandoning his usually urbane and mordant style for one closer to Bernhardt's own.

Literary critic and Symbolist poet Arthur Symons, writing in 1902 about a Bernhardt he considered then past her prime, waxed just as lyrical recalling how her art "spoke to us, once, with so electrical a shock, as if nerve touched nerve, or . . . her voice were laid tinglingly on one's spinal cord . . . as if the whole nervous force of the audience were sucked out of it and flung back, intensified, upon itself, as it encountered the single, insatiable, indomitable nervous force of the woman. [Her acting] mesmerised one, awakening the senses and sending the intelligence to sleep."[50] References to electricity, here and elsewhere, evoked a still novel and mysterious technology that produced almost instantaneous communication via telegraphy and that lit streets, homes, and theatres with new brilliance.[51] Allusions to the electric also touched on the physiological force that powered the brain in ways beyond the mind's control, leaping with magical speed from nerve to nerve and, audiences imagined, from body to body, bypassing cognition. As a result, heightened "senses" meant slumbering "intelligence."[52]

Actors cannot exist without audiences, but the zeal with which critics described Bernhardt mesmerizing theatergoers suggested a wish to be overcome by her that she continually and handily granted. Symons presents Bernhardt's nerves and voice as forming a kind of electrical circuit with the bodies of audience members, a circuit controlled by her "indomitable nervous force," which amplifies, gathers, and directs the audience's energy, diminishing their will while enhancing her own. The resulting dynamic is quintessentially illiberal: the star is "indomitable," the audience "mesmerised." In mid-nineteenth-century England, people believed that mesmerism proved that one person could excite actions and reactions in others without their conscious assent. As Chauncy Hare Townshend put it, in mesmerism, "the one impels, the other obeys impulsion."[53]

BERNHARDT'S EXTERIORITY EFFECTS

Why did hundreds of thousands the world over, including drama critics hired to be professional skeptics, find Sarah Bernhardt so powerfully attractive and so attractively powerful? One answer lies in Bernhardt's cultivation of acting techniques that required and displayed formidable control over her face, voice, and body. In contrast to Rachel, who sometimes appeared to be experiencing the same "self-oblivion" as her characters, Bernhardt was perceived as wielding supreme agency even when portraying emotional or physical collapse.[54] Henry James praised the young Bernhardt for "understand[ing] the art of motion and attitude as no one else does."[55] Other critics lauded her "easy control over all her limbs down to her long taper fingers" and noted how "in depicting human suffering, she seems to absolutely control every organ of her body."[56] Bernhardt's superlative management of her own body accentuated the difference, inherent to theater, between the actor and those who watched her.

A rarely cited 1880 article about Bernhardt's dress rehearsals shows how deliberately she approached her performances and those of the actors she hired and managed. After leaving the Théâtre-Français, Bernhardt became the director of her own theater troupes and oversaw each production in which she starred. While rehearsing Victor Hugo's *Hernani* in 1880, she mounted a ladder to make the portraits in the background of one scene look more antique by smearing them with a dirty cloth. The reporter observing Bernhardt's rehearsals stressed the "tireless drudgery" needed to produce some of her most powerful effects. A backward tumble into a chair in *Le Sphinx* had the star personally sawing down the chair's legs to the perfect height. Both the laborious rehearsals and the apparently effortless performance that resulted affirmed Bernhardt's determination to execute her own intentions. Everything was "subjected" to her "controlling judgment and direction," including the head of the actor playing Armand in *La Dame aux camélias*, which she "turned and wrenched . . . twenty different times . . . so as to indicate the precise posture producing the most telling effect."[57]

By many accounts, Bernhardt grabbed and manipulated theatergoers' attention as authoritatively as she did the head of the actor playing Armand. In an era when the modern theater director had yet to be invented, Bernhardt was both actress and impresario, regulating her own movements and those of her fellow performers. The same reporter cited above describes her shifting between the stage and auditorium to adjust blocking, costumes, and props, as well as explaining character motivation to actors who "obey" her with "instantaneous deference."[58] More than ten years later, a journalist watching her rehearse pronounced, "Sarah Bernhardt notices everything, controls everything."[59] That Bernhardt allowed reporters to witness her active management of her troupe attests to her willingness to showcase, rather than conceal, her executive powers.

Richard Schickel, Christine Gledhill, Felicity Nussbaum, and Joseph Roach have all argued that celebrity depends on "interiority effects" and "public intimacy," on members of the public feeling that they know what celebrities are really like inside and offstage.[60] To care about what stars are like offstage, however, fans first need to be attracted by what they do on it. Celebrities as varied as Edward Kean, Mae West, Michael Jackson, and Kim Kardashian have attracted interest through what I will call *exteriority effects*: arresting facial expressions, vocal acrobatics, and extravagant, riveting bodily movements.[61] Interiors and exteriors cannot be easily separated, and performance theory and practice have long aligned actors' bodies and minds.[62] But where interiority connotes inner consciousness along with the unconscious, exteriority evokes visible, audible, and palpable physical actions.[63] Drama critic Jules Lemaître identified Bernhardt's "powerful attraction" with her corporeality: "She does what none before her dared to do, she performs with her entire body."[64] Dancer Maud Allan, in her autobiography, recalled playing the piano as a child while thinking "of Sarah Bernhardt's wonderful talent, of the beautiful movements of her body."[65] The youthful Allan was not alone in her strong response to the star's exteriority effects. In 1885, after seeing Bernhardt perform in Paris, medical student Sigmund Freud wrote about the experience to his fiancée: "Every inch of that little figure lives and bewitches. . . . it is incredible what postures she can assume and how every limb and joint acts with her."[66]

For over thirty years, Bernhardt performed exclusively in French for audiences around the world who, even when equipped with bilingual playbooks, often did not fully comprehend the words she uttered. As a result, many scholars have noted, she relied on physical gestures and vocal inflections far more than on the meaning of the words she declaimed.[67] Bernhardt herself remarked that because US audiences did not "fully understand French," she had to "play at her best tension" in order to attract their "attention" and "arouse their sympathies."[68] Audiences whose lack of French meant they had little or no idea what the lines Bernhardt spoke meant became bellwethers for testing the expressive power of her gestures, movements, and vocal tone: "It is a sincere tribute to her artistry," wrote one critic, "that a theater public . . . should sit through four solid hours of dialogue they cannot understand with a rapt silence not untouched with awe."[69]

What did Bernhardt do, exactly, to have such a formidable effect? A 1909 review, preserved in a Midwesterner's theater scrapbook, offers an excellent starting point for unpacking Bernhardt's magic. It describes the gifted comic Cecilia "Cissy" Loftus enacting a Bernhardt impersonation that identified and exaggerated Bernhardt's most recognizable techniques:

There, like a page of memory, suddenly called to vivid and vocal life, is the old Bernhardt that always caught the hanging when she entered or left a room; that cried shrilly in her throat; that could tumble her speech and her feeling into floods of nasal words; that liked to brush her eyes and press her bosom; that invariably looked one way while her hands wandered in another; that liked to pause and palpitate and palpitate and pause again, before she departed in tigerish glide.[70]

A good mimic is a keen observer, and Loftus noticed and reenacted Bernhardt's key exteriority effects:

1) **Hyperextension**, a tendency to send different body parts in opposing directions (as when the actress looks one way while her hands wander in another).

2) **Tempo variation**, seen here as an alternation between rushing and pausing, stillness and gliding.

3) **Framing**, a protocinematic ability to fix the audience's attention, either by using dramatic exits and entrances to alternate between presence and absence, or by isolating body parts, as when the actress grabs a wall hanging, brushes her eyes, or presses her bosom.

4) **Mobility**, already implied in the three preceding techniques: a deliberate and even exaggerated use of movement, enacted in the quote above by the head that turns, the body that enters and leaves, the hands that brush, press, and wander, and the voice that tumbles and floods as it shifts between chest and head, throat and nasal passages.[71]

Bernhardt tended to use all of these techniques simultaneously, but a rarely reproduced sketch of her performing *La Dame aux camélias* in 1880 (figure 2.7) offers an unusually clear understanding of her use of hyperextension, the technical term for taking a body part beyond its normal range of motion. This 1880 illustration was included in the lavish souvenir "Bernhardt Edition" of *La Dame aux camélias* sold during the star's first tour of the United States and Canada as part of a massive publicity campaign to drum up interest in the French star. Intended to justify the unusually high prices for Bernhardt tickets, the editions' illustrations showcased her most characteristic and moving poses. A loosely drawn sketch that could have been made during a performance or rehearsal, the image captures the dynamics of a live stage performance in ways that photographs from the same era could not, because the long exposure times still prevalent in 1880 meant that anyone being photographed had to adopt poses that could be held for many minutes. When Napoleon Sarony took a photograph of Bernhardt in *La Dame aux camélias* the same year as the Bernhardt Edition appeared, he depicted her in the play's final death scene, reclining, and apparently expired, on a sofa, albeit at a precarious angle that suggests she may at any moment drop to the floor (figure 2.8). By contrast, the

FIGURE 2.8. Napoleon Sarony, photograph of Sarah Bernhardt as Camille, 1880.

illustrator of the Bernhardt Edition has tried to convey an action in the process of unfolding onstage. The broad strokes at the bottom of the sketch and the prominent hatching marks used to render the male figures suggest a drawing made rapidly on the spot; the whiteness of the dress mimics the strong contrasts typical of theatrical lighting circa 1880.

The sketch (figure 2.7) provides a telling view of what Bernhardt did when performing the role of Marguerite Gautier. The illustrator has chosen one of the play's most celebrated moments, at the end of act 3, when Marguerite's lover Armand confronts her at a party, erroneously believing that she has flightily betrayed him. After he humiliates her by throwing money at her, she collapses. The sketch shows Bernhardt rotating, inverting, flattening, and arching different parts of her body to perform what becomes an almost literally pivotal scene. Even as Bernhardt enacts Marguerite's distress, her use of hyperextension flaunts her virtuosic control over her body. The sections, seams, and flourishes of her costume cannily articulate the different segments of her pose as she arches, twists, and angles her head, trunk, and limbs in different directions, emphasizing her flexibility, extension, and balance. Her left hand presses her forehead down, while her face turns ever so slightly upward and to the right, toward the beholder. The odd backward bend of the torqued right wrist turns Bernhardt's arm into a sinuous curve but also conveys strain by implying that she is supporting her entire body on the back of her hand in a failing attempt to stay upright.

By thrusting her chest upward while pulling her pelvis back, Bernhardt creates the deep S curve for which she was so well known. This is, as it were, the signature posture of a star, born Rosine, who later chose a first name beginning with the letter S. Difficult to achieve and difficult to ignore, this pose is carnal and hyperbolic, involving as it does the performer's entire body, from her supine head to the lifted foot whose pointed toes help to keep her upright. Of course, nobody actually falls like this. Bernhardt's posture highlights a split between the performer, who deliberately sends her limbs in different directions and holds them there, and the character she plays, whose involuntary swoon resembles the responses of audience members overwhelmed by Bernhardt. The trendiest and most compelling styles of any given era inevitably look dated to later generations, and today we might view Bernhardt's pose here as artificial and almost campy. But critics in the 1870s and 1880s saw the star's expressive use of her entire body as precisely what made her acting seem more natural and realistic than that of her predecessors.[72]

Combining tempo variation with mobility, Bernhardt used deceleration and acceleration to inspire strong emotion. Praised by one of her acting students as a "master of pace," Bernhardt often shifted between rapid, forceful movements and slowly extended ones.[73] She also varied the speeds of her acclaimed vocal delivery: "She sang, she hammered, she accelerated the cadence into a gallop which suddenly rolled, mounted, pranced, tumbled into a silence which nothing broke but a repeated sob."[74] Attempting to explain how Bernhardt "Could Surely Move Crowd," journalist Archie Bell wrote, "There was a staccato in her diction, an intensity . . . and a speed that perhaps has never been equaled."[75] The London *Times* drama critic Arthur Walkley observed that she alternated between elongating words and "hammering" them out in a "rapid patter."[76] Trying to describe "the voice that this age can never forget," another journalist sent his own words cascading: "It purls, it coos, it chants."[77]

A final example, never before cited in the vast literature on Sarah Bernhardt, offers an opportunity to see all of Bernhardt's exteriority effects at work simultaneously. In 1910, a twenty-seven-year-old Chicago drama critic named Sheppard Butler published a remarkably observant review of Bernhardt's performance in *La Tosca*, a play written for her by Victorien Sardou in 1887 and still known to audiences today through Giacomo Puccini's 1900 opera adaptation. Butler offers a clear and detailed account of Bernhardt's stage business in the penultimate act, during the moments after Tosca, an opera diva, murders Scarpia, the villainous police chief who has tortured her revolutionary lover and then attempted to rape her.

> No sobs now, not even a shudder. Hardly a muscle of the woman's face moved. Only her eyes roved about pitifully, almost casually.
>
> Quietly she stepped to the table, picked up a napkin, moistened it, and, finger by finger, scrubbed the blood from her hand. Carefully she plucked at her skirt, dabbing at one or two spots she saw there. Dead silence, silence that seemed almost unbearable. A ripple of applause started. Soft, impatient hisses stopped it. No need of language to follow the action now. This was universal language.
>
> Methodically she blew out two candles. Two more she took and, stooping slowly, placed them at the head of the body. Always she

moved as would a tired housewife putting the last room to rights. And always there was that face, grim, wan, ghastly, with the restless, roving eyes.

Outside a trumpet and a grating roll of drums. The woman swept one last glance over the room, crept to the door and listened. Then she stepped through, closing it carefully, so as to make no sound. The curtain fell, silently.[78]

Butler's liberal use of verbs conveys the different tempi at which the star moves: the actress scrubs, plucks, blows, stoops, places, creeps, and steps. His description helps us see how Bernhardt used alternately slow and rapid motions to focus attention on particular body parts, such as the "restless, roving eyes" that move while the rest of her face stays still. When she scrubs the blood from her hand individual finger by individual finger, she protracts that action almost unbearably, as she also does when carefully dabbing and plucking at her skirt or "slowly" stooping to place candles by Scarpia's corpse. The slow dabbing of each finger also invites spectators, especially those using opera glasses, to frame their own close-ups of the star by training their gaze on each digit as she sets it into isolated motion. Butler also records the audience's strong response. Some sit in rapt "silence," their stillness suggesting both concentration and submission to the compelling action onstage. Others react to Bernhardt's exteriority effects with their own, disrupting her performance to celebrate its power with a mid-scene "ripple of applause."[79] Still others hiss to quell the unruly clappers.

At the very end of this scene, in a bit of stage business almost as famous as her placement of candles on either side of Scarpia's head, Bernhardt glided through a half-closed door in a way that similarly combined mobility, framing, tempo control, and the sinuous flexibility associated with hyperextension. (We will encounter this signature move again in "Imitation.") Reynaldo Hahn, a composer, critic, and intimate of Marcel Proust, described this moment in even greater detail than Butler, ending his book about the actress with this passage: "Sarah half opens the door, passes her head through it to explore the hallway, then her shoulders follow, then her entire body, with the undulating movement of a reptile; the door closes slowly, slowly, while the train of her dress disappears . . . And while the curtain lowers, one spies Tosca, furtive, trembling, departing alongside the walls, as silent as a shadow."[80] Bernhardt's slow ooze through the doorway showcased her ability to decelerate an action normally executed more rapidly. It also continually reframed her body for the viewer, leaving less and less of her visible while drawing attention to her head, shoulders, and dress train as each passed from view. Her serpentine departure became a fluidly unfolding series of stills, each framing her body differently. The gradually dropping curtain created the same framing effect vertically, successively hiding more and more of the star's body before obscuring it altogether.[81]

Although Hahn's account confines itself to his own point of view, generalized as that of "one" who watches Bernhardt, his careful description of her extended exit attests to his absorption in her performance and helps us to imagine what it might have felt like to witness this moment in a theater. To see Bernhardt as Tosca slowly depart is both to hope that the character will move more quickly to secure her escape and to long for the star performer to slow down her departure so that we will not lose sight of her. By bringing herself in and out of view, often in slow motion, Bernhardt tinged her onstage presence with a sense of fleeting plenitude and imminent absence.

Bernhardt did not confine her use of such effects to *La Tosca*. In many other plays, she captivated audiences by delaying her entrances or playing with her back to the auditorium, another use of framing to heighten and focus audience attention. When other players were onstage, the star knew that, as one of her acting students put it, "she robbed any actor of the audience's attention simply by being there."[82] Such techniques offered a tantalizing combination of fullness and loss more often associated with photography and film. But where those more mechanized media required camera operators and directors to tell actors where to stand and how to move, theatrical stars such as Sarah Bernhardt and Henry Irving devised and managed such effects themselves.

Techniques like these emphasized the celebrity performer's mastery of both her own physical instrument and the audience's responses. The extremes of agency at work in *La Tosca*'s plot mirror the uneven distribution of agency between the excited, enthralled audience and the charismatic, controlled actor, who exercises an agency both liberal (managerial, executive, controlled) and illiberal (violent, sensational, despotic). As Tosca listens to Mario being tortured, she resembles the audience members who felt helpless before Bernhardt's power. When Scarpia wrests from Tosca the kind of involuntary response that critics described Bernhardt as wringing from theatergoers, he deprives a diva known for her consummate vocal control of her customary agency, reducing her to groans, cries, and pleading. When Tosca stabs Scarpia, the diva reclaims her imperious agency, reuniting the character with the commanding performer and authoritative stage manager who played her. Just as Bernhardt could, in Arsène Houssaye's words cited earlier, "strike" spectators "right in the chest with some direct and pointed words," Tosca strikes Scarpia in the heart with a pointed dagger.[83] Like a playwright penning stage directions or a director instructing a performer how to move, Tosca orders Scarpia to "Die! . . . Die! . . . Die! . . ."—and die he does, ceding his agency, in that moment, to her voice and her words. When Tosca places candlesticks beside Scarpia's corpse, she is a Catholic moved to express pity for her victim and torturer—and a theater director arranging stage lighting.

Bernhardt did not limit her use of exteriority effects to the theater; she also used mobility and framing when meeting with journalists. Throughout one 1910 interview, for example, she repeatedly buried her nose in a bunch of roses, hiding her face, then lifting it back into view. In a gesture that echoed Tosca scrubbing blood from her hand one finger at a time, Bernhardt busied herself throughout the conversation by plucking petals from each rose in her bouquet and then letting them drop, one by one, to the floor. Shifting between gestures that subtracted (removing petals, hiding her face) and restored (letting petals pile up, revealing her face), Bernhardt managed to rivet everyone's attention even while seated. At interview's end, she rose to stand on a carpet of flowers.[84]

If celebrity is a contest over agency, it seems reasonable to assume that each party would want to prevail over the others. Sometimes, however, journalists and publics would rather relinquish agency than claim it. Bernhardt, like many celebrities before and after her, used thrilling exteriority effects to hold sway over audiences who then as now relished a show of theatrical strength. Most critics and theatergoers appreciated rather than censured the star performer's ability to move and even to overpower them. Neither an oppressed victim of the male gaze nor a role model seeking to empower others, Bernhardt consummately managed her face, voice, and body in ways that placed her at the top of an illiberal hierarchy in which audiences pleasurably ceded their wills to hers.

Celebrity performers, however, did not always successfully rule their audiences, who could be willful and obstreperous, particularly in the first half of the nineteenth century. In 1825, actor Junius Booth (father of Edwin and John Wilkes), after being booed in New York, published an "apologetical and supplicatory" letter in a local newspaper in order to make a show of submission to audiences he had offended, one that "completely allayed the excitement against him at New York."[85] Nor, as we saw in the first chapter, did the press always find celebrities alluring and attractive. There is already more than a hint of grotesquerie in the references to Bernhardt figuratively stabbing audience members or administering electric shocks. As the next chapter shows, at least some journalists became critical of Bernhardt's exteriority effects, especially when they spilled outside the theater's confines. Cartoonists in particular were keen to imagine the mayhem that might result when a celebrity transmitted his or her outsized power to fans.

CHAPTER 3

SAVAGERY

In 1957, Elvis Presley held a concert in Vancouver, BC. The young singer had been having a good run since the release of his debut studio album the year before. Radio exposure, record sales, television appearances, and live tours were making him rich and famous. Everywhere he went, Elvis caused a sensation. During one of his 1957 concerts, audience members reportedly wept, moaned, clutched their heads, and even got down on all fours. His consummate management of his own body, even when he seemed to be letting loose, provoked an electric response. But that same popularity attracted its fair share of irate opposition from pundits, who denounced "Pelvis Presley" for his unbuttoned shirts, skintight pants, and wriggling hips.[1] Many an editorial belittled the new star as a "virtuoso of the hootchy-kootchy" whose "bump-and-grind routine," reminiscent of "the blonde bombshells of the burlesque runway," was "odious coming from a man."[2]

Over time, journalists would come to recognize Elvis's merits. In hailing him as a king of rock and roll, they downplayed his debts to African American and female performers. But during those early days, many found his ability to move his audiences repugnant—especially when it came to the effects that his "blonde bombshell" gyrations had on female fans. Just before Elvis performed in Vancouver, the local *Sun* ran a front-page editorial by a reporter who had recently seen Elvis in Spokane. The experience had left the journalist all shook up. Elvis "did the most grotesque and imbecilic things with his body," but far worse were the reactions of the "fresh-faced girls" in the audience, who "screamed, and quivered, and shut their eyes, and reached out their hands to him as if for salvation." His own conclusion was even more violent than the reactions he attributed to Elvis's female public: "If any daughter of mine broke out of the woodshed tonight to see Elvis Presley in Empire Stadium, I'd kick her teeth in."[3]

Other reporters focused less on how Elvis affected audiences than on how people acted after seeing him perform. On September 3, 1957, a few days after the Vancouver concert, the *Sun* ran a front-page photograph of Presley fans, characterized as a "demented army," running toward the camera (figure 3.1). The accompanying article called the teens the "big show" of the evening. Elvis had transformed them "into writhing, frenzied idiots of delight by [means of] the savage jungle beat music." The result: "the most disgusting exhibition of mass hysteria and lunacy this city has ever witnessed."[4] The *Sun*'s accusation that Elvis fans were overreacting

FIGURE 3.1. "Presley Fans Demented," front page of the *Vancouver Sun*, September 3, 1957.

to the star was itself an overreaction, since even the police quoted in the article described them as "just excited kids." On a day when the governor of Arkansas had summoned the National Guard to prevent school integration, a bunch of teenagers milling around a parking lot was hardly front-page news.

A conservative Canadian newspaper in 1957 had historically specific reasons to worry about the burgeoning teen culture and US cultural dominance associated with Elvis. But the *Sun*'s decision to cast Elvis fans as a seething mob was not unique to its politics or location. That same year, *Variety* reported that in Kansas City, "hysterical teenagers," mostly girls, were breaking through police cordons, swarming onstage, and tearing off Presley's clothes, and that in Atlanta, a fight had broken out at a Bill Haley concert.[5] Nor were tales of willful, unmanageable fans confined to rock stars or to the post–World War II era. As we will see, this was a tale as old as modern celebrity culture itself.

Celebrities by definition attract large followings, but their very popularity usually inspires a vocal minority to resist the general euphoria. What better way to take down the latest celebrity than to cast a newborn star's devotees as gullible, ignorant, and unruly? The previous chapter focused on theater reviewers who contentedly understood celebrity culture as a stable hierarchy in which sensational stars held sway over enthralled admirers. This chapter focuses on newspapermen who disdained celebrity culture as an illegitimate, anarchic force that encouraged celebrities and fans to run wild. Some expressed their concerns through elaborate cartoons that depicted rowdy mobs threatening to take even the most captivating icons captive. Such images presented celebrities as unable to control fans who belonged to groups—women, African Americans, Native Americans, Mormons—that the cartoonists deemed incapable of rational self-rule. By portraying fans as savages whose illegitimate violence turned star power itself into a disability, journalists used their agency to portray celebrities and fans as misusing theirs.

The most successful celebrities connect with fans in ways that bypass the media. Media workers often react to that by portraying fans as dangerously out of control. Reporters who see themselves as cultural gatekeepers sometimes paint those who ignore their dictates as bestial gatecrashers. The photographer who snapped the picture on the front page of the Vancouver *Sun* later recalled Elvis fans trampling him "like a herd of cattle."[6] In that instance and others, tensions between media platforms add fuel to the fire. Elvis owed his rapid ascent in 1956 not only to radio and records but also to television, an upstart but increasingly popular technology. His live performances worried film distributors concerned that 1956 movie attendance was down because teenagers preferred to spend their money on concerts.[7]

During the 1870s and 1880s, when modern celebrity culture experienced a global growth spurt, international stars and their admirers became targets of similarly hostile coverage. Celebrities also earned abundant kudos, particularly from reviewers whose job was to decide which performers were most worthy of admiration (see "Sensation"). Nineteenth-century journalists were expected to have strong opinions, and sometimes those opinions were positive. But the press also liked to see itself as leading public opinion, not following it, and certainly not as mindlessly promoting a few celebrated individuals. Some reporters fretted, not without cause, that colleagues might lose their bearings around celebrities such as Sarah Bernhardt. When one newspaper man exclaimed, after shaking Bernhardt's hand, "I feel her warm flesh still, clear to the tips of my fingers. It sent a thrill all over me. To touch divinity and live!," a fellow journalist quoted him with a sneer: "And this is written for grown men and women who live in an age that is supposed to be intelligent."[8] The implication: reporters who gushed like fans insulted a public presumed to be mature, restrained, and reasonable, surrendering their own authority in the process.

In an era before technology made it easy to capture stars in their less scripted moments, one key way for the press to assert its independence from celebrity culture was through the genre of caricature. Before 1881, French law required illustrators seeking to publish caricatures of public figures to first secure permission from the famous individuals they depicted.[9] After an 1881 law waived that requirement, newspapermen took full advantage of their newfound freedom, shifting from cartoons heavy on allegorical figures and abstract social types to lampoons of living individuals.[10] Caricatures proliferated of Bernhardt as a repulsive circus attraction and of her fans as savages. Although comic newspapers in France often espoused republican values, they did not necessarily embrace the kind of radical democracy associated with the revolutionary Commune that the Third Republic had violently suppressed in 1871. Many of the cartoons caricaturing the Bernhardt phenomenon aimed to curb fans' dangerous enthusiasms by offering cautionary tales about celebrity fever as an outlaw source of misrule, and did so by rendering the latest star attractions as objects of repugnance.

THE CELEBRITY ATTRACTION

To this day, those dismayed by celebrity culture are quick to associate it with low entertainment. Sarah Bernhardt made her mark in classical tragedies as well as boulevard melodramas and was, even at her most sensational, more Meryl Streep than Miley Cyrus. But that did not stop skeptical journalists from describing her as a sideshow attraction better suited to the menagerie, the circus, or the colonial exhibition than to the loftiest theaters. French journalist Victor Fournel, already alarmed that Bernhardt's London success was leading her to abandon art to become a curiosity, became even more irked when Bernhardt announced a plan to entertain "the Yankees."[11] "People go to see her as a species of freak," wrote one critic of her 1890s *Cleopatra*.[12] Another described the star's ambition as "sufficiently strong to send her to the top at once, after the manner of the young woman who is shot out of a cannon in the variety halls."[13] One reporter imagined Bernhardt trying something "in the acrobatic line," while jokes about the bizarrely thin "microscopic artist" affiliated her with pseudo-scientific exhibits such as the flea circus.[14] Even admirers sometimes evoked the lingo of the circus barker: "There she stands," proclaimed a 1910 article preserved in a theatrical scrapbook, "the Ajax of two centuries, the Most Wonderful Woman in the World."[15] Sword swallower, tiger tamer, world's thinnest woman: it is difficult to come up with a circus act to which Bernhardt was *not* compared.[16]

Though Bernhardt affiliated herself with high art, frequently giving poetry readings and resurrecting obscure dramas such as Alfred de Musset's *Lorenzaccio*, she also embraced associations with more outlandish forms of popular entertainment. In 1905, when she agreed to tour the US vaudeville circuit, often performing in literal circus tents, a satirical article imagined the French star comparing her performances to Buffalo Bill's Wild West extravaganza, with its "big shots of emotion and smoke of sentiment . . . full of boom, pouf of passion."[17] The actress's decision to continue acting into her seventies, even after a 1915 leg amputation, only cemented her association with the freak show. After learning of her operation, the head of the Shubert theaters' press office wrote a memo suggesting that she do a

"Post-Amputation Tour," predicting that it would be a "great success . . . because of the news interest attached to seeing a woman of her age and her standing appearing with a cork leg. The newspapers will eat this up."[18] Tour she did, performing on a litter to full houses across the United States.[19]

George Bernard Shaw may have had all this in mind when he accused Bernhardt of claiming an "unquestioned right . . . to posture in a traveling show."[20] Shaw was not the only one to associate Bernhardt with "charlatanry."[21] French actress Marie Colombier, who accompanied the star on her first North American tour, compared her to a juggler and Indian fakir, able to maintain her cool while deceiving the public.[22] In a thinly veiled exposé, Colombier presented her former boss as "Sarah Barnum," merging the French actress with American huckster P. T. Barnum, whose marketing feats included convincing many that Joice Heth, an African American slave, was George Washington's 161-year-old former mammy and exhibiting members of Sioux and Winnebago tribes.[23]

Journalists seeking to make Bernhardt's attractions repugnant often emphasized her Jewishness, which they presented as a combination of unattractive physical and personal traits. Though nineteenth-century France was by no means uniformly hostile to qualities perceived as Jewish, 1880s France saw a sharp rise in public expressions of anti-Semitic sentiment. Colombier's book formed part of that wave.[24] The Sarah Barnum on Colombier's cover is crowned with a Jewish star and shown in profile with a prominent nose and comically unruly hair (figure 3.2). The image resembles illustrations of fictional Jewish villains such as Fagin and Svengali who embodied the greed and excessive ambition that Europeans had long associated with Jews. (Even moderate ambition seems excessive to those who have contempt for those exercising it.) By 1894, when French army officer Alfred Dreyfus was convicted of selling state secrets to the Prussians, many had begun to fear the hidden dangers that even assimilated Jews might pose to the nation's safety.

There is nothing hidden about the threat posed by Colombier's female Barnum, whose pushy energy could not be more apparent. She appears to leap out of the hoop that frames her, and though her carriage has no horses, its propulsive force creates a zephyr-like vortex that swirls around the letters spelling "ARAH" and presses the letters spelling "Barnum" forward, toward the picture plane, so that they seem on the verge of falling off the page. The text itself harps even more on Sarah Barnum's Jewishness, repeatedly calling Bernhardt's mother "La Juive," the Jewess; attributing

FIGURE 3.2. Marie
Colombier, *The
Memoirs of Sarah
Barnum*, 1884.

to Sarah Barnum "the commercial intelligence inherent in her race"; and remarking that, "a real daughter of Israel . . . [,] Barnum was dirty," leaving little doubt about the pejorative meaning of the six-pointed star on the cover.[25]

Colombier was not unique in linking Bernhardt's skillful self-promotion to a Jewishness that placed her outside civilization but also made her consummately gifted at swindling legitimate citizens. British journalists commented on how the "great show-woman" shared her assertiveness, shrewdness, and love of gain with Benjamin Disraeli, the celebrated Jewish prime minister who became Lord Beaconsfield: "There is a rumour that Sarah Bernhardt has undertaken a bust of Beaconsfield. His lordship will tax all her skill; it is not easy to chisel him."[26] As late as 1899, a French journalist attacked Bernhardt's "childish, almost savage procedures . . . of publicity and shameless theatricality" by comparing her to Judith in the

Old Testament: "She went to the Holophernes-Public . . . and . . . has its head, which she flatters, caresses, inebriates, insults. . . . She is Woman, she is the Jewess, and she is Success."[27] Over the course of Bernhardt's career, many journalists favorably compared her to rulers and divinities, praising her as a goddess, a high priestess, and a queen, the "Napoleon of women," who "never had a Waterloo."[28] Others, however, went to the opposite extreme, casting her as an interloper who dominated the public not to please it but to destroy it.

The press proved even more anxious about the crowds who gathered to celebrate the star. In Copenhagen, Bernhardt's reception proved so enthusiastic that "some of the inhabitants, unaware of what was going on, asked if the excitement meant a change of government."[29] Writing about Bernhardt's first visit to London in 1879, poet and cultural critic Matthew Arnold worried that "the extraordinary attraction exercised upon us by the French players" might cause the English public to lose its sense of "measure." He wrote: "All this has moved . . . a surviving and aged moralist here and there amongst us to exclaim: 'Shame on you, feeble heads, to slavery prone!' The English public, according to these cynics, have been exhibiting themselves as men of prostrate mind, who pay to power a reverence anything but seemly."[30] Having himself "yielded to infatuation" for Rachel in his youth, Arnold made clear that he did not intend to "cast a stone" at those "running eagerly" after the new generation of French players. But the space he accorded the "moralist" view lent credence to its equation of fandom and "slavery," as did his citation of a Wordsworth poem decrying the "feeble heads" that had capitulated to Napoleon. Where the reviewers cited in "Sensation" described Bernhardt's power to enslave as a function of her prodigious talent, Arnold used the same metaphor to present fans as having lost the strength essential to the exercise of free citizenship. Ventriloquizing that view without fully embracing or rejecting it, Arnold nonetheless left the reader with a vivid sense of celebrities as tyrants whose attractions any self-respecting audience member should stalwartly resist.

Journalists began to refer to a Bernhardt "craze" around 1880.[31] A decade later, the word "fan," with its roots in "fanatic," linked strong interest in celebrities with impaired reason. "Fans" initially referred only to baseball aficionados. By 1914 journalists were also applying the term to actors' most devoted admirers, although still placing it within quotes to mark it as novel slang.[32] Concerns about out-of-control fans were rife, with many seeing celebrity culture as promoting unruly public action by those least capable of self-government. The previous chapter cited many who saw Bernhardt as an all-powerful despot who managed herself and her public with consummate skill. The less sanguine view was that no one was minding the celebrity store. Stars were not canny tyrants deftly running their own performances and orchestrating public responses. Instead, they were themselves subject to the passions they unleashed and victims of their greatest devotees. Even those who conceded that celebrities owed their success in part to talent and hard work worried that star worship might make fans lose their bearings. That concern only increased in the twentieth century, when fascists used mass media to create cults of personality.

Theater has always had champions ready to praise its capacity to improve morality, foster critical insight, and promote direct democracy. Tributes to enthusiastic fans, however, are rare. Indeed, pundits have long feared that celebrity culture licenses subordinate groups to run amok. Nineteenth-century caricaturists imagined women, Mormons, African Americans, Native Americans, Africans, Indians, and Turks succumbing to Bernhardt mania and fomenting mayhem. Far from assuming that democracy should be as complete as possible, many in 1880s France, the United States, and the United Kingdom worried more about too much democracy than too little. The middle-class and elite white men who dominated politics and the press were not all convinced that equality was an unlimited good. Britain had only definitively abolished slavery in 1833, France in 1848, the United States in 1865. Each country still imposed severe limits on who could vote. In 1880, the United States, still smarting from its civil war, was in the process of undoing Reconstruction efforts to extend full citizenship to former slaves. France, subject throughout the nineteenth century to frequent revolutions that left the country oscillating between democratic and autocratic extremes, remained haunted by the revolutionary Communards of 1871 and was, in 1880, only beginning to liberalize its Third Republic.

Celebrity culture especially vexed those anxious that democracy might combine the worst aspects of monarchy and mob rule. In a liberal democracy, representatives are chosen by an electorate whose right to vote stems from a presumed capacity for reason and self-control that in turn fosters willingness to follow rules and procedures. But many nineteenth-century figures considered democracy a potential nightmare that might allow the people and the individuals they elevated to wield unchecked power. Liberal democracy imposes order; illegitimate democracy foments chaos.[33] Those fears about democracy surfaced in cartoons that pictured both Bernhardt and her fans fainting, drowning, shooting guns, scalping elected officials, and engaging in torture and cannibalism. No longer would the strong passions unleashed by celebrities be contained within the theater. Instead, a celebrity's expressive powers might inspire acts of grotesque violence in real life. These extravagant visions implied that only the press retained enough freedom from celebrity culture to see its dangers clearly.

Caricature works by selecting a few key features to amplify, reverse, and ridicule. As nineteenth-century cartoonist Harry Furniss put it in his autobiography, "a caricaturist is an artistic contortionist. He is grotesque for effect," turning the sublime into the ridiculous, mixing "the gigantic" with the "infinitely little," the "animal" with the "ethereal."[34] Because cartoonists depicting real people need their subjects to be recognizable despite those distortions, they often focus, as historian Patricia Mainardi has observed, on "news that everyone already knows."[35] The principle of exaggerating the familiar operates throughout a full-page color cartoon purporting to depict frequently reported chapters in the life of Sarah Bernhardt (figure 3.3). The cartoon was executed by Henri Demare (1846–1888) and published on February 18, 1883, in *Le Grelot*, a four-page weekly whose cover always featured a full-page illustration, often with a political bent but sometimes focused on arts and entertainment.[36] The image illustrates famous episodes from Bernhardt's life offstage: her work tending soldiers during the Franco-Prussian war, her balloon ascent, her forays into self-portraiture, her toast to Alsace and Lorraine, and her return from a United States tour that, the caption claims, left her "missing her fatherland." Most of the figures exhibit some degree of distortion. At top left, the cartoonist grafts an adult Bernhardt's head onto a baby's body; at bottom right, Bernhardt's lover, the painter Louise Abbéma, is depicted with a disproportionately large head and wearing pants, though in real life Abbéma confined her taste for masculine dress to tailored jackets worn over skirts.

Even as this cartoon reinforces Bernhardt's star power by multiplying her image, it also undoes it. By showcasing the artists who produce the images on view, the cartoon makes Bernhardt an effect rather than a cause. At bottom right, we see Abbéma holding a brush and palette, putting the finishing touches on the central vignette. This painterly flourish assigns the authorship of even the self-portraits we see Bernhardt painting and sculpting to another. Abbéma's signature appears twice, the cartoonist Demare's once, Bernhardt's not at all. The words "pinxit" ("painted") and "delinearet" ("sketched") appended to Abbéma's and Demare's signatures

FIGURE 3.3. Henri Demare, caricature of Sarah Bernhardt, *Le Grelot*, February 18, 1883.

elevate their status as image makers. Bernhardt, by contrast, does not name herself; she is named, repeatedly, in captions ("Birth of Sarah!") that infantilize her by presuming that both cartoonist and public are on a first-name basis with the star.

The cartoon further punctures Bernhardt's stardom by belittling her fans. The lower left-hand panel portrays Bernhardt waving farewell as she heads toward an erect, fully draped figure of France, portrayed as a noble sculptural allegory of liberty and white womanhood. To Bernhardt's right kneels a woman with skin shaded dark brown in the color original, who is kneeling and appears to be either worshipping the star or begging her not to depart. The Bernhardt figure's large ears, long nose, and high cheekbones all signal an unattractive Jewishness underscored by the Jewish stars at the top of the page.[37] The figure of the rotund African American woman evokes the iconography of slavery. She is barefoot, clad in a shabby, short-sleeved striped garment, and kneels with hands raised in an imploring gesture reminiscent of the widely reproduced imagery that had in previous decades accompanied the abolitionist slogan "Am I not a man and a brother?"

With fans like these, the cartoonist implies, who needs celebrity? The vignette recasts the star's success as failure, her elevation by fans as their mutual debasement. Bernhardt's first voyage to North America had gained her a new following abroad. With it came a financial independence that allowed her to bypass censorious French reporters, still angry that she had left the Théâtre-Français. Bernhardt's success outside France, however, initially did nothing to rehabilitate her standing inside it. On the contrary: French cartoonists depicted her new American followers as lacking status and judgment. The African American woman's subservient posture and rapt gaze make the dollars that she and others like her have conferred on the star worthless. Indeed, the cartoonist equates the fan with the moneybags whose exaggerated rotundity she shares; in the color original, both the bags and the kneeling woman's striped dress and hat are shaded yellow, as are the Jewish stars at the top of the image. The cactus next to the African American woman slyly suggests, with dubious geographical accuracy, that Bernhardt could succeed only in a cultural desert. As portrayed here, the star herself scorns the American nation that worships her by turning her back on her lowly admirer to approach a tricolor image of France. Disgusted by her devotee, the star even seems to abandon her earnings, so eager is she to recover her "patrie," the French fatherland.

UNRULY PUBLICS

French cartoonists loved to show Bernhardt causing proper citizens to lose their heads and noncitizens to act like outlaws. An elaborate cartoon by Albert Robida (1848–1926), published on February 19, 1881, in *La Carica-ture*, a Parisian weekly with a middle-class readership, offered a delirious vision of the political violence unleashed by "The Conquest of America by Sarah Bernhardt" (figure 3.4). As out of control as the fans it depicted, the cartoon sprawled over the newspaper's two-page centerfold.

A lengthy tongue-in-cheek subtitle aligns the fanciful image with up-to-the-minute reporting by presenting the cartoon as based on photographs and sketches provided by the paper's correspondents. The elaborate composition mixes small, crudely rendered sketches with larger, more realistic engravings of actual photographic portraits that circulated widely during the publicity blitz accompanying Bernhardt's US tour. The thin black lines framing those photographic images set them apart as portraits whose shadings gesture at a three-dimensional realism absent from the more cartoonish drawings. But Robida also undermines those images' relative dignity by allowing cartoon elements to invade their frames. A careful look at the portrait of Bernhardt as Frou-Frou in the top left corner, for example, shows a cloud drifting in from one scene and teepees jutting into it from another.

The captions to the photographic images transform their grandeur into grandiosity. Underneath the image of Bernhardt as Marguerite in *La Dame aux camélias*, for example, we read that while playing a courtesan, the actress suggestively promised to deliver some sermons "in the flesh" at a local cathedral, a pun that conflates the performer with the fallen woman she portrays and presents her acolytes as either gullible or corrupt. The text under the image of Bernhardt as Adrienne Lecouvreur describes her acting in Arkansas for fur trappers and several grizzly bears who are all deeply moved by her performance, a joke that reinforces the cartoon's key theme: the animal nature of the star's most adoring spectators. Below the image of Bernhardt as Phèdre, her most exalted role, we read that when performing Racine in Mohican translation, the actress drew tears from "all the warriors and their squaws," who "pitilessly scalp" the few spectators suspected of coldness.

Many of the other panels similarly deflate Bernhardt's success in the United States by depicting her North American admirers as brutes who force others to submit to Bernhardt fever. We see her inspiring Mormon wives to "revolution" in a chaotic image that shows a mob of women, white and black, armed with brooms, an umbrella, and a banjo (figure 3.5). The caption explains that Bernhardt has encouraged the women to overthrow Brigham Young, arrest their husbands, burn Salt Lake City, and scheme to replace polygamy with polyandry. Other panels endow the star with an uncanny ability to deprive white men of both their dignity and their hair. The final panel, discussed in more detail below, shows a swarm of bald, scalped senators acclaiming Sarah as emperor while she towers over them, wearing a cloak made from their shorn locks. Elsewhere, kneeling men swallow an entire Great Lake to show their admiration for Bernhardt, who wears a bathing costume covered in stars and stripes.

Yet another outlandish image portrays a white man who disappears into a sausage machine to become the star's lunch, while, to the left, a waiter with darkly inked black skin, wildly curly hair, and exaggeratedly large lips serves Bernhardt the results (figure 3.6). America appears here as a place whose outsized appetites level differences, a point underscored by the resemblance between Bernhardt and the waiter, both shown leaning over the sausages at similar angles, with Bernhardt's nose almost as overstated as the waiter's lips and hair. Behind them, a sign trumpets the vast quantity of sausages sold. Its two rows of zeroes underscore the message that America is a land of inflated but empty values; not for nothing do the sausages resemble coins that in turn resemble ciphers. Indeed, as processed human flesh, the sausages are worse than worthless. The caption offers a gruesome take on the all-consuming nature of fandom, with the directors of the sausage factory hurling themselves into a machine marked "Pig's Entrance" in order to have the honor of being included in "the divine artist's" lunch.

Several panels further deflate Bernhardt's agency by suggesting that she has conquered America only to be conquered in turn by its indigenous peoples. One caption imagines her delivering long lectures in English, Comanche, and Iroquois. At the very center of the composition, Robida places an image of Bernhardt covered in inky marks: "To honor the Apache nation," reads the caption, "Sarah plays Phèdre with national tattoos" (figure 3.7). The image is one of childish defacement, akin to drawing a mustache on the *Mona Lisa*, but the hand at work here is also artistically knowing (Robida was *La Caricature*'s founding editor) and the image reminiscent of the cartoon process itself. Robida's use of blank space foregrounds the

FIGURE 3.4. Albert Robida, "La Conquête de l'Amérique, par Sarah Bernhardt," *La*

FIGURE 3.5. Detail, Albert Robida, "La Conquête de l'Amérique, par Sarah Bernhardt," *La Caricature*, February 19, 1881.

Sarah encourage une révolution chez les Mormons hostiles. Le pouvoir de Brigham Young est abattu. Salt-Lac City est brûlée. Les maris sont chassés ou arrêtés. Quelques esprits exaltés parlent d'établir la polyandrie.

FIGURE 3.6. Detail, Albert Robida, "La Conquête de l'Amérique, par Sarah Bernhardt," *La Caricature*, February 19, 1881.

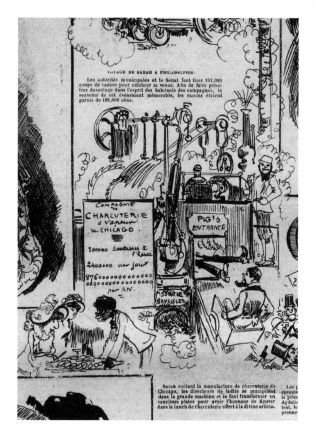

Sarah visitant la manufacture de charcuterie de Chicago, les directeurs de ladite se précipitent dans la grande machine et se font transformer en saucisses plates pour avoir l'honneur de figurer dans le lunch de charcuterie offert à la divine artiste.

FIGURE 3.7. Detail, Albert Robida, "La Conquête de l'Amérique, par Sarah Bernhardt," *La Caricature*, February 19, 1881.

FIGURE 3.8. Detail, Albert Robida, "La Conquête de l'Amérique, par Sarah Bernhardt," *La Caricature*, February 19, 1881.

tattoo lines and encourages us to look at them more closely. Some of the marks suggest pagan idolatry—a serpent, crescent moons, a stick-like figure bearing a tomahawk on horseback. Others fail to resolve into recognizable objects or letters, suggesting a barbarism of representation as well as of self-presentation. Bernhardt's upcast eyes evoke a classical pose that contrasts uneasily with her slightly parted lips, open enough to show her teeth, often a sign in nineteenth-century caricatures of a lack of social decorum. The loss of status implied by Bernhardt's savage appearance is underscored by the caption's observation that it is Bernhardt who honors the Apaches with her performance, not they who honor her.

Over and over again, the cartoon depicts celebrity and fandom unleashing political havoc. The star's motley fans attack everyone who fails to admire their idol. Celebrity becomes military coercion when Bernhardt marches on Broadway in a soldier's uniform, gun in one hand, sword in another, leading her troops as she steps over a cannon (figure 3.8). Bernhardt precipitates a second civil war when, as the caption puts it, "populations shattered

FIGURE 3.9. Detail, Albert Robida, "La Conquête de l'Amérique, par Sarah Bernhardt," *La Caricature*, February 19, 1881.

FIGURE 3.10. Detail, Albert Robida, "La Conquête de l'Amérique, par Sarah Bernhardt," *La Caricature*, February 19, 1881.

by the tragedian" beg her to accept the presidency of the United States, leading to "immense agitation" and the resistance of some states. US democracy is portrayed as chaotically violent, with two white men pointing guns at each other while others stuff ballot boxes with votes for Sarah. In a swipe at American ignorance that is also a visual joke about a world turned topsy-turvy, two of the political banners promoting Sarah have reversed the first letter of her name (figure 3.9). To help decide whether or not to proclaim the actress president, the Sioux loyal to Bernhardt "invade" Washington, DC, and scalp US senators (figure 3.10).

In the final image, at the top of stairs so steep that they appear to constitute a ladder, Bernhardt towers over the now bald senators, a very long sword in one hand, a crown in the other, while a dark-skinned Sioux holds the senators at bay, standing guard with a large musket (figure 3.11). The star's spotted ermine robe echoes that worn by Napoleon for his 1804 coronation as emperor of France. The caption reads: "Sarah Opening Congress. All the senators converted by scalping acclaim Sarah empress of all the Americas. The anti-Bernhardt states surrender, and the country is entirely pacified." In contrast to the actual Civil War, which ended slavery and strengthened the union, Bernhardt's civil war enforces subordination to the star and topples democratic institutions.

Although Robida's cartoon claims to be about the United States, it is, of course, really about France. In 1881, the Third Republic had only very recently entered the liberal phase that followed a decade dominated by reaction against the 1871 revolutionary Commune. The Commune had in turn overthrown a dictatorial imperial regime that had severely restricted the press for two decades, just as Louis-Philippe and Napoleon had earlier in the century. The new freedoms of 1881 licensed journalists to ridicule public figures long protected by punitive libel laws. But, as so often in France, progressive politics did not translate into truly egalitarian democracy. For decades, most white Frenchmen, even those involved in the nation's democratic revolutions, had cited their superior rationality and cultivation as alibis for imperial conquest and as reasons to exclude women from political participation. Throughout the century, French leaders cited ideas about religious and racial difference to justify incursions into Egypt and Africa.[38] The new journalism often ridiculed feminist calls to let women vote, attend university, and enter professions. Shortly after Robida satirized Bernhardt's conquest of America, he produced another cover for *La Caricature* mocking French women's demands to participate in elections and government.[39]

This historical context alerts us to the double valence of Robida's decision to represent a popular Jewish actress inspiring the enfranchised and disenfranchised alike to overthrow elected officials in order to install her as their autocratic female ruler. The cartoon deflates Bernhardt's achievements as a theatrical celebrity by depicting her fans as unruly outcasts, which in turn inflates the threat that she and they pose. It offers an antagonistic commentary on celebrity culture as empowering the lowest strata of society to unseat the elevated few who might curb their passions. Only the salutary ridicule of a free press, the cartoon implies, can correct these excesses.

FIGURE 3.11. Detail, Albert Robida, "La Conquête de l'Amérique, par Sarah Bernhardt," *La Caricature*, February 19, 1881.

SAVAGE FANS, DEBASED CELEBRITIES

In contrast to the vision of a dangerously omnipotent star, a May 15, 1880, cartoon published in *La Caricature* imagined Bernhardt's popularity as making the star pathetically powerless rather than disruptively powerful (figure 3.12). Here, instead of leading fans into revolt, the celebrity falls victim to their barbarism. The "Aventures et mésaventures de Séraphiska" consists of six images that depict Turks, Native Americans, Africans, and Borneans interacting with a Bernhardt figure renamed Séraphiska, a distinctly un-Gallic variation on "Sarah."[40] Each

FIGURE 3.12. "Aventures et mésaventures de Séraphiska,"

episode of this elaborate narrative purports to sketch the consequences of Séraphiska's "popularity," a word that recurs in many of the captions. We begin with a pickpocket placing Séraphiska in a box intercepted by Sioux, whose preponderance in these cartoons, along with the Iroquois, may owe something to the French origins of their names. The caption "Séraphiska observes her popularity among the natives" contrasts ironically with a crude image that shows the actress gagged, silenced, and orally violated when the Sioux use her mouth as the target for a bowling ball. "Popularity," far from strengthening Bernhardt's agency, deprives her of it by making her a target for those who find cruelty an amusing sport.

rre, sur mer et dans le ventre des bêtes féroces

ricature, May 15, 1880.

The remaining panels depict Bernhardt's fans around the world as savages. Once again, a cartoonist imagines Bernhardt performing for Native Americans, but this time she is more victim than victor. A caption explains that the natives have used "violence" to make the star sign with "the Grand Theatre of Tomahawk-City," a cartoonish reversal of the real Bernhardt's decision, months before, to break her contract with the Théâtre-Français and tour America as a free agent (figure 3.13). In a warning about the dangers that fandom poses to the rule of law, the cartoon contrasts the legitimate power of a French bailiff to the illegitimate violence exercised by the Sioux. The bailiff tries to use his official authority to make the actress honor her contract with a French theater, but finds himself scalped, then tattooed each morning with a notice of Séraphiska's evening performance. The legal writ represented by his subpoena cedes power to a violent and violating inscription. Like the Sioux, Bernhardt causes the white man's law to crumble, but she escapes the legal censure of the French state only to fall prey to the brutal energies she releases.

Far from being in Séraphiska's thrall, the native spectators hold her captive. The cartoon almost literally erases the star by rendering her in faded, barely discernible lines that appear even more faint when contrasted

FIGURE 3.13. Detail, "Aventures et mésaventures de Séraphiska," *La Caricature,*
May 15, 1880.

to the saturated black ink used to represent the hair, headdresses, and
tattoos of the Sioux audience members. The cartoon combines myths of
savage warriors armed with tomahawks and captivity narratives in which
indigenous groups kidnap white women and force them to assimilate to
tribal ways. Such myths experienced a resurgence in the 1870s, at precisely
the moment when the US government was waging genocidal violence
against Native Americans.[41] Mocking as the French newspapers were of
the United States, they uncritically replicated its invidious depictions of
native peoples.

Cumulatively, the cartoon presents a variation on Homi Bhabha's description of the colonized Other as "not quite / not white."[42] Séraphiska is
just civilized enough to highlight the savagery of her fans, but not civilized
enough to tame their desires to annihilate her. The remaining panels show
one colonized group after another attacking the star, their enthusiasm in-
distinguishable from aggression. In a parade of imperialist stereotypes,
we see a Turkish grand vizier drown his eight hundred and twenty-five
wives to impress the actress, while Hindus place her on a pyre that evokes
suttee. Other panels equate the public's attraction to the star with a drive
to destroy her through ingestion, regurgitation, or starvation. In India, a

snake swallows the star, then disgorges her; in Egypt, it is a crocodile. A Nubian king forces Séraphiska to sculpt him. Anticipating the association of Africa with cannibalism that would repeat itself in an 1892 exhibit of "human sacrifice in Dahomey" at the Paris wax museum, another panel depicts an African king and his court "literally go[ing] crazy for the great artist. . . . [They] love her so much that they decide to eat her."[43] In order to make the too-thin Séraphiska more appetizing, they force-feed her. She then becomes so fat that even after a French circus impresario rescues her, "she is no longer recognizable in the theater of her former success." The cartoon ends with Bernhardt so sad about her lost celebrity that she abandons the legitimate stage to become the lowliest kind of popular attraction: a giant woman at a fair. The suggestion, however, is that this is only a return to Séraphiska's base origins, since an earlier panel depicts an elephant recognizing her from their shared past at a Paris boulevard theater.

An even more violent take on celebrity culture's dangerously democratic excesses appeared on the cover of the same February 19, 1881, issue of *La Caricature* containing the two-page cartoon "Sarah Bernhardt's Conquest of America" discussed earlier. The cover anticipates the full cartoon's vision of "popular enthusiasm" for Bernhardt capsizing the political order. To present the star with the key to the city of Chicago, white male officials line up in their nightshirts, ropes around their necks. "Enthusiastic" Native American spectators scalp Bernhardt to turn her hair into souvenirs, scalp their wives to provide her with a wig, and then proclaim Bernhardt their tribe's female leader. Bernhardt's theatrical tour becomes a martial campaign in which she mounts a horse in full military regalia and leads an army that includes her fellow actors, many of them women in soldier's uniforms.

As with the other caricatures we have looked at closely, this image (not reproduced here) plays with inflation and deflation, taking distortions to grotesque extremes. Two relatively flattering and quasi-photographic images of Bernhardt on the cover's lower half look oddly gigantic in contrast to the cartoonish antics around them. The gratuitous violence that Robida attributes to Bernhardt and her followers reaches a gruesome apotheosis in a panel that depicts a large ship capsizing as a captain in the foreground shoots at it. The caption reads: "So that no-one can ever again tread upon a ship on which Sarah has placed her divine foot, the captain of the steamboat that had the honor to carry Sarah over the Hudson blows his brains out along with those of 800 male and female passengers, who include 45 negresses in an interesting situation." The image of a tilting, exploding boat presents Bernhardt's celebrity and her admirers' fervor as overturning even the most solid structures and generating a kind of free fall. The reference to "45 negresses" alludes to a famous legal case in which British slave traders threw slaves overboard to drown, then claimed insurance damages for lost property. It is difficult to tell whether Robida is criticizing callous indifference to black women's lives, reproducing it, or both. From any of those angles, the image presents celebrity worship as a fall from the emancipated citizenship African Americans had achieved by 1880. Bernhardt mania revives antebellum slavery and its harsh indifference to black suffering. In this hysterical critique of celebrity hysteria, fandom poses a mortal danger to the powerful and the powerless alike.

In contrast to worshipful theater reviewers who bolstered Bernhardt's celebrity and vaunted their own discernment by praising her, caricaturists asserted their freedom to ridicule both the star and her admirers. Unlike the mainstream drama critics who lauded Bernhardt's hypnotic ability to control her own body and the bodies of theatergoers, caricaturists portrayed the star as grotesque, her followers as abject and violent, and fandom as a passion that no one, least of all the star herself, could control. *La Caricature*, a leading Parisian humor magazine, depicted the celebrity as a demagogue and her fans as terrorists, singling out for parody African Americans, Native Americans, Indians, and Africans, all groups who were in fact being subjected to considerable violence at the time. With the contradictions typical of racist and imperialist discourse and of caricature itself, French cartoonists presented victims of state domination as enemies of the state, and an actor who performed exclusively in French for audiences that included many highly educated people as unable to control her hordes of brutish admirers. With ingenious nastiness, cartoonists devised scenarios that simultaneously exaggerated the threat posed by celebrity worship and diminished celebrity merit.

For all its aggressive devaluation of celebrity, however, caricature was an essentially reactive, parasitic form. Making Bernhardt repulsive only inverted her very real powers of attraction. Cartoonists could spoof the star precisely because she commanded so much recognition; their parodies made sense to French readers only because French newspapers reported Bernhardt's London and North American successes so avidly and in so much detail. The caricatures reproduced here, it probably does not need stating, were outlandish inventions. Unlike theater reviews, which painstakingly described actual stage performances, cartoons bore little relationship to reality. There are, alas, no records of Bernhardt inspiring women and Native Americans to wage armed revolt, although her extensive tours of the United States did occasionally take the star into Indian Territory and one early twentieth-century article described a pro-suffrage group greeting her with flowers upon her arrival in Chicago. Although many French newspapers used anti-Semitic imagery to ridicule Bernhardt, there is only one recorded incident of an actual anti-Semitic attack on the actress: after an Odessa mob shouted "Down with the Jewess! Give us money!" and threw stones and sticks at Bernhardt's carriage, the actress diverted her attackers by throwing "stage jewels" at them. When they scattered to chase them, she escaped to her hotel, where she reportedly asked if the mob thought she was going to "throw pearls before swine."[44] Nor is there any evidence that African or Native Americans were especially strong Bernhardt fans, although nineteenth-century playbills and letters to newspaper editors attest to African Americans being excluded from the best seats and confined to segregated sections of New York and Boston theaters.[45] However, as the next chapter shows, caricaturists were neither completely wrong nor completely alone in imagining how much fans longed to get closer to their favorite celebrities.

CHAPTER 4

INTIMACY

Celebrity is all about drama. This axiom holds for fans as well as stars. This is why only the most extreme fans make the news: a Madonna devotee tattooing her album covers on his back; a woman pretending to be a hotel maid in order to gain access to tennis star Andy Murray's room so that she could stroke his arm while he slept.[1] Novels and films from Irving Wallace's *The Fan Club* to Martin Scorsese's *The King of Comedy*, Stephen King's *Misery*, and Sofia Coppola's *The Bling Ring* tend to depict fans either as groupies desperately seeking to turn celebrities into real-life friends or lovers, or as stalkers threatening stars' safety and even their lives.

To be sure, a very small number of highly visible fans have literally killed or attempted murder in desperate bids to gain the attention of stars as varied as Andy Warhol, John Lennon, and Jodie Foster—and in order to enter the limelight themselves. But the notion that the typical fan is more active than passive is itself a fantasy, one set in motion two decades ago by media scholar Henry Jenkins when he influentially argued that fans are not gullible, passive consumers but creative, savvy producers.[2] Setting out to redeem fandom, Jenkins trained his attention on enthusiasts who lobbied studios to keep their favorite shows on the air, forged communities by dressing up as their favorite characters and stars, or wrote fiction based on their favorite TV shows or science fiction books. His aim: to redefine fans as critics and collaborative authors who form "adversarial" collectives that resist and oppose dominant powers and mainstream culture.[3]

By extending insights drawn from feminist studies of female spectators to fans in general, Jenkins radically transformed celebrity studies, but did little to alter the value system that had trivialized fans in the first place. In that hierarchy, activity trumps passivity, production matters more than consumption, and critique has more prestige than admiration or enjoyment. To make this argument, Jenkins focused on fans who respond to celebrated works and genres by creating new, freestanding works: "Fans do not simply consume preproduced stories; they manufacture their own fanzine stories and novels, art prints, songs, videos, performances, etc."[4] Some do. But the majority of fans focus on celebrated *people*, not famous works, and take great pleasure in consuming preexisting materials in ways that hover between full activity and utter passivity. Only a handful of fans express themselves by producing original and autonomous objects. Reading Jenkins today, one comes away with the impression that his textual poachers are like characters in *Game of Thrones*, jousting to establish the legitimacy of their own meanings. But faced with a choice between being in *Game of Thrones* and watching *Game of Thrones*, most fans would choose to sit back and enjoy the show.

What if the kinds of extreme independence and activity that Jenkins valorizes are overrated? Most fans are tranquil daydreamers, not aggressive stalkers, happier to commune with representations of their favorite stars than to pursue them in real life. Furthermore, the rare fans who hyperactively pursue celebrities are more likely to reinforce the status quo than to challenge it. Fans who crave contact with the famous rarely aim to overturn established hierarchies; instead, they want a share of the celebrity's wealth and status. Those few who pursue and harass celebrities, far from operating from what Jenkins characterizes as "a position of cultural marginality and social weakness," replicate the dominant and domineering belief that women and men in the public eye exist solely for the pleasure of others.[5] Nor should authorship and the production of autonomous artworks be the measure of what makes fandom matter. Most fans who craft their own artifacts favor genres such as scrapbooks and fan mail, which foster proximity, familiarity, and interdependence. Fans tend to recycle preexisting representations, not generate new ones. The majority contentedly surf the intricate surface of celebrity culture, rarely modifying what they find there. For each devotee energetic enough to try to enliven celebrity culture by silhouetting a magazine image, making a GIF, visiting an actor backstage, or crafting an elaborate prequel to a favorite author's work, there are millions content simply to hang a poster of Audrey Hepburn on their wall, listen one more time to their favorite Bruce Springsteen album, or follow Rihanna on Instagram.

Whether compiling hard copies of images and texts in scrapbooks or importing digital ones into Tumblr and Pinterest sites, most fans curate and collage ephemeral materials handed to them by others. Rather than dismiss such efforts as parasitic or attempt to redeem them as more autonomous than they are, this chapter explores how fandom inhabits zones between the extremes of heroic activity and catatonic passivity. Fandom blurs the distinctions between reading and writing, production and consumption.[6] Fans rarely direct their own fates or those of others, and few become auteur-like creators of freestanding artworks. But at the same time, almost no fan is utterly passive, completely acted upon by determining forces. Instead, most fans inhabit a middle state of play that involves collecting, assembling, arranging, framing, transposing, classifying, displaying, daydreaming, contemplation, and immersion. Though fans enjoy mimicking stars (see "Imitation") and trenchantly criticizing them (see "Judgment"), the impulse to admire, appreciate, and celebrate is even more basic to fandom than desire, identification, or antagonism. Fans, when questioned, remain keenly aware of all that prevents them from ever seducing or becoming like the glamorous, accomplished, talented figures they idolize.[7] Although many take pleasure in seeing celebrities topple, stars can only fall after having first risen on a tide of widespread interest and acclaim.

BASKING IN EPHEMERA

The majority of fans pursue intimacy, connection, and proximity, not with real people, but with the heaps of stuff generated by celebrity culture. Internet sites such as Tumblr replicate, in more collective, interactive, and public form, practices that date back over a hundred years. Long before the digital age, a host of fans lovingly preserved, collated, and occasionally reworked the many texts and images that described and depicted celebrities. The theatrical scrapbooks that became something of a craze between the late 1880s and early 1920s offer the clearest surviving evidence of these practices in the late nineteenth and early twentieth centuries.[8] Neither secret nor crafted with a public audience in mind, those scrapbooks existed mainly to record their compilers' theatergoing activities or their interest in particular performers. Most of the scrapbooks in theater archives today are anonymous or compiled by people who led unremarkable lives. Their very blandness is what makes albums extraordinary evidence of what ordinary fans do.

Today, archives around the world house hundreds of theater scrapbooks, most of them assembled between the 1890s and the 1910s. Thousands more remain in closets, basements, and attics or were consigned long ago to landfills. Some of these myriad scrapbook makers documented weekly attendance at local theaters by arraying programs, playbills, and reviews, usually in chronological order. Others preserved memories of summer vacations that involved nightly trips to vaudeville shows or collated souvenirs of extended foreign travels that included multiple visits to theaters and concert halls. Some albums focus on performers rather than performances; however, albums devoted to a single performer are rare and were usually compiled by the performers themselves or by their family members, not by fans. In a few rare cases, scrapbooks substituted for actual theater attendance. For over a decade, Burrill H. Leffingwell of Rochester, New York, encyclopedically documented the New York City entertainment scene, covering opera, ballet, film, and a range of theatrical productions, from variety shows to the avant-garde. Leffingwell seems rarely to have attended any performance in person, but for years he faithfully clipped articles from several newspapers and magazines, including trade publications such as *Variety* and the *Dramatic Mirror*. Today, his oversized volumes burst at the seams with thousands of brittle clippings that despite having yellowed with age still convey the vitality of a bygone era's prodigious entertainment culture.[9]

In addition to tracking personal outings and documenting theater history, albums enabled fans to bask in vivid images of their favorite stars. The golden age of theatrical scrapbooks coincided with technological advances in photography and printing that made lifelike images cheaper and easier to produce. One example is a tinted picture of Maude Adams (figure 4.1), preserved by a young woman named Helen Henderson in a 1904–5 album whose hand-lettered and misspelled title page announced its subject as "Actoresses and Actors I Have Seen in New York."[10] Everything about the image works to intensify the viewer's sense of proximity to its celebrity subject; it is easy to see why Helen Henderson chose to place it in her album. The heavy paper stock on which it is printed supports bold, saturated shades that arrest the viewer's attention and convey a sense of vitality, especially noticeable (in the color original) in the flush of the actress's cheeks, the warmth of her brown eyes and chestnut eyebrows, and the varied tones of her reddish hair. The image is large, taking up almost an entire 12.5" × 10" album page, which contributes to its lifelikeness and promotes absorption by leaving no room for distraction by other images or clippings. The spare background similarly focuses the viewer on Adams,

FIGURE 4.1. Maude Adams, TRI Scrapbook #162.

while its green hue highlights, by contrast, her auburn hair and flushed skin. The directness with which Adams looks at the camera creates the impression that she is looking at and acknowledging us, even as her bold, confrontational stare seems to keep the viewer at bay. The figure's loosened hair suggests that we are being afforded a private view of a relaxed moment, even as the actress's costume and the image's caption remind us that this is Adams in a specific role.

Helen Henderson did nothing more, or less, than tear this page out of one sheaf of bound pages and glue it into another, but even that minimal act added value to the image. Scholars today use the term "remediation" to refer to the act of transferring data from one format to another—vinyl LPs to MP3s, film to video, printed images to JPEGs, TIFFs, and PDFs. But fans spend far more time on what we might call *resituation*, which involves moving objects from one location to another without effecting any significant change in medium. Resituation matters less as authorship or artistry in its own right than as a way of recording brief acts of atten-

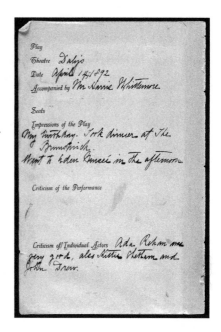

FIGURE 4.2. TRI Scrapbook #137.

tion. The presence of a Maude Adams image in an album, as opposed to in a magazine, attests to its consumption (someone actually looked at this image); marks a reader and theatergoer's choices (someone singled out this image among many others); and registers appreciation (someone liked this image enough to preserve it for repeated viewing).

Resituation matters all the more because so few compilers ever wrote in their albums (for more about those who did, see "Judgment"), even when invited to do so. By the 1890s, several companies were publishing blank books whose covers were embossed with titles such as "Plays I Have Seen" and whose pages offered preprinted rubrics soliciting "Impressions of the Play," "Criticism of the Performance," and "Criticism of Individual Actors" (figure 4.2). Even when nudged to unleash their inner drama critics, most compilers abstained. Instead, they confined themselves to filling out entries requesting the most basic information: the name of the play seen, the date of the performance, the theater attended, where they sat, who accompanied them. The example above comes from an album covering the years between 1892 and 1899, compiled by the future Mrs. Harris Whittemore, who saw shows in New York, Boston, Philadelphia, and London.[11] Although she carefully inserted ticket stubs and playbills from many performances into her album, she usually either skirted the album's request for her "Impressions of the Play" or used that space to note, as on the page reproduced above, an afternoon outing before the performance and a birthday dinner after it. (For the rare occasions on which she expressed herself more assertively, see "Judgment.")

Most compilers felt more at ease commenting on stars than on scripts or staging. Actors mattered far more to most nineteenth- and early twentieth-century theatergoers than playwrights or plays did, just as movie stars later counted far more with audiences than most film directors or screenwriters.[12] As the above example shows, "Criticism of Individual Actors" often proved more compelling than "Impressions of the Play" or "Criticism of the Performance." In this case, the compiler stayed on point, however unimaginatively, by noting, "Ada Rehan was very good." Compilers who organized their albums around performers emphasized proximity to their images and stories. The young woman who assembled a 1912 album that included keen, if slangy, criticism of several plays shifted into a more enthusiastic mode when talking about a favorite performer: "Rose Stahl wasn't a bit good-looking but you couldn't help loving her just the same."[13] To record a performance by ballet dancer Anna Pavlova, the same compiler combined three sets of materials: a soulful photograph of the dancer (figure 4.3), the front page of a theater program (figure 4.4), and a magazine article on "Pavlowa's [sic] Art and Its Meaning" (figure 4.5).[14]

Compilers who annotated their albums years after making them often showed the most emotion when recalling personal history with favorite performers. As a young woman, Louise Hannah attended many plays in Chicago between 1910 and 1914. Revisiting her album as an adult, she jotted "First time ever saw her" next to images of Ethel Barrymore and Maude Adams.[15] Her laconic comment spoke volumes about the feelings of intimacy generated by fandom, which could inspire a theatergoer to mark anniversaries of landmark encounters with cherished stars.

Most scrapbook compilers were indifferent to the subtleties of graphic design, content to cut and paste materials excised from theater programs and periodicals and to arrange them in more or less chronological order. A few, however, manipulated their clippings in ways that animated them and brought their favorite performers closer. Louise Hannah, for example, put her keen sense of page layout to work assembling evocative montages of stars. In one instance, Hannah placed three very

FIGURES 4.3, 4.4, 4.5. Anna Pavlova clippings, TRI Scrapbook #144.

FIGURE 4.6. Johnston Forbes-Robertson clippings, TRI Scrapbook #111.

different images of the lauded British actor Johnston Forbes-Robertson on facing leaves (figure 4.6). A frontal pose shows most of his body; a profile provides a more intimate view; a production still places his face and figure at a distance that accentuates the visual proximity afforded by the other two images.[16] The result showcases the actor's introspective persona and familiarizes anyone viewing the page with several facets of the same celebrity.

On another page of the same album, Hannah, who carefully recorded how much money she spent on the souvenir programs and theater magazines

FIGURES 4.7 and 4.8. Images of E. H. Sothern and Julia Marlowe, TRI Scrapbook #111.

she disassembled to populate her album pages, seems to have acquired two copies of the same image in order to present it differently on two facing pages. On the right-hand page of her album (figure 4.7), we see a portrait of E. H. Sothern and Julia Marlowe, a married couple in real life, as it would have appeared in the original source. On the album page to the left (figure 4.8), Hannah has taken the same image, cut out each of the actor's faces, and placed them closer to each other. By bringing husband and wife into greater proximity, Hannah also brought their images closer to her, creating a love scene on the page between two actors whose theatrical romances had an extra frisson for viewers who knew that the onstage couple was also an offstage one. Wielding scissors and glue as a live spectator might have used opera glasses, Hannah created a private moment that closed the gap between the players themselves and between celebrities and fan.[17]

FIGURE 4.9. TRI Scrapbook #12.

Where photographers transferred live performers to a medium that fixed them on paper, some scrapbook compilers altered those images in ways designed to simulate mobility and liveness. Many used contouring to make images of actors "pop" off the page, as in this image from one of the Leffingwell albums (figure 4.9).[18] Louise Hannah, in the example below, used scissors to silhouette the entire body of the actress playing "Polly at the Circus," but cut out only the top contour of the horse (figure 4.10).[19] The result accentuates the equestrian's buoyant poise as she balances on her mount's narrow back with upraised arms. Another compiler used a similar technique to accentuate an image of actress Doris Keane (figure 4.11).[20] Even as the careful scissor work outlining the top of Keane's head reminds us that this image is nothing but ink on paper, the silhouetting also makes the image look more like an actual body part. The image's placement at the very top of the album page and the actress's pose make her seem about to rise from her seat and even from the album page itself to approach us. Keane leans forward while perched on the side of the chair, pressing one hand on her seat for leverage, the other on her waist for support. Her outlined head breaks through the rectangular frame around the image to touch the page's topmost edge. Released from the magazine where it originally appeared, the scrapbooked image seems about to escape the album's confines as well.

The minimal act of clipping images from a print source conveyed intimacy with the material itself and with the subject depicted, especially

FIGURE 4.10. TRI Scrapbook #111.

FIGURE 4.11. Image of Doris Keane, TRI Scrapbook #13.

FIGURE 4.12. Image of Marguerite Sylva, TRI Scrapbook #178.

when scissor work showcased the deft handling of the materials assembled. Consider the image (figure 4.12) of opera and musical theater star Marguerita Sylva (1875–1957) preserved in one of several small albums devoted to a number of female performers popular around 1900.[21] The careful outlining of the actress's face, hair, and bared shoulders conflate vision and touch. To observe how carefully the compiler has moved their scissors around every wave of Sylva's hair and around the tight negative space between her throat, neck, and left shoulder is almost to feel that one is touching, if not the person depicted, then the piece of paper holding her image. The slight clumsiness of the decoupage around the nose and chin contrasts almost poignantly with the defter outlining of the figure's exposed back. Where the original image probably took full advantage of the tonal gradations that rotogravure made possible after the 1890s, the silhouette created for the album produces a charmingly awkward break between the shadows outlining the actress's face and the flat monotone of the album page. The result effectively combines proximity and distance. It stands out from the page in a way that makes the image livelier. And it registers work that hovers between production and consumption, looking and making, and speaks above all to a desire to bask in celebrities' presence by collecting, handling, and holding their representations.

APPROACHING CELEBRITY

The relatively placid immersion of the scrapbook compiler represents the typical fan far better than the stalkers and groupies most people picture when thinking about those who crave intimacy with their favorite celebrities. But there are many degrees between these two extremes. Some literally dream about celebrities; there are entire books devoted to recounting the dreams that ordinary people have had about figures as different as Queen Elizabeth II and Madonna.[22] Given the connections that film theorists have long drawn between film and fantasy, it is not surprising that in the age of the moving image, figures seen on screens remain on our minds while we slumber.[23] But dreams about celebrities predate cinema and even the commercialization of photography; the media saturation that defines celebrities means that they have been slipping into our sleep for centuries. In 1848, the poet and magazine editor William Allingham wrote in his diary: "Dream—dine with the Queen, who asks me to try her custard pudding. I ask if Her Majesty knows the song of " 'Miss Baily,' and recite it to her."[24] Allingham had never met Queen Victoria in person, and her photographic image did not become widely available until 1860. But the broad dissemination of paintings, prints, and newspaper articles focused on the young monarch had made her part of his mental landscape.[25] The same convergence of performance and print culture that could popularize the lyrics to "Miss Baily" could also collapse the distinction between intimates and strangers, just as Allingham's dream salaciously combined a mundane custard pudding with "Her Majesty's" grandeur.

Similar feelings arose when members of the public chanced upon celebrities in waking life. Even a seasoned journalist known for his sophisticated parodies could find himself succumbing to the glamor that celebrity
sightings cast over the most mundane events, as when theater critic Max
Beerbohm felt a "romantic thrill" upon seeing Queen Victoria drive by
in her barouche: "Strange, to see her with my own eyes . . . on her way to
Paddington Station."[26] Others were more aggressive. In 1895, diarist Lady
Monkswell was walking in London with her young son when she spotted
the Queen of Holland and her mother about to get into a carriage. Lady
Monkswell's social position gave her frequent occasion to meet dignitaries
in person, but that did not dampen her excitement: "Eric and I whipped
out on to the pavement." After her son doffed his hat to the royals, "they
both gave him a little bow. He was immensely delighted to have a bow from
two Queens. We followed them down Piccadilly, and numbers of people,
even those on omnibuses, bowed and smiled at the little girl."[27] Monkswell
offers a glimpse of the famous as public property as she unselfconsciously
records how she and her son suspended decorum to pursue royals down
the street, joined by others similarly intent on acknowledging and being
acknowledged.

In the highly theatrical scene Monkswell sketches, recognition of a
famous person spawns a desire to be recognized by them in turn. This
scene also offers a cautionary tale about celebrating active fandom over
its more passive expressions. Monkswell shows no awareness that the famous individuals whom she hounds might prefer maintaining their privacy
in public to being followed down the street. Actress Stella ("Mrs. Patrick") Campbell recorded her discomfort with the "intolerable curiosity"
people expressed about her private life, her horror at being recognized
and mobbed in public, and her dissonant sense of being public property
while at the same time feeling that "no one seemed to really care who
I was."[28] Although most nineteenth-century fans avoided the bizarre extremes imagined by the cartoonists who pictured Sarah Bernhardt's fans
as rampaging outlaws (see "Savagery"), in an age that revolved almost
exclusively around live performance, most celebrities found themselves
contending on at least a few occasions with the public's forceful zeal.[29]
Singers and actors Mary Anderson, Jenny Lind, Lotta Crabtree, Christine
Nilsson, and Adelina Patti all found themselves subject at some point
in their careers to incidents like the one in which Sarah Bernhardt, en
route to an 1881 matinee, "found the road blocked with women who made
her write her name on their cuffs and forced gifts of jewelry upon her."[30]

Members of a Sydney crowd shook Bernhardt's "hand with such good-will, but misplaced energy, that on arrival at her hotel it was swollen almost beyond recognition."[31]

Most fans attempting to make contact with celebrities did so through writing. In 1956, a devoted Italian fan sent Marilyn Monroe a collage he had created in her honor.[32] A century or so earlier, as soon as it became possible to send letters cheaply through the post, strangers had begun to deluge celebrated authors and performers with missives requesting autographs, money, and matrimony. Most celebrities responded positively, since signing a piece of paper was an easy way to make contact and maintain renown without sacrificing personal privacy. In 1851, a man from Palmyra, Missouri, sent a notecard to Jenny Lind asking for the world-famous Swedish opera singer's autograph, explaining that he had never heard her sing, but wanted her signature because "the name of Jenny Lind is familiar to everyone."[33] David Henkin's history of antebellum US postal culture has shown that as print became more common and people began to exchange letters with unprecedented frequency, handwriting began to signify individual personality. Expanded mail routes and lowered postal rates launched a craze for collecting autographs of well-known public figures and expanded the reach of the commercial newspapers promoting celebrities. The autograph craze was a way for readers to transform abstract, homogenized newspaper print into distinctive bodily traces. Henkin writes of a woman who by 1858 had an extensive autograph collection that included abolitionist leaders, aristocrats, and a senator; Jill E. Anderson has found that between 1844 and 1865, the poet Henry Wadsworth Longfellow alone received 410 requests for his signature.[34]

Many correspondents aimed simply to express their admiration or care for the celebrities to whom they wrote. In the nineteenth century, actor Edwin Booth, opera singer Pauline Viardot, and poet Longfellow all received numerous missives from the public that each chose to preserve for posterity (figure 4.13). Their correspondents lavished praise, doled out criticism (see "Judgment"), and offered condolences, religious counsel, and medical advice. Some engaged in outright begging or barter; many requested acting lessons or editorial advice; others asked for money and sometimes received it, given how many thank-you notes Edwin Booth preserved that had correspondents gratefully acknowledging his gifts, usually of one hundred dollars.[35] As Anderson has shown, Longfellow's correspondents often sought to trade their letters for signs of the poet's bodily presence. They requested likenesses, locks of hair, the pencil he used to write *Hiawatha*, and

FIGURE 4.13. Pamphlet sent to Edwin Booth, circa 1870s.

handwritten verses already available in print. Others entreated the poet to use his influence and talent on their behalf, asking him to comment on their poems or help to publish them. One writer even requested permission to court Longfellow's daughter: "From the necessity of her parentage she must be a lovely girl."[36] Scholar Peter Brown has interpreted the early Christian worship of relics associated with ancient saints as a recasting of classical patronage networks, since pilgrims often hoped that saints would intercede on their behalf.[37] At least some modern fans, in writing to their idols, similarly hoped to convert celebrities into benefactors.

While some fans were eager to extract favors from the celebrities they approached, others aimed to give, not receive. Even in a twenty-first century dominated by online media, pop star Taylor Swift received thousands of letters and packages daily: "sparkly envelopes . . . lovingly decorated with glitter," declaring the senders' admiration and affection, sometimes accompanied by chocolates, stuffed animals, or (some things never change) unusual sexual proposals.[38] In the nineteenth century, many of Sarah Bernhardt's most dedicated female admirers bestowed jewelry on their idol without violently thrusting it upon her; a list of Bernhardt items for sale at an 1883 auction included pieces given to her by an Italian queen, a Russian princess, and an array of European and North American women, including "five young English ladies [who] contended, or rather combined, for the honour of offering [a] bracelet."[39] The actress lavished enthusiastic compliments on them in return, telling an interviewer that she preferred her female fans to her male ones, and inscribing a photograph to "the most charming of all women."[40]

A handful of fans took their desires for intimacy much further. Nineteenth-century newspapers reported many incidents, both real and fanciful, that today we would call stalking. An 1882 report in the *New York Clipper* described an Indian prince for whom Sarah Bernhardt's "undulating personality" had become "the eidolon of his pet delirium." In a flagrantly Orientalist scenario, the prince kidnaps Bernhardt and confines her in an apartment furnished with a pet leopard and dancing girls. He demands a private command performance, exhorting her to "Flash upon me with the tenderness of Adrienne, with the passion of Phaedre, with the divine pity of Medea!" He then attempts to rape her, but is foiled by a street urchin who bursts in to save the day.[41] Though clearly spurious, the article presented itself as news, perhaps because it described a desire seldom acted upon but no less real: to capture those who had captivated public attention and reverse their dominion. An 1895 article similarly conveyed how hostile the relationship between celebrities and fans could sometimes become. It reported that a young woman had threatened to shoot Bernhardt onstage, because, she claimed, the actress had housed her and promised to adopt her, then "tired of her society," "turned her out of doors," and had the young woman committed after she protested this ill treatment. At that point, the young woman's mother threatened to throw vitriol at the star. Bernhardt claimed never to have met the young woman, who was known to be using morphine and had "harassed" Bernhardt's niece. The article reported that the woman's "letters were on file with the prefecture of police," a detail that suggests that Bernhardt had a routine for dealing with what may have been common threats.[42]

The intimacy that fans sought with performers was often sexual, even if only in fantasy; recall the suggestiveness of William Allingham dreaming that Queen Victoria had invited him to try her custard. Far from being cultural renegades challenging the status quo, such fans simply enacted a very conventional tendency to equate performers, particularly female ones, with the easy availability attributed to prostitutes.[43] That said, the most esteemed female stars were far less likely than supporting players and extras to be seen as courtesans or streetwalkers. From the 1880s on, Sarah Bernhardt, though perceived as sexually free, was also well known to be financially independent, rather than a kept woman. Her successful European and North American tours had made her wealthy enough to manage her own theaters and popular enough to sidestep journalists and theater reviewers. When the teenaged Pierre Loüys wrote to Bernhardt in 1888, his diary explicitly characterized his letter to the forty-four-year old performer at the height of her career as more "decent" (*convenable*) than the missives he had addressed the year before to a younger, less eminent actress.[44]

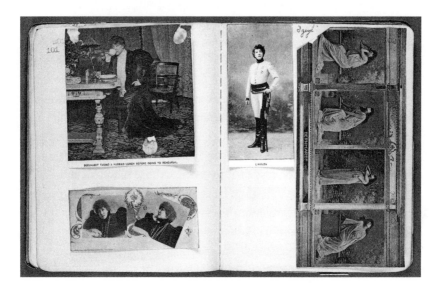

FIGURE 4.14. Images of Sarah Bernhardt, TRI Scrapbook #79.

Fans who took female celebrities as occasions for aggrandizing their own sexual agency tended to fixate on younger actresses working in music halls, variety shows, and burlesque entertainments—another instance of more active fans replicating rather than challenging existing hierarchies. The anonymous compiler of ten small, red-leather-covered theatrical scrapbooks created between 1898 and 1901 expressed a similar distinction between sexually available actresses and more elevated, less accessible ones. Each of the ten unusually small albums, at 8" x 6.5" about half the size of most theatrical scrapbooks, was divided into sections. The front pages featured august female stars heralded around the world for their serious dramatic roles; the back pages displayed risqué images of starlets with more local followings. The sections devoted to venerable figures such as Sarah Bernhardt, Ada Rehan, and Henrietta Crosman, "leading actress of legitimate roles," document their career highlights, illustrate their imposing homes, and depict them costumed for their most significant parts, as in one set of pages from the album featuring Sarah Bernhardt (figure 4.14).[45]

Arrayed almost surreptitiously in the back pages of the same volume are racy images of Paula Edwardes, the "Belle of New York," described in one caption as a "semi-legitimate . . . [who] has gone into vaudeville" (figure 4.15).[46] At the very back, we find one Mazie Follette, leaning against a wall

FIGURE 4.15. Images of Paula Edwardes, TRI Scrapbook #79.

FIGURE 4.16. Images of Mazie Follette, TRI Scrapbook #79.

in a filmy wrap and pouting for the camera in a strapless gown (figure 4.16). The caption to one photo of Follette and another young woman dismissively refers to them as "display[ing] two pretty faces and four shapely limbs."[47] At other points, however, the materials gathered in these albums dissolve the very hierarchies they seek to reinforce. Some clippings report on the marriages of established stars and budding starlets to diamond brokers and stock market millionaires, but one item announces actress Marie Wilson's resignation from the Florodora Company after making her own $750,000 killing on Wall Street.[48] The most august female celebrities could find themselves defined more by their husbands' achievements than their own, while "ain't-she-sweet girls" could sometimes attain respectability and financial independence.[49]

Fans who sought intimacy with actual celebrities often came into conflict with stars determined to keep the public at bay. How a given celebrity negotiated the perception of public availability varied with gender, age, career stage, family ties, and personal temperament. In the years between 1879 and 1881, when Bernhardt first gained international attention, journalists frequently described the still youthful star as a trendy attraction for men, including the queer "greenery-yallery" Aesthetes who went "raving mad" for Bernhardt when she first came to London.[50] As the Kansas *Atchison Globe* put it when Bernhardt visited the United States in 1882, "now we know what aesthetic means. Sarah Bernhardt is Oscar Wilde's idea of true beauty."[51] Far more often, however, humor magazines made ribald jokes about the heterosexual male "swells" who hoped to marry the actress.[52] Newspapers wrote of princes, czars, and maharajahs lavishing jewels and honors on Bernhardt, pining for her in vain. In 1879, after London papers reported that Bernhardt might play the young Shakespeare in a new one-act play, *Fun* described young men about town "languishing" to "enjoy the opportunity of beholding the French Inimitable" in a doublet and hose, while another reminded readers of the actress's erotic availability: "A special postal service has been arranged for the benefit of the young gentlemen who will propose to Mdlle. Sarah Bernhardt."[53] That same summer, a British newspaper reported that *Le Figaro* had printed the addresses of all the female members of the visiting French acting troupe, along with details about the precise rooms they occupied and the exact rents they paid.[54]

By the 1880s, critics would almost universally portray Bernhardt as dominating theatergoers of all stripes through her talent and intensity. But in 1879, when she was still establishing her global reputation, newspapers and magazines directed at young male readers tended to depict attraction to the female star as bolstering their agency at the expense of hers. An article by "an infatuated contributor" made a leering reference to Bernhardt's thinness: "Would that she were *bone* of *my* bone. . . . What matters it that she is a Dutch-Jewess?"[55] Another article, entitled "Sarah Bernhardt on the Brain," described a "virulent" Bernhardt mania whose symptoms included "a fierce longing to besiege the Gaiety stage door, and demand a prominent part as 'Sarah's Young Man.'"[56] Even when stricken by illness, the suitors "besiege" and "demand," refusing to settle for bit roles or supporting parts. A *Punch* article on the opening night of the Comédie-Française kept things simple when writing about the troupe's leading male performers: "*Punch* salutes the Brothers COQUELIN." But in writing about Bernhardt, the author got more personal: he praised "the feverish fire and passionate grace of SARAH BERNHARDT (at whose feet *Punch* prostrates himself, and kisses the hem of her *peplon*)."[57] In the act of playfully imagining himself submitting to Bernhardt, the author also pictures himself invading her by kissing the ruffle covering her hips. A columnist personifying a louche young man about town similarly remarked, after seeing the actress's London premiere of *La Dame aux camélias*, "I admire Madame Bernhardt's clinging white garment."[58] The sexual politics of the commercial theater empowered male theatergoers in particular to picture themselves as freewheeling men about town with the power to judge actresses like horseflesh and select at will those who pleased them most.[59]

Bernhardt risked becoming a commercial erotic attraction even when creating, displaying, and selling images of others. Many journalists reduced the artworks she made and exhibited to mere curiosities. *Le Figaro* described her 1879 show in a Piccadilly gallery as "an exhibition of her works and of her person."[60] In a column called "Seeing Sarah," the comic newspaper *Funny Folks* put it even more bluntly: "We had gone nominally to look at her pictures and sculptures; but really, I believe, to gaze on the picturesque Sarah herself as she struck graceful attitudes amongst her works of Art."[61] For all her acknowledged artistry, Bernhardt acquired celebrity and earned money by displaying herself onstage and posing for photographs that shopkeepers fought to "possess . . . as an attraction for their windows."[62] Not surprisingly, the early years of her fame also found her associated with commodities linked to male self-indulgence. One columnist mused about cigars sporting Bernhardt's name: "Can fame aspire further? The weeds, being long and attenuated, convey a delicate compliment to the comedienne by their resemblance in shape to herself."[63] The mock gallantry of the advertisement's rhetorical question notwithstanding,

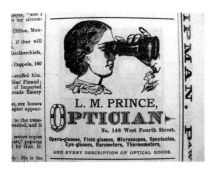

FIGURE 4.17. Program advertisement, TRI Playbill 341.

the Bernhardt cigars elicited fantasies about manhandling the star's person and sending her up in smoke.

The desire to have the fan's sexual agency prevail over the star's was not limited to men accosting female celebrities. Women of all classes attended the theater in large numbers throughout the nineteenth century, and advertisements for "optical goods" in theater programs often depicted their ideal customers as women eager to get a better view of the stage (figure 4.17).[64] Female fans did not hesitate to wield the power of the look and directed their attention equally to feminine and masculine performers. In the middle decades of the nineteenth century, ballerina Marie Taglioni attracted female fans across Europe and North America, as did actor Charlotte Cushman, known for her ardent Romeo and imposing Lady Macbeth.[65] Actor Edwin Booth preserved several of the letters his female admirers sent him, labelling some of the missives requesting assignations "mash notes."[66] One correspondent offered to meet him after his performance: "Tonight—after the Theatre (I shall be there!)—at the Temperance Hall.—a pink domino—on the left cheek marked a small cross—the word—'Eros'—you will speak first."[67] Another requested that he acknowledge her while onstage: "When Iago dies to-night, will he in pity, give a last parting look to one who will indeed treasure it as one treasures the last look of the 'dead.' A devoted admirer, Parquet Circle, 'right.'"[68] Out of two hundred letters that boyish comedian Elsie Janis received from "unknown admirers . . . two-thirds were from girls," whom Janis described as "her staunchest supporters," adding that "she like[d] the girls best," except when it came to playing football.[69]

Sarah Bernhardt owed her 1879 London success to her crossover gender appeal; she was able to "wind her way not only into the heart of the prosperous city merchant, but also into the protesting bosom of his spouse." Nor did she appeal to only one type of woman; she was as interesting to fashionable society dowagers as to the "young and spectacled ladies" seeking Oxbridge educations.[70] Female aristocrats traveled from London to Paris just to see Bernhardt perform, and scores of women waited outside theaters morning and night to hand her flowers and "steamy letters."[71] As

Bernhardt aged, her fan base became more female. So did the mainstream theatrical public. In 1915, when Bernhardt was in her seventies, female impersonator Julian Eltinge described the "middle-aged woman" as "the backbone of the theater's attendance."[72] A 1906 article noted that most of those who stood for hours waiting to buy tickets to Bernhardt performances were women, while a 1916 feature described the only men in the seventy-two-year old star's US audience as dragged there by spouses: "There were gray-haired critics who had followed the career of the most wonderful woman of today. . . . There was the woman who couldn't understand French, and there was the woman who knew a few words, and there was the man whose wife had forced him to come against his will."[73] The crowd standing vigil outside the actress's home in Paris as she lay dying in 1923 also consisted mostly of women, although the tributes that dominated the press for weeks after her death came mainly from male journalists, drama critics, playwrights, and performers.[74]

Female fans did not confine themselves to looking at women, nor to looking alone. A 1905 US headline described Bernhardt "Mobbed by Cheering Women at the Pier" who "pelted her with flowers" when she disembarked in New York.[75] In St. Petersburg in 1882, "Not content with raining flowers on the stage, ladies in the audience jumped over the partition separating them from the pit, so that they could approach the great artiste as closely as possible."[76] Women pursuing their favorite male stars could be as invasive and inconsiderate as the men whom London humor magazines imagined pestering Bernhardt in 1879. In the 1860s, women went "daft" for Edwin Booth's Hamlet, sending him up to five hundred letters a week containing flowers, hair, and other mementos. In Boston, women accosted him from windows and haunted a drugstore he frequented, purchasing large quantities of slippery elm and jujube paste in the hopes of encountering their idol; one "pretty blonde" was reported to have bought over a hundred toothbrushes.[77] In 1887, R. D. Blumenfeld wrote of Buffalo Bill Cody in London being "embarrassed by an overwhelming mass of flowers which came hourly from hosts of female admirers," and in the 1890s, "matinee girls" became notorious for having "crushes" that had many acting "less discreet than their fond mammas imagine them to be."[78]

Although tales of aggressive fans abound, many stories also circulated about fandom as self-abnegation. A Frenchman who wrote over forty letters to Bernhardt after seeing her in *Hernani* reportedly had to be treated in an asylum for the melancholy that resulted when she did not reply; "he languished for 15 years, always in the fixed idea that he would one day become the husband of Dona Sol."[79] The cover of an 1880 issue of the sophisticated Parisian journal *La Vie moderne* imagined white men in suits and top hats drowning as they rush to give Bernhardt flowers before she departs for the United States by steamship.[80] Inside, the magazine presented a sketch of firefighters in provincial France dwarfed by their floral tributes to the actress. The accompanying article, presented as the "Diary of a Stage Prompter," tells the story of a fictional fan who realizes his dream of getting closer to his idol by becoming the theater staff member who stands in a box below the stage to feed the star her lines. Still not satisfied, he longs to be locked in Bernhardt's trunk with her dresses: "Oh, to live and die in this trunk, what a dream!" His fantasies revolve around self-effacement; as a prompter, he serves his idol by standing in the shadows, whispering lines that enable him to declare, but only indirectly, his "timid passion."[81] Although the story is fictional, and seems implausible today, when most celebrities would be leery of any fan seeking such close contact, as late as the 1990s, a Japanese newspaper article about a beloved all-female theater troupe reported that their most devoted fans drove favorite stars to and from the theater, cooked their meals, acted as their secretaries, and managed the flow of gifts presented by other fans.[82]

COURTING REPULSION

Stars devised several ways to resist the loss of agency that came with being an erotic attraction. One newspaper reported in 1874 that a forty-year-old Edwin Booth publicly demonstrated his indifference to one devotee by taking a gold chain she had sent him containing her hair and placing it on a friend's cat.[83] Bernhardt deflected a marriage proposal from a Russian count who "fell madly in love with her" and "followed" her to Vienna by reportedly telling him "she could not marry a man, because she was married to her art."[84] In 1879, Bernhardt volunteered at a London charity fair and was accosted by a man who "offered to give her all he possessed in the world for a *petit baiser*." She "promptly ordered him to be 'fired out,' which he instantly was."[85] She confided to a fellow actress that after an Englishman who hosted an 1879 supper party in her honor tried to kiss her, she "did not speak to him again for years. It was *abominable*, she said, *abominable*. It showed he had no respect for her."[86]

Actors had to balance the need to attract public notice with their desire to maintain some degree of privacy. Bernhardt developed an unusual
method for doing this: actively courting repulsion. Late in life, Bernhardt
encouraged actors to embrace ugliness: "No human frailty, no ugliness,
no abnormality of mind or body must repel you."[87] She followed this advice
throughout her career, beginning with her request, when cast in the 1876
play *Rome vaincue*, to play a blind grandmother rather than the starring role
of a beautiful vestal virgin condemned to live burial after losing her chastity.
To save her granddaughter from such torture, the grandmother contrives
to kill her with a dagger. Because she is blind, she must find her daughter's
vital organ by touch, asking her, "Is this your heart?"[88] The combination of
pathos and gore and Bernhardt's performance made the otherwise turgid
five-act tragedy a success.[89] Henry James, writing as a drama critic for *The
Nation*, called the play "pompous and tedious" but noted that audiences
were arriving at ten o'clock in order to catch the last two acts, which featured Bernhardt's strongest moments.[90] Even before the play premiered,
the London *Examiner* noted, "A great attraction of the piece will be Mlle.
Sarah Bernhardt's playing, at her own request, an old blind woman."[91]
The thirty-two-year old Bernhardt found a way to simulate blindness by
showing only the whites of her eyes and chose to "muffle . . . her youth
and beauty in long veils and grey tresses," covering her trademark curls
under a wig.[92]

Offstage, Bernhardt balanced attraction and repulsion with paintings
and sculptures that fascinated the public by embracing the grotesque.
In *Après la tempête*, a large marble work that the actress made and exhibited at the 1876 Paris Salon, Bernhardt updated Michelangelo's *Pietà*
by depicting a haggard grandmother mourning her adolescent grandson,
whose drowned body lies draped upon her lap (figure 4.18). The elderly
woman is almost fully clothed; the focal point is the young man's supine,
almost nude corpse. The monumental sculpture was designed to awe, not
to seduce. Although the slender grandson's arched posture invited comparison with Bernhardt's famously torqued poses, the artist encouraged
reporters to align her with the grandmother figure, telling them that she
had modeled the old woman's grief-stricken expression on her own face.
A few years later, in 1880, Bernhardt exhibited a painting at the Paris
Salon entitled *Young Woman and Death*, a "very *bizarre* picture" that attracted a crowd of curious visitors. It depicted a young woman in a violet
dress and feathered hat standing with a veiled skeleton. One critic, who
found the image "incorrect, but full of subtle charm" and its subject "most

FIGURE 4.18. Sarah
Bernhardt, *Après la
tempête*, 1876, white
marble sculpture, 29
1/2" × 24" × 23".

strange," singled out the skeleton's unappealing appearance: "It might
have been made to look more attractive, and one understands the hesita-
tion of the young girl to throw herself into his hands."[93] His observation
missed Bernhardt's intention: to depict a seduction attempt from which
both the woman in the painting and the viewer standing before it would
recoil. The image's startling juxtaposition of death and life seized viewers'
attention but also repelled them. In 1882, Paul Fresnay reported having a
similar reaction to the notorious photograph of Bernhardt sleeping in a
coffin: "There is certainly something a little too strong in this comedy of
Death."[94] Bernhardt's "leanness" and "colourlessness" made her "ghastly"
resemblance to a corpse strong enough to interfere with the visual pleasure of this critic and other male fans eager to imagine female celebrities
as theirs for the taking.

Through live performances and media saturation, celebrities have for centuries become so pervasive that members of the public find their dreams

haunted by renowned people whom they have never met nor even glimpsed in person. Some fans actively each out to celebrities in ways ranging from circumspect to certifiable. Most are content to limit their desires for proximity to their favorite stars to words and images. Nineteenth-century periodicals directed at male readers often imagined young men having free access to attractive young women in the public eye, but women as well as men openly took an erotic interest in celebrities of both sexes, increasingly so as the century progressed. Female stars, especially as they aged, inspired an especially loyal enthusiasm among other women, who expressed their affection for their favorite performers by bestowing gifts or making heroic efforts to see them in person. But by far the majority of fans occupied a zone between the aggressive stalker and the docile, mindless consumer. The scrapbooks bequeathed to us by nineteenth- and twentieth-century theatergoers attest to the many fans who found contentment by immersing themselves in representations of celebrities, basking in ephemeral materials that, as the next chapters will show, portrayed celebrities as simultaneously distinctive and almost infinitely reproducible.

CHAPTER 5

MULTIPLICATION

Fans want to believe in the uniqueness of their favorite icons. Stars, assisted by journalists and photographers, accordingly work to distinguish themselves, both from ordinary mortals and from other stars.[1] Received wisdom would therefore have it that multiplying the star's image dilutes celebrity and undermines the star's uniqueness. Received wisdom should spend a few minutes thinking about Marilyn Monroe. Like any celebrity, Monroe became a distinctive star not simply by standing out from the crowd but also by multiplying herself. To read a single article about Marilyn Monroe was often to encounter many Marilyns, since editors and page compositors rarely limited themselves to one picture of the star; some of her most famous imagery consists of serial poses from a single photo shoot (figure 5.1).

"The most photographed girl in the world" was also known for coining quips that circulated as widely as Internet memes do today. Asked, for example, what she had on when posing for a nude calendar photo, she replied, "The radio," a witticism reproduced almost as often as the image that inspired it.[2] Even the initials of the professional name that Norma Jean Baker gave herself embodied the replication on which celebrity depends: each of the two letters making up the monogram *MM* reproduces the other, just as the letter *M*'s vertical symmetry makes it a mirror of itself.

Celebrity involves contests over who will create, define, and appraise those known, in their lifetimes, to more people than can possibly know one another. For individuals to become famous on such a large scale, their images, names, and stories must proliferate, gaining rather than losing interest and resonance as they travel. The economy of celebrity does not operate according to a simple metric of supply and demand in which the more images there are of a star, the less value they have. Instead, once the star has secured the public's and press's interest on other grounds, such as defiance, sensation, and merit, *the more copies, the more celebrity*. With each new series of multiples, the celebrity becomes all the more singular.

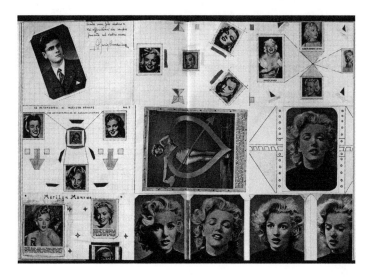

FIGURE 5.1. Collage sent by young Italian fan to Marilyn Monroe in 1953.

Celebrity culture expands every time a new technology makes it easier and cheaper to produce and distribute copies on multiple scales, in multiple media. As scholar Clare Pettitt has shown, reporter Henry Morton Stanley became famous for tracking down missionary David Livingstone in Africa in 1871 because images of their encounter appeared in newspapers, books, stage productions, dioramas, toy shops, Tussaud's Wax Museum, and even billboards advertising patent medicines.[3] The iconic image of Marilyn Monroe standing above a subway grate, her white dress billowing upward, first appeared on the front pages of newspapers, then in a film, and has since been reproduced on postcards, posters, murals, fabric, and wallpaper. You can encounter this image as a public sculpture in Chicago, or find it in a Massachusetts thrift store, decorating a dinner plate (figure 5.2). When Andy Warhol blew up photos of Monroe, Elizabeth Taylor, Jacqueline Kennedy, and other icons, then silkscreened them to create grids that repeated the same image multiple times in different colors, he created meta-celebrity objects whose form reproduced the reproduction intrinsic to stardom. The result: beings who are neither purely individual nor simply plural but who toggle constantly between the singular and the multiple in ways that do not dilute identity but concentrate it.

Even as Monroe perfected the celebrity skill of proliferating as many images of herself as possible, she also incarnated the celebrity self as a tissue of citations.[4] She famously posed for *Life* magazine as a series of

FIGURE 5.2. Marilyn Monroe plate.

earlier sexpots, including Lillian Russell, Clara Bow, and Marlene Dietrich, acknowledging her debts to stars past while flaunting her ability to surpass them in the present. By establishing herself as a distinctive type, Monroe also made herself available to be imitated by many others, an invitation taken up by her contemporaries Kim Novak, Jayne Mansfield, Mamie Van Doren, and Sheree North, as well as by later figures, including Madonna, Christina Aguilera, Gwen Stefani, and Lady Gaga. As scholar Paige Baty has written, "the icon lives as copy."[5] Celebrities and fans alike become connoisseurs of the flashy similarities and subtle distinctions produced by the multi-plications that spawn celebrity. To this day, celebrity magazines encour-age readers to track resemblances among celebrities by publishing "trend reports" that show different stars sporting similar styles—embroidered dresses, asymmetrical sleeves, iridescent fabrics. Other features allow read-ers to hone their skills at differentiating celebrities by juxtaposing two stars wearing identical dresses and asking readers to vote on "who wore it best."[6]

There is nothing new about these ways of encouraging publics to see stars as simultaneously unique and derivative. Early in her career, many remarked on Sarah Bernhardt's resemblance to her predecessor Rachel: both flaunted their Jewishness, neither had a conventional marriage, and each clashed with the management of the Théâtre-Français. Once Bern-hardt became an established star, journalists compared other women to her. One reporter, for example, described Cosima Wagner as "a woman of the Sarah Bernhardt type," because both were intelligent, dressed well, had personal "magnetism," and looked Jewish.[7]

THE HALO OF THE MULTIPLE

The more singular a celebrity, the easier they are to replicate. When Fanny Davenport (1850–1898) played Sardou's *Cleopatra* in 1891 (figure 5.3), the same year that Bernhardt originated the role in France, the US actress had no trouble copying the French star's look (figure 5.4). Others followed suit, including Olga Nethersole (1867–1951), "the English Bernhardt," who incorporated Bernhardt's style into the portrayal of a wayward nun (figure 5.5). Silent film star Theda Bara (1885–1955) made no secret of her affinities with Bernhardt (figure 5.6). Born Theodosia Goodman, Bara

FIGURE 5.3. Fanny Davenport as Cleopatra.

FIGURE 5.4. Sarah Bernhardt as Cleopatra.

FIGURE 5.5. Olga Nethersole as Sister Beatrice, TRI Scrapbook #3.

FIGURE 5.6. Theda Bara as Salome, TRI Scrapbook #8.

did little to conceal her Jewishness; tackled Cleopatra and Camille, two of Bernhardt's signature roles; and, as the French star had done in the 1870s, proclaimed an interest in drawing and sculpting.[8] Despite their age difference, Bara's resemblance to Bernhardt struck one scrapbooker enough that he overlapped images of the two women striking similar poses (figure 5.7).[9] Around the same time that Bernhardt was photographed reclining on a leopard skin (figure 5.8), the now forgotten Valeska Suratt adopted the same animal-print decor and supine pose, not once but in at least two different photos, which one scrapbook compiler brought together on a single album page (figure 5.9).[10]

Typing buttresses individuality because it highlights differences as well as similarities. Davenport, Nethersole, and Bara all emulated Bernhardt's look, but their common hairstyles and costumes also accentuated each star's distinctive traits: Davenport's solidity, Nethersole's elusive inwardness, Bara's campy excessiveness. Even Suratt distinguished herself from her model by upping the ante: where Bernhardt lounged on a leopard skin, Suratt went her one better with an assortment of zebra, tiger, and jaguar pelts. The use of replication to establish individual celebrities as clearly identifiable types also extends to male celebrities. Boxer Muhammad Ali became a celebrity thanks not only to his superlative athletic skill but also to his memorable tag lines, easily remembered and repeated: "I am the greatest," "Float like a butterfly, sting like a bee." Marlon Brando modeled himself on Montgomery Clift and was in turn emulated by James Dean and Paul Newman.[11] Marilyn Monroe's second husband, Joe DiMaggio, resented sharing her with the public but was equally enmeshed in celebrity culture: as a baseball star, he too existed as both singular and multiple. DiMaggio stood apart from other

FIGURE 5.8.
Image of Sarah
Bernhardt, TRI
Scrapbook #21.

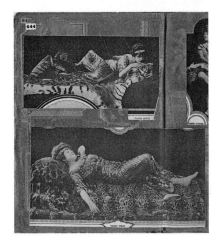

FIGURE 5.9. Images of Valeska Suratt, TRI
Scrapbook #3.

players thanks to his record-breaking achievements, his Italian American ethnicity, and his style of play. At the same time, DiMaggio recalled older Yankees stars such as Babe Ruth and Lou Gehrig and, like any celebrity, had his likeness reproduced in myriad photographs, baseball cards, and figurines.

Intellectuals writing about celebrity have long exposed stars' failures to be truly singular and distinctive. But the debunkers share the mythologists' assumption that publics, celebrities, and media workers value pure singularity above all else, then fool themselves into thinking that stars are absolutely singular when they are not. In a statement echoed by many scholars of celebrity, Max Horkheimer and Theodor Adorno argued that "in the cultural industry the individual is an illusion. . . . Pseudo individuality is rife: from the standardized jazz improvisation to the exceptional film star whose hair curls over her eye to demonstrate her originality."[12] Walter Benjamin, in his essay on the work of art in the age of mechanical reproduction, linked the advent of celebrity to compromised singularity when he speculated that the film industry emphasized stars' offscreen personalities to compensate for the loss of aura that actors suffered in the transition from stage to screen. Benjamin developed the concept of aura to explain how the modern ability to reproduce copies of artworks mechanically had changed their value. In archaic times, unique objects associated with religious rituals were located in faraway places and possessed a distinctive cult value. By contrast, modern industrial techniques enabled the masses to purchase cheap reproductions of artworks and hang them in their drawing rooms. The existence of so many copies deprived artworks of their aura, endowing them instead with an exhibition value in a marketplace of spectacles. By analogy, Benjamin argued, stage actors had an "aura" tied to "presence; there can be no replica of it." On film, he wrote, "the aura that envelops the actors vanishes" because the camera deprives viewers of direct access to the performer's "whole living person," allowing them to see only the fragments that machines recorded.[13]

Benjamin was a brilliant and subtle thinker, as alert to mass culture's possibilities as to its limitations, but he was simply incorrect to say that film invented celebrity culture. As we have seen throughout this book, and as dozens of scholars have documented, theatrical stars with vivid personalities and compelling offstage stories had mass appeal long before film. Nor does Benjamin's opposition between film and theater hold up, since stage actors embraced photography and phonography as soon as those techniques were invented. Far from precluding or avoiding mechanically reproduced images, theater thrived on them. Actors sat for studio portraits by photographers who also developed techniques for taking production stills. By the 1890s, theater audiences spent intermissions gazing at dozens of paintings, pastels, and photographs of actors for sale in lobbies and foyers.[14] An 1895 theater review mentioned that each week of a play's run, "every lady" attending a Saturday matinee would receive a different large-format photograph of one of the lead actors.[15] Spectators arriving and departing from shows encountered images of actors in glass cases displayed on theater building facades.[16] By 1907, theatrical postcards were not only being sold in theaters but were also widely available through newsagents, stationers, and tobacconists, in cities and suburbs, at railway stations and seaside kiosks.[17]

More importantly, Benjamin's claim that film's mechanical reproduction destroyed the actor's singular aura, while technically correct, ignores the allure of multiples themselves. That allure has many sources. In film and photography, it derives in part from what scholars call the indexical quality of those media; just as smoke indexes, or points to, the actual presence of fire, photographic plates register the actual presence of whatever faced the lens. Photographic images, easy both to produce and to reproduce, also radiate the plenitude associated with all printing processes: there is a euphoria to knowing how rapidly an image, text, or sound recording can multiply, how far and how abundantly those multiples can travel. Art historian Jennifer Roberts has written eloquently about how difficult it was to transport paintings in the late eighteenth and early nineteenth centuries, and how easily the transmission of large, bulky canvases could break down or be delayed.[18] By contrast, the commercialization of photography that began in the 1860s had the opposite effect of alerting people to the relative ease with which visual information could circulate on a mass scale. To this day, iconic photographs of celebrities evoke the many other people encountering, purchasing, and enjoying them. Images of a young Sarah Bernhardt posing for photography pioneer Nadar, of Audrey Hepburn standing in front of the window of Tiffany's, of Muhammad Ali triumphing over Sonny Liston—all radiate their own distinctive glamor and shimmer with the energy of the multitudes who have looked at them.

The age of mechanical reproducibility gave rise to its own version of aura; call it the "halo of the multiple." By virtue of being multiplied, celebrities come to seem unique; their apparent singularity is *intensified* by copying. The more versions of them we see, the more distinctive they come to seem. Copies do not dim the celebrity's halo; they brighten it. That is why so many celebrity artifacts explicitly highlight the star's multiplicity—variously expressed as citations of other stars, replication by other stars, enactment of multiple roles, and proliferation across myriad artifacts and media, from the coins and statuary that publicized the rulers and athletes of the ancient world to twenty-first-century websites and applications such as Tumblr and Pinterest, whose users often do no more—and no less—than transfer images from one Internet location to another. Celebrity culture thrives neither on singularity nor multiplicity alone but on their superimposition. Far from being a fall from the grace of individuality, multiples and acts of multiplication have their own appeal, and media workers, celebrities, and publics actively collaborate to discern the unique in the multiple and the multiple in the unique.

CELEBRITY AND THE CULTURE OF MULTIPLES

Techniques for making copies have existed since antiquity. Casting, molding, and printing, whether of coins, reliefs, statues, movable type, engraved plates, incised woodblocks, inked lithographic stones, or photographs, are all common and longstanding techniques for producing multiples. Such techniques have many uses besides propagating renown, but, by the eighteenth century, many publishers, authors, and artists were using printed words and images to satisfy the public appetite for information about well-known authors, artists, monarchs, and performers, living and dead.[19] By the 1840s, technical and commercial improvements to printing processes were yielding increasingly accurate copies at ever quicker speeds and often falling costs. Any nineteenth-century middle-class household could express its admiration of genius by purchasing a plaster bust of Beethoven, Voltaire, Goethe, or Liszt to place on a mantelpiece. Likenesses of living celebrities appeared in books; as porcelain figurines and on the heads of walking sticks; and on fans, screens, snuffboxes, playing cards, decorative tiles, and enamel miniatures.[20]

Performance has long had an especially close relationship with print; celebrity can be understood as resulting from their combination. The multiplication of two-dimensional images of actors established them as celebrities long before the inventions of cinema, photography, and even newspapers. In seventeenth-century Japan, the new theater form of kabuki emerged alongside the new genre of ukiyo-e woodblock prints; as printmakers began to depict popular actors in scenes from recent plays, each genre publicized the other.[21] Oil paintings, drawings, sketches, and caricatures of actors abounded in late eighteenth-century Europe. The most popular paintings were reproduced as prints, using techniques including mezzotint and stipple engraving, which produced large numbers of high-quality copies. At the time, the average number of images that could be produced from a single plate using the mezzotint process was thirty, a thousand when using cheaper stipple engraving processes.[22] Often these illustrations found their way into the memoirs, biographies, and scandalous chronicles then attracting an increasingly robust audience. City dwellers lined up to gawk at the images of celebrities covering the windows of urban print shops. Those who could spare a shilling, sixpence, or penny purchased these relatively cheap prints to hang on their walls.[23] One scholar estimates that John Bell's editions of British plays, illustrated with plates depicting contemporary actors, sold about five thousand copies.[24]

Five thousand copies sounds like a lot, until we compare that number to the over 300,000 purchasers of an 1867 photograph of the Princess of Wales, or consider that in the 1860s, a single photograph studio in London (Mayall's) sold roughly 500,000 commercial photograph portraits per year.[25] Over 100,000 copies of the Sarah Bernhardt photographs taken by Napoleon Sarony during her first visit to New York City sold between 1881 and 1882 alone.[26] As a result, within a year those images had become recognizable enough in France to feature in caricatures published in a Parisian newspaper in 1881 (see "Savagery")—at a time when images could cross the Atlantic only via steamship. Over a decade later, a photograph of Bernhardt in *Munsey's Magazine* reportedly led to the June 1896 issue selling 700,000 copies.[27]

Robert Darnton has aptly observed that almost every era experiences an information explosion relative to its predecessors.[28] Some information explosions, however, are bigger than others, and the number of printed words and pictures circulating in the nineteenth century dwarfed anything that came before. Nor was it simply the quantity of multiples that increased; the distances they traveled and the speed at which they multiplied also grew dramatically across the nineteenth century. The limestone slabs used to print lithographs in the middle of the century allowed printers to pull one hundred sheets an hour. By the 1890s, soft zinc plates that could be rolled on rotary presses allowed printers to pull one hundred sheets *a minute.*[29] Concurrently, the time required to transport and transmit multiples also decreased. Eighteenth-century newspapers were delivered by horses and sailing ships. After the 1840s, news sped around the world via steamships, trains, and telegraph cables.

Photography was by no means solely responsible for the nineteenth century's image explosion. When P. T. Barnum brought opera singer Jenny Lind to the United States, in 1841, her daguerreotypes sold in large numbers. The daguerreotype format, however, yielded only one image per exposure, which meant that Lind had to sit for a new portrait every time she visited a new city. As singular rarities, daguerreotypes commanded a high price; they could reach a large audience only when reproduced in other formats. Lind's image began to multiply only after Matthew Brady, who became famous by taking pictures of celebrities, sold his daguerreotype of Lind to a commercial lithographer who made and sold reversed transfer prints of Brady's unique image.[30] Even after a photographic process emerged in the 1860s that enabled easy reproduction of many positives from a single negative, publishers continued for several decades to reproduce photographic images using transfer, etching, and intaglio processes. The resulting prints illustrated sheet music, as well as candy, cigar, and soap boxes.[31] The final results combined, to different degrees, the realistic precision of photography with the more handmade aesthetic typical of engraving, as in this print (figure 5.10), based on a photograph of Sarah Bernhardt in *L'Etrangère* (figure 5.11).[32]

The heavily illustrated weeklies that began to appear in Paris, London, and New York in the 1830s used woodcuts and other types of engravings to illustrate their pages. As late as 1886, even magazines devoted to photography illustrated their many advertisements for the latest lenses, tripods, and fixatives not with photographs but with engravings.[33] When Joseph Byron sold his photographs of Edwin Booth's funeral cortege in 1893 to the *New York Herald*, the newspaper reproduced them as line drawings.[34] Only around 1900 did improvements to the halftone process finally make it easy to integrate text with images that replicated photography's subtle tonal variations. The result was an explosion of illustrated magazines in the early twentieth century, including the theater magazines so often disassembled by scrapbookers.

Well before 1900, however, celebrity and photography spurred each other's growth. In 1854, the same year that Félix Nadar published a "Pantheon" featuring caricatures of three hundred celebrities, he also opened a photography studio and began to sell portraits of renowned artists, scientists, and politicians, including Charles Baudelaire, Richard Wagner, and Ulysses S. Grant. By 1860, his studio was flourishing enough for him to be able to afford to have his signature cast in transparent material, placed on the building's facade, and lit at night by gas. "Professional beauties" such as Lillie Langtry, who later took to the stage, became celebrities primarily by having their photographs taken and sold.[35] Street peddlers hawked freestanding celebrity photographs to passersby, while booksellers, stationers,

FIGURE 5.10. Charles A. Walker, Engraving of Sarah Bernhardt as Mrs. Clarkson, 1880.

FIGURE 5.11. Photograph of Sarah Bernhardt as Mrs. Clarkson, circa 1880.

and photography studios displayed the same images in the large plate glass windows that characterized modern nineteenth-century commercial buildings. In 1865, Jane Carlyle wrote to her husband, Victorian pundit Thomas Carlyle, "the greatest testimony to your fame seems to me to be the fact of my photograph . . . stuck up in Macmichael's shop-window."[36] *Anthony's Photographic Bulletin,* which ran a column entitled "Our Picture Gallery," noted the magazine's receipt of "a number of pictures and portraits of Indian celebrities," including "Comanche John," and explained that such images held great interest, "as they are pictures of people we hear a great deal of, but never see."[37] Images of performers whom large numbers of people did often see were in even more demand. Jose Maria Mora, a theatrical photographer working in New York in the late 1870s, reported sales of over three hundred thousand pictures of theatrical celebrities in one year alone.[38]

How did these many new techniques for reproducing likenesses affect celebrity? To answer this question, we can turn to Sarah Bernhardt, whose stardom coincided with the emergence of commercial photography, and who became the biggest star of the nineteenth century by, as one French journalist put it, "multiplying herself."[39] Reporting on her 1880 performances in Toulouse and Marseille, one journalist commented that everywhere he went, he found Bernhardt: "In the window of every bookstore, one sees only portraits and photographs of Sarah Bernhardt as Doña Sol, as Zanetto, as Adrienne, as L'Etrangère, as Frou Frou."[40] Bernhardt befriended Parisian newspaper editors and gave frequent press interviews around the world.[41] She sat for her first photograph in 1864, at age 20, for Félix Nadar. From the 1870s on, she worked with leading commercial photographers in most of the major capitals that she visited: Paul Nadar (Félix's son) in Paris, Napoleon Sarony in New York, the Downeys in London. The consistency in Bernhardt's poses, facial expressions, and costumes across photographs taken by different studios suggests that she took an active role in deciding how she would appear. Later female stars did the same: Marlene Dietrich informed cinematographers exactly how to light her, and Richard Avedon reported that Marilyn Monroe would examine contact sheets for hours.[42] On Bernhardt's first trip to the United States, in 1881, she met Thomas Edison and made an early phonograph recording, followed in later years by many commercial recordings of herself reciting poems and important speeches from plays in her repertory, which remain our only access to her legendary voice. An early adopter of film, she also made hundreds of movies, most now lost.[43] Her lifelong habit, when touring, of playing several roles in a single week or even, in old age, several roles in a single night, added to the sensation of seeing many Bernhardts simultaneously.

Perhaps photography's most significant effect on celebrity was to make it much easier to identify different images as representing the same person. Today, examining the dozens of paintings, drawings, and sculptures depicting Sarah Siddons, whose career ended in 1812, or of Rachel, who died in 1858, it is difficult to find any resemblance among them. Before photography, the proliferation of multiple portraits of the same person did not establish their visual identity; rather, it underscored the protean nature of human physiognomy and the variability of human perception. By contrast, the dozens of photographs for which Sarah Bernhardt, Henry Irving, Ellen Terry, Mark Twain, Abraham Lincoln, and Oscar Wilde posed helped each of them to impress upon the public a consistent, distinctive appearance. In the photographic era, replication did not dilute celebrity uniqueness; it concentrated it.

Even images that blended realist and cartoonish aesthetics found ways to use multiplication to reinforce singularity. Consider an 1896 image (figure 5.12) of Sarah Bernhardt wearing a dress imprinted with images of herself in her most iconic roles and signature poses.[44] Like many of the cartoons explored in the "Savagery" chapter, this image gathers multiple likenesses of Bernhardt within a single frame and juxtaposes distorted, even grotesque representations with a more realistic, even flattering one. The artist has rendered Bernhardt's hair, features, and ruffled collar photographically, using shading to soften her features and to simulate detail and depth. By contrast, the images populating Bernhardt's dress appear to be quickly roughed-out sketches that exhibit the abstraction and exaggeration typical of caricature. Knowledge of Bernhardt's best-known props, costumes, and gestures enable the informed fan to recognize images of her as Hamlet, Tosca, Adrienne Lecouvreur, Camille, and Doña Sol printed on the dress's sleeves and just below its Empire waistband. Toward the bottom of the

FIGURE 5.12. George Luks, "The Great Bernhardt in Her Robe and Roles," *New York World*, May 24, 1896.

dress, we see more-distorted figures enacting some of Bernhardt's typical poses: spiraling, twisting, diving to the floor, flinging arms wide open, or turning away from the viewer. The figure just to the right of the black-suited Hamlet, with its jerky, narrow angularity, and the figure at bottom left, which appears to be diving headfirst onto the ground, are particularly cartoonish. All of the line drawings lack detail, especially facial detail; the seated figure on Bernhardt's torso, for example, has no nose, and several have no visible eyes or mouth. While some of the sketches emphasize torsion and folds, others flaunt their flatness.

If we take a step back, we see a picture of a single individual whose distinctiveness exists in and as multiples. Indeed, multiplicity is the image's central visual theme. The cartoons on Bernhardt's dress copy not only well-known photographs of Bernhardt in her most famous roles, but also one another. The black figure on white ground to the viewer's left reverses the white one on black to the viewer's right. At least one of the images appears twice: the torso-level image of Bernhardt on a chair holding a scepter repeats itself slightly below it, angled, reversed, and reduced. We have here an inadvertent visual pun on poet Walt Whitman's notion of a single charismatic individual containing multitudes. In this case, those multitudes are the many well-known versions of the celebrity herself. The star's dress is a tissue of self-citations, a screen on which to project multiple images of herself—an early version of the scene in the film *Being John Malkovich* in which the actor John Malkovich, playing himself, goes through a portal that allows people to become him, and finds himself in a crowded restaurant where every patron is played by Malkovich in a different guise.

Meditations on multiples were not limited to fanciful cartoons. Scrapbookers filled their albums with images that multiplied individual stars. Some used special effects to present the same star several times over, a favorite technique for depicting celebrities who specialized in stunning metamorphoses. One compiler preserved an image of female impersonator Julian Eltinge that shows him dressed as a man rowing four different versions of himself dressed as a woman (figure 5.13). Tellingly, the caption describes this image of Eltinge in quintuplicate as "unique."[45] Another trick photograph, found in a scrapbook devoted to the popular comic impressionist Elsie Janis, depicts twelve Janises gathered around a table, all wearing the same hairdo and the same high-necked dress (figure 5.14). These similarities focus attention on Janis's many facial expressions, each presumably so characteristic of the celebrity being imitated that the editor felt comfortable not providing readers with a key to the stars Janis mimicked.[46] The caption explains that Janis imitates the distinctive traits of other celebrities "in a manner entirely her own." Because of her unique approach to multiplying others, theatrical managers saw in

FIGURE 5.13. Image of Julian Eltinge, TRI Scrapbook #3.

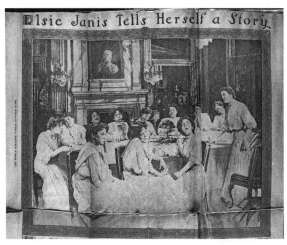

FIGURE 5.14. TRI Elsie Janis Scrapbook.

her "the making of a star." A 1905 article about Janis similarly entangled uniqueness and replication when it noted that although "Little Elsie" was in her youth considered "the pocket edition of Cissy Loftus," a professional mimic thirteen years her senior, she was "anything but a pocket edition now and she does not require comparison with Cissy Loftus or any other imitator, for her work is essentially original."[47] Multiplicity and singularity reinforce each other: an actor whose stage work consisted explicitly of imitating others could be seen as both a copy of a more famous impersonator and, after becoming a celebrity in her own right, an "essentially original" mimic.

Formats unique to photography enabled and encouraged viewers to focus simultaneously on minute variations in expression *and* on the shared traits that made it clear that all these different images represented the same individual.[48] The prefabricated photograph albums that hundreds of thousands of people around the world bought during the 1860s and 1870s had slots designed to hold four images per page, making eight simultaneously visible on facing pages. This accustomed people to seeing many images at once, many of them human likenesses. Visitors to commercial photography studios often perused sheets containing multiple images of the same person, each slightly different from the others but all taken during the same sitting.[49] Customers visiting New York City theater photographer Jose Maria Mora in the 1870s and 1880s could select their favorite prints from sheets containing fifty-six images of the same star.[50]

Theater scrapbooks also juxtaposed multiple images, but their blank pages encouraged compilers to mix and match images of different sizes and drawn from many sources.[51] In the early twentieth century, new printing techniques enabled magazines to emulate this collage-like layout; in turn, scrapbookers often gravitated to magazine compositions that already looked like album pages. One example (figure 5.15), drawn from a special issue of a theater magazine devoted to Sarah Bernhardt just after her death and preserved in a 1923 album, presents five images of the star within a single frame, with a diamond-shaped image at the center transforming the remaining four into pentagons.[52] Compositions like these trained publics to perceive a star's continuity across roles, scales, and perspectives: on one page alone, we see Bernhardt dressed as a man and as a woman, in profile and in close-up, facing left, right, and center. Such compositions also catered to fans' euphoric obsessiveness. The collector's drive to assemble every known image of a favorite star merges with a kind of orgiastic relish in having so many representations simultaneously within view. As a penciled annotation on a different scrapbook

FIGURE 5.15. Images of Sarah Bernhardt, TRI Scrapbook #21.

page containing nine images of one actress put it, "all Mrs. Leslie Carter." The sheer fact of proliferation supports a childlike satisfaction in pointing at one's accumulated treasures: there she is, and there she is again, and again, and again.

CREATING DISTINCTIVE TYPES

Scrapbookers were as keen as magazine compositors to arrange multiple images within the same album, often foregrounding how stars stayed identifiably the same across their diverse incarnations. In this way, members of the public contributed as much as stars themselves to establishing the parameters of a particular celebrity's *type*, their consistently present, relatively distinctive, and readily identifiable traits.[53] The more distinctive the star, the more readily they become a type, something easy for others to copy that maintains its identity across multiple iterations. The star's type expresses the qualities that define them from one role to the next. Sarah Siddons exemplified tragic majesty; Edmund Kean passionate energy; Edwin Booth delicate intelligence; Henry Irving quirky intensity; Ellen Terry statuesque grace; Eleonora Duse restrained inwardness. As soon as Bernhardt became an independent agent free to choose her own roles and mount her own productions, she made herself into what one critic described as an "embodiment of Oriental exoticism: the strange, chimaeric idol-woman: something not in nature, a nightmarish exaggeration, the supreme of artifice."[54] Despite periodically venturing into more wholesome roles, such as Joan of Arc, Bernhardt never denied acting to type. Indeed, when explaining to an interviewer why she avoided Ibsen's naturalist dramas, she noted that were she to perform in one, "the public would say, 'No, no, that is not a Bernhardt play.'"[55]

Typing enables self-replication, but also makes celebrities more available for imitation, enabling others to duplicate more easily a given star's signature traits. The careful observer of the image of Bernhardt wearing a dress imprinted with multiple Bernhardts (figure 5.12) will have noticed that it contained one figure who is not Bernhardt: US performer Mrs. Leslie Carter, often called the "American Sarah Bernhardt." Toward the bottom of the page, the illustrator depicts Carter copying Bernhardt, in multiple senses. She wears slippers that resemble those Bernhardt wore while sculpting. She is painting, which was one of Bernhardt's hobbies. And, though Carter's painting remains out of view, her position facing Bernhardt and the caption stating that she is taking "notes for future use" both imply that her canvas represents the star she takes as her model.

A Columbus, Ohio, scrapbook covering the years 1903–5 offers an example of an ordinary member of the public using multiplication to chart singularity. The compiler belonged to a college sorority whose Greek letters she inscribed on the front cover, and her album devotes many pages to individual actresses, including Minnie Maddern Fiske, Sarah Bernhardt, Maxine Elliott, and others. Her album features glossy images culled from magazines rather than theater programs, which suggests that instead of recording actual theater visits, her scrapbooks became a vehicle for expressing interest in selected performers. On two facing pages (figure 5.16), the compiler arranged eight images of Ethel Barrymore, plus two others of male performers. Barrymore, now known best from films in which she played elderly matriarchs, was in her youth one of Broadway's most glamorous stars. Varied as these portraits are, they all telegraph the traits that distinguished Barrymore from other stars: she is winsome but strong-willed, modest but confident, and errs on the side of projecting innocence, virtue, and good breeding even when wearing a sparkling, low-cut gown. The fan's appetite for many images of the same star even extended here to outright duplicates: the page on the left includes two

FIGURE 5.16. Images of Ethel Barrymore, TRI Scrapbook #63.

versions of Barrymore with fur stole and muff, one full-length, one smaller and cropped at hip level.[56]

Being original and repeating oneself by acting to type were two sides of the same coin. One of Bernhardt's favorite anecdotes recounted her youthful mistake of trying to replicate one of her great predecessors, the French actress Marie Favart. Though successful as an imitation, she found that the performance rang false, and "at that moment Sarah Bernhardt decided she would be herself."[57] Critics seconded her sense of her own singularity, so central to the establishment of a celebrity. "No one was exactly like her," wrote one journalist just after Bernhardt's death, in 1923, echoing Mark Twain's famous witticism: "There are five kinds of actresses: bad actresses, fair actresses, good actresses, great actresses, and Sarah Bernhardt."[58] Twain was making a joke about the quality of Bernhardt's acting, but he was also confirming the widespread belief that she was a genre unto herself: "*Sarah, c'est Sarah!*"[59] Anton Chekhov chastised Bernhardt's "thirst for originality" as "insatiable."[60] Novelist and drama critic Alphonse Daudet expressed a more positive take on her distinctiveness when he praised her for giving familiar lines uniquely personal readings.[61] An otherwise skeptical Virginia Woolf referred to Bernhardt's "curious face, so unlike any other face," for one brief phrase sounding like a fan convinced of the exceptional qualities of a favored and favorite star.[62]

THE MIRROR OF CELEBRITY

Exaggerated as many of the claims for Bernhardt's originality sound, comparing images of Bernhardt to those of other actresses supports the notion that she owed her status as the world's greatest celebrity to her canny sense of how to do what every star had to do—distinguish herself. Bernhardt consistently avoided adopting poses and gestures common to most female performers. French, US, and British publications and publicity materials from the 1860s through the 1890s typically depicted actresses gazing upward or sideways, as in these three examples, all published around 1880. The first (figure 5.17), an 1880 engraving from the sophisticated French cultural review *La Vie moderne*, presents an image of a female performer turning her face away from the viewer. The second image (figure 5.18) is a frequently reproduced photograph of Helena Modjeska in which she casts her eyes heavenward. The third (figure 5.19), a popular print of actress Clara Morris, depicts her

FIGURE 5.17. Mlle. Baretta, by Felix Lucas, *La Vie moderne*, October 23, 1880.

FIGURE 5.18. Helena Modjeska.

FIGURE 5.19. Clara Morris.

gazing off to the side. In all three images, the women depicted avoid confronting the beholder. Bernhardt, by contrast, adopted a direct, confrontational gaze in many paintings, prints, and photographs. Frequently, she stares directly outward, as in an image (figure 5.20) from a souvenir program produced for her 1880–81 tour of the United States. That tour began in New York City, where Bernhardt performed at the same theater and in many of the same roles as Modjeska and Morris, making the differences among their poses all the more significant.

Even when playing the frivolous, flirtatious Frou-Frou (figure 5.20), or with her face softly framed by lace, ruffles, and a flower (figure 5.21), Bernhardt wielded a steady gaze that faced the viewer head on.

The only other female performer of the 1870s and 1880s who regularly adopted a similar pose was Charlotte Cushman, shown here in a print based on a photograph taken around 1874 by Napoleon Sarony, who also photographed Modjeska, Morris, and Bernhardt (figure 5.22). Even Cushman's forthright gaze drifts a bit to the viewer's left, her demeanor softened by the way her hand touches her face (a gesture rarely adopted by male actors). Though Cushman appears matronly in this image, she was well known for parts that departed from decorous femininity: she played Romeo in her youth and witches, gypsies, and beggars in middle age. As one 1871 reviewer put it, "The more feminine graces Miss Cushman truly has not at command."[63] Like Cushman, Bernhardt also played trouser roles, but unlike Cushman, Bernhardt stared aggressively

"FROU-FROU."

FIGURE 5.20. Sarah Bernhardt as Frou-Frou.

at the beholder even when pictured in hyperfeminine roles such as Frou-Frou, Fedora, and Camille. Bernhardt was not the only female celebrity to stare down her beholders; one can find images of equally formidable actresses such as Gabrielle Réjane, Maxine Elliott, and Alla Nazimova doing the same. But in doing so, they followed a precedent set by Bernhardt.[64]

Although male celebrities did sometimes appear in profile, most prints, paintings, and photographs of well-known men portrayed them facing the viewer, as in an 1880 image (figure 5.23) of actor Henri Mounet-Sully from *La Vie moderne*. In an image (figure 5.24) that illustrated the programs from the joint national tour that Edwin Booth and Helena Modjeska undertook between 1889 and 1890, Booth faces the viewer while his female costar, Modjeska, gazes slightly upward and off to the side with her gaze turned in his direction, which makes her seem defined relative to him while he seems more independent of her.[65] Although Modjeska's pose makes her face less available for viewing, it also allows the viewer to stare at her from a position

FIGURE 5.21. Sarah Bernhardt, Booth Theatre program for Wednesday, December 1, 1880.

FIGURE 5.22. Charlotte Cushman.

of invulnerability. Not so with Booth, whose confrontational gaze is slightly unsettling, in a way that registers his trademark intensity. Though both images are engravings, Booth's face appears rendered more photographically and realistically than Modjeska's schematic features. Booth also seems more distinctively himself because we see his entire face, while Modjeska's image seems more generic because a profile offers less visual information than a frontal pose. Indeed, without the text naming her, it would be difficult to identify Booth's costar from the image alone.

The Booth-Modjeska program highlights two other distinctive features of Bernhardt's iconography. First, one of her most original maneuvers was to appropriate the directness, self-assertion, and boldness that men sitting for portraits adopted more frequently than women did. Bernhardt did this not once or twice, but over and over again, in multiple images and for many decades. Second, another way that Bernhardt differentiated herself from female stars such as Modjeska, Ellen Terry, Ada Rehan, and Julia Marlowe (each of whom found other ways to appear singular) was to rarely pose alongside a male costar. In most paintings, drawings, posters, and publicity photographs, Bernhardt stood alone. With the exception of production stills based on actual performances, where even Bernhardt had to share the stage with other actors, she rarely included anyone else in the frame with her aside from the occasional pet. Although W. C. Fields warned actors never to share a stage with an animal or a small child, Bernhardt's fondness for posing with wolfhounds and lion cubs only reinforced her ability to command the viewer's attention in the same way that she commanded the obedience of highly strung dogs and wild beasts.

Comparing hundreds of images in many dozens of scrapbooks reveals another visual convention that Bernhardt rejected: the pose in which a performer, almost always female, was pictured in front of or alongside a looking glass. Facing pages of an album compiled by Charles Ackley between 1891 and 1918, for example, depict multiple images of Olga Nethersole, each conveying her signature traits of sensuality, drama, intimacy, and luxury, all slightly neutralized by a consistent air of well-padded dignity (figure 5.25). The image at lower right shows Nethersole seated before a vanity. Her eyes in the mirror appear to meet the viewer's, but only because the seated figure is looking at herself. In another scrapbook image (figure 5.26) containing materials from a similar period, the eyes of the female performer's mirror reflection appear to meet ours, with more impact than in the

MOUNET-SULLY, par DE LIPHART.

FIGURE 5.23. Henri Mounet-Sully, by Ernest de Liphart, *La Vie moderne*, October 23, 1880.

BOOTH   MODJESKA

FIGURE 5.24. Edwin Booth and Helena Modjeska, detail from theater program, circa 1889.

Nethersole image, because the small oval hand mirror frames the performer's eyes more tightly and brings her reflection much closer to the picture plane. Even here, however, the mirror reduces the impact of her reflection because the small frame truncates her face, as does the profile view.

A woman looking at herself in the mirror was not a power pose. To be sure, these images all depict women who had achieved enough celebrity to be featured in a theater magazine and included in a scrapbook, and to that extent the pose provides an example of celebrity multiplication. But the precise duplication at play in mirroring tends to undermine distinctiveness instead of promoting it. The motif evoked misogynist associations of women and vanity. It also tended to reduce and fragment either the woman or her reflection, transforming multiplication into subtraction and division. In most cases, both the woman depicted and her reflection avert

FIGURE 5.25. Images of Olga Nethersole, TRI Scrapbook #48.

FIGURE 5.26. Image of Marie Tunison, TRI Scrapbook #3.

their eyes from the viewer, as in two images (figures 5.27 and 5.28) that appeared in the same scrapbook.

Some mirror poses display a childlike narcissism, as in a photograph of the young Lotta Faust slyly kissing herself in the mirror (figure 5.29), placed in one of six small albums compiled by the same person around 1901, each covered in red leather and devoted entirely to images of actresses.[66] Others took the mirroring to elaborate extremes, as in another image from one of the red leather albums (figure 5.30). Here, in a doubling of doubling, actress Miriam Nesbit stands in front of a large framed mirror while looking at herself in a handheld glass.

FIGURE 5.27. Image of Clara Palmer, TRI Scrapbook #3.

FIGURE 5.28. Image of Elfie Fay, TRI Scrapbook #3.

FIGURE 5.29. Images of Lotta Faust, TRI Scrapbook #79.

In avoiding the mirror pose, Bernhardt differentiated herself from other female performers in two ways: she rejected a visual cliché and refused to use multiplication in ways that diminished the figures duplicated by cutting off their features and masking their eyes. Tellingly, one of the few images that did place Bernhardt in front of a mirror had her standing with her back to the glass and made her reflection invisible (figure 5.31).[67]

FIGURE 5.30. Image of Miriam Nesbit, TRI Scrapbook #81.

FIGURE 5.31. Image of Sarah Bernhardt, TRI
Scrapbook #79.

Bernhardt by no means rejected putting herself on display. She lent herself
to multiple portraits in many media, adopting different poses, costumes,
and expressions. At the same time, she cultivated traits that made it easy for
viewers to identify the unity across that diversity. Her ability to maintain
that unity of type no matter who painted or photographed her positioned
her as the ruling personality, governing intelligence, and creative director
of her own image. By contrast, the precise duplication of a mirror reflection, like the relationship between a photographic positive and negative,
seems easy, automatic, and creepily redolent of the uncanny loss of individual agency that fictional characters feel when they encounter a double.

Bernhardt was very drawn to the notion of the double; she entitled
her autobiography *My Double Life* and wrote two novels featuring female
lookalikes, *Petite idole* and *Joli sosie*. But when it came to purveying her
own image, she avoided any pose that might compromise her appearance
of singularity, whether that meant removing others from the frame or
avoiding being seen next to a mirror image of herself. Instead, as all celebrities aim to do, she harnessed replication to present herself as matchless,
exceptional, and instantly identifiable, and successfully resisted poses that
led the many other female celebrities who assumed them to appear less

assertive and more interchangeable with one another. As the next chapter shows, this conjunction of multiplicity and singularity also made celebrities available for imitation by ordinary members of the public. Though journalists and photographers happily used new print formats to help celebrities replicate themselves, they proved less tolerant when ordinary members of the public sought to emulate celebrities.

CHAPTER 6

IMITATION

Celebrities multiply themselves through paper and pixels, but also through people. From the most dedicated Elvis impersonators to sports fans casually wearing sneakers endorsed by LeBron James, ordinary men and women like to imitate famous ones. In the 1910s, women bobbed their hair to look like dancer Irene Castle's, spent theater intermissions sketching costumes they had just seen onstage, and purchased Billie Burke dresses, named for the popular theater star who later played Glenda the Good Witch in the 1939 film *The Wizard of Oz*.[1] Little wonder that in 1935, a Japanese magazine listed "copycat" as one of the five types of fan associated with a popular theater troupe.[2] A 1964 *Life* magazine article on the most popular stars of the year reported that British boys were paying the equivalent of $1.85 for a Beatles haircut (figure 6.1) and that twenty thousand Beatles wigs had been sold. One schoolboy, threatened with expulsion if he adopted a bowl cut, chose expulsion.[3] Whether reproducing Farah Fawcett's feathered flip in the 1970s, donning black rubber bracelets and lace gloves à la Madonna in the 1980s, or posing in the 2010s for photos collected on a site entitled "Lesbians Who Look Like Justin Bieber," the relatively unknown have for many decades deliberately emulated those well-known enough to be called celebrities.[4]

It's easy to dismiss those who pattern themselves on celebrities for having surrendered their freedom and individuality—their agency—to the hypnotic effects of mass culture. Theodor Adorno, never one to take the rosy view, argued that even spontaneous-seeming reactions to mass culture, such as dancing to jazz music, merely imitate the gestures associated with true pleasure. The results of this "mimesis" are grim: "The behaviour of the victims . . . recalls St. Vitus's dance or the motor reflex spasms of the maimed animal." What Adorno considered "forcibly" produced imitations looked to him more like injury, disease, and death than genuine "self-expression and individuality."[5]

Many, however, have long seen celebrity imitation as serving more useful and happy purposes in constructing a sense of self. Although few celebrities aim to share their freedom and status (see "Sensation"), that does not stop publics from claiming the right to copy anything about stars that they can. Lord Palmerston, advocating the opening of the British National Portrait Gallery in 1859, assumed that people would seek to imitate "those who have done things which are worthy of our admiration" even more avidly if they could see the features of the admirable replicated in "the visible and tangible shape of portraits."[6] His statement

FIGURE 6.1. "They Crown Their Country with a Bowl-Shaped Hairdo," *Life Magazine*, January 31, 1964.

evoked the Enlightenment belief that emulation could be a democratizing, egalitarian activity. In 1994, film scholar Jackie Stacey's pioneering work challenged the characterization of female film spectators as passive by eliciting British women's memories of viewing Hollywood films in the 1940s and 1950s. Stacey found that ordinary women saw female stars as representing a glamor and abundance that offered a temporary respite from wartime austerity. Identification did not always express itself as imitation, but Stacey quotes many instances when it did. The women she surveyed recalled copying hats, shoes, hairstyles, and eyebrows seen in films; brushing their hair to look like Bette Davis's in *Dark Victory*, buying a suit after seeing Marilyn Monroe wear one in *Niagara*, or wearing boleros because Deanna Durbin favored them.[7] Sociologists studying responses to Princess Diana's death, in 1997, learned that many people turn to celebrity biography to glean solutions to common personal problems, such as eating disorders and unfaithful partners.[8] Others have found that blockbuster Hollywood stars model ways to express positive emotions, while indie actors provide templates for voicing skepticism, alienation, and defiance.[9] Postgame interviews with athletes similarly illustrate how to voice winning and losing, satisfaction and disappointment. Like the deportment and elocution manuals so popular before the rise of radio and television, media coverage of celebrities can offer the general public guidelines for how to be in the world.

These two schools of thought assign very different values to imitation, but both assume that copying comes easily. One considers imitation an unavoidable reflex, while the other tends to assume that anyone who wants to imitate a celebrity is free to do so without encountering obstacles or attracting censure. What, however, if celebrity imitation is not automatic, effortless, and open to all, but rather a choice, a skill, and a privilege that members of dominant groups often seek to deny those in subordinate ones?

An anecdote about the novelist Henry James illustrates just how deliberate, difficult, and restricted celebrity imitation can be. Given his high standards and elevated style, James may seem an unlikely candidate for fanboy, but he began his career in the 1870s as a theater reviewer and continued for many decades to publish essays about playwrights and actors. Despite his interest in drama and performance, James strongly criticized modern celebrity culture in works such as *The Aspern Papers* and "The Death of a Lion," which showcased the dangers of paying more attention to the private lives of artists than to their work.[10] Though James admired Sarah Bernhardt's talents as an actor and praised her performances early in her career, in 1879 he rebuked her for becoming a "celebrity, pure and simple," thanks to her "advertising genius" and a taste for publicity that had made her "the muse of the newspaper."[11]

Much as James disapproved of Bernhardt's publicity-seeking ways, he continued to admire her acting, as we learn from the diaries of Alice Comyns Carr, a gifted theater costume designer married to a drama critic and theater manager. In a rarely cited passage from her *Reminiscences*, published in 1926, Carr recalled how, decades earlier, James had entertained the daughters of *Punch* cartoonist George du Maurier by attempting to replicate Bernhardt's famously sinuous exit (discussed in "Sensation") in the penultimate act of *La Tosca*:

> Henry James had a very critical appreciation of dramatic impersonation, and he often amused the du Maurier girls by his imitation of theatrical celebrities. . . . He had just come from seeing Sarah Bernhardt in *Tosca*, and undertook to give a "representation of the great actress." But when he came to the point where he had to squeeze himself through a crack in the door, Henry James forgot that he was not so slim as the divine Sarah, and his plump figure stuck half way.

For "years after," Carr adds, the girls would tease James by asking him "to please be Sarah."[12]

As this anecdote illustrates, imitation is not easy. James tries to slip into a star's skin, only to find himself wedged in a doorway. Much as he admired actors, in this instance he could not translate his "critical appreciation" of their work into an equally skilled performance of his own. The crack in the doorway that he fails to squeeze through is small, but the gap it exposes between his dramatic talent and Bernhardt's is wide. Nor does James himself consider imitation a heedless, involuntary reflex. In saying he would give a "*representation* of the great actress," James used a term that meant both an actor's interpretation of a role and an author's creation of a text. Representations frame the world, deciding what is worth including or excluding, and thus imply an ambition to do more than merely copy reality. By offering to give his own "representation" of Bernhardt, James implied that his imitation would deploy all of his considerable artistic acumen. If his artistic creation fell short, it was not for lack of intentional effort.

Finally, imitation is not equally open to all. There's more than a hint of gay shaming in Carr's account of young women ridiculing an older man for so enthusiastically trying to imitate a female celebrity, and failing. As a novelist, James prided himself on his self-consciousness and keen observation, counseling novice writers to try to be people "on whom nothing is lost."[13] How embarrassing, Carr implies, for "the Master" to get caught in the act of forgetting the difference between his "plump" body and the "divine Sarah's" slim one. Try as he might, Henry could not "be Sarah," although his botched imitation did achieve the highly theatrical goal of drawing attention to himself.

THE IMITABLE CELEBRITY

James was no ordinary imitator, and his attempt to copy a celebrity failed in part because he ambitiously tried to reproduce an extraordinarily demanding piece of stage business. Most people who imitate celebrities content themselves with repeating catch phrases, buying products, or adopting looks associated with their favorite stars, all ways of imitating celebrities that existed well before the rise of radio, film, television, and YouTube. Until the eighteenth century, images of celebrated leaders, artists, and performers had emphasized resemblance to an abstract classical ideal. But around 1750, portraitists and the many printmakers who copied paintings began to focus on realistic, quirky details that differentiated one individual from another. Images depicting Rousseau wearing an unusual kind of cap or Byron with his broad shirt collar open made it easier for ordinary men to imitate the small traits of great ones.[14] As the previous chapter showed, celebrity originality often produces a type available for others to copy. Precisely because the poet Lord Byron grew his hair longer and left more shirt buttons undone than most other well-known men who sat for portraits, an 1868 diarist could remark that a friend's father in his youth displayed "all the grace of Byron about the head and throat," while an 1883 article could similarly remark that Oscar Wilde's newly shortened hair was "now arranged exactly like that of the elder and inferior poet whom Mr. Wilde condescends to honor by this imitation. That bard has only to adopt the Byronic collar to complete a general resemblance which would illustrate the continuity of poetic genius."[15]

During the nineteenth century, industrial modernity not only led to an explosion of imagery that culminated with the commercialization of photography in the 1860s; it also increased the sense that bodies could and should be transformed for the better, through what historian Michael Anton Budd has called the drive to sculpt the physical self.[16] In the 1840s and 1850s, the acolytes of Edwin Forrest, an actor renowned for his robust physique and rough manners, often copied his facial hair. A few decades later, a journalist reported that Sarah Bernhardt's "smallest gestures were noted, copied, exaggerated by a multitude of idolatrous women."[17] Only a very small number went as far as the woman who shot herself at a 1903 performance of Sarah Bernhardt in *Werther*, "imitating in every movement Madame Bernhardt's portrayal of the suicide"—but that act itself echoed the rash of copycat suicides that had followed the initial publication of Goethe's novel, in 1774.[18]

What were celebrity imitators trying to achieve? The mostly male journalists who wrote about Bernhardt's mostly female imitators saw them as seeking to emulate her eccentricity, originality, defiance, energy, desire, and will, as well as the seductiveness and emotional intensity that characterized her signature roles. Matthew Arnold, in his essay on the French theater's 1879 visit to London, wrote of the "great ladies who are seeking for soul, and have found it in Mdlle. Sarah Bernhardt."[19] But it was easier to seek soul and even to find it than to incarnate it, as Bernhardt did, and many who aspired to imitate the star contented themselves with purchasing products associated with her. Although the celebrity endorsement business developed exponentially in the last decades of the twentieth century, the practice of using celebrities to advertise goods has existed for at least two hundred years. Carriage manufacturers named phaetons and surreys after Sarah Bernhardt because she represented energy and speed; a Sarah Bernhardt Hair-Waver and Curler invited women to recreate the star's unruly locks; and an exhibitor of a Bernhardt pelargonium suggested that woman and flower shared a vivid elegance.[20] The stormy Edwin Forrest found his name attached to locomotives, steamers, and fire engines; people named babies and mint juleps after Clara Fisher, a child star of the 1820s; Helena Modjeska became a brooch, a line of soap, and a caramel marshmallow biscuit.[21]

Many nineteenth-century advertisers attached stars' names to goods without permission, but some paid celebrities to vouch for products that they claimed to use. Bernhardt, for example, was compensated to provide testimonials for wigs, water, and the Edison Record company.[22] In 1939, Mary Pickford was no longer actively working in films, but she advertised her own cosmetics line in movie magazines using taglines that played on the public's desire to model themselves on celebrities: "She made it HER powder—just as you will make it YOUR powder."[23] For decades, female celebrities tended to endorse cosmetics and clothing, while male celebrities touted alcohol and tobacco. In the 1970s, television commercials presented Orson Welles using his distinctively orotund voice to announce that Paul Masson would serve no wine before its time; well into the twenty-first century, the magazine covers of *Cigar Aficionado* showcase a different male celebrity each month, posing with stogie in hand.

In the nineteenth century, many people copied how stars dressed both onstage and in the studio photographs displayed for sale in shop windows on almost every city street. Like modern celebrity, modern fashion involved creating patterns, types, and models and distributing them to ever growing numbers of people over increasingly large distances and at an increasingly fast pace. Actors are not the only celebrities to influence how people dress and wear their hair, but theater and fashion had especially close connections in the nineteenth and early twentieth centuries; as theater historian Marlis Schweitzer has shown, many women went to the theater to observe and replicate the latest styles.[24] Commenting in 1882 on the social influence of the typical Parisian actress, a journalist observed that "the most virtuous women study [the actress], learn her by heart, copy her outfits [*toilettes*], her posture, her manners, her eccentricities."[25] This was certainly the case with Sarah Bernhardt. When Bernhardt toured provincial France in 1880, *Le Figaro* reported on how interested their female readers ("lectrices") were in her costumes and fancifully reported how "even in churches, young girls dream . . . of Sarah Bernhardt's outfits between Bible verses."[26] Bernhardt's sartorial influence extended to England, where one could buy a "Bernhardt costume" at a French dressmaker's in Covent Garden. British fashion magazines advertised Bernhardt gloves, bonnets, dresses, bodices, corsages, blouses, perfume, hair styles, and hair dye.[27] After the 1860s, when many middle-class women acquired their own sewing machines, the fashion press also began to include detailed patterns in every issue, with instructions on how to make outfits worn by numerous female stars. One magazine advised a reader to "Copy the 'Sarah Bernhardt' toilette in this JOURNAL," while another directed a reader from South Africa how to make a Sarah Bernhardt ruffle depicted in a previous issue.[28]

Wearing an item of clothing associated with Bernhardt enabled fans to approximate her essence by imitating her appearance. Paradoxically, the Bernhardt trait that admirers most wanted to emulate was her "inimitable originality"; fashion was yet another arena in which replication only intensified the star's aura of uniqueness (see "Multiplication").[29] In many cases, the dresses Bernhardt wore onstage were too elaborate and expensive to be widely copied, but accessories such as the Sarah Bernhardt gloves advertised in theater programs were easily produced and purchased.[30] In piecemeal fashion, many elements of Bernhardt's costumes became the new normal. As a fashion journalist explained, "for some time she wore eccentric sleeves . . . ; our very newest sleeves are made in this way." Bernhardt wore large bunches of flowers to be more visible onstage; "now nothing is considered more elegant." Bernhardt adopted white kid gloves, "and for a long time no lady appeared at a ball without white gloves." She changed to Swedish gloves, in which the smooth kid surface lay next to the skin with the rough surface facing outward, and though once "one hardly dared appear in the street in them, now they are universally adapted."[31]

FASHION, IMITATION, AND AGENCY

Fashion is particularly susceptible to being seen as suffering from what art historian Robin Kelsey, writing about photography, has called an "intention deficit disorder."[32] To many, it appears obvious that celebrities adopt new styles arbitrarily and that people copy them automatically. Anticipating Adorno's association of mimesis with contagion and disease, in 1879 a journalist joked that Bernhardt's first visit to London had spawned a new illness, Sarah Bernhardt mania, whose symptoms included buying her photograph and "investing in all the Bernhardt scarves, gloves, braces, collars, costumes, hats and hair-dyes."[33] To this day, cultural commentators single out women copying female performers as especially mindless, echoing the common bias that women are inherently passive and that performers, especially female ones, are only secondarily creative, limited to repeating words scripted by others rather than originating their own ideas and visions. In the nineteenth century, however, costumes represented an arena of relatively autonomous self-expression for actors, in contrast to the twentieth century, when Hollywood studios employed designers such as Adrian and Edith Head to dress film stars. Even after the studio system broke down, late twentieth-century female stars continued to be marquees for couturiers, so that we now associate Audrey Hepburn with Givenchy, Liza Minelli with Halston, Cher and Tina Turner with Bob Mackie. Well into the twenty-first century, celebrity magazines report avidly on the designers who dress female stars for various awards ceremonies. In recent times, only a few rare performers, such as Prince, have designed their own outfits.

Nineteenth-century actors, by contrast, obligated to purchase their own costumes, were also relatively free to choose how they would look.[34] Journalists writing about Bernhardt's style highlighted the active role she took in inventing fashions that others then adopted; one even identified "the costumes of to-day" as her "creation."[35] An article on "individuality in the costumes of Mme. Bernhardt" noted that she "may be said to have created a style of her own in dress as well as in acting."[36] Far from being seen as an inert form on which to hang someone else's designs, Bernhardt was lauded for having invented new standards for others to copy. Drama critics considered the costumes she wore onstage expressions of the same artistic impulses that led her to paint and sculpt.[37] Just as today we attribute authorship to the fashion designer who sketches pictures of clothes, rather than to the workers who cut and sew them, the nineteenth-century fashion press accorded Bernhardt the status of author in the Romantic sense: a person whose imagination generates new and original ideas.[38] "As all the world knows, Sarah Bernhardt has a perfect genius for designing costumes," wrote one British reporter. Others noted that Bernhardt had fabrics woven for her according to her own drawings ("dessins"). When she did work with well-known designers, she sometimes "departed from the design submitted to her."[39] Bernhardt explained to one interviewer, "I always design my own gowns; they are meant to express moods. They must be individual. I have never copied anyone else."[40] Here, authorship equals ownership ("my own gowns") and originality ("individual," "never copied"). Even, or especially, at their most whimsical, those costumes registered the execution of a deliberate intention: "they are *meant to* express moods." Like Oscar Wilde, who wrote that the aim of art is "simply to create a mood," the actress as fashion designer combined the seriousness of high art with the authoritative whimsy of the dandy or aesthete who sought to capture fleeting sensations in dress.[41]

While journalists writing for the women's press focused on the intelligence Bernhardt exercised when inventing new fashions, those writing for humor and sports publications with primarily male readerships focused on ridiculing the women who imitated her. For these reporters, the women who copied Bernhardt dresses, bonnets, and hairstyles were the sartorial equivalents of Henry James stuck in a doorway: striving to reproduce the star's distinctive look, they only exposed their failure to achieve it. An 1892 review by an avowedly "captious critic" of Bernhardt's *Cleopatra* in *The Illustrated Sporting and Dramatic News* noted that even in June, a month when most playhouses were deserted, "it is still the fashion apparently to have seen Bernhardt, and—as in matters of fashion the fair sex takes the lead—there has been quite a rush of ladies to *Cleopatra*. . . . Nine out of every ten women whom we saw in the vestibule had evidently made up after the familiar portraits of the actress," especially in "arrangement of the hair."[42] For this commentator, Bernhardt's glamor as the Queen of the Nile, famous for her powers of seduction, became tarnished when mirrored by her less appealing followers, who transformed the rare into the common.

Some journalists mocked celebrity imitation by imagining it taken to comic extremes. A cartoon in an 1883 issue of *Funny Folks* (figure 6.2) showed a woman with gloves so long that they need to be held up by her maid. A man in top hat and monocle, standing in for the supercilious male reader, observes the scene.[43] The caption reads: "The gloves worn by Sarah

Bernhardt in *Fédora* were four and a
half feet long. Aristocratic Lady Amateur: Well, Mr. Spangler, I may not
be so good an actress as Sarah Bernhardt, but my gloves are six inches
longer!" The gloves caricatured here
were indeed world famous; even the
Rocky Mountain News reported on
them.[44] The cartoon aims to deflate
them, literally and figuratively, by
exaggerating them even further;

FIGURE 6.2. "The One Thing Needful,"
Funny Folks, August 4, 1883.

the glove fabric that would have been tightly compacted on Bernhardt's
arm appears here stretched and sagging to the point of formlessness. The
cartoon parses imitation as a form of competition; unable to improve on
Bernhardt's acting, the aristocratic amateur boasts of exceeding the star's
already excessive glove length. The cartoon's chief target is the copycat
whose vanity leads her to boast of outdoing Bernhardt when she has failed
even to equal her. But it also pokes deadpan fun at Bernhardt's extravagance
in wearing gloves four and a half feet long, suggesting that imitation belittles
both the imitator and the model imitated.

Women's fashion magazines encouraged readers to copy how celebrities dressed as well as the traits their styles expressed. By contrast, men's
magazines challenged both the idea that fashion might embody a celebrity's essence and the possibility that ordinary women might succeed at
imitating stars. Nineteenth-century male satirists ridiculed women whom
they imagined expressing aspirations for independence and public attention by emulating Bernhardt. An 1891 Russian burlesque entitled "Sarah
Bernhardt, or Loge No. 2 in the Dress Circle," for example, spoofed a
variety of women inspired by the "international celebrity" known for her
"eccentric personality." When a husband forbids his wife from going
out to see the actress, she retorts, à la Bernhardt, "I'll do whatever I
want." One character takes up painting after discovering that "Sarah
Bernhardt's . . . artistic temperament is like mine." Others foolishly
believe that, like Bernhardt, they will become the focus of public attention: "During the intermission they won't be able to take their binocu-
lars off me," says one woman; "Me neither," echoes another, who later
in the play walks onstage, "moving dramatically," to ask the audience,
"Don't you think I look remarkably like Sarah Bernhardt?"[45] Not only is

the answer no; the very question exposes how poorly her self-knowledge matches her self-regard.

Satires like these posit both imitation and imitability as a privilege denied to the majority of women. From one vantage point, such caricatures seem designed to correct unseemly self-regard and excessive accumulations of status. From another, they seem intent on mocking anyone who dares to rise above her appointed station. As ideals, however unattainable, for those aspiring upward, celebrities and their imitators often became targets for those who wanted to limit social mobility.

RACIAL BARRIERS TO IMITATION

Though the majority of parodists poked fun at white women getting above themselves by imitating Bernhardt, a small but significant number presented celebrity imitation as a racial privilege confined to white people. As we saw in "Savagery," several French cartoonists expressed their view that Bernhardt was dangerously, even tyrannically appealing by linking her to Native and African Americans. The worry that the relationship between celebrities and publics might overturn racial hierarchies similarly comes through in this French journalist's comment about Bernhardt: "If she has treated Negroes [*les nègres*] like Parisians, she has even more so treated Parisians like Negroes."[46] This quote, which took for granted that Parisians were white and as such should occupy a higher position than Negroes, similarly construed the celebrity's supposedly good treatment of the latter as a sign that she had demoted the former.

In a catch-22 typical of racism's double binds, cartoonists depicted members of nonwhite groups as abject whether they succeeded in imitating white celebrities or failed. Consider an 1881 advertisement for La Diaphane, a rice powder endorsed by Bernhardt (figure 6.3). Designed to take up an entire page, the busy image consists of four corner panels that, from top left to bottom right, tell the story of Bernhardt's departure from France, her arrival in New York's harbor, the dispersal of her name throughout Europe, and her popularity in even the remotest areas of America. The image associates the celebrity with the product advertised both by suggesting that the powder has actually touched the star's skin and by offering, at bottom center, a facsimile of Bernhardt's practically illegible handwriting. Since we cannot actually read the star's testimonial to the powder's wonders, its

FIGURE 6.3. 1881 advertisement for "La Diaphane" powder.

main purpose is to make us feel closer to her body by offering an image
of writing produced by her own hand. The ad also presents the celebrity
and the good for sale as metaphors for each other, since "La Diaphane"

L'amérique nous envoie ses fleurs parfumées, le myrthe, la verveine, le magnolia ; Sarah lui en rapporte les parfums dans sa *Diaphane*, cette merveilleuse poudre de riz.

FIGURE 6.4. Detail from 1881 advertisement for "La Diaphane" powder.

refers both to the powder and to Bernhardt herself. Both are delicate and filmy. Both move quickly; the caption to the panel at the bottom left explains that Bernhardt's fame moved through Europe "like a train of powder." Both maintain their freshness even when traveling around the world. Both are aesthetic, aristocratic, and grand: the elaborate device at the top of the frame presents Bernhardt's name in rococo lettering, superimposed on a disc that resembles a label for rice powder, while the emblems of painting and sculpture at the top corners of the frame allude to Bernhardt's forays into the visual arts. The circular medallion at the bottom of the frame contains the quasi-noble motto that Bernhardt devised for herself, "Quand même," whose meaning approximates the 2017 catchphrase "Nevertheless, she persisted."

Perhaps most importantly, but also most ambiguously, both the powder and the performer are white. Celebrity endorsements typically invite identification and imitation. Thousands of ads like this one have suggested that by purchasing products associated with stars, consumers can become more like them. Scholars customarily associate this kind of commodity fetishism, which confuses people and things, with the loss of agency associated with error and delusion. It is therefore striking that two vignettes in the advertisement for La Diaphane mock the act of imitation by caricaturing both the imitators and the imitated as seeking to exercise *more* agency than they would normally be allotted. At top left (figure 6.4), the image of a grotesquely magnified Bernhardt with an equally huge powder box invites the viewer to perceive the reputation of the product's celebrity endorser as unjustifiably inflated. At bottom right (figure 6.5), the advertisement depicts two female figures presented as black. The caption to this vignette suggests that though many are called to imitate Bernhardt, not all succeed in doing so, even when they adopt the products associated with her. The caption reads: "In America, the enthusiasm is general.—What you doing there?—Me put on Sarah Bernhardt powder. Me no longer want to be poorly whitened." The use of the present tense suggests that one of the figures is meant to be represented in the act of applying the powder, but both figures' faces are so darkly shaded that it is difficult to discern their features, which encourages the viewer to doubt the powder's effectiveness as a whitening agent.

The caption to the vignette at bottom right suggests that imitation of Bernhardt has become so "general," so common, that it has spread to those whom the cartoonist considers the lowest members of society. To be sure, the image also

En Amérique l'enthousiasme est général. — Quoi toi faire là ? — Moi mettre poudre Sarah Bernhardt. Moi plus vouloir être mal blanchie.

FIGURE 6.5. Detail from 1881 advertisement for "La Diaphane" powder.

gestures toward the exotic allure often attributed to both Bernhardt and to African American women. But image and caption both find ways to establish the black figures' subordinate position in a racial hierarchy. By presenting one of the black women as wanting to correct her "poorly whitened" (*mal blanchie*) skin, the caption presents whiteness as both norm and ideal. By depicting one of the women in a gracelessly contorted pose that may be meant to suggest a poor attempt at imitating one of Bernhardt's famous onstage gestures, the image associates blackness with the savage and grotesque. White minstrel performers often did the same when claiming to imitate black movement and speech, often presenting both as failed imitations of elevated white behavior.[47]

Many scholars have noted how dominant groups deny subordinated groups agency by depicting them as mere mimics. But copying can itself be intentional, creative, and ambitious. For that reason, dominant groups have also frequently denied oppressed people the right to imitate their supposed betters.[48] By presenting the two black female figures in dresses whose short sleeves and skirts expose their arms, ankles, and feet, the image associates them with an abject poverty impossibly distant from the delicate beauty associated with the advertised product.[49] Compare their faces, poses, and garb to the idealized renderings of genteel white women at bottom left, whose elaborately tailored dresses have high necks and long skirts, and who appear surrounded by elements of modern urban infrastructure such as sandwich boards and streetlights. The fashionable white women occupy the same space as Bernhardt: at top right, they wait to see her disembark; at bottom left, they read an ad for one of her public appearances. By contrast, the black women appear in an isolated tropical setting far from the realms of fashionable urbanity. Their exposed dark forearms reverse the long white gloves Bernhardt wears in the ad's central image. They know Bernhardt only through the powder named after her, making the links between the celebrity and these imitators as flimsy as the powder's ability to whiten their dark skins.

The bizarre self-contradiction of this advertisement replicates a tension within celebrity and consumer culture between egalitarianism (anyone can be a star, or at least powder up like one) and exclusion (some people can never rise above their appointed stations). Both vignettes defy a fundamental principle of advertising: to claim miraculous powers for products and their celebrity endorsers. The top left image undercuts the celebrity's grandeur by inflating it beyond credibility, while the bottom right image mocks a consumer for believing that the advertised product might work. Tellingly, both vignettes spoof the product itself by exaggerating the size of the round powder box that looms large at the top left and bottom right corners, anchoring the entire composition. Advertising touts glamor, but risks cheapening it by expanding its purview to anyone who can afford a box of rice powder. Celebrity elevates stars by making them known to multitudes, but by definition those multitudes will include society's least prestigious groups. The black women who inflate Bernhardt also debase her, and caricature seeks to put both imitator and imitated in their proper places.

Taken as a whole, the advertisement for La Diaphane seems designed not only to sell a commodity but also to assure the middle-class white women it targets that celebrity status and imitation cannot overcome hierarchies of class and caste. The sardonic image of the oversized Bern-hardt implies that despite her glamor and success, her status as an illegiti-mate, unmarried working woman remains lower than that of bourgeois women of leisure firmly attached to fathers and husbands. The image of the black women too dark to be lightened by La Diaphane similarly conveys that while everybody *wants* to use the advertised good, not everybody *can*. The attempt to imitate celebrities may be universal, but only those at the top of the racial hierarchy are allowed to be seen as successfully copying the stars. Celebrity and commodity culture work by appealing to large numbers of people who hunger for status and distinction. One common critique is that both do so in ways that cultivate illusions about capitalism fostering equality for all. This advertisement, however, makes no effort to reconcile the contradiction between elitism and populism; instead, it seeks to limit celebrity culture's potential to level the differences between stars and their least privileged followers.

Another set of images, these from the United States, circa 1882, sim-ilarly mock low-status ethnic groups who seek to raise themselves by imitating a celebrity.[50] The first gives us a series of ethnic Oscar Wildes (figure 6.6). These images depend on a coarse racism that exaggerates features considered typical of each respective group. The Jewish Oscar has the long nose and high cheekbones familiar from Bernhardt cari-catures (see "Defiance" and "Savagery"). The African American Oscar has spiky hair, exaggeratedly full lips, and (like the women in the rice powder ad) exposed legs and bare feet. The German Oscar wears leder-hosen and drinks beer from a stein that doubles as a vase for a lily. The Asian American Oscar has sallow skin, a pigtail, and a long mustache. The Irish Oscar at top left highlights how celebrity offers individuals upward mobility in ways that trigger caricaturists to reinforce social hierarchies: Wilde was himself Irish, and the coarse features and fancy dress of the "Irish Wilde" portrayed here point both to the real Oscar's pretention in trying to rise above his station and to the impossibility of masses of Irishmen following suit.[51]

The humor here, such as it is, depends on mingling the rarified with the base, the lily and the sunflower with a pig, a mug, and a jar labeled "for sale." We are asked to laugh at the distance between the celebrity and the abject ethnic groups who strive and fail to imitate him. Imitation only widens the gulf between Wilde's interest in beautifying everyday life and

FIGURE 6.6. E. B. Duval, caricatures of Oscar Wilde in ethnic dress, circa 1882.

the Jew's venal commercialism, Wilde's fancy dress and the ragged state of the barefoot and pantless African American, his aestheticism and the Asian's utterly foreign garb, decor, and music. For this cartoonist, a Jew or Irishman who tries to mimic Wilde's style succeeds only in accentuating his distance from it.

Even as these images play on the gap between the white Wilde and his ethnic others, they also lower Wilde to his imitators' level. Their point is not simply that a Jewish or black Wilde would be ridiculous, but that Wilde himself is ridiculous, with his long hair, extravagant costumes, and interest in home decor. An article in the humor magazine *Moonshine* took a similar swipe at the celebrity aesthete when it reported that "in Rochester they dressed up an old negro in full aesthetic costume" on the occasion of his stop in that New York city during his 1882 lecture tour of the United

States. Ventriloquizing Wilde's reaction to the sight in verse, the article continued:

> And then to flout my faultless figure
> They mocked me with an old fat nigger,
>   Aesthetically spick and span.[52]

This racist doggerel sees Wilde's ethnic imitators taking him down even when they copy him perfectly. The more "aesthetically spick and span" their reproduction of his signature look, the more they "flout" and "mock" him. Taking Wilde as a model defied the boundaries separating male from female; the same *Moonshine* article mentioned that "one man said he should call him 'she,' as he was a 'Charlotte-Ann' [charlatan]."

Cartoonists mocked the possibility that by imitating Wilde, ethnic and racial groups whom the dominant classes wanted to keep out of sight, quietly serving others for little or no pay, might take center stage and draw attention to themselves. Consider a spoof of the contagious effects of Wilde's dandyism (figure 6.7).[53] Here, again, an image derides an African American figure for attempting to imitate a white celebrity. Scholar Monica Miller has shown that for several centuries, white satirists reduced black dandies to failed impersonators and belittled African Americans who exercised agency by dressing up.[54] The dandy pictured in the foreground of this 1882 image, part of the Currier and Ives "Darktown Comics" series, has caught "the aesthetic craze." His imitation is imperfect: his pants, bright yellow in the color original, have ragged hems; a large feather threatens to overwhelm his too-small hat. But his finery does differentiate him from the black women on either side of him, who wear drab, worn clothing and whose bared arms signify their engagement in manual labor. The young woman in the background wears an apron, which suggests that she works as a cook, while the older woman closer to the foreground is actively engaged in washing, a job that maintains the finery of those who can afford to keep their clothes as spotless as the white shirt visible in the laundry basket at bottom left. The cruel joke of the cartoon is that a figure who should know his place in a realm of harsh necessity has dared to make himself purely aesthetic by wearing finery in a work yard and by turning a laundry basin into a vase for a sunflower.

Making the dandy look so different from the women in the image marks his social transgression as individual, even idiosyncratic, and

THE ÆSTHETIC CRAZE.

What's de matter wid de Nigga ?   Why Oscar you's gone wild !

FIGURE 6.7. Currier and Ives, "The Aesthetic Craze," circa 1882.

unrepresentative of his race. The skeptical commentary of the older female figure highlights his strangeness, in dialect itself marked as deviating
from white speech and normal spelling: "What's de matter wid de nigga?
Why Oscar you's gone wild!" That comment presents a black man daring
to imitate a white celebrity as "wild," engaged in an isolated and savage
bid for freedom that inevitably fails. At the same time, the pun on "wild"
and the fact that the young black man is also named "Oscar" suggests
that imitating Wilde does effectively, if absurdly, differentiate the dandy
from other black men. Like the defiant celebrities discussed in chapter 1,
Wilde appears here as a potential resource for those wishing to assert their
freedom from social norms and constraints.

Although the cartoon reinforces the notion that copying celebrities is a privilege not available to African Americans, the adoring gaze of the young woman in the background provides this failed imitation of Wilde with at least one appreciative spectator. Her presence suggests that although Wilde and his imitators were usually perceived as defying normal masculinity, their fancy dress might have attracted women who both desired and identified with dandies. Even as the caption dismisses the African American Oscar's pretensions as a bemusing form of wildness in need of cure or quarantine, it also implies a fear that Oscar Wilde and others like him might inspire ordinary members of the public to dissolve old social bonds and form new ones.

IMITATION AS RACIAL PRIVILEGE

While journalists, cartoonists, and advertisers discouraged ordinary women from imitating female stars and set racial limits on who could emulate white celebrities, white nineteenth-century audiences applauded and rewarded white men who imitated women and African Americans. Minstrel acts, popular around the world well into the 1920s, featured white performers in blackface makeup who pretended to dance, sing, speak, and dress like cartoonish distortions of black people. Scholar Eric Lott has called minstrelsy "an affair of copies and originals" and noted the affinities between cartoonists and minstrel performers, both of whom exaggerated traits in order to create buffoonish, distorted types.[55] In some cases, minstrels were white people claiming to imitate black people whom they alleged were trying to imitate white people, but failing. The recurring character Zip Coon, for example, represented a black dandy whose pretentions to gentility inevitably end in malapropism and mayhem.[56] Many minstrel troupes also parodied high art performers such as opera singer Jenny Lind, tragedian Tommaso Salvini, and Sarah Bernhardt, who became the subject of several minstrel performances after her first tour of the United States in 1881.[57]

Minstrel performers tended to do two kinds of female impersonation. In the first type of act, slender white men donned elegant fashions in order to impersonate female celebrities or coquettish, light-skinned African American beauties with haughty and delicate manners.[58] White male performers like the Only Leon, who impersonated Sarah Bernhardt throughout his career, did not always use blackface makeup in their refined depictions of elegant women in fancy dress. During the period when Oscar Wilde lectured across the United States, Leon also performed as Miss Patient Wilde, a lover of sunflowers and lilies, whose first name evoked the Gilbert and Sullivan operetta *Patience*, which included a character based on Wilde.[59] In the second, more buffoonish type of act, a white man blacked up and put on a coarse dress and headwear to impersonate a large and ungainly African American woman whose dimensions and demeanor made any conventionally feminine behavior on her part seem absurd, particularly in the many skits that depicted such women "awkwardly aping their betters."[60]

The Bernhardt minstrel acts popular in the early 1880s favored the second type of impersonation. They converted Sarah Bernhardt into "Sarah Heartburn" and "Sarah Barnyard" and the high tragedy of Camille into the low farce of "Calmeel, or the Fate of a Croquette."[61] The burlesque transformed the flighty coquette of the Dumas play, who sacrifices all for love and dies of consumption onstage, into a croquette, a heavy piece of fried dough "solid enough to depend on." Advertisements for "Sarah Heartburn" also touted the fashionable accessories coveted by Bernhardt fans. The promotional campaign when the act first opened in Philadelphia included a wagon that drove around town filled with trunks labeled "Heartburn's laces, gloves, etc.," evoking the numerous costumes that made the news when they accompanied Bernhardt on her 1880–81 North American tour.[62]

Minstrel spoofs of Bernhardt became international hits, performed throughout the United States and in London for decades. One Ohio newspaper described an 1887 performance of William Henry Rice's "original creation" of Sarah Heartburn as popular enough to have the theater turning people away at the door. The act remained in Rice's repertory for close to thirty years.[63] By 1896, "Calmeel" had morphed into "Clam Eel"; by 1911, the act combined Sarah Barnyard and Sarah Heartburn and the subtitle had evolved into "The Fate of a Chicken Croquette."[64] Minstrel troupes often timed their tours to coincide with actual Bernhardt performances.[65] In June 1881, for example, Rice followed Bernhardt across the Atlantic to perform "Sarah Heartburn" in London's St. James's Hall at the same time that Bernhardt appeared in *Camille* at London's Gaiety Theatre.

One painstaking review of "Sarah Heartburn" ascribed its appeal to popular interest in comparing pseudo-black copies with white originals: "Numbers have seen the 'great white Sarah,' as the Americans call her, and nothing could be more natural than to compare the great black Sarah with the original." Somewhat humorlessly, the critic underscored the difference between the two versions: "We are sorry we cannot pay Mr. Rice the compliment of calling his sketch a caricature of Mdlle. Bernhardt. Save in a few peculiarities of manner, it is curiously unlike the original."[66] Rather than a genuine imitation of Bernhardt, the reviewer writes, the minstrel is

> merely . . . a grotesque *artiste* . . . A performer who stumbles about in a very awkward fashion and falls over his long skirts, which the original *artiste* manages with such cleverness. . . . [Theatergoers] hear a performer shout in a husky voice and mix up references to the topical absurdities of the day when it is to her exquisite elocution and her silvery tones that Mdlle. Bernhardt owes so much of her fascinating power. They see the burlesque representative drinking water out of a pail, and telling the attendant who brings a chair to "sling it round the other way." They observe the mock Camille presenting the lover with a lettuce as the token of her affection, and receiving, in return, a bottle of zoedone [a non-alcoholic sparkling beverage of the day]. They watch the imitator of Mdlle. Bernhardt smear off the burnt cork in order to present a ghastly face, half black and half white, for the grotesque death scene.[67]

The journalist's indignation, though gallant, suggests a lack of familiarity with the conventions of minstrelsy, whose very point was to give white men a platform for highlighting that blacks were and always would be the lesser opposite of whites.[68] As another reviewer put it, "Sarah Heartburn" gave audiences "a sort of Sarah Bernhardt reversed, or, nigger-ly speaking, turned '*Topsy*-turvy'"—an allusion to the character of Topsy, a young female slave in *Uncle Tom's Cabin*, whose representation in stage adaptations of Harriet Beecher Stowe's novel exemplified racist ideas about black peoples' imperviousness to pain.[69] "Topsy" here is shorthand for a reductive idea of blackness as negating Bernhardt's performance of whiteness. Where the white Bernhardt was graceful, the blackface Bernhardt is clumsy. Where the white Bernhardt received flowers and drank champagne, the blackface Bernhardt gives lettuces and swigs zoedone. The white Bernhardt poetically recited, the blackface Bernhardt huskily shouts. Bernhardt was known for twirling and falling backward in Camille's death scene; Rice dives headfirst into a divan.[70] Everything about this performance presumes and reinforces the gulf between prestigious whiteness and lowly blackness, including its gambit that the performer's status as a white man, revealed at the very end when he smears off half of his makeup, can survive his impersonation of a black woman.

By presenting themselves as distinctive types whose images and stories could be easily multiplied, celebrities made themselves available for imitation. The proliferation of consumer goods associated with celebrities might seem only to confirm the longstanding theory that stars are themselves commodities, objects to be bought and sold. But as we have seen, celebrity imitation had far more complicated meanings. Fans paid homage to Sarah Bernhardt's artistic agency when they copied the fashions she created. While copying often seems like a submissive action that confirms the imitator's secondary status, many satirists construed celebrity imitation as a privilege reserved for the higher orders (which included themselves, since parody is itself a form of imitation). A comic Russian play burlesqued grandiose elite women inspired by Bernhardt to rebel against the husbands they are supposed to venerate and obey. Advertisers, cartoonists, and minstrel performers depicted African Americans and others in low-status ethnic groups who emulated Bernhardt and Wilde as trying, but failing, to exceed the limits placed on them. Fashion magazines presented imitation as enhancing both imitator and imitated, while caricatures often demeaned both, even as they emphasized the gap between celebrity models and copycat fans. Perhaps the clearest sign that imitating celebrities might benefit the imitators was how eager many white men were to restrict the pleasures and advantages of celebrity imitation to themselves.

CHAPTER 7

JUDGMENT

In the twenty-first century, everyone's a critic. Within seconds of viewing a movie or TV show or watching an athlete or politician perform, any of the billions of people with access to the Internet can post snarky or effusive comments for all the world to see. It is tempting to view this phenomenon as radically new, with digital media liberating audiences that had for the previous two centuries grown increasingly docile. Many historians have argued that over the course of the nineteenth century, theater audiences became increasingly quiet and deferential, with twentieth-century spectators falling into even more passive habits, particularly during the decades when many spent hours in front of the "boob tube," content to absorb the limited fare provided by broadcast programming.[1]

But did the fact that, about a hundred and fifty years ago, many audience members stopped spitting, heckling, and rioting also mean that they lost their critical edge? Nineteenth-century fan letters and theater scrapbooks tell a different story. Spectators who stayed quiet during performances and refrained from hurling rotten fruit at inadequate performers still found ways to pass judgment and make their views known. The documents they produced survive to this day in archives around the world. Rarely consulted, their pages nonetheless speak volumes about the long history of the public's zeal for judging everything, including celebrities.

Nineteenth-century fan mail and scrapbooks offer fresh answers to important questions about celebrity culture. As we saw in "Sensation," many celebrities deliberate strategically about how to move their publics. Can publics and media also be rational and discerning about those they choose to adore? Celebrity is a contest—for status, wealth, and recognition. Is it a fair one? Fair contests require sound judges; how do publics and media evaluate celebrities, and do those judgments ever have substance?

The most influential studies of celebrity have, as we saw in the introduction, answered these questions with a resounding "no." To this day,
critics continue to ring the changes on Theodor Adorno's denunciation
of celebrities as interchangeable commodities churned out by a corporate
culture industry that encourages mindless acceptance of institutions better
questioned or overthrown. In the 1970s, some scholars began to embrace
a less corrosive view of popular culture and took closer looks at what fans
of film, television, and music actually think and do.[2] For Henry Jenkins,
whose ideas we examined in "Intimacy," at least some fans produce and
transform culture rather than passively consume it.[3] Nonetheless, the sense
persists that publics mindlessly accept celebrities at face value instead
of judging them on their merits. Even as interest in celebrity seems to
have reached historic highs, the value we ascribe to celebrities and to those
who make them famous has reached an all-time low. Contemporary usage
links celebrity with superficiality, artifice, and irrationality, and many now
equate celebrity with worthlessness. In 2015, I participated in an online
"Ask Me Anything" discussion about celebrity on the social media platform Reddit, whose users can vote posts up or down. The most popular
questions described celebrities as merely "famous for being famous" and
asked me to comment on why so many people confuse "celebrity" with
"importance" and expertise, leading them "to listen to celebrities instead
of facts."[4] In 2008 presidential candidate John McCain ran a campaign
ad against Barack Obama that began: "He's the biggest celebrity in the
world. But is he ready to lead?" By calling his opponent a celebrity, Mc-
Cain charged Obama with being all flash and no substance and reduced his
supporters to the ultimate in undiscerning irrationality: "adoring fans."[5]
    Pundits taking aim at celebrity culture usually have female stars with
mostly female fans in their sights. McCain's attack ad on Obama put him
in the company of Britney Spears and Paris Hilton. The Reddit users who
participated in my 2015 "Ask Me Anything" discussion repeatedly evoked
"Kim Kardashian" as shorthand for celebrity culture's vacuity and lack of
real value. Novelist Salman Rushdie did the same in a 2015 commence-
ment address that exhorted graduates to "plunge" into life and report on
"what's really going on in people's heads, what music is in there, what movies, what dreams, which Kardashians," only to qualify his recipe for om-
nivorous enthusiasm: "Apart from the Kardashian part. If possible, avoid
that part."[6] The best-known Kardashians are all women, and their social
media feeds, which emphasize self-fashioning, play to interests coded as

feminine. Journalists have associated indiscriminate fandom with women since at least the 1890s, when reporters mocked the "matinee girls" who flocked to daytime performances and openly announced their crushes on handsome male stars. In the 1920s, newspapers circulated stories about crazed female fans who committed suicide after the untimely death of silent film star Rudolph Valentino. In the 1940s, journalists smirked about the young singer Frank Sinatra's skills in "the art of how to make girls faint" and photographers trained their lenses on the adoring gazes of his young and largely female audiences.[7]

Those who dismiss celebrity culture may be more motivated by un-conscious gender bias than by reasoned assessment. Ask people to name celebrities who deserve their fame and the results will yield many more examples of men admired mostly by men than women admired mostly by women. When pointing to the silliness of celebrity culture, critics circa 2010 were far readier to cite Kim Kardashian, Britney Spears, and Lindsay Lohan than Zac Efron, James Franco, and Tiger Woods. The more femi-nized the fan base, the less seriously the press takes the star: millions of women must be wrong. In 1964, when the Beatles first visited the United States, *New York Times* journalists mocked Beatlemania as the effusion of "a gaggle of giggling girls." Though today many men remember liking the Beatles of "I Wanna Hold Your Hand," reporters at the time contrasted the "hysterical squeals emanating from developing femininity" to the stal-wart resistance of lone male "dissenters" such as a "tall youth" holding up a sign declaring "Alonzo Tuske Hates the Beatles" or a boy muttering, " 'Look what America's coming to, man,' . . . shaking his head sadly."[8] Not incidentally, the same reporters in 1964 disparaged the Beatles themselves as a talentless boy band whose popularity, they predicted, would not last long.[9] Time proved the teenaged girls to be the more prescient and dis-cerning critics.

Celebrity, however, has not always been so feminized. As the intro-duction noted, throughout the nineteenth century, male celebrities far outnumbered female ones. When photography pioneer Nadar drew a pantheon of the 249 most celebrated living persons in France in 1854, he included only eleven women. Nadar depicted most of the men as full-length figures in modern dress and all of the women as busts, with ten of the disembodied female heads clustered together on a tray.[10] The bulk of the "popular celebrities" caricatured in the 1860s Paris newspaper *Les Célébrités populaires* were male politicians such as Garibaldi, Léon

FIGURE 7.1. Chess celebrities, *Illustrated London News*, July 14, 1855.

Gambetta, and Jules Ferry.[11] Celebrity had an equally masculine cast in England and the United States. In 1855, the *Illustrated London News* ran a sketch featuring seven "chess celebrities" (figure 7.1).[12] Also in 1855, a Boston minister published a book entitled *Visits to European Celebrities*. The figures he discussed included abolitionist William Wilberforce and scientist Alexander von Humboldt. In 1879, when Edmund Yates began to reprint his journalistic profiles of *Celebrities at Home* in book form, seventy-eight of the eighty-two people featured were men. An 1890 *Cabinet Portrait Gallery* published by a London studio specializing in celebrity photographs focused on clergymen, professors, barristers, military leaders, and aristocrats. Sarah Bernhardt, one of the few actresses featured, appeared sandwiched between the Archbishop of Canterbury and the Duke and Duchess of Fife.[13] As late as 1912, a US theatrical manager could call politician and lexicographer Daniel Webster a "national celebrity" and mean it as a compliment.[14]

Perhaps not surprisingly, during the many decades when the term *celebrity* comprised a host of august men, it had mostly positive connotations and was strongly associated with merit. The same was true of the widespread admiration that created those celebrities; British critic Thomas Carlyle, in his 1841 book *On Heroes, Hero-Worship, and the Heroic in History*, based on popular lectures delivered the year before, influentially exhorted the public to be more, not less, worshipful. To be sure, nineteenth-century celebrity culture had its critics, particularly among avant-garde authors seeking to demonstrate their independence from the popular marketplace.[15] But for every Henry James who claimed to disdain celebrity, a Walt Whitman cultivated it for himself and appreciated it in others.[16] By the late 1870s, the term evoked both the notoriety spawned by publicity stunts and the worthier fame that resulted from persevering effort. An 1887 compendium of *Celebrities of the Century* could still use the term in a fairly neutral sense to describe itself as a "Dictionary of Recent and Contemporary Biography," with entries on poet Robert Browning, composer Daniel Auber, and abolitionist William Lloyd Garrison.[17] To leaf through a nineteenth-century book with "celebrities" in its title was to encounter Charles Dickens, Abraham Lincoln, and Mark Twain. British Prime Minister William Gladstone and Member of Parliament John Bright signed autograph albums, unconcerned about placing their names alongside those of poets, actors, and opera singers.[18] Even in the early decades of the twentieth century, scrapbook clippings about performers might appear alongside news items featuring politicians, authors, and celebrated sites, because Anna Pavlova, the New York Stock Exchange, Theodore Roosevelt, and George Bernard Shaw (who loved getting his photograph into the papers) all fell under the same category: celebrity.[19]

Nineteenth-century publics enjoyed reading about the private lives of public figures and, as we saw in "Sensation," relished submitting to the overpowering attractions of mesmerizing stars. But they also saw themselves as making informed judgments about celebrities' talents, skills, and achievements. Even when the press and public criticized individual celebrities, they did so on the assumption that some deserved adulation more than others. When George Bernard Shaw attacked reigning star Sarah Bernhardt in an 1895 review, he did so to point out the greater merits of the lesser-known actor Eleonora Duse. His aim was not to banish celebrity altogether but to anoint a newer and worthier star.[20] Few nineteenth-century commentators naively believed that celebrity was simply the natural outcome of hard work and talent. Many perceived Bernhardt, for example, as a skilled marketer, unrivalled in "the sensational art of *réclame*."[21] But it did not follow that celebrities who relied on publicity tactics lacked all merit. Even journalists who suggested that Sarah Bernhardt might be more of a "Sarah Barnum" than "*The* Sarah Bar-none" conceded that she also owed

her success to her talent, to "the virile force of her intelligence," and to the
energy that made her "capable of more work than ten men."[22]

RESPECT FOR ACTING

A hundred and fifty years ago, "celebrity" was a term commonly used to
praise someone who excelled at an activity considered worthwhile. Perhaps even more surprisingly, serious dramatic acting numbered among the
worthiest of worthwhile activities. Today, most people equate celebrity
with performers and consider performers intrinsically undeserving of renown. Nineteenth-century publics did not agree that the best entertainers
merited less admiration than authors, statesmen, inventors, entrepreneurs,
and athletes. An 1889 "Panorama of the Nineteenth Century" devoted to
picturing French history included images of actresses Rachel Félix and
Sarah Bernhardt alongside such venerable figures as General Lafayette,
composer Charles Gounod, and artist Honoré Daumier.[23] In the 1887
volume listing *Celebrities of the Century* referred to above, Jenny Lind
followed Abraham Lincoln, Sarah Bernhardt came after scientist Claude
Bernard, and ballet dancer Marie Taglioni appeared just before literary
critic Hippolyte Taine.

Many now think of nineteenth-century Britons and Americans (less so
the French) as steeped in what scholar Jonas Barish influentially dubbed
the "anti-theatrical prejudice."[24] But for the past two decades, scholars have
complicated that thesis by showing that members of all classes valued, even
envied, theater people—for their collectivity, their protean fluidity, their
commercial success, their embrace of self-fashioning and role-playing,
and their rhetorical skills and physical expressiveness.[25] Avant-garde mod-
ernists and stringent moralists found surprising common ground in their
shared suspicion of performers, but the majority of Europeans and Americans embraced acting, not only for professionals but also for amateurs of
all classes. An early nineteenth-century scrapbook devoted to theatrical
news items included an 1823 report of a Lady Normanby who had appeared
in a production at the Duke of Devonshire's villa, with no suggestion that
it was improper for a woman to act.[26] Though playing in private homes,
amateur performers never hid from public view. "Private theatricals to
no end!" exclaimed an 1880 society column, noting that they were the
"rage" of the London season and reporting on the "crowded" tableaux at

the home of a Mrs. Freake (who wrote the play performed at her house) and the "dainty and delicate performance" of "the new amateur star," Miss Williams.[27] Men of great stature and influence who had a theatrical bent openly displayed it. Edward Flower (1805–1883), a brewer who became the mayor of Stratford-on-Avon, acquired a taste for private theatricals while still a schoolboy. In 1857, his wife wrote indulgently of his performance as "a very surprising" Queen Eleanor in a play that Flower himself scripted and that their family performed at home.[28] When providing information for an 1890 biographical sketch, a British member of Parliament and barrister who was later knighted listed his participation in "amateur theatricals" alongside his memberships in elite clubs.[29] Amateurs sought to acquire some of the poise, expressiveness, and clear diction that they admired in trained actors; the Ohio compiler of one turn-of-the-century scrapbook was interested enough in the question of what constituted good acting to save an article describing an acting school's curriculum.[30]

Individuals and institutions alike held the best and most renowned professional performers in the highest esteem. In 1906, after dining with opera singer Nellie Melba, the aristocratic Lady Ribblesdale (1858–1911) remarked in her diary, "What power a great cultivated talent becomes, and how small and insignificant one feels in its presence."[31] By the end of the nineteenth century, France began to award the Legion of Honor to actors and actresses, though usually for their work as writers and teachers, not as performers. Dignitaries and royalty regularly conferred honors and tributes on performers. The young British monarch gave France's greatest actress a bracelet inscribed "Queen Victoria, to Rachel" and presented singer Jenny Lind with a lapdog that accompanied her when she toured the United States.[32] In 1880, an enthusiastic Danish crowd presented Bernhardt with an album signed by "a great number of persons of distinction."[33] Henry Irving received three honorary degrees, gave the 1898 Rede Lecture at Cambridge (on "The Theatre in Its Relation to the State"), and in 1895 accepted the knighthood first offered him in 1883. In 1916, after the New York City French Drama Society elected Bernhardt as its Présidente d'Honneur, a judge wrote to the organization on municipal court stationery anxiously inquiring whether his club, the city's second oldest, might be allowed to hold a reception in her honor.[34] The week after Bernhardt's death, the queen of England ordered a mass for her at London's Westminster Cathedral; similarly, after actress Helena Modjeska died, St. Stanislaus Church in New York City held a requiem high mass for the actress of Polish origin.[35] High society never fully accepted Bernhardt as one of their own, but by the time she reached her fifties, the world's elites saw her theatrical stardom as a kind of nobility conferred not by inheritance but by merit.

RESPECT FOR ACTRESSES

Female celebrities were a minority for most of the nineteenth century, but the majority of that small number of female stars were either royals or performers. Theater was one of the few arenas where the public deemed women as capable, gifted, and intelligent as men and where men proved as willing as women to admire female accomplishment.[36] In the 1830s, when someone suggested to Judge Joseph Story that "his Puritan ancestors would not approve of all his theatergoing," the Supreme Court Justice and Harvard law professor replied by emphatically praising actress Fanny Kemble: "I only thank God I'm alive in an era with such a woman."[37] The crowds for opera singer Jenny Lind's first New York concerts in 1850 included far more men than women, who came not to leer but to appreciate both the virtuosity and the virtue of the gifted soprano who often donated her considerable earnings to charitable causes.[38] Highly reputable men in positions of authority extended respectful invitations to performers. Harvard professor Edward S. Everett invited Jenny Lind to visit him on campus, joined by the governor and lieutenant governor of Massachusetts. The audience at the singer's Washington, DC, concerts included the president, cabinet members, senators, and generals.[39]

While the public viewed many actresses as sexual spectacles, it also distinguished between female performers appreciated mainly for their looks, who often lacked talent, and those hailed as serious artists, who often lacked beauty.[40] The text for the 1890 *Cabinet Portrait Gallery*, for example, snidely noted that two novice actresses pictured in that volume "owe[d] their success" to "personal attractiveness" and were not "likely to rival Rachel."[41] Conversely, Rachel did not need to be personally attractive to become a byword for excellence and to remain one for decades after her death. A scrapbook compiler commenting on an 1888 Ellen Terry performance similarly noted that she looked a "little old," but added, "acting perfect."[42]

Many even proved willing to attach the term "genius" to female performers. As scholar Gustavus Stadler has shown, nineteenth-century writers saw genius as compatible with popular celebrity, and even if they could never quite agree if geniuses of any sex were exceptionally creative individuals or vessels for external forces, the term always designated exceptional achievement and talent.[43] The notable US theater producer David Belasco cited a long list of figures, from Nell Gwynn to Ada Rehan, as examples of the actress as a "woman of genius."[44] Reporters did not use the word "genius" lightly. Even when describing Rachel at the height of her career, for example, the *New York Times* demurred that "Many, while allowing her wonderful *talent*, deny that she has genius."[45] At the same time, genius was not a realm from which female performers were barred. A 1923 Bernhardt obituary observed, "The death of the most famous actress in the world is a fresh reminder that the stage still opens the widest door to the richest realm in which women win honor, fortune and popularity by their own talents and genius."[46]

Bernhardt did not need to die for still another reporter to call her "a queen by right of genius and rare intelligence."[47] In the years after she emerged as a global celebrity in 1879, a consensus developed that, as Lady Monkswell wrote in an 1880 diary entry after seeing Bernhardt perform, "Whatever people say Sarah Bernhardt has genius."[48] In a 1926 article syndicated by US periodical *McClure's*, an American man described visiting the Paris graves of Balzac, Chopin, Corot, Cuvier, La Fontaine, Patti, and Molière with his son, only to find that "the sight that most fascinated him and me was the grave of Sarah Bernhardt," decorated with offerings by men from all nations: "humble Frenchmen, two Spaniards and a dark-skinned man from some far-off colony. We talk much of internationalism and of immortality; we know little of either; but at Bernhardt's tomb one realizes one thing at least—great genius and great art are both international and immortal."[49]

JUDGING FANS

Nineteenth-century fan mail, theater playbills, programs, and even theater reviews often trafficked in hyperbole. As such, they might seem to offer proof that nineteenth-century celebrities owed their success not to merit, but to puffery: airy, inflated advertising rhetoric designed to lure in unsuspecting customers presumed incapable of telling good performances from bad ones. Indeed, in his classic study of the public sphere, political theorist Jürgen Habermas opposed theater spectatorship to critical acumen. In the eighteenth century, he argued, the emergence of civil society transformed the middle class from an audience passively watching a spectacle into, as historian Sarah Maza puts it, a "judging, debating, criticizing entity—a public."[50] His devolutionary narrative argued that by the twentieth century, public relations tactics had reduced active, critical thinkers to docile, naive consumers.

Many scholars have since complicated Habermas's narrative of decreasing agency and questioned his association of spectacle with passivity. They have argued that theater promoted direct democracy and that even consumerism empowered publics, especially women, to see themselves as exercising choice, to judge the famous for themselves, and to take pleasure in unmasking them.[51] Readers of the nineteenth-century commercial press were no respecters of persons, and within the limits allowed by the law, newspapers in England, France, and the United States thrived by exposing the peccadilloes and crimes of illustrious individuals. Although theater and concert audiences were increasingly required to sit in silence and to demonstrate self-control and decorum, they still found ways to express opinions. Indeed, precisely because new practices such as darkened auditoria encouraged those attending plays to pay more attention to the stage than to one another, spectators became more interested in assessing actors and made their judgments known at concentrated times and places, such as curtain calls.[52]

The opinions of nineteenth-century fans are more difficult to reconstruct than those of today's online commenters, but some left abundant records of their views in diaries and letters.[53] A treasure trove of nineteenth-century fan mail lovingly preserved in a famous US actor's historic home bears witness to how much nineteenth-century audiences loved judging actors and saw themselves as actively working to "arriv[e] at a fair estimate of dramatic talent."[54] In 1888, Edwin Booth, the greatest American actor of his generation, the owner of several successful New York theaters, and beloved for his portrayals of Shakespeare characters, purchased a mansion on Gramercy Park South. Booth lived on the top floor, surrounded by theatrical memorabilia that included the skull he used when playing Hamlet. The rest of the house became the Players Club, an all-male association that Booth founded to help actors improve their status by mingling with elite professionals. For decades, the building housed a library filled with paintings, sculptures, books, and documents donated by performers over the years. Among the most valuable materials are several folders containing dozens of letters, cards, and notes that Booth received between the 1860s and 1890s and chose to save. Some were "mash notes" seeking assignations or proposing marriage. Others requested money, employment, or acting lessons. Many sent condolences after reading news of illness and deaths in Booth's family. A remarkable number of letter writers plied the actor with quack remedies or sought to convert him to their particular brand of Christian salvation (see "Intimacy"). Dozens sent extremely long verses that combined all of the above.

Not all the letters focused on Booth's private life, however. A significant number offered discerning amateur drama criticism. Some emphasized the strength of their responses to Booth's acting, while others offered detailed performance notes that pitted the actor's agency as a master interpreter of celebrated dramas against the letter writers' own powers of observation and judgment. Some correspondents positioned themselves as experts who could teach Booth a thing or two about acting. One advised Booth how to read lines from *Hamlet*; another noted that the actor's guise as an aged Richelieu might appear more realistic if he donned "Spectacles or what served for Spectacles in those days."[55] An 1866 letter from "an old Theatre habitué" praised Booth's performance but advised him to ask one of his fellow actors "if he would not produce a better effect by studying not to mouth his words nor run his sentences one into the other so that it is extremely difficult to understand him."[56] A detailed and very long 1866 letter offered several pointers for improving Booth's Richard III. "Your appearance was not sufficiently stern and sombre," the writer complained, advising Booth to don a mustache or whiskers, adopt a harsher voice, and wear a darker costume. "You might also . . . have a larger hump on the back & a more infirm gait as you move on the stage." With some final suggestions about exactly how best to move in one scene ("It strikes me it would be more powerful if you were slowly to stagger from the tent") the frustrated stage manager signed off, adding in a postscript, "The lights on the stage could be lowered in some of the scenes to give a more sombre appearance where necessary."[57] Far from being passive and acquiescent, audience members like this one saw theatergoing as an occasion to exercise their acumen and did not hesitate to advise a celebrated young actor on how to improve his performances.

Some critiques were less polite. A card from a correspondent signing off as "Shakespear N° 2" offered some pungent advice in a scrawl that grew larger with each line: "Mr Booth Your Hamlet is overdone. Your constant

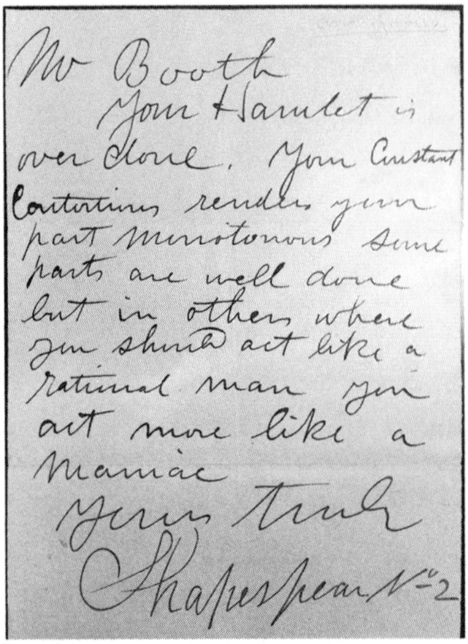
Mr Booth
Your Hamlet is
over done. Your Constant
Contortions render your
part monotonous Some
parts are well done
but in others where
you should act like a
rational man you
act more like a
maniac
Yours truly
Shakespeare No 2

FIGURE 7.2. Undated letter to Edwin Booth.

contortions render your part monotonous. Some parts are well done but in others where you should act like a rational man you act more like a maniac" (figure 7.2).[58] Another spectator, also disappointed in Booth's take on the melancholy Dane, wrote, "Don't you go into such awful antics when the Ghost is speaking to you. I was disgusted with that part of your acting and thought 'Oh would some power the giftie gie us.'"[59] An even less elevated correspondent objected to the bangs the actor adopted in *Julius Caesar*: "Dear Mr. Booth, Don't wear those dreadful frizzers. 'Brutus is noble,' and why would you conceal that 'front of Jove' which indicates a noble character, and is also one of the chief beauties of your face."[60] Not only did theatergoers have a range of opinions about how actors should move, speak, and wear their hair, they were willing to go to a great deal of trouble to express them.

Those explaining what made Booth excellent were careful to justify their praise by demonstrating how well they observed and assessed the subtlest stage business. "You were admirably successful in grasping vividly the knowing ideas of the character," wrote one theatergoer in 1867 of Booth's Iago, which he had seen the actor play more than once.[61] Another correspondent evaluated the evaluators by offering a detailed ranking of the drama critics who had reviewed Booth's performances. He awarded the prize for the most "eminently truthful and judicious" analysis to a writer for the New York *Albion*.[62] A journalist who had himself reviewed Booth's Charleston performances for the local newspaper included his clippings for the star's perusal, a telling commentary on how much influence celebrity actors wielded, even on the professionals appointed to evaluate them.[63]

The close attention that fans trained on beloved performers sometimes transformed initially appreciative spectators into disappointed ones. In 1883, Mary Isabella Stone of Framingham, Massachusetts, sent Booth a check for $1.00 and a letter requesting that he send her copies of the 1878 editions of his most frequently performed plays, since she had been unable to obtain those volumes from booksellers. Explaining that "Hero-worship is good for youths and maidens, especially when it can be shared by their elders," she presented herself as a loyal but thoughtful documenter of the ephemeral art of stage acting: "To study the plays, to write descriptions of the acting, and collect the best criticisms, is my habit; in order to refresh the memory in old age, and to leave some dim reflections of your noble impersonations for certain dear little ones who may not be grown up in season to see and feel for themselves the power of that personality which has been to us so truly a blessing."[64] Booth returned the check when he mailed Stone the books that she proceeded to annotate obsessively, using a color code to key her comments to the many different dates on which she had seen Booth perform the same roles.

In pages that appear to have been added to the original volumes, Stone noted everything she could remember about the performances she had seen: costumes, stage blocking, Booth's gestures, the position of his head and hands, the tone of his voice, the direction of his movements. Attempting to render his reading of the line "Ah, ha," for example, she described it as "part groan, part gasp, & he seems choking with horror." Yet even this avowed enthusiast found room to be critical. Displaying remarkable self-consciousness about the act of spectating itself, she mapped the different aims of successive experiences "of hearing Booth. 1st time, For enchantment. 2nd, For impression & recollection. 3d, For criticism. 4th, For comparison." Upon seeing Booth perform Hamlet for the sixth time, Stone found herself growing distinctly jaded, criticizing his choice of a "dreadful wig" not once but twice. After asking herself, "Why am I not as deeply impressed as before?" she speculated that the effect of seeing him repeat the identical effects on separate occasions meant that "It seems less *reality*, more *acting*."[65]

Some of Booth's correspondents had more mundane takes on how he could improve his performances. An 1867 letter writer suggested that Booth stage a dramatic version of Coleridge's poem the *Rime of the Ancient Mariner*.[66] A young woman asked him to schedule a matinee for a Monday or Tuesday in a year when Lent began on Wednesdays, because "Ma won't let us go to the theater in Lent." Another correspondent requested that he stop performing *Much Ado About Nothing* exclusively on Friday nights and Saturday afternoons so that the Jewish community to which she belonged could see him as Benedick.[67] Letters like these overturn received historical narratives about the taming of nineteenth-century audiences. Disruption and violence are not the only markers of audience activity, and even newly disciplined audiences found polite ways to be almost comically active spectators, eager to judge what they heard and saw and even, in some instances, to shape it.[68]

Fan mail often combined adoration with assessment. Opera singer Pauline Viardot (1821–1910) carefully preserved the many encomia she received in the 1860s, when she became famous for her Parisian performances of two Gluck roles: Orphée and Alceste. Many of her correspondents used the word "transported" to describe how strongly Viardot had moved them, but those ecstasies never prevented them from being careful, even fussy observers. Commenting on Viardot's costume when performing Lady Macbeth, an 1860 letter writer observed that "Viewed from behind, the veil, though exact, is a bit short, but from the front and in three-quarter view, it's magnificent!" The same writer suggested that "Madame Viardot repeats perhaps a bit too much the movement of the hand that washes itself. . . . with slight pauses this would become perhaps even more sinister" and reserved special praise for a twice-repeated gesture in which Viardot torqued her right arm.[69] Another amateur critic offered advice about how Viardot handled a crescendo in one of Alceste's arias. Even as he modestly anticipated that she might find his "pedantry . . . absurd," he pompously offered to pay her a visit if he noticed her adopting his suggested "amendment."[70] (The mansplainers we have long had with us.) Another correspondent provided two pages of careful praise, thanking Viardot for seeming so "real" (*vraie*) as Orpheus and keying each of his compliments to a specific episode in the opera. He signed off: "Since yesterday, I have become acquainted with Orpheus, and I will never in my life forget him."[71] Many of Viardot's most effusive letter writers ratified their reactions to her artistry by evoking the figure they considered the singer's ultimate judge, the composer of the music she sang. One woman, for example, reported that her husband had remarked, "Gluck would be very happy if he saw Orpheus represented by Mme. Viardot. This woman is sublime."[72]

Even hyperbolic publicity materials, however exaggerated their claims, appealed to the public's interest in identifying the best and judging their greatness for themselves. An 1861 poster described actress Charlotte Cushman as standing "peerless and alone" as Romeo; an 1878 playbill for Helena Modjeska hailed her as "the only Camille"; another program named Sarah Bernhardt "the great one."[73] Advertisements for the play *Love and Law* equated the "reputation" of its 1884 "star cast" with their "ability."[74] An 1858 poster for performer Charlotte Cushman linked her stature as a "celebrated artist" to her standing as "the greatest living actress"—not the sweetest, nor the most beautiful, but the greatest.[75] Even bad actors became occasions to assert stardom's basis in merit. When society woman Cora Brown Potter took to the stage with no training or experience, critics were swift to point out that her deficiencies would *prevent* her from becoming "a dramatic star." As one headline put it, "She Is Far from Being an Actress—She Attempts a Short Cut to Fame, But Fails to Reach It."[76]

SCRAPBOOKS AND THE CULTURE OF EVALUATION

Scrapbookers, who focused on clipping and arranging publicity materials and theater reviews, often used their albums to accord different degrees of status to the many plays and performers they viewed. Oliver Sayler (1887–1958), a professional theater critic and press agent, organized his many scrapbooks into sections, reserving the front of each book for material related to the plays he considered the most important, usually Shakespearean.[77] Another compiler put together an album in which, on most pages, multiple images of many different performers crowded together, jostling for space (figure 7.3). But the same compiler reserved an entire page for a large picture of a single performer: Sarah Bernhardt in

FIGURE 7.3. Album pages, TRI Scrapbook #1.

FIGURE 7.4. Image of Sarah Bernhardt,   FIGURE 7.5. Postcard of Elsie Janis.
TRI Scrapbook #1.

L'Aiglon (figure 7.4).[78] Bernhardt's photograph dominates the page and even effaces the image of another actress by covering it.

Other scrapbookers similarly gave Bernhardt materials special treatment, lavishing an entire page on a single, carefully centered program from a Bernhardt performance while crowding as many as four cast lists onto other pages.[79] Still others expressed their opinions more directly. Even after it became less common for live audiences to talk back directly to the stage, members of the public freely added comments to theatrical promotional materials. The purchaser of a postcard of comedian Elsie Janis (figure 7.5) wrote in the narrow margin beneath the actress's image: "Dear G & B, Liked this individual's impersonations, but didn't care particularly for anything else."[80] Janis, as we saw in "Multiplication," was an early twentieth-century theatrical star best known for her spot-on impressions of other actors. This postcard, itself an artifact of celebrity culture, attests to the commercial value and popularity of her image and also shows how seriously the public took even a young comic actress. For a mass-produced image, the card is surprisingly redolent of high art. The truncation of Janis's figure at chest level makes her resemble a classical portrait bust. The soft modeling and rich use of shading around her neck make the image more painterly, as do the contrast in tone and echo in texture between Janis's dark ringlets and the intricate pattern of her white lace dress. The card's purchaser follows suit by taking Janis's celebrity seriously, assessing her performance and finding her superior to her supporting cast. One simple sentence speaks volumes about how an average theatergoer fused the subjective emotions of attraction (to like, to care for) with a more objective ability to separate worthy from unworthy performers.

Theatrical scrapbookers could rival fan mail writers in their obsessive evaluation of plays and players. As registers of theater attendance, all scrapbooks encode value judgments about what their compilers deemed worth seeing and commemorating. Many scrapbooks included theater reviews, in which professional journalists evaluated actors' merits. A significant subset of compilers also recorded their own terse but firm assessments of plays and performers. One painstakingly inserted capsule reviews into the small space between character names and actor names on the program for an 1890 performance of *As You Like It*, distinguishing the "stately . . . but stage" Olivia from the "vivacious" Maria, the "artistic" Malvolio, the "manly" Sebastian, and the "graceful—sweet—refined" Viola, whose voice was "at times too high."[81] An 1897 compiler wrote of lead performer E. S. Willard: "There is no doubt he is a fine actor and overshadows every one in the caste [*sic*]."[82] In spidery handwriting, the person who began keeping a scrapbook in 1881 opined that Modjeska in *Much Ado About Nothing* in 1888 was "Charming— Graceful. Sweet voice." Ten years later, the same compiler found Modjeska "Perfect" in a production of *Mary Stuart* and was sufficiently impressed to add two rare exclamation points after her name on the cast list pasted into the album. No soft touch, the amateur critic sometimes gave more mixed reviews. In red ink, on the cast list of Augustin Daly's production of *As You Like It*, next to the role of Jaques, they noted "Good voice, not magnetic," while Lilian Olcott in an 1886 version of *Theodora* was a "V.G. and careful actress. Poor voice—cold. Best in Act 1 Scene 2."[83] Damning the performer with faint praise and noting in exactly which scene she had done her feeble best, this compiler emulated the fine distinctions made by discerning professional reviewers and occupied the position of a connoisseur for whom only the best acting would elicit the highest praise.

A few compilers assessed plays rather than players, laconically doling out grades. Though some scrapbook compilers were enthusiasts, many

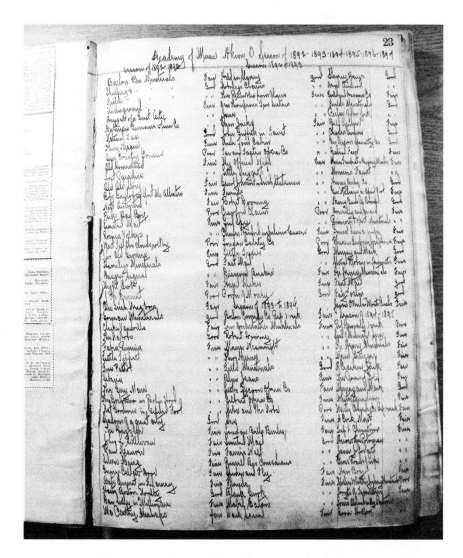

FIGURE 7.6. Index to WRHS Akron Academy of Music Scrapbook, 1892–1917, TRI Scrapbook #1.

adopted a highly discriminating attitude and used their albums to demonstrate that they were not easily pleased. The compiler of an 1898 Cleveland scrapbook kept an index of every play seen and assigned each the rank of good, fair, poor, or fine (figure 7.6).[84] A young New York woman who went to the theater about once a week used the slang of the day to rate the plays she saw. Those she disliked were "punk," "rotten," and "vile"; those she enjoyed ranged from "fair," "very fair," and "very good" to "great," "splendid," and "perfectly marvelous."[85]

Preprinted theatrical albums became popular starting in the 1890s, with fixed rubrics on each page inviting compilers to inscribe their "Impressions of the Play," "Criticism of the Performance," and "Criticism of Individual Actors." These albums were luxury items, tooled in leather, with decorative end papers. A young woman who kept one such album between 1892 and 1899 was from a family wealthy enough to take her to shows in New Haven, New Jersey, Boston, New York, Philadelphia, Chicago, and London. While keeping this album, she became engaged to a Mr. Harris Whittemore, whose own albums attested to a passion for Wagner operas. The future Mrs. Whittemore, though presumably educated, had less elevated tastes, and made only sparing comments on the hit plays that she saw. Often, she devoted more space to recording who accompanied her to the theater than to her opinion of the play, but over the years even she mastered the art of the one-line review: she summed up Lillian Russell's 1894 production of *The Grand Duchess* as "Crazy" and dismissed *The New Woman* that same year with "Did not care for it" (figure 7.7). By contrast,

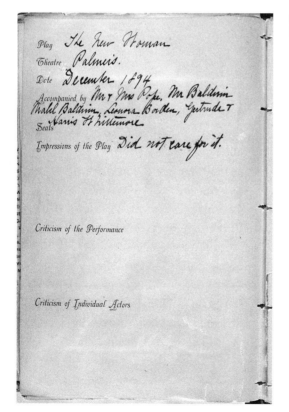

FIGURE 7.7. Album page, TRI Scrapbook #37.

FIGURE 7.8. Album page,
RBML 7.4, Ms. #1767.

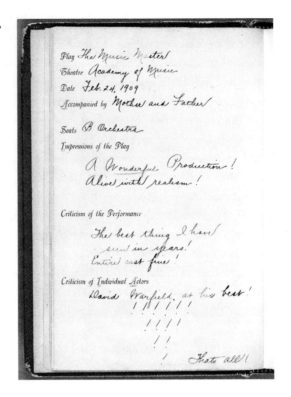

she found *Trilby* at New York City's Garden Theatre in 1895 "Very, very good."[86] Another amateur critic often wrote "Trash" next to the playbills he pasted in his album's pages, although he continued to attend the musicals, burlesques, and comedies he loved to hate.[87]

Some compilers proved exceptionally energetic and loquacious critics. One commentator deemed the 1909 *Music Master* "A *Wonderful* Production! Alive with realism" and declared the play's star to be "David Warfield at his best," festooning that point with an inverted triangle of exclamation points that cascaded down the album page (figure 7.8).[88] In 1912, a young theatergoer deemed Verdi's opera *Aida* "an awful heavy play but ... the singing beautiful." She responded better to ballerina Anna Pavlova, who "was certainly marvelous. She could imitate that beautiful music, so well that you could almost tell what the piece was by watching her dancing." Over time, she became more critical, writing of a 1913 play subtitled "A Modern Cinderella," "I should say almost the same old fairy-tale.... *Ancient* Cinderella." The budding critic wrote of that play, "There were no especially admirable characters in it," but of another, "It was awfully clever and I couldn't imagine how it would turn out until the very end."[89] Others took a more sociological approach, commenting on how theater reflected national differences. A Quebecois man kept an album bursting with the souvenir programs he collected during trips abroad between 1906 and 1908, including one for the Parisian play *Paraître*, which he thought reflected poorly on the state of marriage in France relative to his home country. After filling the entire space dedicated to "Impressions" with a handwritten critique of the play, he concluded: "Vive le Canada!"[90]

Others only commented on plays they especially liked. The "Theatre Book of the Misses Comstock," with its brown linen cover and leather corners, frugally used an old notebook already filled with meeting minutes as a repository for the theater programs and cast lists that the two sisters collected between 1886 and 1898 while living in Columbus, Ohio. They penciled in very few notes, making it all the more significant when they did write "Very Good" above the program for one play or "*Splendid*" on another.[91] An 1887 theatergoer enjoyed assigning plays relative grades, commenting that the historical play *Claudian* was "Very good but not so good as Clito. (Saw Clito again Mch. 9)."[92] Another compiler noted when a play had been seen "twice" or "three times," indicating yet another method audiences used to confer merit: voting with their feet.[93]

The enjoyment theatergoers had in judging the relative merits of genres, productions, playwrights, and performers often vied with their disappointment at a bad performance. One aspiring playwright decided to use his scrapbook to train his dramatic sense by summarizing each play he attended. He wrote an earnest headnote to the 1896 section of his album: "It is my desire to keep a copy of all programmes and an accompanying description of each play."[94] Upon seeing *The Count of Monte Cristo*, he provided a detailed critique of James O'Neill's adaptation of the Alexandre Dumas novel:

Although an admirer of Dumas I am forced to say that the presentation of Monte Cristo on the stage was to me scarcely listenable. From all I can gather from persons with whom I have spoken to, I feel that O'Neil [*sic*] has lost the very essence of the grand novel. To say that I was disappointed does not express my feeling. Having

[*sic*] had for two years yearned to see Monte Cristo, and then on seeing it, in what I call its uncouth shape, it sunk lower than any play
which might have been acted and dramatized by a child six years old.
In the dramatization of any novel the great lesson which it teaches
should not be lost to [make] scenic effects, which do not appeal to
the higher educated classes.

What this compiler lost in admiration for O'Neill he gained in a sharpened
sense of his own critical skills and his ability to distinguish between the
play's sensational qualities and its moral ones.

In the twenty-first century, *celebrity* has become synonymous with an
empty renown that has no basis in merit or achievement.[95] By this account,
fans lack judgment, all celebrities are pseudo-celebrities, and the press
can only participate in hoaxes or debunk them. By contrast, nineteenth-
century usage assigned *celebrity* both positive and negative meanings, and
most of the figures identified as either having celebrity or being one were
respected artists, authors, statesmen, scientists, inventors, and religious
leaders. Even actors, a less exalted group, elicited high regard from many
journalists and members of the public, who hailed the very best performers
as geniuses. Throughout the nineteenth century, a majority of the press and
public considered acting an important and worthy aesthetic activity and
accorded far more attention and distinction to performers than to plays
or playwrights.

Fan mail and scrapbooks attest to a genuinely popular interest in evaluating the most celebrated performers. In this permutation of the drama of
celebrity, every player exercised agency: the celebrity actors who strove to
give excellent performances, the theatergoers eager to demonstrate their
critical acumen, and the reporters, publicists, and photographers who
produced the materials used to assess and rank celebrities. An 1890 profile
of Sarah Bernhardt, musing on the difficulty of separating her notoriety
as a "personality" from her successful "embodiment of subtle art," concluded, "our great-grandchildren will not easily make up their minds upon
her merits."[96] However difficult the task of evaluation, such comments
assumed that far from being mindless and undiscerning, publics enjoyed

judging a celebrity's real worth. As we saw in "Sensation," celebrity culture has always had its irrational elements, but as this book's next and final chapter, "Merit," will show, celebrities themselves have long encouraged professional critics and ordinary theatergoers to assess, measure, and rank their achievements as stars.

CHAPTER 8

MERIT

How do publics and journalists who see celebrities as deserving their renown measure celebrity merit? Entertainers—singers, dancers, and actors—offer a better route to answering this question than other kinds of celebrities because their abilities seem especially resistant to objective appraisal. This was especially the case in the nineteenth century. In the twentieth century, entertainment industries invented a series of awards in order to rank and reward the best performers: the Oscars in 1929, the Emmys in 1949, the Grammys in 1959. The judgments implied by these prizes may not have always been accurate—was Judy Holliday, who won the 1950 Oscar for *Born Yesterday*, really a better actress than Bette Davis, who made *All About Eve* that same year? But despite the occasional glitch, for many people these awards stand for legitimate assessments of merit, thanks to formal voting procedures and institutional longevity.

In the twenty-first century, anyone with access to the Internet can rate just about anything, and every day millions spend time deciding how many stars, likes, and tomatoes to award to performers eminent and obscure. Measuring celebrity has never been easier, and the sheer number of data points lends these judgments authority, even when those ranked are not widely known. Jenna Marbles may not be a household name, but given that she had over eighteen million subscribers to her YouTube videos in 2018, it's hard to deny that she must be doing something well.

Celebrity culture, however, has existed for much longer than the Internet or the film industry. When modern celebrity culture was experiencing its first major growth spurt, how did people find ways to rate and rank the celebrities? And did celebrities themselves try to avoid these judgments, or did they encourage them?

Contests produce trustworthy assessments of merit when judges use consistent, well-defined criteria to rank comparable skills and strengths. Given how much tastes vary, artistic performance does not lend itself to standardized evaluation. But just because ballet dancers don't have batting averages does not mean that Margot Fonteyn became a ballet star thanks only to her pretty face. The nineteenth-century stage performers who created the template for later forms of stardom found several ways to encourage audiences to evaluate actors on their merits. Between the 1840s and the 1910s, the practice of performing the same plays around the world for many decades made it easy for audiences to compare different actors in the same roles, in three distinct kinds of contests. The first was a general *historical competition*, in which audiences made it a habit to measure newcomers against the greatest actors of the recent past, asking, for example, whether the young Henry Irving of the 1870s was inferior or superior to his predecessor Edmund Kean in the 1820s. The second was *shadow repertory*, in which contemporary actors frequently took on the same roles, facilitating comparisons such as those made in the 1880s between Irving's and Edwin Booth's interpretations of Hamlet, or Sarah Bernhardt's and Helena Modjeska's performances of Camille. Finally, the less common *mirror repertory* put star actors in direct competition. Londoners in 1881, for example, could watch Edwin Booth play Othello to Henry Irving's Iago on one night, and then see the two actors switch roles on the next. Such gimmicks sold tickets because audience members enjoyed debating which actor was the better tragic hero and which excelled as the villain. Thanks to steamship and railway travel, audiences and critics from Lisbon to Louisville could engage in global comparisons. Digital platforms make it exponentially easier and quicker for billions of people to rate entertainers and to make their assessments known. But the impulse to weigh celebrity merits is not new. Debating merit has always been a core feature of celebrity culture, even when doing so required a significant investment of time and energy. Far from relying on personality alone, nineteenth-century theatrical stars, aware that the public associated celebrity with merit, embraced any strategy that made it easier to evaluate their work as actors.

GLOBAL REPERTORY

The existence of a relatively stable international repertory of frequently performed works made it almost impossible for nineteenth-century publics not to compare different actors in the same roles. Theaters needed to make money to stay open. The fact that nineteenth-century troupes performed the same plays for many decades suggests that audiences liked comparing different actors in the same roles, and theater scrapbooks support this: many compilers saw the same play more than once, usually with different casts. In this respect, nineteenth-century theater was very different from twentieth-century film and television. Movies and television, despite the occasional remake, invite the best actors to claim a monopoly on roles that they originate. Al Pacino is not the best of many Serpicos; his greatness as an actor means that he *is* Serpico, just as Bette Davis is Margo Channing and James Gandolfini is Tony Soprano. Since the twentieth century, critics and publics have also measured film actors by how different they can be from one role to the next, valuing Al Pacino because his Michael Corleone (figure 8.1) bears so little resemblance to his Frank Serpico (figure 8.2), and lauding Meryl Streep for the disparity between her appearances in *Sophie's Choice*, *Out of Africa*, and *Silkwood*.

Nineteenth-century theater fans were not averse to versatility. In 1906, a Bernhardt enthusiast gushed: "What a range the woman has; the incestuous Phèdre, the sexless Jeanne d'Arc, the crafty Fédora, the delicious Princess Faraway, and now the saintly Thérèse, and she revels in them all."[1] At least three of these roles, however, also enabled publics to compare Bernhardt to the many other performers who tackled those same roles before, after, and sometimes at exactly the same time as she did: a number of other stars around the world played Phèdre, Joan of Arc, and

FIGURE 8.1. Al Pacino as Michael Corleone in *The Godfather*, 1972.

FIGURE 8.2. Al Pacino as Frank Serpico in *Serpico*, 1973.

Fedora during the many decades covered by Bernhardt's long career. To be sure, many of the best nineteenth-century stage performers became identified with a particular role that few others dared to play. Charlotte Cushman owned Meg Merrilies in the dramatization of *Guy Mannering*; as a theater critic observed, when Mary Anderson "rashly ventured to challenge comparison" with Cushman in that role, she only "offered a conclusive demonstration of her own artistic inferiority."[2] Henry Irving had few challengers as Mathias in *The Bells*. But to be seen as worthy of accolades, Cushman and Irving also had to perform roles such as Lady Macbeth and Hamlet, played often by many others.

US scrapbooks attest that between the 1840s and the 1910s, theatergoers in New York, Ohio, Chicago, Boston, Washington, DC, and other cities regularly saw a core group of works that remained almost constantly in repertory: *The Lady of Lyons, Caste, The Lights o' London, Richelieu, The Corsican Brothers, Uncle Tom's Cabin, Camille, Tosca, Fedora, Frou-Frou, Gismonda, Sapho, Zaza, Chu Chin Chow,* and a number of Shakespeare plays.[3] This repertory was global in both origin and terminus. Thanks to the absence of strictly enforced dramatic copyright laws, these works, most of which began life in English or French, ended up translated into many languages and produced on stages across Europe, the Americas, and Asian and African outposts of the British and French empires. In 1901, a Chicago theater even staged the French play *Gismonda*, by Victorien Sardou, in Yiddish adaptation.[4] Thanks to steamships and railways, actors from many countries could perform the same plays in cities large and small around the world. Philadelphia theatergoers could compare Lillie Langtry, Helena Modjeska, and Ellen Terry in *As You Like It* within the space of a few years.[5] As a theater critic for the *Los Angeles Times* put it in 1901 about another Sardou play, "The revival of 'Diplomacy' at the Empire afforded experienced playgoers an opportunity of forming some intelligent estimate of the relative merits of the players in well-known characters with those who played the same parts some years ago in other theaters." In this case, the critic ruled, "The verdict will not be in the favor of the Empire cast."[6] Audience members had numerous chances to compare how different actors interpreted identical moments or recited the same passages.[7]

Professional reviewers offered nuanced assessments of actors' relative merits: "Mr. Edwin Booth is America's leading tragedian. But that is not saying that he is a great actor. This does not seem to be the time for great actors. . . . Booth is the best in the collection, always remembering that the collection is not first class."[8] To make a claim so precise about Booth's standing required placing him in a wider pool of contenders, a practice that extended well beyond fussy critics paid by the word. Even Booth's most effusive admirers bolstered their credibility by comparing their idol to other actors: "When I inform you [Booth] that I have seen the Great Actors Charles Young, Charles Kemble, Macready, and greatest of all (the child of Genius) Edmund Kean in their best days, and that I consider your rendition of Hamlet superior to them all, you will think mine is not slight praise."[9] These were the words of a Philadelphia fan, writing in 1868, who signed off hoping that Booth's success would equal the merit of his Hamlet, considered by many the best male role in any nation's dramatic repertory. An Englishman from Maidstone similarly justified his 1880 praise of Booth's performance as Richelieu by noting that he had seen "nearly all the great Stars of the past thirty years."[10]

Even those performing less venerable parts than Hamlet could be readily compared to other performers in the same roles. When Sarah Bernhardt performed Hermann Sudermann's *Magda* for US audiences in 1906, one theater critic noted that the play was "in the repertory of so many prominent actresses that not to know Magda indicates a nonattendant at the theatre."[11] Another was able to list how different actresses interpreted a single moment in Sudermann's play: "Sarah Bernhardt screamed. Minnie Maddern Fiske trembled violently. Helena Modjeska became mute with the shock and almost fainted. Mrs. Patrick Campbell, turning her wonderful bare back to the audience, sent a visible chill running down her spine. But Duse merely gazed at the man, and slowly a flush spread over her pale face."[12] Even for comic actors, comparability mattered. A Buffalo reporter could declare that impressionist Elsie Janis did "not require comparison with Cissy Loftus or any other imitator" only because he had seen both imitate the same person, whom he had also directly experienced in action. His conclusion: "Miss Loftus does not do Edna May particularly well, so that she rather loses in a comparison of the two imitators this week."[13]

Another sign that comparisons helped link celebrity to merit: the biggest stars actively promoted their comparability to other famous performers throughout their careers. In 1900, having outdone all the great female performers of the previous century, Sarah Bernhardt took on the great male actors as well when she decided, at 56, to play Hamlet. Reviewing Bernhardt as the melancholy Dane, theater critic Max Beerbohm lamented that *Hamlet* had become "a hoop through which every very eminent actor must, sooner or later, jump."[14] Bernhardt made the same point more positively: "I will play 'Hamlet,' for 'Hamlet' is the titan of tragedy. . . . I will wear the male garments of the period and will be compared with the great Hamlets gone, and that should make it a success of curiosity. I shall challenge the Hamlets—all men."[15] Bernhardt was not the first woman to play Hamlet, but she was the most explicit about doing so to compete with male performers.[16] By playing the "titan of tragedy," she would vie for the highest degree of merit. Always happy to present herself as exercising a strong will, Bernhardt stated a clear intention ("I will play 'Hamlet'") that expressed an ambitious desire to scale the heights of her profession ("for 'Hamlet' is the titan of tragedy"). Her comments articulated a canny understanding of celebrity as both attraction and merit; her Hamlet would be "a success of curiosity" but would also allow her to "challenge" and "be compared with the great Hamlets gone."

HISTORICAL COMPETITION

Like the many other theatrical stars who chose to "be compared with the great Hamlets gone," Bernhardt, Booth, and others engaged in *historical competition*. Like Hamlet himself, the would-be theatrical celebrity had to contend with a ghostly predecessor in order to honor *and* surpass an older generation's paragon of merit. Historical competition blends usurpation and reincarnation. The novice performer must first emphasize her likeness to her rival, to establish comparability. Only then can she unfold the distinctive persona that will ultimately efface her predecessor. Historical competition is a useful foil to theater scholar Joseph Roach's concept of "surrogation": the process by which performers evoke forerunners in order to help groups resurrect lost pasts.[17] Surrogate attempts to incarnate history are often incomplete, ambivalent, and uncanny, driven by agents not entirely conscious of their interest in keeping the past alive in the present. By contrast, the actors engaging in historical competition and the critics and publics judging their competitions were fully aware of comparing newcomers to acclaimed predecessors.

At the outset of her career, Bernhardt had several opportunities to make herself comparable to her best female predecessors. As Doña Sol in Victor Hugo's *Hernani* in 1877, she revived a role originated by Mlle Mars (1779–1847), one of the greatest actresses of the early nineteenth century. The play's author hailed Bernhardt's performance by comparing her to each actress who had played the role before her: "You have not only shown yourself the rival, but the equal of those great actresses, Mdlle. Mars, Madame Dorval, and Madame Favart, who preceded you in the character of Doña Sol. I shall go farther. You have surpassed and eclipsed Mdlle. Mars. You are crowned by yourself twice a queen—a queen by beauty and a queen by talent."[18] Not everyone agreed; an 1878 review of *Hernani* praised Bernhardt but found that she did "not quite come up to Mdlle. Mars."[19] But both articulated how, to become a star, an actor had to try to equal or outdo a highly regarded predecessor, and the clearest way to do so was to interpret a role identified with that forerunner. Hugo put such contests in the realm of attraction by calling Bernhardt a "queen by beauty," but he also underscored the role of merit by referring to her crowning "talent." Nor did he claim a monopoly on star making. The original French, "Vous vous êtes vous-même couronnée reine," emphasizes Bernhardt's agency by repeating "vous" three times. The grammatical subject who elevates Bernhardt is not a critic, audience member, or playwright, but Bernhardt herself.[20]

The most important target of Bernhardt's historical competition was the renowned tragedian Rachel, whom we have encountered in previous chapters. A critical and commercial success, Rachel specialized in French tragedies by Racine and Corneille and developed a performance style that infused classical gravitas with the intensity characteristic of the new melodramas. Like Bernhardt, Rachel was widely known to be Jewish and had a reputation for being strong-willed. In 1838, with her first performances, Rachel so quickly established herself as a new standard for greatness that soon after that debut, the previously reigning Mlle Mars temporarily retired, "eclipsing herself out of fear of being eclipsed." Mars agreed to resume acting only if she could perform a role no one had ever played before, since she could hope to achieve a "triumph" only by avoiding comparison with the new star—a refusal to compete that only helped to cement Rachel's victory.[21] When Rachel first performed in London, in 1841, she once again had to convince spectators that she could vie with the greatest English actress of the preceding generation, Sarah Siddons (1755–1831), whom older spectators still remembered seeing. She did not always succeed. Although Rachel pleased the young Queen Victoria, Henry Crabb Robinson unfavorably compared her to the British star in an 1850 diary entry: "A Frenchman only can be excited to enthusiasm by such merits. She wants the magical tones, and the marvellous eye, and the majestic figure of Mrs. Siddons."[22] To be compared with Siddons at all, however, was to have reached acting's highest echelons, and lack of unanimity about the contest's victor only fanned the public's curiosity to judge for itself.

Rachel remained a global standard for merit in acting long after her premature death, in 1858. When Bernhardt first began to acquire an international reputation, a *New York Times* article noted, "To surpass Rachel is the aim and study of her life."[23] That aim may explain why Bernhardt, born Rosine, changed her name to the more Jewish-sounding Sarah, which invited comparison with France's other Jewish star. Early in Bernhardt's career, the highest praise critics could bestow on her was to deem her acting "worthy of Rachel."[24] On her first tours of England and the United States, Bernhardt included two parts closely identified with Rachel at her peak: Ernest Legouvé and Eugène Scribe's Adrienne Lecouvreur and Racine's Phèdre.[25] Bernhardt courted comparison with her great predecessor in order to make it easy for critics to see her worthiness. Critics rose to the bait, deeming her 1879 performance in London of Phèdre "one of the greatest exhibitions of tragic art seen probably since the days of Rachel herself," noting that "but one short act of the tragedy was . . . enough . . . to settle at once and for ever the claims of this incomparable artiste."[26]

Not all saw Bernhardt as the winner of these contests. A *New York Times* article from 1879 noted that Bernhardt had "been placed upon a pedestal far higher than her merits deserve. It is not necessary, in paying tribute to her undoubted talent, that we should dethrone Rachel, or forget the genius of Siddons."[27] Author Mary Ward became a Bernhardt devotee in 1874, upon first visiting a Paris theater, but could not convince her uncle, the poet and critic Matthew Arnold, that the new generation's greatest French performer had surpassed the old: "Never did I come so near quarreling with 'Uncle Matt' as when . . . after having heard my say about the genius of Sarah Bernhardt, he patted my hand indulgently with the remark, 'But, my dear child, you see, you never saw Rachel!' "[28] Far from making stardom a purely arbitrary affair, lack of unanimity about who was the better actor only sharpened observations of actors' relative merits.

Rachel's premature demise, in 1858, left Parisian audiences eager to find an equally great actress to replace her. Audiences compared Bernhardt to her predecessor even when the younger actress played parts that Rachel had never performed. Max Nordau recalled how after witnessing Bernhardt's 1876 premier, in *Rome vaincue*, "a loud murmur filled the hall. 'Rachel!' went from mouth to mouth. . . . 'This is a royal talent! We have found a new Rachel!' . . . The legitimate heiress had at last appeared;

public and criticism united in placing the diadem and mantle of Rachel upon Sarah Bernhardt."[29] Nordau describes an audience so committed to historical comparison that the highest praise it could give a new actress was to identify her with an older one.

By the early twentieth century, few remained who had seen Siddons and Rachel, and the living Bernhardt had become the new standard of greatness. In 1881, an actress billed as Madame Walter was still being hailed as "the Austrian Rachel," but the year before, *La Presse* had already praised Polish actress Mlle Marie de Ryng by dubbing her the "Sarah Bernhardt" of Warsaw.[30] The US actress Mrs. Leslie Carter cultivated her reputation as the "American Sarah Bernhardt," and in 1900 Japanese performer Sada Yacco, when touring Europe, billed herself as the "Sarah Bernhardt of Japan."[31] A 1906 review ratified its high praise of actress Margaret Anglin by explaining that her impressive voice "may be compared only to Mme. Bernhardt's."[32] By 1900, at least one reviewer concluded that "the only standard by which Sarah Bernhardt may be justly criticised is the standard of her own acting."[33]

SHADOW REPERTORY

To establish their merits, stars also made themselves easily comparable with living actors. To do so, they adopted roles already played with great success by *living* stars, generating what I will call *shadow repertories*. Sometimes older stars tried to seem more modern by adopting roles associated with younger performers. The practice continues to this day in pop music: Sarah Vaughan did a Beatles cover album in 1981, when she was in her late fifties; late in his career, country-and-western singer Johnny Cash began to cover songs by much more contemporary groups, such as the industrial rock band Nine Inch Nails; in 2015, a sixty-four-year old Paul Anka released swing versions of hits by Nirvana, Soundgarden, and others. Sometimes young performers seek celebrity by tackling roles performed very recently by established stars. Ballet and opera today continue to depend on shadow repertory, with critics and aficionados able to compare multiple interpretations of *Giselle* or *Turandot* from year to year and even within the same season. In both cases, the shadow acquires definition from the light cast by the trendier or better-known performer. Bids to be hip and modern can cast a harsh glare on an older star's age, but they can also help those in danger of becoming antiquated secure a foothold with younger generations.

Conversely, even if ultimately critics and audiences find the novice inferior, new performers acquire gravitas by being compared to better-known and well-respected figures. In both cases, competition spurs the press and public to treat the performing arts as tests of measurable skills.

Throughout her career, Bernhardt chose to play roles associated with the most popular and the most esteemed living actresses. In tackling Adrienne Lecouvreur in London in 1880 and in New York in 1881, Bernhardt not only claimed a role that Rachel had played decades earlier but also one that Modjeska and Ristori, two of the most internationally lauded performers of the day, had played around the world only a few years before. In turn, when touring Poland in 1882, Modjeska chose roles that enabled her to compete directly with Bernhardt.[34] In 1905, while touring Chicago, Bernhardt chose to play the lead in Sardou's *La Sorcière*, a role that Mrs. Patrick Campbell had played in the same city only a year earlier, to poor reviews. Where Campbell failed, Bernhardt triumphed. The same year, 1905, Bernhardt also debuted as Fanny in Daudet's *Sapho*, a part that until then had been the property of Réjane and Jane Hading in France and that US audiences associated with Olga Nethersole. Chicago critic James O'Donnell Bennett made the comparison explicit: "She is not the sordid Fanny Mme. Réjane played; she is not the half maniacal slave of passions Miss Nethersole extracted from the gutter." In this case, comparability did not establish Bernhardt as the best exponent of the role. Instead, it affirmed her skill as a distinctive interpreter by highlighting her as the only actress "able to make Fanny Le Grand an interesting figure and a sympathetic one."[35]

From the 1870s through the 1930s, the most important role in the female repertory was Marguerite Gautier in *La Dame aux camélias*, often referred to outside France as *Camille*. By 1906, so many actresses had played the role that one reviewer joked "it would require the talent of a statistician to compute how many emotional actresses have followed Eugenie Doche" in portraying the title character.[36] A 1909 advertisement for a film based on the play explained that "ambitious actresses aspire to play Marguerite Gautier . . . because it gives a woman on the stage the opportunity of showing off the variety of her histrionic gifts."[37] The role became such a staple in Bernhardt's repertory that critic William Winter, who considered Modjeska its "best" exponent, dubbed Bernhardt's appearance in it as inevitable as death and taxes.[38] In the same 1906 interview where Bernhardt announced that she would play Hamlet to challenge the great male actors, she explained that she would also continue to perform the Dumas play:

"In 'Camille' I shall challenge all the women, for the feminine star has ever loved 'Camille' and it is known of all, and the least adept in the art of the stage can follow, understand, compare and criticize."[39] Bernhardt's comment articulated how repertory linked celebrity to merit in ways that empowered actors and audiences alike. Precisely because theatergoers knew *Camille* so well, both as Alexandre Dumas fils's widely translated play and as Giuseppe Verdi's opera *La Traviata*, even the "least adept" spectators could "understand" Bernhardt's French performance and produce sound criticism of it by "compar[ing]" her to others.

In 1881, when Bernhardt first brought *La Dame aux camélias* to London and the United States, the title role still bore the imprint of two eminent young performers, Helena Modjeska and Clara Morris.[40] Bernhardt's agent, Henry Edgardo Abbey, had organized Modjeska's and Morris's recent visits to England, so he was well placed to advise the French actress about roles that would heighten curiosity about whether the newcomer might outdo her competitors. Though Bernhardt eventually came to be considered a far better actor than either Morris or Modjeska, in 1881 the outcome of their competition was far from predictable: only three years before, Modjeska had been proclaimed "The Only Camille." Even after Bernhardt added Marguerite to her repertory, some continued to deem Modjeska its better exponent. One British critic noted that her "playing... has certainly a method more agreeable to English taste than the more animal and Frenchy style of Bernhardt."[41] Others were surprised to find that "when put to the test, La Dame *à la mode* has actually proved nearly equal to La Dame *à la Modjeska*."[42] (British critics did love a pun.) Bernhardt set her stamp on the role by deliberately excising several bits of stage business associated with her two best known predecessors.[43]

Once Bernhardt made her mark as Camille, other actresses assayed the role in order to become comparable to an international star at the top of her powers. As with Magda, comparability helped critics discern what made each performer's interpretation distinctive. A 1906 article deemed Bernhardt "the exaggerated type. . . . the Camille for the Parisians; and with them there is no other." Duse was a more Mediterranean Camille, fragile, pitiable, and pure of heart; Olga Nethersole's Camille was "human and real," a victim of modern life.[44] Greta Garbo appeared in the film version of *Camille* in 1936; her tackling of a role identified with Bernhardt became one reason the Swedish film star was considered to play Bernhardt in a 1947 biopic that never got made.[45]

MIRROR REPERTORY

Despite the logistical challenges involved, a surprising number of performers chose to play the same roles simultaneously, usually at different theaters but in the same city and on the same or alternating days. In these cases, shadow repertory became what Bernhardt scholar Patricia Marks calls "mirror repertory."[46] So central was comparison to the nineteenth-century public's enjoyment of theatrical star turns that audiences were willing to pay to see different actors perform the same role in rapid succession. The practice continues to be popular; in 2017, Laura Linney and Cynthia Nixon alternated the roles of Regina and Birdie in a Broadway production of Lillian Hellman's *The Little Foxes*. Even at astronomical 2017 ticket prices, the *New York Times* advised those trying to choose one configuration of *The Little Foxes* to "see it twice."[47] Simultaneous appearances, far from cutting ticket sales in half, increase curiosity about both performances. In 1883, when London became home to three simultaneous productions of *Fedora*, including one starring Bernhardt in a role written expressly for her, a journalist observed that the overlap seemed to have "stimulated rather than satisfied public curiosity concerning the original."[48]

In the United States, Fanny Davenport (1850–1898) made a long career out of following Bernhardt from city to city in English versions of the plays that Bernhardt presented in French. Davenport had established herself as a major presence in the United States in the years just before Bernhardt became well known outside France. The publicity materials for an 1877 national tour vaunted Davenport as "pronounced by press and public the ne plus ultra of dramatic art"—an overstatement, but one that showed ambition, and a desire to appeal to audiences interested in serious plays.[49] Even before Bernhardt first arrived in the United States, in 1881, Davenport specialized in English versions of roles that Bernhardt originated in Paris, such as Postumia in *Rome vaincue*, mounted as *Vesta* in the United States. In 1877, Davenport's repertory included Anglophone staples outside Bernhardt's ken: *London Assurance*, *As You Like It*, *Pique*, and *School for Scandal*. During the 1880s and 1890s, however, when Bernhardt became a regular visitor to the United States, Davenport found a new niche as, in effect, Bernhardt's double. The English-speaking counterpart to the French star arranged to appear in New York, Philadelphia, Boston, and Detroit just before or just after Bernhardt, performing in English roles that, even in the United States, Bernhard staged exclusively in French: *Fedora, Gismonda, Tosca, Cleopatra,* and *Camille.*[50]

When playbills referred to Davenport's "matchless rendering" or "incomparable impersonation" of Fedora, they did so knowing that many audience members could literally contrast Davenport's performances to Bernhardt's from one night to the next.[51] As one reviewer of Davenport's Cleopatra put it, "Americans have seen both Sarah Bernhardt and Fanny Davenport as the beautiful sorceress of the Nile and while many are apt to remember that comparisons are odious they can not [*sic*] help compare the methods of the great French actress of her times with those of the gifted American artiste."[52] In 1896, Harvard undergraduate Richard Maynard reported to his parents that after failing to appreciate Bernhardt the first time he saw her play Phèdre, he returned to see her a second time as *Camille*—while a friend of his chose instead to attend the Fanny Davenport version of the Dumas play.[53] Another theatergoer saw Davenport play Gismonda but selected an image of Bernhardt in the role to crown the page on which he placed the playbill from the Davenport production (figure 8.3).[54] It is difficult to say who won this contest: the performer who obtained the ticket sale, or the one whose image was chosen to represent the role.

Mirror repertory was not unique to Bernhardt, nor was it confined to female performers or to those performing in different languages from each other. After alternating as Othello and Iago at the Lyceum Theatre in London in 1881, Edwin Booth and Henry Irving simultaneously played dueling Hamlets three years later at different Boston and New York theaters. Julia Marlowe (1865–1950) and Mary Anderson (1859–1940) both played *The Lady of Lyons* in Philadelphia within weeks of each other, at different theaters, and a scrapbook demonstrates that at least one theatergoer attended both performances, no doubt eager to compare two leading US actresses.[55]

So successful was mirror repertory at enabling performers to advertise, translate, and rival one another that Bernhardt herself adopted this strategy during a 1901 tour of the United States, inviting US actor Maude Adams (1872–1953) to play the title role in Edmond Rostand's *L'Aiglon* one week apart from Bernhardt, first in the same New York City theater, then in a Cleveland venue. In 1901, Bernhardt was fifty-seven, Adams barely thirty, although the younger performer had been onstage since childhood and was at the peak of her popularity after starring in several hit comedies by James Barrie. Unlike Bernhardt, Adams was not yet associated with historical drama or with trouser roles, although a few years later she became famous for playing Peter Pan. In 1901, however, the character of the Eaglet, Napoleon's sickly but histrionic young son, was a stretch for Adams. This was not surprising, since French playwright Edmond Rostand had written *L'Aiglon* expressly for Bernhardt. Although the play became a hit immediately upon its March 1900 premiere at the Théâtre Sarah-Bernhardt in Paris, its intense nationalism and intricate rhyming couplets made it an unlikely candidate for translation or export. Nonetheless, after hearing that Maude Adams was slated to premiere the English version in New York, Bernhardt added it to the repertory of her 1900–1901 US tour.

Even those US critics who protested that "comparison" between Adams and Bernhardt was "futile" engaged in just that.[56] Some predicted that Adams would "survive . . . comparison" with Bernhardt; others, having seen both, called Bernhardt next to Adams "a leopard alongside a kitten."[57] One Ohio scrapbook compiler lovingly preserved the press's detailed coverage of this celebrity face-off. In Cleveland, the two actresses performed *L'Aiglon* at the same theater, with Adams going first, serving as a preliminary live translation for Bernhardt's all-French production.[58] Reviewers noted the marked dissimilarities between the "rival performances."[59] One saw Adams as by far the better performer and evoked box

FIGURE 8.3. Image of Sarah Bernhardt, program for Fanny Davenport in *Gismonda*. WRHS Scrapbook #139.

office as an index of merit, noting that Adams made more money despite charging lower prices for tickets.[60] Another hesitated to compare the two because doing so would require him to "overthrow" his idol, Adams, while a third wrote that "Bernhardt stands head and shoulders above her rival; almost dwarfs her, in fact."[61] The younger and slighter Adams was better suited physically to impersonating a frail young man, but, for some, Bernhardt took the "palm" for artistry precisely because she did not look the part but wore "the breeches in her mind."[62] In cooperating to compete, both actresses encouraged the press and public to compare their respective merits, reinforcing the equation of celebrity with genuinely worthy and superior skills and of fandom with rational judgment as well as passionate feeling.[63]

GLOBAL PERFORMANCE NETWORKS

The larger and more varied a comparison pool, the more substantive the resulting judgments. The readiness of many nineteenth-century performers to circumnavigate the world lent even more credibility to comparisons between actors. Audiences across Europe, the Americas, Africa, and Asia could and did see actors from many nations on a regular basis, lending some plausibility to advertisements that hailed certain performers as the "world's greatest." A New York critic writing in 1906 noted that because Rachel, Ristori, Modjeska, Bernhardt, and Duse had all visited the East Coast, "It is therefore possible for some to make comparisons between all five of these eminent women by recalling plays given here in Manhattan." Even before touring the United States, Ristori had traveled to Paris in the 1850s as the "open and avowed competitor" of Rachel, "the brilliant Frenchwoman whose reign had become monotonous."[64]

Critics credited the global theater circuit with improving audience taste and discernment. When French actors Bernhardt and Coquelin toured the United States in 1900, one reporter argued that their appearances would ameliorate audience taste and judgment and improve American actors by affording comparisons with European ones.[65] Twenty years earlier, another reviewer described Edwin Booth as able to "stand a comparison with all but one whom Europe has in recent years sent over to us. Mr. Booth would himself shrink from a comparison with Salvini, but we know of no other artist with whom he cannot stand on the most honorable footing." The critic then praised the Italian actor as superior to other "foreign celebrities of inferior merit," weighing Booth on both a national and international scale and concluding that "there is no other American interpreter of the great characters of Shakespeare with whom he can justly be named in the same breath."[66] Even when slightly diminished, Booth's merits seemed more substantial when placed in so capacious a frame.

Appreciation for international actors was not limited to a United States still in cultural thrall to Europe. An 1880 article in London's *Daily Telegraph* noted that international comparison had become endemic to theatergoing: "The public have been able to study acting, and to compare the representatives of various and varied styles. Fechter, Jefferson, Ristori, Lafont, Janauschek, Aimée Desclée, Salvini, Sarah Bernhardt, and Modjeska have sparkled in the dramatic firmament, creating interest and discussion."[67] The comparison list named the best-known actors of the day, who hailed from France, Italy, Poland, Czechoslovakia, and the United States. The reference to stars sparkling in the firmament was more than a dead metaphor; it captured the reach of actors whose careers often took them around the planet. As a 1905 Quebec newspaper article put it, "Stars are travelers."[68]

Long before film, celebrity was a global phenomenon. As we saw in "Multiplication," with the advent of telegraphy, news of stars could move around the world in a matter of minutes; affordable images circulated more slowly, but widely. Famous people were almost as portable as the media portraying them. Numerous North American actors performed in London, including Charlotte Cushman, Edwin Booth, Clara Morris, Olga Nethersole, and Lotta Crabtree. A host of English performers made frequent and lucrative tours of the United States: George Arliss, Forbes Robertson, Mrs. Patrick Campbell, and Henry Irving, who first toured the country in 1883, shortly after Bernhardt's initial visit and, like her, returned regularly, often with Ellen Terry. The many programs from the Irving-Terry tours preserved in US scrapbooks attest to the transatlantic successes that helped to support Irving's expensive Lyceum productions in London.[69] Saint Petersburg and Rio de Janeiro, among others, became "internationalised" theatrical capitals with polyglot audiences accustomed to viewing foreign performers. Celebrity performers also traveled to more peripheral, far-flung locales. Until she retired in 1885, Adelaide Ristori played "in almost every country of the world, from Egypt to Mexico, from Denmark to Honolulu," as Oscar Wilde observed, with some relish, in a review of her autobiography.[70] After the 1870s, numerous Anglophone actors shuttled between England, North and South America, Ireland, Australia, South Africa, and India, using internal railway networks to cover extensive ground within those territories.[71] Not all performers making the colonial rounds were stars; some toured the colonies after declining from their peak or failing to move into the first ranks. Often, however, an international tour allowed successful actors to extend and cement already stellar reputations.

The global scale of Bernhardt's international fame itself became an important element of her celebrity.[72] In 1879, the *New York Times* called Bernhardt "an Alexander in petticoats—she sighs for new worlds to conquer." By the time producer Daniel Frohman presented Bernhardt with a gold laurel wreath in 1913, the rhetoric of global dominion had soared even higher: "With your golden voice you have conquered all the nations of the world. You made the universe your slave."[73] As we saw in "Savagery," in the 1880s, when Bernhardt first became a global star, it became common for caricaturists to lampoon her far-flung travels. One portrayed her as "always on the move," able to leap from California to Istanbul to an iceberg in a single bound.[74] A 1912 British tribute to Bernhardt included signatures from Fiji, the South Polar Regions, Alaska, and Siberia.[75] A French theater journal, summing up the star's achievements, described her as "a queen and priestess before whom frontiers did not exist. . . . her prestige was such, universally, that a sort of international religion arose around her."[76] To see Bernhardt was not only to commune with a particular French performer but to dissolve national barriers by connecting with the many others around the world who had also been in her presence. Celebrities like Bernhardt become hubs connecting far-flung members of geographically disparate publics; similar communities have, since the eighteenth century, formed around icons as disparate as Napoleon, Richard Wagner, Anna Pavlova, Charlie Chaplin, Audrey Hepburn, Maria Callas, Michael Jackson, Princess Diana, Madonna, and Beyoncé.

The opportunity to compare actors from many lands could also sharpen awareness of national differences, and many who achieved international fame remained identified with a particular country. Performers hailed abroad acquired more prestige at home, in part because their international fame bolstered their native land's cultural capital. The Polish-born Modjeska remains a treasured figure in her home country to this day, not despite but because she spent the most successful portion of her career living in the United States. When touring abroad, Bernhardt performed exclusively in French, was supported by actors born and trained in France, and used sets and costumes billed as originating in Paris theaters; as a result, audiences outside France saw her as a representative of her nation.[77] In 1881, Dutch musicians greeted her arrival at the Amsterdam train station by playing "La Marseillaise"; that same year a Montreal newspaper described her as giving Québecois "the illusion of being transported into the middle of Paris."[78] Years later, in Melbourne, audience members sang the French national anthem on Bernhardt's first night there, before the curtain rose.[79] By the early twentieth century, Bernhardt had become France's "Greatest Missionary."[80] A memorial service held for her in Cleveland in 1923 ended with renditions of the French and US national anthems.

French theater critics did not at first take kindly to the notion that France's superiority needed ratification by other nations. In the 1870s and 1880s, many French journalists professed indifference or hostility to Bernhardt's international success. *Le Globe* carped about Bernhardt's popularity with Britons: "Is it now from London that we need to be illuminated by a ready-made opinion concerning our actors?"[81] Far from wanting Bernhardt to conquer foreign lands, French journalists praised her when, in August 1879, she renounced—temporarily, as it turned out—her plans to tour the United States.[82]

In later years, however, French citizens began to appreciate Bernhardt's ability to represent France to the world. In 1905, the French consul in Chicago addressed a poem to the actress on behalf of the "French colony" that addressed her as "Grande Française, adorable génie," and in 1916 Bernhardt undertook a US tour designed to convince Americans to aid the French in fighting the Germans during World War I.[83] Upon the star's death, French journalists vaunted her merits as a "powerful ambassador" who had extended their nation's prestige by "incarnating French thought" abroad as the best-known French person in the world since Napoleon.[84] On November 28, 1944, soon after being liberated from the Nazis, Paris held a centenary anniversary celebration for Bernhardt, whose statue had been torn down and whose theater had been stripped of her name during the German Occupation. As part of the program for the gala event, the text noted that "because so many times across the world . . . French thought has been named Sarah Bernhardt, we celebrate that name tonight."[85]

In the nineteenth century, when Paris had no rival as a global theatrical capital, to be the "greatest living actress in France" was also to be "the greatest in the world," and Bernhardt stressed her internationalism as often as she did her Frenchness.[86] Her posters often advertised the distant countries where she had most recently performed.[87] Bernhardt and other global celebrities understood that the world performance circuit allowed audiences as well as actors to compete over merit. In an interview from around 1905, Bernhardt told a Chicago reporter, "Every time I come back to America I find audiences that are more keenly in touch with me and my plays. You are becoming cosmopolites and I feel it over the footlights."[88] The ability to value foreign actors measured a public's standing in the cultural arena. When the Comédie-Française visited London in 1879, the *Sporting Gazette* prefaced a discussion of "Bernhardt mania" by praising the English for being able to appreciate the French theater troupe:

> That taste is not so utterly gone in England as some would have us believe—that as a nation we are not given up on the one hand to beer and skittles, or on the other to limbs and licentiousness—was proved by the representative character of the audience at the Gaiety on Monday night to greet the Comedie Francaise [*sic*]. A true appreciation of what is best in art is in the Englishman and in the Englishwoman.[89]

In the United States, the ability to appreciate Bernhardt's merits enabled US cities to measure themselves against one another and the world. Theatergoers and journalistic boosters competed over whose turnout and applause for Bernhardt would best demonstrate their lack of provincialism. Even New York felt enough theatrical rivalry with Boston to report that its 1881 reception of Sarah Bernhardt compared favorably to theirs.[90] Chicago incorporated its reception of Bernhardt into its image of itself as a world metropolis with headlines such as "Huge Cosmopolitan Audience Greets French Artiste."[91] The Midwestern city's leading theater critic suggested in 1906 that the large audiences flocking to see Bernhardt perform proved "Chicago's great achievement in turning out as it did. It is now on a par with London, New York, Vienna, St. Petersburg and Copenhagen in patronizing a foreign artist."[92] Chicago in turn had its own regional competitors, since Columbus, Cleveland, Akron, and St. Louis all had lively theater scenes.

Because cities acquired merit when visited by performers at the apex of the dramatic hierarchy, they vied over which could show the most appreciation for the best actors. When Edwin Booth toured the United States in 1881–82, after having had great success in England, France, and Germany the previous decade, he represented several different sites of sophistication: New York, Europe, Shakespeare's England. Accordingly, an article on "Booth's Welcome" pasted in a scrapbook documenting the aforementioned tour noted that his large crowds in Memphis reflected well on the city: "The lawyers and merchants and doctors have turned out as well as the young clerks and businessmen, and the great tragedian has had a welcome from a cosmopolitan audience, and one reflecting the best character of the people."[93] Noting that people had come to Memphis to see Booth from all over Tennessee as well as from Arkansas and Mississippi, the author took the success of Booth's engagement as "a vindication of the intelligence and refinement of this city" and thought it might mean that in the future, "Patti will not be compelled to give us the go-by because it is not possible to get enough people in the house to justify her coming." Other articles in the same scrapbook made similar points about other cities; a good turnout for Booth in St. Louis, for example, proved that its citizens were "liberal patrons of amusements."[94]

Many French performers toured the United States, including Coquelin, Réjane, and Yvette Guilbert, but few visited as often as Bernhardt did (ten times between 1880 and 1918) or stopped in as many far-flung places. Her 1905–6 tour of the vaudeville circuit included stops in Salisbury, North Carolina; Battle Creek, Michigan; Waco, Texas; Venice, California; and Muskogee Indian territory.[95] Bernhardt's coverage of the entire country made her visits an especially good occasion for different regions and cities to compete over which could best demonstrate its merits by appreciating hers.[96] A 1906 article on "Bernhardt in the Corn Belt" praised the theatergoers of Kansas City, Missouri, for turning out to see Bernhardt, boasting of "the largest audience that ever in the world gathered together to witness a dramatic performance . . . in Kansas City, this state, at Convention Hall. A $10,000 audience. New York couldn't do it, nor Paris, nor Chicago, nor London. Our own Kansas City did it in a canter, easily, without a whoop or yell, just naturally, without turning a hair. But our theme is not Kansas City."[97] Readers might be forgiven for thinking that it was.

In the nineteenth century, the ease with which publics and the press could compare actors helped to define acting as a worthy activity and actors as meritorious figures. As we saw in "Judgment," theatrical scrapbooks attest to the average theatergoers' enthusiasm for evaluating plays and performers. Reconstructing global repertory and performance networks helps us to understand what made those evaluations credible. Male nineteenth-century actors, like their present-day counterparts, could be compared in Shakespeare roles, while female performers could draw on a sizable global repertory of works by Scribe, Dumas, and Sardou. This gave critics and audiences in major capitals and smaller cities alike regular occasions to see how actors from around the world executed the same roles.

Like many star performers, Sarah Bernhardt knit celebrity to merit by making herself easy to compare to other actors. Early in her career, she engaged in historical competition by playing roles identified with her most accomplished predecessors, Mlle Mars and Rachel. During the key period between 1879 and 1886, when Bernhardt became a truly international star, she embraced shadow repertory by choosing roles that had very recently been successes for her most celebrated contemporaries. Soon, other actresses began to shadow her, performing roles that she had originated, with some even mirroring her by playing the same parts as she did, at the same time, in the same cities. Late in her career, Bernhardt kept herself up-to-date by shadowing or mirroring younger performers.

Although journalists often described the greatest performers as incomparable, stars only come to seem unique by making themselves comparable to many others. The widespread use of historical, shadow, and mirror repertory made the most renowned actors into global standards of comparison, thus cementing a connection between celebrity and qualitative merit. Today, journalists often reduce celebrity to metrics, defining the biggest stars as those who earn the most money, sell the most albums, win the most awards, break the most records, or attract the largest numbers of Google hits, Twitter followers, and YouTube views. In this system, fans have agency only in the aggregate and celebrity is often seen as the enemy of art, lacking any real value. Nineteenth-century critics and publics shared that passion for ranking stars, but their reliance on nuanced comparison rather than unambiguous metrics encouraged individuals to assess celebrity achievements for themselves. The result was a consensus, now vanished, that celebrities, especially those who had stood the test of time, owed their fame to genuine and highly esteemed merits.

CONCLUSION

The man known for his flamboyant headgear and his public boasts about sleeping with other men's wives was an unlikely candidate for political office. He dismissed his critics as vermin, insisting that only he could set the record straight. He brushed off people who mocked his lapses in grammar and spelling, then wrote a best-selling autobiography, using collaborators to help with the pesky grammar and spelling issues. He claimed to be taller and thinner than he actually was. He bragged about taking women by storm, but issued denials when accused of sexual misbehavior. He crowed about how much money he made, even though his risky financial ventures often failed. He conceded that he knew nothing about government but ran for national office anyway, to spite someone who had joked that he could never be elected. When he did win, he boasted obsessively about how many votes he'd gotten and how little money he'd spent obtaining them, thanks to his knack for connecting with crowds. His provocative crudeness made him especially popular with white Americans who felt alienated from the country's East Coast elites. Over time, he came to be associated with racial slurs against immigrants, African Americans, Native Americans, and Mexicans and his name became a rallying cry for jingoistic nationalism, misogyny, and white supremacy.[1]

I refer, of course, to Davy Crockett (1786–1836), whose career in many ways anticipates that of twenty-first-century celebrity politician Donald Trump. Important differences distinguish the two men: Crockett did actual military service, for one; he was not born into wealth, for another. And though Crockett waged war against Native Americans, he also broke with his party by voting against President Andrew Jackson's Indian Removal Act. Both Crockett and Trump, however, understood celebrity. The new media of the 1820s and 1830s helped Crockett rise to fame and political power. Engravers and printers reproduced his portraits; publishers used his name to sell almanacs; actors made a fortune impersonating him onstage.[2] Almost two hundred years later, tabloid journalism, reality television, and Twitter similarly boosted Trump. Reporters latched onto both men because their showmanship made for good copy. Like most successful celebrities, Crockett and Trump understood how to leverage tensions between their supporters and representatives of the media. Both favored direct appeals to the public and both often dismissed what others printed about them as lies.

In providing a history of celebrity culture, this book has also offered a theory of how it works and why it fascinates even its fiercest detractors. Most histories of celebrity culture emphasize change over time and variation across media; this one has highlighted continuities. The similarities between Donald Trump's and Davy Crockett's celebrity exist because the Internet did not invent celebrity culture and because Hollywood did not create the star system. Twenty-first-century social media platforms and twentieth-century entertainment industries simply capitalized on a much older phenomenon spawned by a nexus of popular journalism, commercial photography, and newly rapid forms of travel.

Yes, celebrity culture has changed over the last two hundred years. The theatrical culture that in the nineteenth century gave rise to the first global celebrities distributed autonomy and influence fairly evenly among actors, audiences, playwrights, and critics. The Hollywood studio system shifted the balance of power by concentrating control in studio heads—although even they depended on public taste, and could find themselves bested by their most popular stars. How we gender and value celebrity has also shifted. In the nineteenth century, the typical celebrity was a mature man venerated for his professional accomplishments. By the early twenty-first century, the typical celebrity was a young woman judged primarily on her appearance and likely to find her success derided and dismissed even when it was the result of exceptional talent. That change, however, did not originate with celebrity culture, but with larger social transformations. When married women did not own their own wages or property and almost no women could enter professions or obtain university degrees, it posed no threat to existing hierarchies to admire a handful of anomalous female geniuses. Once feminism began to make real gains, female celebrities, as women of wealth and ambition, could be viewed as proxy soldiers in the battle for women's equality even when they themselves were far from feminist. No longer unthreateningly distinct from the majority of women, female celebrities came to be judged as all women unwilling to accept lesser status are judged. The results have not been pretty.

Technological changes have also had real effects. Any invention that increases how far and how fast communications can travel will amplify celebrity culture, and the Internet has been no exception. Digital media have sped up communication between celebrities and fans, and made their exchanges more public. They have increased celebrity culture's reach and scale, and made it easier to quantify celebrity. But many Internet platforms merely allow people to combine activities that used to be separate, such as pasting images into scrapbooks, sending fan mail, copying celebrity fashions, and ranking celebrities by talent or earning power. Whether conducted via paper, pixels, or in person, such practices sustain celebrity culture, but they do not define it, any more than concepts such as ideology, commodification, or public intimacy do.

Celebrity culture, whether A-list or Z-list, Bollywood or Hollywood, consists of interactions between celebrities, media, and publics. Each of these groups is too internally varied and has too much force for anyone to say in advance whose vision will prevail. Each tries to influence who will become a celebrity and how celebrities and fans will be valued. Each has partial, contested, but real agency, and each uses that agency to collaborate and tussle with the others. The energy expended in these skirmishes and alliances drives celebrity culture. Celebrities might try to undercut the media, as the eighteenth-century English actor David Garrick did when he responded to hostile reviewers by publishing his own anonymous rebuttals of their critiques.[3] They might try to use media to reach the public, as Sarah Bernhardt did when she wrote letters to newspaper editors that, once published, would influence newspaper readers. Or they might turn media workers into allies, as Hollywood star Constance Bennett did when she cultivated reporters whose positive articles improved her standing with the public.[4]

Celebrity culture's triangular structure has proven durable precisely because it is so flexible. When norms change and new media take off, publics may temporarily find themselves more influential, stars may briefly acquire more clout, media companies may momentarily seize the upper hand. But such shifts do not magically transform a three-way drama into a monologue. Celebrity culture exists only when publics, media producers, and well-known individuals engage with one another. If one group were to drop out or ignore the others, celebrity and fandom would disappear.

Each of this book's chapters has explored a different permutation of the drama of celebrity. Defiant celebrities occasionally spark real change, but by and large, stars exist in states of social exception. Their popularity may irritate the reporters forced to write about them, but it also offers ordinary people the vicarious freedom of admiring the few who ostentatiously ignore rules followed by many. Often, defiant celebrities and their fans relish disregarding cultural gatekeepers who might censure one celebrity for being too thin, another for being too fat. In other instances, however, both journalists and publics enjoy ceding their agency to talented orators and performers who use their exquisite control over their own bodies to craft sensational performances that many find irresistibly alluring. But nothing about celebrity culture is ever definitively settled. The celebrity who bores some publics may inspire passionate devotion in others, or overly excited fans and the stars they adore may become the target of critics who caricature them as savage: emblems of excessive, outlaw agency. The common desire to achieve intimacy with celebrities may lead to extreme forms of aggression such as stalking, but it can also express itself in the minimal but real activity of recyclers happy to immerse themselves in representations of their favorite icons that they enjoy moving from one site (a magazine, a theater program) to another (a scrapbook, a website).

Many aesthetic traditions dismiss copying for trafficking in illusion and replacing original creations with secondary shadows. But modern celebrities use mechanical reproduction to establish their singularity and find their value increasing as their images multiply. Celebrities, publics, and media all cooperate to propagate that imagery, and the ability to turn the self into copies proves essential to anyone wanting to become an original type. Once typed, celebrities become available for emulation. Those who imitate celebrities, far from being mindless automatons, often aim to bolster their own agency, and can find themselves mocked for that ambition, especially if they belong to subordinated groups. Although many have associated celebrities and fans with uncritical passivity, celebrity culture is also fertile ground for critical practices of observation and evaluation. Publics and media workers have long joined forces to assess and rank celebrities in various walks of life. Some fan mail demonstrates that enthusiastic acolytes can also be discerning critics, and many celebrities embrace practices that make them comparable to others, including competitions that equate fame with merit.

I began researching this book in September 2008, when Barack Obama was running for president. While combing through the Sarah Bernhardt archives in Paris, I would jump up every hour to check the library computer for the latest news on CNN. I completed this book after Donald Trump took office as president, in 2017, often breaking from final revisions to read about his latest tweets on my smartphone. In 2008, many highly educated progressive voters felt cautious optimism about new media and even about celebrity culture, because both had brought a leader they admired to power. In late 2016, soon after Trump won the Electoral College vote, Alex Ross published a New Yorker piece entitled "The Frankfurt School Knew Trump Was Coming," voicing the sentiments of the many millions who blamed celebrity culture for helping to put a despicable man in office. But Ross's article, which equated Trump's election with the rise of mass media, could just as easily have been entitled "Pessimists Are Likely to Be Right 50% of the Time." Tempting as it is to blame reality television for what ails us, celebrities were more likely to denounce Trump than support him, as the anemic lineup at his inauguration proved. Numerous stars have spoken out against Trump, including Meryl Streep, Robert De Niro, Lin-Manuel Miranda, John Legend, George Takei, Alyssa Milano, and LeBron James, many of whom have larger Twitter followings than he does. Every US president, from Abraham Lincoln to Franklin Delano Roosevelt, John F. Kennedy, and Ronald Reagan, has been what Ross claims only Trump has been: "as much a pop-culture phenomenon" as a "political one."[5] And though mainstream media outlets profited by covering Trump, most (with the exception of Fox News) also took him to task for his lies, his racism, his misogyny, his failure to release his tax returns, and his lack of political experience.

The history and theory of celebrity teach us that we get the celebrities we deserve. Capitalism does not foist any particular celebrity on us, even if capitalist ideology finds many affinities with celebrity culture's exaltation of individuals. Ever since the 1830s, when the commercial press first helped give rise to modern celebrity culture, the journalistic landscape has been too fractured and chaotic for the press alone to manufacture celebrities. Publics have proven difficult to influence. As we have seen throughout this book, even concerted publicity campaigns can fail, and reporters can be surprisingly hostile to the most popular entertainers, from Byron to the Beatles. Conversely, publics alone cannot a celebrity make, because their access to celebrities is always mediated by photographers, journalists, film producers, disc jockeys, concert bookers, software developers, and celebrities themselves. Though stars are never self-anointed, many play a key role in crafting their personae, and this book should serve as a cautionary tale about the dangers of underestimating celebrities or viewing them as pawns. If nothing else, most stars possess a shrewd grasp of how to manage the media and attract public attention.

Most writing about celebrity culture warns that it's worse than you fear. This book has argued that celebrity culture is too dynamic and complicated to warrant the many reductive jeremiads it has inspired. In some instances, it can turn out better than its harshest critics could ever imagine; in others, it descends to lows that even the grimmest dystopian would fail to predict. Sometimes cause for joy, sometimes for despair, celebrity culture is neither panacea nor plague; it is what all the groups whose interactions create celebrity culture make of it. As a result, even those who ignore celebrity culture are implicated in its travails—not because society demands that everyone stay on top of the latest celebrity gossip, but because failing to pay attention to this particular status system can have consequences for society at large. Celebrity culture is always a debate about whom and what we value. The slightest interventions can matter in contests for agency where no single person or force can ever be assured of permanent victory. Precisely because no one group or individual controls the drama of celebrity, each of us has a limited but real role to play in shaping the course it takes.

ACKNOWLEDGMENTS

To James Eli Adams, Danielle Allen, Giada Alessandroni, Noah Altshuler, Amanda Atwood, Ellis Avery, Sarah Balkin, Robin Bernstein, Stephen Best, the staff of the Bibliothèque nationale de France, Katherine Biers, Joseph Boone, the staff of the British Library, Karl Britto, Christy Burns, Jennifer Callahan, Anne Cheng, Amanda Claybaugh, Deborah Cohen, Liz Cohen, Margaret Cohen, Sarah Cole, the staff of the Columbia University Rare Book and Manuscript Library, Nena Couch, Patricia Crain, Nicholas Dames, Mary Davis, Carolyn Dean, Andre Dombrowski, Sierra Eckert, Margaret Edsall, Philip Fisher, Emily Fitzell, Fumiko, Diana Fuss, Dehn Gilmore, Eric Glassgold, R. Darren Gobert, Neil Goldberg, Erik Gray, Rae Greiner, Jonathan Grossman, Marah Gubar, The Guggenheim Foundation, the staff of the Harvard University Houghton Library, David Henkin, Pembroke Herbert, Margaret Homans, Jean Howard, Martha Howell, Margaret Hunt, Annamarie Jagose, Eleanor Johnson, Jane Kamensky, Eric Klinenberg, Ivan Kreilkamp, Thalia Leaf, Jennifer Lee, Caroline Levine, Jessica Lilien, Heather Love, Michael Lucey, Deborah Lutz, Deidre Lynch, Josh Macht, Alison Mackeen, David Madigan, Bathsheba Marcus, Sid Maskit, Liz Maynes-Aminzade, Andrew Miller, Derek Miller, Toril Moi, Barbara Morris, Alondra Nelson, Anahid Nersessian, Karen Newman, the staff of the New York Public Library, Felicity Nussbaum, Brigid O'Brian, Carol Ockman, Clare Pettitt, Ben Platt, John Plotz, Rashmi Poddar, Leah Price, Martin Puchner, the Radcliffe Institute for Advanced Studies, Rose Razaghian, Joe Rezek, Linda Reilly, Maurice Samuels, Anne Savarese, Elaine Scarry, Vanessa Schwartz, Laurence Senelick, Lucy Sheehan, James Simpson, Vanessa Smith, Eric Smoodin, Deborah Steiner, Jenny Stephens, Dale Stinchcomb, Abigail Struhl, Karen Tongson, Vina Tran, Francesca Trivellato, Irene Tucker, Clara Tuite, Stephen Twilley, Judith Vichniac, Nancy Vickers, the staff of the Victoria & Albert Museum, Judith Walkowitz, Rebecca Walkowitz, Lee Wallace,

Peggy Waller, Nicholas Watson, Adam Watt, Raymond Wemmlinger, the staff of the Western Reserve Historical Society, Victoria Wiet, Carolyn Williams, Matthew Wittman, Sally Yi, Pauline Yu, Caitlin Zaloom, Susan Zieger:

Thank you.

NOTES

INTRODUCTION

1. Circulation figures for *Life* provided in Edith Evans Asbury, "Time Inc. to Revive *Life* as a Monthly," *New York Times*, April 25, 1978, https://www.nytimes.com/1978/04/25/archives/time-inc-to-revive-life-as-a-monthly-picture-magazine-to-be.html.

2. Daniel Boorstin, *The Image: A Guide to Pseudo-Events in America* (1961; repr., New York: Knopf, 2012), 57, 75, 61. On the importance of media, see also Leo Braudy, *The Frenzy of Renown: Fame and Its History* (New York: Vintage Books, 1986).

3. On the celebrity of Boorstin's soundbite, see Sharrona Pearl and Dana Polan, "Bodies of Digital Celebrity," *Public Culture* 27, no. 1 (January 2015): 185. In a review essay, Michael Newbury observes that academic studies of celebrity are "dominated by an idea of falsity." "Celebrity Watching," *American Literary History* 12, nos. 1–2 (March 2000): 276. Richard Schickel, in *Intimate Strangers: The Culture of Celebrity* (Garden City, NY: Doubleday, 1985), aimed to puncture the illusion that the public intimacy celebrities foster offers access to their real selves. For more complex views of the constructed nature of celebrity, see Christine Gledhill, "Signs of Melodrama," in *Stardom: Industry of Desire*, ed. Christine Gledhill (London: Routledge, 1991), 207–229; and S. Paige Baty, *American Monroe: The Making of a Body Politic* (Berkeley: University of California Press, 1995).

4. For an economist who argues that celebrity is an efficient mechanism for identifying the cultural products most worth our attention, see Moshe Adler, "Stardom and Talent," in *Handbook of the Economics of Art and Culture*, vol. 1, ed. Victor A. Ginsburgh and David Throsby (Amsterdam: North-Holland, 2006), 895–906. In 2011, best-selling sociologist Duncan J. Watts updated "known for being well known" for the big-data era, claiming that because celebrity is nothing but an arbitrary network effect, lamentably bad books, movies, and performers have the same chance as truly excellent ones of attracting millions. Duncan J. Watts, *Everything Is Obvious: Once You Know the Answer* (New York: Crown Business, 2011). Kerry Ferris, *Stargazing: Celebrity, Fame, and Social Interaction* (New York: Routledge, 2011), details how contemporary journalists and scholars pathologize those who engage with celebrity culture as simultaneously too passive and susceptible and too active and obsessed.

5. On celebrity culture as reinforcing commodification and ideological fictions of individualism, see Theodor W. Adorno, in *The Culture Industry: Selected Essays on Mass Culture*, ed. J. M. Bernstein (London: Routledge, 2001); Guy Debord, *Society of the Spectacle*, trans. Fredy Perlman et al. (Detroit: Black & Red, 1967); P. David Marshall, *Celebrity and Power: Fame in Contemporary Culture* (Minneapolis: University of Minnesota Press, 1997); and Chris Rojek, *Celebrity* (London: Reaktion Books, 2001), 19, 25. Richard Dyer, in his foundational book *Stars* (London: British Film Institute, 1979), briefly discusses how a star like Greta Garbo exerted some control over her image by battling with the studio over scripts, but concludes that the ultimate "author

of Garbo is ideology" (155). Joshua Gamson, in *Claims to Fame: Celebrity in Contemporary America* (Berkeley: University of California Press, 1994), acknowledges that publics can be knowing about how celebrity is constructed but focuses on the commodification of attention. For a more recent example of the use of commodification theory to understand celebrity, see Thomas Mole, *Byron's Romantic Celebrity* (London: Palgrave Macmillan, 2007). For a recent example of ideology critique, see Sean Redmond, who writes: "Celebrity culture is centrally involved in producing the illusion of greater democratization but in fact masks the truth that power remains in the hands of the select few." "Introduction to Part Two," *A Companion to Celebrity*, ed. P. David Marshall and Sean Redmond (Chichester, UK: Wiley Blackwell, 2016), 80. Karen Sternheimer similarly argues that early movie fan magazines "reinforce[d] the belief that inequality is the result of personal failure rather than systematic social conditions." *Celebrity Culture and the American Dream: Stardom and Social Mobility* (New York: Routledge, 2011), 4.

6. Adorno, "Culture Industry Reconsidered," in *The Culture Industry*, 106.

7. For a study that emphasizes the qualities inherent to stars themselves, see Joseph Roach, *It* (Ann Arbor: University of Michigan Press, 2007); biographies of celebrities also tend to assert their subjects' agency. See, for example, an excellent work by Adrienne McLean, *Being Rita Hayworth: Labor, Identity, and Hollywood Stardom* (New Brunswick, NJ: Rutgers University Press, 2004). For influential arguments that fans drive celebrity culture, see Jackie Stacey, *Star Gazing: Hollywood Cinema and Female Spectatorship* (London: Routledge, 1994), and Henry Jenkins, *Textual Poachers: Television Fans and Participatory Culture* (New York: Routledge, 1992). The academic argument that the media drives celebrity, whose earliest scholarly proponents included Theodor Adorno, Leo Lowenthal, Daniel Boorstin, and others cited above and below, continues to command extensive public support. In 2015, when I participated in an online "Ask Me Anything" discussion about celebrity on the social media platform Reddit, whose users can vote posts up or down, the most popular questions presented celebrities as owing their success primarily to their publicists rather than to their talents, as wielding undeserved authority, and as famous merely for being famous. "I'm Professor Sharon Marcus, from Columbia University, and I study celebrity culture in the past and in the present, AMA!," Reddit, March 17, 2015, https://www.reddit.com/r/science/comments/2zca5c/science_ama_series_im_professor_sharon_marcus/.

8. To take another example, in April 1939, the popular film magazine *Modern Screen* gave actor Jeffrey Lynn the full celebrity treatment, lauding his first major role as a "brilliant success," praising his "sympathetic charm," and devoting half a page to photos meant to illustrate his "ascent to fame." It didn't work. Lynn lived until 1995, working steadily in film and television, but he never became anything remotely resembling a star. Elisabeth French, "Success—The Hard Way," *Modern Screen* 18, no. 5 (April 1939): 36–38, 89–90.

9. See Michael Warner, *Publics and Counterpublics* (New York: Zone Books, 2002).

10. See Robert Turnock, *Interpreting Diana: Television Audiences and the Death of a Princess* (London: British Film Institute, 2000).

11. Tina Brown in *The Diana Chronicles* (New York: Broadway Books, 2007) discusses how Diana's marriage with Charles coincided with an expansion of the tabloid press in England (77–8); Diana's skill at charming many individual journalists, not least by helping them to do their jobs (129–132); and her "cool understanding of the peril as well as the power of media attention" (131), derived in part from the fact that Diana "studiously" reviewed her coverage in tabloids and broadsheets "on a daily basis" (222). Though poorly educated and in many ways unsophisticated, in romancing and

marrying Charles, Diana "had at last found something that she was good at: media relations" (132)—a talent not to be taken for granted, as other members of the royal family who lacked Diana's insightfulness and skills soon learned. On the taboo that Diana broke by shaking hands with AIDS patients without wearing gloves, see 286. On Diana's bond with the public and how it shaped media coverage (rather than vice versa), see 343.

12. I use the term *drama* to refer to interactions whose outcome is not preordained and that therefore generate a tension that feels suspenseful; in this sense, my use of the term has some affinities with Victor Turner's concept of the *dramatic* in *Dramas, Fields, and Metaphors: Symbolic Action in Human Society* (Ithaca, NY: Cornell University Press, 1974), 32. Turner also uses the term to refer to breaches of norms, a topic I take up in chapter 1, "Defiance," although I part company with Turner's assertion that social dramas inevitably move through stages of crisis and redressive adjustment (38).

13. On the rise of commercial photography, see "Multiplication."

14. Joe Kember, *Marketing Modernity: Victorian Popular Shows and Early Cinema* (Exeter: University of Exeter Press, 2009), 136, 144.

15. For example, Jack Benny first appeared on the radio in 1932, as a guest of Ed Sullivan; Benny and Sullivan were both later among the first to become television stars. See Susan Murray, *Hitch Your Antenna to the Stars: Early Television and Broadcast Stardom* (New York: Routledge, 2005), and Mary R. Desjardins, *Recycled Stars: Female Stardom in the Age of Television and Video* (Durham, NC: Duke University Press, 2015).

16. See Sharon Marcus, "Celebrity 2.0: The Case of Marina Abramović," *Public Culture* 27, no. 1 (January 2015).

17. In *Unbelievable: My Front-Row Seat to the Craziest Campaign in American History* (New York: Dey Street Books, 2017), television journalist Katy Tur compares Franklin Delano Roosevelt to Donald Trump and observes that in 2016, no single company had the prestige—or the monopolistic control—that the National Broadcasting Company hosting Roosevelt's radio talks enjoyed in the 1930s. She also shows how Trump exploited the twenty-first-century proliferation of media channels to bypass outlets and journalists whose coverage displeased him (89–90). Matthew Jordan notes that although Trump demonized the media, he "served them well," because his sensationalist, controversial campaign attracted viewers and readers; leading cable news networks realized far higher profits in 2016 than they had forecast. "In a Post-Truth Election, Clicks Trump Facts," *The Conversation*, October 25, 2016, https://theconversation.com/in-a-post-truth-election-clicks-trump-facts-67274. Anachronistically, however, Jordan identifies the monetization of attention, which has existed for over two centuries, as originating with digital journalism.

18. Swift published an open letter to Apple on her Tumblr page; see Kim Hillyard, "Taylor Swift Writes Open Letter to Apple Music: 'We Don't Ask You for Free iPhones,'" *New Musical Express*, June 21, 2015, https://www.nme.com/news/music/taylor-swift-134-1225572.

19. Alfred Ng, "Rihanna Slams Snapchat over Controversial Ad: 'Shame on You,'" CNET, March 15, 2018, https://www.cnet.com/news/rihanna-slams-snapchat-over-controversial-ad-shame-on-you/.

20. "Beliebers Revolt Against Their Deity, Justin Bieber, Over New Girlfriend Sofia Richie," *Daily Beast*, August 14, 2016, https://www.thedailybeast.com/beliebers-revolt-against-their-deity-justin-bieber-over-new-girlfriend-sofia-richie.

21. On Barrie's young fans, see Marah Gubar, "*Peter Pan* as Children's Theatre: The Issue of Audience," *Oxford Handbook of Children's Literature*, ed. Julia L. Mickenberg and Lynne Vallone (Oxford: Oxford University Press, 2013).

22. "A disk jockey, Murray the K, conducted a popularity poll on the individual Beatles. Mr. Starr seemed to come in ahead of Mr. McCartney by several decibels." John O. Wilson, "2,900 Voice Chorus Joins the Beatles," *New York Times*, February 13, 1964.

23. On medieval saints, see Thomas J. Heffernan, *Sacred Biography: Saints and Their Biographers in the Middle Ages* (Oxford: Oxford University Press, 1992).

24. On eighteenth-century celebrity, see Felicity Nussbaum, *Rival Queens: Actresses, Performance, and the Eighteenth-Century British Theater* (Philadelphia: University of Pennsylvania Press, 2010); Deidre Shauna Lynch, *Loving Literature: A Cultural History* (Chicago: University of Chicago Press, 2015); Brian Cowan, "News, Biography, and Eighteenth-Century Celebrity," *Oxford Handbooks Online* (September 2016), http://doi.org/crzx; Stuart Sherman, "Garrick among Media: The 'Now Performer' Navigates the News," *PMLA* 126, no. 4 (October 2011); and Antoine Lilti, *Figures publiques: L'invention de la célébrité, 1750–1850* (Paris: Fayard, 2014). Lilti's survey, which offers a wealth of evidence that celebrity culture was already thriving two centuries ago, adopts a theoretical perspective that repeats the standard take on celebrity: that it has little to do with actual accomplishment (6, 272); is epitomized by the public exposure of private lives and the illusory feelings of false intimacy that result (7); was "never really legitimate," despite also being a form of prestige (8); can best be understood in terms of commodification and consumer culture (281); and represents mass media's ability to dominate the public and suspend its capacity for rational, critical judgment (9–10). Here and below, unless otherwise noted, all translations from the French are my own.

25. Ruth Cowen, *Relish: The Extraordinary Life of Alexis Soyer, Victorian Celebrity Chef* (London: Weidenfeld & Nicolson, 2006), 3–4, 49, 61.

26. On nineteenth-century advertisements involving celebrities, see "Imitation." In 1877, actor Sarah Bernhardt helped to organize a benefit performance for people wounded in Russia; see Émile Abraham, "Revue des théâtres," *Le Petit journal*, August 19, 1877, Gallica; years later, she also did a benefit performance for a children's hospital; see *Some Letters from a Man of No Importance: 1895–1914* (London: Jonathan Cape, 1928), which mentions that actor Henry Irving also frequently mounted shows for charitable causes (61). Clara Morris, in her 1901 autobiography, *Life on the Stage* (1901; repr., Cabin John, MD: Wildside Press, 1977), noted that events such as a benefit for orphan asylums organized by producer Augustin Daly "had long been a custom," although Daly innovated by arranging "monster programmes, which included the names of every great attraction in the city—bar none" (367). On a benefit performance to help San Franciscans after the 1906 fire, see Clement Scott, "The Playhouses," June 18, 1892, Clippings-Misc., Harvard Theatre Collection at Houghton Library, Harvard University (HTC).

27. For details on how the expansion of leisure time promoted attendance at plays and sporting events and therefore generated interest in celebrities, see Benjamin McArthur, *Actors and American Culture, 1880–1920* (Iowa City: University of Iowa Press, 1984), 126–27. David Grimsted notes that in the US, theater ticket prices "always were low enough to make occasional theatrical attendance possible for most Americans." *Melodrama Unveiled: American Theater and Culture, 1800–1850* (1968; repr., Berkeley: University of California Press, 1987), 52. Though some theaters in England and France deliberately kept prices high, both cities had many venues with a cross-class or working-class clientele. Sarah Bernhardt, a star whose repertory was associated with high art (she performed exclusively in French), reached people of all classes; late in her career, she performed in a London music hall and on the US vaudeville circuit.

28. Article in the *Brooklyn Eagle*, November 19, 1911, "Charles Frohman Ingenuously Defends the 'Star System': Insists That Public and Not the Managers Create Theatrical Luminaries," clipping in Rare Book and Manuscript Library, Columbia University (RBML), Dramatic Museum Scrapbooks collection, Scrapbook 1.24. On the shift from character to personality that began in the 1880s, see Warren Susman, *Culture as History: The Transformation of American Society in the Twentieth Century* (New York: Pantheon, 1984). In *Celebrity and Power*, Marshall notes that contemporary celebrity culture has its roots in nineteenth-century democratization and individualism (6–8).

29. For further discussion of the rise of commercial photography and illustrated magazines, see "Multiplication."

30. Michael Schudson, in *Discovering the News: A Social History of American Newspapers* (New York: Basic Books, 1978), argues that the rise of commercial newspapers in the 1830s and after was linked to a democratic ethos predicated on notions of individual agency. He notes that when newspapers transitioned from the mercantile newsletters of the 1820s, which had names like "advertiser," they adopted names that "express a kind of *agency*—names like 'critic,' 'herald,' 'tribune'" (17). Christophe Charle, in *Le Siècle de la presse, 1830–1939* (Paris: Seuil, 2004), similarly notes that in the nineteenth century, the public became an actor in the process of making a newspaper, by sending letters to editors and affecting sales (17).

31. On the history of newspapers in the United States, including their relationship to changes to the postal system, see Schudson, *Discovering the News;* Jason Hill and Vanessa R. Schwartz, eds., *Getting the Picture: The Visual Culture of the News* (London: Bloomsbury Academic, 2015); and David Henkin, *The Postal Age: The Emergence of Modern Communications in Nineteenth-Century America* (Chicago: University of Chicago Press, 2006). For France, see Claude Bellanger et al., eds., *Histoire générale de la presse française*, 5 vols. (Paris: Presses Universitaires de France, 1969–76); René de Livois, *Histoire de la presse française*, vol. 1 (Paris: Les Temps de la presse, 1965); Patrick Eveno, *Histoire de la presse française: De Théophraste Renaudot à la révolution numérique* (Paris: Flammarion, 2012); and Dominique Kalifa, ed., *La Civilisation du journal: Histoire culturelle et littéraire de la presse française au XIXe siècle* (Paris: Éditions Nouveau Monde, 2011). For England, see Andrew King and John Plunkett, eds., *Victorian Print Media: A Reader* (Oxford: Oxford University Press, 2005); Esther Milne, *Letters, Postcards, Email: Technologies of Presence* (New York: Routledge, 2010); Karin E. Becker, "Photojournalism and the Tabloid Press," in *Journalism and Popular Culture,* ed. Peter Dahlgren and Colin Sparks (London: Sage Publications, 1992), 130–152, which offers a useful overview of the integration of images into British newspapers and periodicals; Celina Fox, *Graphic Journalism in England during the 1830s and 1840s* (New York: Garland Publishing, 1988), a 1974 PhD dissertation published as part of a series devoted to outstanding theses in the fine arts from British universities; and Clare Pettitt, *"Dr. Livingstone, I Presume?": Missionaries, Journalists, Explorers and Empire* (Cambridge, MA: Harvard University Press, 2007).

32. Don C. Seitz, *The James Gordon Bennetts: Father and Son, Proprietors of the* New York Herald (Indianapolis: Bobbs-Merrill, 1928), 62–65.

33. See Charle, *Le Siècle de la presse*, 12–13.

34. On celebrity stories helping to sell newspapers, see Richard Terdiman, *Discourse/Counter-discourse: The Theory and Practice of Symbolic Resistance in Nineteenth-Century France* (Ithaca, NY: Cornell University Press, 1989), 134 n23. Charle, *Le Siècle de la presse*, notes a shift to a "press of personalities" around 1848 in France (103).

35. Hill and Schwartz, *Getting the Picture*, 216.

36. James Keeley, "Newspaper Work: An Address Delivered before the Students in the Course of Journalism at Notre Dame University, November 26, 1912," pamphlet in the library of the Chicago Historical Society, quoted in David Paul Nord, *Communities of Journalism: A History of American Newspapers and Their Readers* (Urbana: University of Illinois Press, 2001), 249. Keeley worked for the *Chicago Tribune*. The French press baron Arthur Meyer similarly observed in 1919 that the press was unable to direct public opinion and could only follow it; quoted in Bellanger, *Histoire générale de la presse française*, 1:ix.

37. Clipping in RBML 4. The actors were Thomas King and John Philip Kemble.

38. In 1825, *Le Constitutionnel,* one of the best-selling Parisian newspapers of the time, had 16,000 subscribers; by 1865, another Paris daily, *Le Petit journal,* was selling more than 250,000 copies a day, a number that had more than doubled fifteen years later. Bellanger, *Histoire générale de la presse française*, 2:18, 24; 3:137.

39. See Simone M. Müller, *Wiring the World: The Social and Cultural Creation of Global Telegraph Networks* (New York: Columbia University Press, 2016); Pierre Frédérix, *Un Siècle de chasse aux nouvelles: De l'agence d'information Havas à l'agence France-Presse, 1835–1957* (Paris: Flammarion, 1959); and M. Michaela Hampf and Simone Müller-Pohl, eds., *Global Communication Electric: Business, News, and Politics in the World of Telegraphy* (Frankfurt: Campus Verlag, 2013), 8.

40. See itinerary in a scrapbook devoted to the 1889–90 Booth-Modjeska tour, in the Hampden-Booth Theatre Library, New York. During one 1887–88 tour, Booth appeared in seventy-two different towns; see McArthur, *Actors and American Culture*, 62. Strolling players had traveled across Europe long before the advent of rail travel, but not in the large numbers or at the high speeds enabled by nineteenth-century industrial technologies. McArthur notes that in 1840 there were fewer than 3,000 miles of railroad, compared to 30,000 in 1860 and 129,000 in 1885 (9–10). By 1904, there were 420 US companies touring the nation (10); evidence from scrapbooks points to a steady influx of foreign performers annually as well. For further discussion of the existence of a national star system and entertainment circuit in the late nineteenth-century US, see Andrew L. Erdman, *Blue Vaudeville: Sex, Morals, and the Mass Marketing of Amusement, 1895–1915* (Jefferson, NC: McFarland, 2004), 7, and David Mayer, *Stagestruck Filmmaker: D. W. Griffith and the American Theatre* (Iowa City: University of Iowa Press, 2009), 31–35, which also notes that some regional rail routes were even named for the theater companies that regularly used them (46).

41. Although it has become less prevalent to argue that Hollywood invented the star system, many still influential works argued that stars did not exist before cinema. See, for example, Edgar Morin, *Les Stars* (Paris: Seuil, 1957), 6, and Richard deCordova, *Picture Personalities: The Emergence of the Star System in America* (Urbana: University of Illinois Press 1990). Dyer, in *Stars*, focuses on Hollywood icons and argues that film techniques such as the close-up created stars (16), although he also acknowledges, in passing, that stars originated in the theater (102).

42. Quoted in Eleanor Gordon and Gwyneth Nair, *Murder and Morality in Victorian Britain: The Story of Madeleine Smith* (Manchester: Manchester University Press, 2009), 90. For a set of essays that makes the case for celebrity existing in the theater long before the invention of cinema, see Mary Luckhurst and Jane Moody, eds., *Theatre and Celebrity in Britain, 1660–2000* (Basingstoke: Palgrave Macmillan, 2005).

43. For statistics on theater attendance, ticket prices, and numbers of theaters in London, New York, Philadelphia, Chicago, and Paris, see Tracy C. Davis, "The Sociable Playwright and Representative Citizen," in *Women and Playwriting in Nineteenth-Century Britain*, ed. Tracy C. Davis and Ellen Donkin (Cambridge: Cambridge

University Press, 1999), 19, and *The Economics of the British Stage, 1800–1914* (Cambridge: Cambridge University Press, 2000); Thomas Postlewait, "George Edwardes and Musical Comedy," in *The Performing Century: Nineteenth-Century Theatre's History*, ed. Tracy C. Davis and Peter Holland (Basingstoke: Palgrave Macmillan, 2007), 98; Michael R. Booth, "The Social and Literary Context," in *The* Revels *History of Drama in English*, vol. 6, *1750–1880* (London: Methuen, 1975), 20; clippings with theater statistics in RBML 1.6; Patsy Stoneman, *Jane Eyre on Stage, 1848–1898* (Aldershot: Ashgate, 2007), 3; Bruce McConachie, *Melodramatic Formations: American Theatre and Society, 1820–1870* (Iowa City: University of Iowa Press, 1992), 256; Michel Autrand, *Le Théâtre en France de 1870 à 1914* (Paris: Honoré Champion, 2006), 15–16; Anne-Simone Dufief, *Le Théâtre au XIXᵉ siècle* (Paris: Bréat, 2001), 61; Catherine Naugrette-Christophe, *Paris sous le second empire: Le théâtre et la ville* (Paris: Librairie théâtrale, 1998); Lenard Berlanstein, *Daughters of Eve: A Cultural History of French Theater Women from the Old Regime to the Fin de Siècle* (Cambridge, MA: Harvard University Press, 2001); and Anne Martin-Fugier, *La Vie elégante, ou, la formation du Tout-Paris, 1815–1848* (Paris: Fayard, 1990), 308–314.

44. On international performance networks in the nineteenth century, see Sharon Marcus, "The Theater of Comparative Literature," *A Companion to Comparative Literature*, ed. Ali Behdad and Dominic Thomas (Chichester, UK: John Wiley & Sons, 2011), 136–54, and the essays in *Nineteenth Century Theatre and Film* 41, no. 2 (Winter 2014), a special issue coedited by Katherine Biers and Sharon Marcus. On the early internationalism of the US stage, see Elizabeth Maddock Dillon, *New World Drama: The Performative Commons in the Atlantic World, 1649–1849* (Durham, NC: Duke University Press, 2014), 20.

45. On D. W. Griffith's early and ongoing engagement with theater, see Mayer, *Stagestruck Filmmaker.*

46. See Emily Carman, *Independent Stardom: Freelance Women in the Hollywood Studio System* (Austin: University of Texas Press, 2016). On film directors as celebrities, see Eric Smoodin, *Regarding Frank Capra: Audience, Celebrity, and American Film Studies, 1930–1960* (Durham, NC: Duke University Press, 2004).

47. On the restrictiveness of film studio contracts, see Arthur Nolletti Jr., "Classical Hollywood, 1928–1946," in *Acting*, ed. Claudia Springer and Julie Levinson (New Brunswick, NJ: Rutgers University Press, 2015), 53. See also Emily Carman's discussion of what she terms "dependent stardom," *Independent Stardom*, 19.

48. Leo Lowenthal, "The Triumph of Mass Idols," in *Literature, Popular Culture, and Society* (1994; repr., Palo Alto: Pacific Books, 1968).

49. One Bernhardt obituary remarked, "It is doubtful if even Charlie Chaplin or Mary Pickford has won wider renown than Mme. Sarah Bernhardt did." "Sarah Bernhardt," March 27, 1923, otherwise unidentified clipping in HTC, SB Box 3 of 3, "Mounted Clippings." A 1906 poll in the newspaper *Le Petit parisien* ranked Bernhardt sixth in a list of the most illustrious French people of the nineteenth century (cited in Berlanstein, *Daughters of Eve*, 236). Writing in 1931, author Rebecca West remarked on Bernhardt's ubiquity: "She played everywhere. Practically everybody I know who is older than myself saw her several times, practically everybody I know who is of my generation saw her at least once. I saw her four times before I was sixteen, and I lived in Edinburgh." Rebecca West, "The Hardy Fleur-de-Lis," in *Ending in Earnest: A Literary Log* (1931; repr., Freeport, NY: Books for Libraries Press, 1967), 28.

50. Bernhardt to *Le Figaro*, 1878, quoted in Louis Verneuil, *La Vie merveilleuse de Sarah Bernhardt* (Paris: Brentano's, 1942), 120.

51. Reported in *La Presse*, April 24, 1879. The journal she sought to sue was *Le Molière*. Other celebrities similarly made sure that their views received a public hearing even

when in conflict with those of journalists, editors, and publishers. In 1866, after the Cracow newspaper *Time* accused actress Helena Modjeska of disrespecting theater-goers by delaying a premiere, she insisted that they publish a letter in which she defended her actions and announced, "Let the public judge." Modjeska letter quoted in Beth Holmgren, *Starring Madame Modjeska: On Tour in Poland and America* (Bloomington: Indiana University Press, 2012), 51.

52. An early adaptor of new media, Bernhardt also made many successful recordings and films, most of them now lost. On Bernhardt's film career, and her careful direction of it, modeled on her experience as director and manager of her own theaters, see Victoria Duckett, *Seeing Sarah Bernhardt: Performance and Silent Film* (Urbana: University of Illinois Press, 2015), esp. 11, 191. Though Duckett's book offers a much-needed corrective to the tendency to neglect Bernhardt's considerable film career, I do not agree with her claim that only with film was it possible for theatrical stars to attain global celebrity; Bernhardt and other theatrical stars achieved world fame well before the advent of film.

53. An analysis of Gale's UK newspaper database shows that during Bernhardt's lifetime, and in the years immediately following her death, British newspapers ran twice as many articles about her as about Charles Dickens during a comparable period in his career and early afterlife.

54. Though these albums are now relatively rare, significant collections exist in several libraries, including the Theater Research Institute of the Ohio State University Libraries; the Museum of the City of New York; the Harvard Theatre Collection at the Houghton Library; and Columbia University's Rare Books and Manuscripts Library.

CHAPTER ONE. DEFIANCE

1. A more complex version of the cultural ideals argument is that celebrities reinforce ideologies by helping to resolve their contradictions. For example, Marilyn Monroe helped people living in 1950s America to reconcile conflicting views of female sexuality by presenting herself as simultaneously innocent and seductive. See Richard Dyer, *Stars* (1979; repr., London: British Film Institute, 1998), 26. Three recent books focus on female celebrities who defy norms, but attend more closely to the opprobrium their defiance has received from some quarters than to the approval that these figures have garnered, as evidenced by their celebrity status. See Russell Meeuf, *Rebellious Bodies: Stardom, Citizenship, and the New Body Politics* (Austin: University of Texas Press, 2017), which argues that stars with nonnormative bodies reinforce dominant neoliberal beliefs about self-improvement (10); Sady Doyle, *Trainwreck: The Women We Love to Hate, Mock, and Fear . . . and Why* (Brooklyn: Melville House, 2016); and Anne Helen Petersen, *Too Fat, Too Slutty, Too Loud: The Rise and Reign of the Unruly Woman* (New York: Plume, 2017), which presents evidence that the media dislikes unruly women far more than the public does, a divergence that this chapter explicitly addresses. Cheryl Wanko dates the appeal of the anomalous celebrity to the eighteenth century; see *Roles of Authority: Thespian Biography and Celebrity in Eighteenth-Century Britain* (Lubbock: Texas Tech University Press, 2003), 14–15.

2. Leo Braudy, *The Frenzy of Renown: Fame and Its History* (New York: Vintage Books, 1986), 6–7, 388, 400, 417. Some scholars point to saints as even earlier examples of figures who gained widespread renown, albeit after their deaths, for ostentatiously departing from worldly norms. See Thomas Heffernan, *Sacred Biography: Saints and Their Biographers in the Middle Ages* (Oxford: Oxford University Press, 1992), who

notes that the tendency to reward saints for their "aura of otherness" (127) faded after the Council of Nicaea made Christianity the state religion.

3. Maureen Cleave, "How Does a Beatle Live? John Lennon Lives Like This," *London Evening Standard*, March 4, 1966; "Madonna Fights Back: Inside *Rolling Stone*'s New Issue," *Rolling Stone*, February 25, 2015, https://www.rollingstone.com/music/news/madonna-fights-back-inside-rolling-stones-new-issue-20150225.

4. On James Dean's eccentricity and nonconformity, and the allure that his "rejection of social convention" had for the public, see Michael DeAngelis, *Gay Fandom and Crossover Stardom: James Dean, Mel Gibson, and Keanu Reeves* (Durham, NC: Duke University Press, 2001), 73–79.

5. Wikipedia, s.v. "Madonna on Late Show with David Letterman in 1994," last modified April 9, 2018, https://en.wikipedia.org/wiki/Madonna_on_Late_Show_with_David_Letterman_in_1994. Alina Simone, in *Madonnaland and Other Detours into Fame and Fandom* (Austin: University of Texas Press, 2016), offers several other examples of how Madonna defied norms of feminine beauty and decorum at various points in her career, despite also coming to embody a very conventional form of feminine glamor (23–25).

6. "Symbol of defiance": Thomas Hauser, *The Lost Legacy of Muhammad Ali* (Wilmington, DE: SPORTClassic Books, 2005), quoted in Robert Lipsyte, "Muhammad Ali Dies at 74: Titan of Boxing and the 20th Century," *New York Times*, June 4, 2016, https://www.nytimes.com/2016/06/04/sports/muhammad-ali-dies.html. See also David Remnick, "The Outsized Life of Muhammad Ali," *New Yorker*, June 4, 2016, http://www.newyorker.com/news/news-desk/the-outsized-life-of-muhammad-ali.

7. Lipsyte, "Muhammad Ali Dies at 74."

8. Quoted in Simone, *Madonnaland*, 23.

9. Erving Goffman, *Asylums: Essays on the Condition of the Social Situation of Mental Patients and Other Inmates* (New York: Anchor Books, 1961), 305, 304.

10. Ibid., 320, emphasis in original.

11. Roland Barthes, *What Is Sport?* trans. Richard Howard (New Haven, CT: Yale University Press, 2007), 53.

12. "Sarah Sees a Prize Fight," *Boston Herald*, April 28, 1891, clipping in Harvard Theatre Collection at Houghton Library, Harvard University (hereafter HTC), Sarah Bernhardt (hereafter SB) Box 3, Obits Folder.

13. Ibid.

14. Hollis Alpert, "It's Dean, Dean, Dean," *Saturday Review*, October 13, 1956, 28–29, quoted in DeAngelis, *Gay Fandom and Crossover Stardom*, 94.

15. Janice Shapiro, "Crushable: John Lennon," in *Crush: Writers Reflect on Love, Longing, and the Lasting Power of Their First Celebrity Crush*, ed. Cathy Alter and Dave Singleton (New York: HarperCollins, 2016), 63. Shapiro cites the Lennon quote without identifying a source; the same quote is attributed to Lennon in Robert Andrews, *The Columbia Dictionary of Quotations* (New York: Columbia University Press, 1993), 515, who cites a *Playboy* interview of September 1980, but the quote is not present in that interview.

16. On Donald Trump as someone who compellingly presented himself on TV as "an outsider and a rule-breaker," and on the dangers of translating that persona into the presidency, see Susan Murray, "Trump's 'Fake News Awards' and the Danger of a Reality TV Presidency," *Newsweek*, January 16, 2018, http://www.newsweek.com/trump-fake-news-awards-danger-reality-tv-presidency-782586.

17. "Approved attributes and their relation to face make of every man his own jailer; this is a fundamental social constraint." Erving Goffman, *Interaction Ritual: Essays on Face-to-Face Behavior* (New York: Anchor Books, 1967), 10.

18. "Harlequin," *Boston Home Journal*, February 28, 1891, in HTC, SB Box 2, 1890s Clippings.

19. Lloyd Charles Sanders, *Celebrities of the Century: Being a Dictionary of Men and Women of the Nineteenth Century* (London: Cassell, 1890), 779. Henry James, "Coquelin," in *The Scenic Art: Notes on Acting and the Drama: 1872–1901* (New Brunswick, NJ: Rutgers University Press, 1948), 206.

20. R. S. Hichens, *The Green Carnation* (1894; repr., New York: Mitchell Kennerley, n.d.), 124, 194.

21. *The Queen*, July 14, 1883, from an article about Wilde's lectures on America in England, in William Andrews Clark Memorial Library, University of California, Los Angeles, Wildeiana Box 10.17A.

22. E. H. Mikhail, ed., *Oscar Wilde: Interviews and Recollections*, vol. 1 (London: Macmillan Press, 1979), 212.

23. Western Reserve Historical Society, Cleveland, Harradence Diary, entry for May 7, 1895. Harradence, a diarist whose first name is not known, also pointed out the agency that Wilde exercised in relation to the press, and vice versa, noting that Wilde was well known for dismissing newspaper criticism, "and such a remark is never forgotten or forgiven." Harradence described Wilde's conviction as the result of a "trial by newspaper."

24. Henry James, "George Sand," in *French Poets and Novelists* (London: Macmillan, 1893), 158.

25. See Jerome Christensen, *Lord Byron's Strength: Romantic Writing and Commercial Society* (Baltimore: Johns Hopkins University Press, 1993); Tom Mole, *Byron's Romantic Celebrity: Industrial Culture and the Hermeneutic of Intimacy* (London: Palgrave Macmillan, 2007); and Clara Tuite, *Lord Byron and Scandalous Celebrity* (Cambridge: Cambridge University Press, 2014), which focuses on how Byron's "effrontery, transgression, and impiety" (xxii) made him one of the first figures to unite fame and notoriety (xv).

26. William Hazlitt, "Lord Byron," in *The Spirit of the Age* (1825; repr., New York: Dolphin Books, n.d.), 88–90, 96.

27. Cited in Christensen, *Lord Byron's Strength*, 89.

28. Ralph Waldo Emerson, "Self-Reliance," in *Ralph Waldo Emerson: Essays and Lectures* (New York: The Library of America, 1983), 261; John Stuart Mill, *On Liberty*, ed. Currin V. Shields (Indianapolis: Bobbs-Merrill Company, 1956), 7.

29. On Wellington, see Peter W. Sinnema, *The Wake of Wellington: Englishness in 1852* (Athens: Ohio University Press, 2006). On Queen Victoria, see Margaret Homans, *Royal Representations: Queen Victoria and British Culture, 1837–1876* (Chicago: University of Chicago Press, 1998). On Lind and Barnum, see Neil Harris, *Humbug: The Art of P. T. Barnum* (Chicago: University of Chicago Press, 1981), 115–116, 120, 139.

30. The press varied in how it described Bernhardt's religious affiliations, but tended to mention both her Christian and Jewish background. In one typical example, *The Pall Mall Gazette* wrote: "Sarah Bernhardt . . . declares herself a Jewess, and refuses to acknowledge the force of the baptismal vows taken in her name." "Letter from Paris," December 19, 1873.

31. *Le Figaro*, May 11, 1864, reporting on Bernhardt's conflict with the manager of the Théâtre du Gymnase. Mary Louise Roberts discusses Bernhardt's defiance in the context of changing notions of womanhood in France in *Disruptive Acts: The New Woman in Fin-de-Siècle France* (Chicago: University of Chicago Press, 2002), 165–219.

32. Edward John Hart, "Illustrated Interviews. No. XL—Sarah Bernhardt," *Strand Magazine*, January 1895: 526–36.

33. Isaac Reed Jr., *Too Thin, or Skeleton Sara* (New York: Evans & Kelly, 1880).

34. "Big dolls," etc.: Henry L. Williams, *All About Sarah "Barnum" Bernhardt, Her Loveys, Her Doveys, Her Capers, and Her Funniments* (London: International Publishing Offices, 1884). For the joke about Bernhardt being flat-chested, see *La Presse*, April 22, 1880. Historian Lenard Berlanstein has shown that between the 1850s and the 1880s, French journalists began increasingly to judge actresses in print on the basis of their sexual attractiveness to men, usually measured by how ample their busts and hips were. *Daughters of Eve: A Cultural History of French Theater Women from the Old Regime to the Fin de Siècle* (Cambridge, MA: Harvard University Press, 2001), 25, 212.

35. *Le Figaro*, March 6, 1876. See also *Le Temps*, August 1, 1870; commenting on Jeanne, the author wrote, "Il est impossible de rêver une blonde plus jolie," and described her as "une figure de Keepsake," while nonetheless chastising her for excessive "décolletage" in the outfit she wore to receive a prize at the Conservatoire. Even the most appealing actresses were not safe from constant policing of their appearance. Here and below, unless otherwise noted, all translations from the French are my own.

36. *Sarah Bernhardt: Paris Sketches* (Boston: Moore, ca. 1880). HTC, FL 398.7.25.

37. "The Seductive Sarah." See also the anonymous *Illustrated Life of Sarah Bernhardt* (New York: A. J. Fisher, 1880), which commented that Bernhardt, "instead of concealing her lack of *embonpoint*, greatly exaggerates it by her mode of dressing" (12).

38. On Streisand's defiant persona, which included emphasizing her overt independence and presenting herself as beautiful, fashionable, and desirable despite features most agreed were homely and excessively Jewish, see Neal Gabler, *Barbra Streisand: Redefining Beauty, Femininity, and Power* (New Haven, CT: Yale University Press, 2016), 6, 36, 47, 159. Gabler describes Streisand as a "self-willed creation" (41) and a "smasher of conventions" (145) as well as an auteur (125)—yet another instance of defiance as a central aspect of a celebrity's appeal, especially in the early stages of the ascent to stardom.

39. "Her blithe willingness to disrobe without shame caused an outburst of censure from viewers." Rebecca Mead, "Downtown's Daughter," *New Yorker*, November 15, 2010, https://www.newyorker.com/magazine/2010/11/15/downtowns-daughter.

40. Simon Hattenstone, "Lena Dunham: 'People Called Me Fat and Hideous, and I Lived,'" *The Guardian*, January 11, 2014, https://www.theguardian.com/culture/2014/jan/11/lena-dunham-called-fat-hideous-and-i-lived. See also Petersen, *Too Fat*, 212, 218–19.

41. Quote in Jules Lemaître, "Sarah Bernhardt racontée par elle-même," *Revue encyclopédique*, December 15, 1893: "Il ne pouvait se douter alors que ma maigreur engraisserait les journalistes."

42. *Le Figaro*, May 7, 1874.

43. "Sarah's Future," *Funny Folks*, May 8, 1880.

44. Circulation figures for *Le Figaro* quoted in an 1876 diary entry in Edward L. Blanchard, *The Life and Reminiscences of E. L. Blanchard* (London: Hutchinson, 1891). See also Patrick Eveno, *L'Argent de la presse française des années 1820 à nos jours* (Paris: Éditions du CTHS, 2003), which describes the paper as directed at a relatively affluent readership and priced on the high side, at 15 centimes an issue (until 1911, when the price dropped to 10 centimes) (31). The highest-circulation newspaper of the 1870s was *Le Petit journal*, at 800,000 in 1880. Its coverage of Bernhardt in the 1870s was mostly limited to relatively terse theater reviews.

45. *Le Figaro*, January 21, 1876.

46. Riffing on a comment originally made by Barbey d'Aurevilly about someone else, one journalist wrote that Bernhardt's knees resembled "two little death's heads." *Le Figaro*, January 19, 1869.

47. This joke, along with several others, appears in "Sarah Bernhardt," *Fishing Gazette*, August 21, 1880.

48. Hatpin joke: *Le Figaro*, May 19, 1878; room joke: *Le Figaro*, May 11, 1874.

49. "A 'Bony' Contention," *Funny Folks*, August 16, 1879.

50. *Le Figaro*, March 7, 1873.

51. *Le Figaro*, October 19, 1880. The same anecdote was also recounted in the "Things Theatrical" column of the *Hampshire Telegraph and Sussex Chronicle*, December 8, 1880, which qualified the bread thrown as a "2 lb. loaf."

52. "Echos de Paris" column, *Le Figaro*, May 6, 1870.

53. *Le Figaro*, November 18, 1874. For another example, see *Le Figaro*, February 18, 1873.

54. On Bernhardt's intense popularity, see Claude Berton, "La Grande Sarah," *La Revue mondiale*, April 15, 1923.

55. The reference to Bernhardt as "rebellious" comes from *La Presse*, April 15, 1874. The figure of 2,300 meters comes from Bernhardt, *Dans les nuages: Impressions d'une chaise* (Paris: G. Charpentier, 1878), 33.

56. "Self-willed": "Our Extra-Special on the Comedie Francaise [*sic*]," *Fun*, June 25, 1879.

57. Margaret Cohen, *The Novel and the Sea* (Princeton, NJ: Princeton University Press, 2010), 11.

58. Victor Hugo quoted in Nigel Gosling, *Nadar* (New York: Knopf, 1976), 16. On scientists and ballooning, see Jennifer Tucker, *Nature Exposed: Photography as Eyewitness in Victorian Science* (Baltimore: Johns Hopkins University Press, 2005), 24–25, and "Voyages of Discovery on Oceans of Air: Scientific Observation and the Image of Science in the Age of 'Balloonacy,'" *Osiris*, 2nd ser., 11, Science in the Field (1996). In "Voyages," Tucker points out that ballooning in nineteenth-century England had strong associations with sensational entertainment, and that scientists were only partially successful in making it compatible with objective data gathering (148); she also notes that ballooning, to the British, sometimes symbolized "social and political defiance" (146) and was lively entertainment (166). In France, where citizens had used balloons to escape or circumvent the Prussians during an 1870 war, ballooning more strongly evoked political liberty.

59. See n. 55.

60. "Courrier de Paris," *La Presse*, July 4, 1879.

61. For references to Bernhardt as a fugitive and runaway, see "La Fuite de Mlle Bernhardt," *Le Figaro*, April 21, 1880, and *La Presse*, April 22, 1880. For a three-column report on the "Voyage Triomphal de Mlle Sarah Bernhardt en Hollande," see *La Presse*, April 1, 1880. For a front-page story about her 1880 London performance of *Adrienne Lecouvreur*, see *La Presse*, May 28, 1880.

62. "Desire for liberty": Henry Lapauze, "Étude biographique: Madame Sarah Bernhardt," *Revue encylopédique*, December 15, 1893. "Outlaw": "Will Mlle Sarah Bernhardt put herself in a state of rebellion against the comité and the minister?" asked *La Presse*, February 2, 1880.

63. The fullest account of the event can be found in an article by Jules Prével in *Le Figaro*, August 26, 1880.

64. "Sensational accounts": "Greeting Mlle. Bernhardt," clipping in HTC, SB Box 2, 1880s Clippings, no other identifying information. Poem: "Our Weekly One," *Judy*, September 8, 1880.

65. "Une nouvelle Jeanne d'Arc," *La Presse*, August 26, 1880.

66. *Le Globe*, September 30, 1880.

67. Ada Patterson, "Sarah Bernhardt—Superwoman," clipping in HTC, SB Box 3, unlabeled folder. "My life": "A Great French Actress. Daily Life of Sarah Bernhardt," *New York Times*, January 12, 1878, in HTC, 1870s Clippings.

68. Jules Huret, *Sarah Bernhardt*, trans. G A. Raper (London: Chapman & Hall, 1899), 62, 3.

69. See, for example, Georges d'Heyli [Antoine Edmond Poinsot], *La Comédie-Française à Londres (1871–1879). Journal inédit de E. Got—Journal de F. Sarcey* (Paris: Ollendorf, 1880), lxxvii.

70. Quoted in Patricia Marks, *Sarah Bernhardt's First Theatrical Tour* (Jefferson, NC: McFarland, 2003), 32.

71. James, *The Scenic Art*, 128–29.

72. "Amusements Dramatic. Bernhardt's Return," *Inter Ocean*, October 4, 1891, in HTC, SB Box 2, 1890s Clippings.

73. "Luxurious criminality": Charles E. L. Wingate, "A New Play: Madame Bernhardt and Her Latest Role," 1892, in HTC, SB Box 2, Clippings-Misc.

74. "Two Plays," *Boston Daily Globe*, January 21, 1906.

75. "Bernhardt Appears in Gismonda," *Chicago Daily Tribune*, June 2, 1895.

76. A clipping in the Jerome Lawrence and Robert E. Lee Theatre Research Institute of the Ohio State University Libraries Scrapbook Collection (hereafter TRI) #21a mentions a hatpin as the weapon of choice; an article on "Bernhardt in 'Ashes,' " in *Evening World*, December 7, 1916, described the weapon as a needle and mentioned the kimono costume.

77. Many of the newspaper stories about Bernhardt published in the 1870s and 1870s mentioned her pets, her sculpting practice, and the coffin. For a newspaper item about the skull on Bernhardt's night table, see *Le Figaro*, January 10, 1873, which also mentioned the satin-lined coffin. For the skeleton, see *Le Figaro*, June 15, 1878.

78. On the ways that the press identified Rachel with male figures, see Rachel M. Brownstein, *Tragic Muse: Rachel of the Comédie-Française* (New York: Knopf, 1993), 23, 58, 87.

79. See Étienne Ganderax, "Sarah Bernhardt et la Comédie-Française," *La Revue de Paris*, June 1, 1930.

80. "Variorum Notes," *The Examiner*, June 10, 1876.

81. Julie de Mortemar, "A Queen of Diamonds," in *Folly's Queens; or, Women Whose Loves Have Ruled the World: Life Sketches of the Most Famous Belles of Cupid's Court for Two Centuries* (New York: Richard K. Fox, 1882), 35.

82. Preface to Jules Huret, *Sarah Bernhardt*, vi.

83. "The Seductive Sarah," *Boston Daily*, October 31, 1880.

84. "Sarah Bernhardt Indignant," December 1880, HTC, SB Box 3, unlabeled folder.

85. An 1875 photograph of Bernhardt and Abbéma with their friends, captioned an "intimate get-together," was reproduced in a 1923 theater magazine soon after Bernhardt's death and carefully preserved in a 1920s scrapbook, TRI #21a. For groundbreaking scholarship on the visual documentation of Bernhardt's relationship with Abbéma, see Carol Ockman and Kenneth E. Silver, *Sarah Bernhardt: The Art of High Drama* (New Haven, CT: Yale University Press, published in association with the Jewish Museum, New York, 2005).

86. "M. Damalas [*sic*] has bought a piece of ground adjoining my hotel . . . on which to build an hotel for himself, with door of communication. It is not true that this ground is for a studio for me, as I have two already." "Sarah Bernhardt and Daria in Brussels," *The Era*, May 20, 1882.

87. Jules Huret described marriage as "la seule excentricité qui manquât à la collection de Sarah." *Sarah Bernhardt* (Paris: F. Juven, 1899), 60. "Paris Gossip" remarked that Bernhardt had "added to her reputation for eccentricity" by marrying Damala, *Globe*, April 6, 1882, clipping in Theatre and Performance Collections, Victoria and Albert Museum (hereafter V&A), SB Personal, Box 7. A clipping with no identifying information similarly commented, "The eccentricities of Miss Sarah Bernhardt have

long been the tale of two continents, but she has hardly ever appeared more eccentric than in the marriage in which she took the leading part yesterday in London." V&A, SB Personal, Box 7.

88. "Letter," *London Era*, December 15, 1880, in HTC, SB Box 2, 1880s Clippings.

89. Ganderax, "Sarah Bernhardt et la Comédie-Française."

90. John Gielgud, *Early Stages* (New York: Macmillan, 1939), 82.

91. On Bernhardt's management of her theaters, see Henry Bauer, "Sarah Bernhardt," *L'Echo de Paris*, 1896, clipping in Bibliothèque nationale de France, Département des Arts du spectacle, Fol-Ico-Per, SB; May Agate, *Madame Sarah* (London: Home and Van Thal, 1946), 116, 126–28; and Noëlle Guibert, *Portrait(s) de Sarah Bernhardt* (Paris: Bibliothèque nationale de France, 2000), 41.

92. On Monroe's production company, which she named Marilyn Monroe Productions and in which she retained a 51 percent controlling interest, see Lois Banner, *MM – Personal: From the Private Archive of Marilyn Monroe* (New York: Abrams, 2011), 41–46. On Brown and the creative and commercial control and resulting profits that accrued to him after he acquired ownership over the master tapes, see Philip Gourevitch, "Mr. Brown," *New Yorker*, July 29, 2002, https://www.newyorker.com/magazine/2002/07/29/mr-brown.

93. "Flagrant": "The Scene at Booth's," *New York Herald*, November 10, 1880, in HTC, SB Box 2, 1880s Clippings; "commonplace," "Bernhardt, France's 'Greatest Missionary,'" *Literary Digest*, April 14, 1923; "unexpected things": *New York Times*, 1879, in HTC, SB Box 2, 1870s Clippings.

94. "Fortunes of the Famous: Instances of Unstable Glory," *New York Times*, July 15, 1879.

95. On Bernhardt, Napoleon, and Ulysses S. Grant, see Clement Scott, "The Playhouses," June 18, 1892, in HTC, SB Clippings-Misc.

96. "The Unconventional Sarah: Why She Was the World's Great Bohemian," *Daily Sketch*, March 28, 1923; "flavorsome individuality": "Sarah Bernhardt," *London Times*, March 27, 1923.

97. Lawrence Vassault, "Sarah Bernhardt," *The Cosmopolitan*, April 1901.

98. "Sui generis": "Amusements Dramatic. Bernhardt," *Inter Ocean*, May 1, 1887, in HTC, SB Box 2, 1890s Clippings.

99. Agate, *Madame Sarah*, 183–84.

100. See Gerald J. Baldasty, *The Commercialization of News in the Nineteenth Century* (Madison: University of Wisconsin Press, 1992), 37–38, 123–24. On the commercialization of the news in France, see Eveno, *L'Argent de la presse française*.

101. Zola article in *Le Messager de l'Europe*, quoted in Eveno, *L'Argent de la presse française*, 12; on promotional contests, see ibid., 47.

102. Charles A. Dana, *The Art of Newspaper Making* (New York: D. Appleton, 1895), 20, 11, 12.

103. All quotes from *Le Figaro*, August 17, 1878.

104. Chas Danner. "Muhammad Ali's Life in Poetry, Activism, and Trash Talk," *Daily Intelligencer* (blog), *New York*, June 4, 2016, http://nymag.com/daily/intelligencer/2016/06/muhammad-alis-poetry-activism-and-trash-talk.html. Only three of forty-six journalists predicted that Ali would defeat Liston. After beating George Forman in Zaire, Ali similarly "leaned down to reporters and said, 'What did I tell you?'" Lipsyte, "Muhammad Ali Dies at 74."

105. Banner, *MM – Personal*, 63, 40.

106. "Marilyn Wins Concessions in Return to 20th," *Variety*, January 5, 1956.

107. For two of many examples, see the references to "prolonged applause" for Bernhardt in *Le Figaro*, June 7, 1877, and to box office receipts in *Le Figaro*, April 16, 1879.

108. John Stokes, "Sarah Bernhardt," in John Stokes, Michael R. Booth, and Susan Bassnett, *Bernhardt, Terry, Duse: The Actress in Her Time* (Cambridge: Cambridge University Press, 1988), 173n38, which describes Bernhardt suing the newspaper *Bonsoir* for attacking the way she managed her theater.

109. "Une lettre de Sarah Bernhardt," *Le Figaro*, April 26, 1880. For other examples of newspapers publishing letters of protest from Bernhardt, see *Le Figaro*, April 23, 1879; *La Presse*, May 27, 1876; and *Le Globe* (Paris), September 13, 1879.

CHAPTER TWO. SENSATION

1. "Stage Stories Retold: Mrs. Sarah Siddons—1755–1831," November 2, 1902; clipping in Rare Book and Manuscript Library, Columbia University (hereafter RBML) 1.1.

2. Elizabeth Butler, *An Autobiography* (London: Constable, 1922), 7. Herzen quoted in Rachel Brownstein, *Tragic Muse: Rachel of the Comédie-Française* (New York: Knopf, 1993), 11.

3. Marie Bashkirtseff, diary entry of January 20, 1876, quoted in Colette Cosnier, *Le Silence des filles: De l'aiguille à la plume* (Paris: Fayard, 2001), 302.

4. William Winter, *Other Days* (New York, 1908), 152–153, quoted in Garff B. Wilson, *A History of American Acting* (Bloomington: Indiana University Press, 1966), 20. Other critics concurred; one wrote of Cushman that "The secret of her attraction is vigor. The masses like vigor." Quoted (with no other identifying information) in William Rounseville Alger, *Life of Edwin Forrest, the American Tragedian* (Philadelphia: J. B. Lippincott, 1877), 2:457.

5. Harriet Beecher Stowe, "Sojourner Truth, the Libyan Sibyl," *The Atlantic*, April 1863.

6. Agnes de Mille, *Dance to the Piper* (1951; repr., New York: New York Review Books, 2015), 48.

7. The commissioner, George H. Chatfield, quoted in "Sinatra Fans Pose Two Police Problems," *New York Times*, October 13, 1944. See also Bosley Crowther, "Lower and Lower," a review of a Frank Sinatra film in the *New York Times*, January 22, 1944, which reported on how the star's "cultists" reacted when he appeared on the screen, and John K. Hutchens, "Visit to the Shrine: Notes on an Evening Among Mr. Sinatra's Admirers at the Saturday 'Hit Parade,'" *New York Times*, November 7, 1943. Image is from Elaine Cunniffe and Gilbert Millstein, "Frank Sinatra Draws Thousands at Paramount Theatre in 1944," *Daily News*, October 13, 1944, http://www.nydailynews.com/entertainment/sinatra-wows-thousands-paramount-theatre-1944-article-1.2381304.

8. Bob Krauss, "Hipster Hexes Hysterical Hepsters," *Honolulu Advertiser*, November 11, 1957.

9. Later in the piece, Gourevitch notes that Brown's "performances are, and have always been, orchestrated to the most rigorous discipline. . . . His outrageousness was carefully calculated to convey that, while he cannot be contained, he is always in control." "Mr. Brown," *New Yorker*, July 29, 2002, https://www.newyorker.com/magazine/2002/07/29/mr-brown.

10. "Her acting thrills . . ." from "Amusements. Columbia," *Inter Ocean*, April 26, 1887, Sarah Bernhardt (hereafter SB) Clippings-Misc., Harvard Theatre Collection at Houghton Library, Harvard University (hereafter HTC).

11. Charles E. L. Wingate, "Mme Bernhardt: Her Reappearance in Boston as Theodora," in HTC, SB Clippings, Box 2, Plays P–Z .

12. Quoted in Gourevitch, "Mr. Brown."

13. de Mille, *Dance to the Piper*, 48.

14. Edward John Hart, "Illustrated Interviews. No. XL—Sarah Bernhardt," *Strand Magazine*, January 1895. For an anecdote about Bernhardt triumphing over a Parisian audience, see May Agate, *Madame Sarah* (London: Home and Van Thal, 1946), 96.

15. James O'Donnell Bennett, "Music and the Drama," April 19, 1906, clipping in RBML 1.9.

16. Joseph Roach, *It* (Ann Arbor: University of Michigan Press, 2007), 6, 184. More recently, Julia H. Fawcett has argued that eighteenth-century actors engaged in what she calls "overexpression" to defend against invasions of privacy by the public, which is persuasive for the cases she discusses but cannot account for less aggressive audience members who described feeling happily overpowered by star performances. *Spectacular Disappearances: Celebrity and Privacy, 1696–1801* (Ann Arbor: University of Michigan Press, 2016), 3.

17. In *Claims to Fame: Celebrity in Contemporary America* (Berkeley: University of California Press, 1994), Joshua Gamson argued, based on ethnographic research, that many fans recognize and enjoy analyzing how savvy publicists manufacture celebrity images. For scholars who show how fans actively rewrite the materials handed to them by celebrity culture, see Jackie Stacey, *Star Gazing: Hollywood Cinema and Female Spectatorship* (London: Routledge, 1994), and Henry Jenkins, *Fans, Bloggers, and Gamers: Exploring Participatory Culture* (New York: New York University Press, 2006).

18. Kim Marra, *Strange Duets: Impresarios and Actresses in the American Theatre, 1865–1914* (Iowa City: University of Iowa Press, 2006).

19. Aimee Cliff, "How Rihanna Maintains Control," *Fader*, April 28, 2016, http://www.thefader.com/2016/04/28/rihanna-needed-me-video-nipples-objectification-control.

20. See Benjamin McArthur, *Actors and American Culture, 1880–1920* (Iowa City: University of Iowa Press, 1984), 155, for a list of US actresses who supported feminist causes.

21. See Susan A. Glenn, *Female Spectacle: The Theatrical Roots of Modern Feminism* (Cambridge, MA: Harvard University Press, 2002), and Felicity Nussbaum, *Rival Queens: Actresses, Performance, and the Eighteenth-Century British Theater* (Philadelphia: University of Pennsylvania Press, 2010). For a similar argument about France, albeit one that depends more on figures such as Bernhardt disrupting notions of natural femininity than providing a role model that could be easily emulated, see Mary Louise Roberts, *Disruptive Acts: The New Woman in Fin-de-Siècle France* (Chicago: University of Chicago Press, 2002).

22. For discussions of liberalism that also attend to emotion and character, see Elaine Hadley, *Living Liberalism: Practical Citizenship in Mid-Victorian Britain* (Chicago: University of Chicago Press, 2010), and chapters 5 and 6 of Amanda Anderson, *The Way We Argue Now: A Study in the Cultures of Theory* (Princeton, NJ: Princeton University Press, 2006).

23. Jules Lemaître, "Sarah Bernhardt racontée par elle-même—Opinions," *Revue encyclopédique*, December 15, 1893. On the structural asymmetry between those who play and those who watch as constituting theater, see Denis Guénoun, *Actions et acteurs: Raisons du drame sur scène* (Paris: Belin, 2005), 9. Here and below, unless otherwise noted, all translations from the French are my own.

24. James O'Donnell Bennett, April 18, 1906 review of Bernhardt in *Tosca*, clipping in RBML 1.9.

25. See William B. Worthen, *The Idea of the Actor* (Princeton, NJ: Princeton University Press, 1984), 84, 75–76.

26. See Joseph R. Roach, *The Player's Passion: Studies in the Science of Acting* (Ann Arbor: University of Michigan Press, 1985), and Joseph W. Donohue, *Dramatic Character in the English Romantic Age* (Princeton, NJ: Princeton University Press, 1970).

27. Alexis de Tocqueville, *Democracy in America*, trans. Gerald E. Bevan (London: Penguin, 2003). "See a play": 570, emphasis added; "turn aside": 541.

28. Frederick and Lise-Lone Marker, "Actors and their Repertory," in *The Revels History of Drama in English*, vol. 6, *1750–1880*, ed. Michael R. Booth et al. (London: Methuen, 1975), 117.

29. Jane Moody, *Illegitimate Theatre in London, 1770–1840* (Cambridge: Cambridge University Press, 2000), 211, 216. Until 1843, only two London theaters had the royal patents that allowed them to perform spoken drama; all other theaters were called "unlicensed" or "illegitimate" and required to perform melodramas, a term originally coined to refer to plays that featured music and mime. See also Victor Emeljanow, *Victorian Popular Dramatists* (Boston: Twayne, 1987); Michael R. Booth, *Victorian Spectacular Theatre, 1850–1910* (Boston: Routledge & Kegan Paul, 1981); and Carolyn Williams, "Melodrama," in *The Cambridge History of Victorian Literature*, ed. Kate Flint (Cambridge: Cambridge University Press, 2012), which notes that "audiences experience melodramatic rhythm as periods of suspenseful absorption pierced by intensified moments of shock, terror, or sentiment" (194). Williams also notes the dependence of typical melodramatic acting on the adoption of static, frozen poses; Bernhardt, by contrast, developed a style that was sensational but took a more fluid approach to tempo variation. Actors had no monopoly on sensational presentation techniques. Authors and reformers on the professional lecture circuit also aimed to thrill. See, for example, the account of an 1847 lecture given by US temperance activist Philip S. White, quoted in Geoffrey Sanborn, *Plagiarama!: William Wells Brown and the Aesthetic of Attractions* (New York: Columbia University Press, 2016), 73.

30. For a fuller discussion of how Kean's emotive style differed from Siddons's more controlled one, see Alan S. Downer, "Players and Painted Stage: Nineteenth Century Acting," *PMLA* 61, no. 2 (June 1946), 524–525, 530, 534.

31. Moody, *Illegitimate Theatre in London*, 209. On Kean's effects on audiences, see also Booth et al., *The Revels History of Drama in English*, 123.

32. George Henry Lewes, *On Actors and the Art of Acting* (London: Smith, Elder, 1875), 14–15, 65.

33. Matthew Rebhorn, *Pioneer Performances: Staging the Frontier* (Oxford: Oxford University Press, 2012), 37, 39; "visceral . . .": William Rounseville Alger, *Life of Edwin Forrest, the American Tragedian* (Philadelphia: J. B. Lippincott, 1877), 2:655.

34. Wilson, *A History of American Acting*, 23.

35. Alger, *Life of Edwin Forrest*, 1:23, 1:179.

36. Bruce McConachie, *Melodramatic Formations: American Theatre and Society, 1820–1870* (Iowa City: University of Iowa Press, 1992), 74, 93 (re working-class fans), 85 (re Napoleonic aura), 93 (for Whitman quote), 70 (re enthusiasm).

37. On Salvini, see "At the Play," *Sporting Gazette*, June 7, 1879. On Hill, see 1891 article quoted by J. S. Bratton, ed., *Music Hall: Performance and Style* (Milton Keynes: Open University Press, 1986), 108.

38. Eimelle, "Marie Dorval Kitty Bell Chatterton Vigny Drame Romantique," *Les carnets d'Eimelle*, December 5, 2012, http://lecture-spectacle.blogspot.com/2012/12/marie-dorval-kitty-bell-chatterton.html. Dorval also required that the many other theaters where she later performed the same role include the staircase in their set design.

39. On melodrama and Romanticism in French theater, see Michel Autrand, *Le Théâtre en France de 1870 à 1914* (Paris: Honoré Champion, 2006); Marvin Carlson, *The French Stage in the Nineteenth Century* (Metuchen, NJ: Scarecrow Press, 1972); Jules Guex, *Le Théâtre et la société française de 1815 à 1848* (Geneva: Slatkine Reprints, 1973); and Florence Naugrette, *Le Théâtre romantique: Histoire, écriture, mise en scène* (Paris: Éditions du Seuil, 2001). Rachel infused the classical repertoire with Romantic passion

but did so by using stillness and restrained, measured, and contained gestures rather than fluid, energetic movement; see Brownstein, *Tragic Muse*, 173, 216.

40. On Bernhardt's combination of classical and Romantic aesthetics, see Gerda Taranow, *Sarah Bernhardt: The Art within the Legend* (Princeton, NJ: Princeton University Press, 1972), xiii. Elaine Aston, *Sarah Bernhardt: A French Actress on the English Stage* (Oxford: Berg, 1989), notes that London audiences responded to Bernhardt's "use of a style based on sensibility" (20). See also Eric Salmon, "Introduction," in *Bernhardt and the Theater of Her Time*, ed. Eric Salmon (Westport, CT: Greenwood Press, 1984).

41. Cited in Aston, *Sarah Bernhardt*, 77.

42. "Convulsed": "How Bernhardt Dresses," *San Francisco Examiner*, May 24, 1891; "electric shocks": "Gaiety Theatre—French Plays," *The Times*, July 10, 1883. There are dozens of examples of these and other metaphors describing Bernhardt's forceful effects on theatergoers. For intensity, see "The Scene at Booth's," *New York Herald*, November 10, 1880, HTC, SB Clippings, 1880s, in which a journalist describing Bernhardt's first New York appearance wrote: "She is simply embodied and intelligent intensity," borrowing a word from physics, where "intensity" refers to an amount of energy radiated over space and time. For magnetism, see "My Impressions of Sarah Bernhardt. By Her American Manager," *New York Theater*, October 1915, in HTC, SB Mounted Clippings, Box 3 of 3. For electricity, see clippings in RBML 1.21 and Agate, *Madame Sarah*, 20. A newspaper poem described Bernhardt as "A coal taken fresh from the altar / A living electrical wire." Edmund Albert Lancaster, "All Hail, Bernhardt!" *New York Mirror*, in HTC, SB Clippings: 1890s, Box 2 of 3.

43. Ann Pellegrini documents this analogy in *Performance Anxieties: Staging Psychoanalysis, Staging Race* (New York: Routledge, 1997), 39–41.

44. Lucy Masterman, ed., *Mrs. Gladstone: Her Diaries and Letters* (New York: E. P. Dutton, 1930), 162; "conquering eyes": "Béranger-Sarah Bernhardt-Bertall," *Étude bibliographique* (Paris: A. Laporte, 1884), Bibliothèque nationale de France, Département des Arts du spectacle.

45. E. C. F. Collier, ed., *A Victorian Diarist: Extracts from the Journals of Mary, Lady Monkswell, 1875–1895* (London: John Murray, 1944), entry for May 27, 1880.

46. "Magnetism": "Sara in the New World," ca. 1880, in HTC, SB Clippings-Misc., Box 3 of 3; "you would": Charles E. L. Wingate, "Fedora," 1892, in HTC, SB Clippings-Misc. For one of many other similar quotes about the force of Bernhardt's personality onstage, see "Madame Sarah Bernhardt. 'L'Aiglon' at The Coliseum," *Daily Telegraph*, September 20, 1910, SB Personal, Box 8, Theatre and Performance Collections, Victoria and Albert Museum (V&A).

47. George Bernard Shaw, "Sardoodledom," *Saturday Review*, June 1, 1895.

48. George Bernard Shaw, "Duse and Bernhardt," *Dramatic Opinions and Essays*, vol. 1 (1895; repr., New York: Brentano's, 1909), 137, 136.

49. Lytton Strachey, "Sarah Bernhardt," *Nation and Athenaeum*, May 5, 1923, 152–153, in HTC, SB Mounted Clippings-Scrapbook.

50. Arthur Symons, "Drama. Sarah Bernhardt," *The Academy*, June 21, 1902. For a similar quote, see "Gaiety Theatre—French Plays," *The Times*, July 10, 1883: "her voice . . . thrills the nerves and fibres of the system to their center."

51. On the nineteenth-century perception of electricity as a "mysterious agency," see Menahem Blondheim, *News over the Wires: The Telegraph and the Flow of Public Information in America, 1844–1897* (Cambridge, MA: Harvard University Press, 1994), 31.

52. See Laura Otis, *Networking: Communicating with Bodies and Machines in the Nineteenth Century* (Ann Arbor: University of Michigan Press, 2011), and Brenton J. Malin, *Feeling Mediated: A History of Media Technology and Emotion in America* (New

York: New York University Press, 2014), 35, 49. On the history of the term *nervous* and its relationship to nineteenth-century theatrical audiences and performers, see Matthew Wilson Smith, *The Nervous Stage: Nineteenth-Century Neuroscience and the Birth of Modern Theater* (New York: Oxford University Press, 2018). I agree with Smith that many nineteenth-century writers thought that the theater could act directly on the nerves of theatergoers. However, my actor-, audience-, and reviewer-focused account diverges from Smith's playwright- and scientist-focused one in a few respects: I found no evidence that references to nerves replaced references to gestures (as Smith argues, 10); rather, theater reviewers presented gestures as creating the charged sensations that interest Smith. Nor did sensation uniformly serve to link audience members with one another or with actors in a relatively egalitarian community; the many examples I cite in this chapter show that charges traveling from actor to audience members could create a hierarchy. Finally, Smith sees the neural subject as replacing an autonomous one (48), but many reviewers perceived Bernhardt as simultaneously autonomous *and* working on their sensations.

53. Chauncy Hare Townshend, *Facts in Mesmerism, with Reasons for a Dispassionate Inquiry into It* (New York: Harper, 1843), 138.
54. On Rachel's self-oblivion, see Russian critic Pavel Annenkov writing about Rachel's performance in *Horace* in Saint Petersburg in 1853–54, quoted in Brownstein, *Tragic Muse*, 121. Annenkov described feeling shattered by Rachel's portrayal of despair (122).
55. Henry James, "The Théâtre Français," in *The Scenic Art*, 91. On Bernhardt acting with her entire body, see also Aston, *Sarah Bernhardt*, 21–22, 24–25, 27–28; and Agate, *Madame Sarah*, 51.
56. "Easy control…": William & Daniel Downey, *The Cabinet Portrait Gallery*, First Series (London: Cassell, 1890), 4; "every organ.…": "'Adrienne Lecouvreur' at Booth's Theatre," *New York Herald*, November 9, 1880; despite this praise, however, the reviewer found Bernhardt's performance to fall short of genius. Theater historian John Stokes notes Bernhardt's "control of gesture and pose," in John Stokes, Michael R. Booth, and Susan Bassnett, *Bernhardt, Terry, Duse: The Actress in Her Time* (Cambridge: Cambridge University Press, 1988), 32.
57. "Sarah Bernhardt's Rehearsals," *Sporting Times*, December 18, 1880.
58. Ibid.
59. Joseph Galtier, *Le Temps*, March 2, 1892, on watching Bernhardt rehearse *Varennes*; quoted in Robert Horville, "The Stage Techniques of Sarah Bernhardt," in *Bernhardt and the Theater of Her Time* (Westport, CT: Greenwood Press, 1984), 38. In the preface to Jules Huret, *Sarah Bernhardt*, trans. A G. Raper (London: Chapman & Hall, 1899), playwright Edmond Rostand similarly described Bernhardt selecting scripts, arranging scenes, directing actors, and adjusting costumes and lighting (xi–xii). A clipping of an article on "La Créatrice de 'L'Aiglon,'" in V&A, SB Personal, Box 8, made a similar point about her attention to detail: "Les décors, les meubles, les costumes, les moindres accessoires furent contrôlés par elle, autant que par l'auteur." May Agate, in *Madame Sarah*, described Bernhardt telling her stage manager "what she wanted in the way of lighting, furniture, and effects" (116).
60. See Richard Schickel, *Intimate Strangers: The Culture of Celebrity* (Garden City, NY: Doubleday, 1985); Christine Gledhill, "Signs of Melodrama," in *Stardom: Industry of Desire*, ed. Christine Gledhill (London: Routledge, 1991), 211–15; Nussbaum on "interiority effects": *Rival Queens*, 18–22 and passim; Roach on "public intimacy": *It*, 16–17 and passim.
61. On Bernhardt's powers of "exteriorization," see Henry Fouquier, "Bernhardt and Coquelin," *Harper's Magazine*, December 1900.

62. See R. Darren Gobert, *The Mind-Body Stage: Passion and Interaction in the Cartesian Theater* (Stanford, CA: Stanford University Press, 2013), 33. On the links between exteriority and interiority in Victorian views of acting, see Lynn M. Voskuil, *Acting Naturally: Victorian Theatricality and Authenticity* (Charlottesville: University of Virginia Press, 2004), 11, 44. On exteriority as a quality of Dickensian performance and a hallmark of the theatricality of Dickensian prose, see Deborah Vlock, *Dickens, Novel Reading, and the Victorian Popular Theatre* (Cambridge: Cambridge University Press, 1999), 28, 40.

63. On Bernhardt acting with her entire body, see Aston, *Sarah Bernhardt*, 21–22; 24–25; 27–8; Agate, *Madame Sarah*, 51; and "French Players: Mlle. Sarah Bernhardt," *The Examiner*, March 18, 1876.

64. Lemaître, "Sarah Bernhardt racontée par elle-même."

65. Maud Allan, *My Life and Dancing* (London: Everett, 1908), 36.

66. Ernst L. Freud, ed., *Letters of Sigmund Freud: 1873–1939*, trans. Tania Stern and James Stern (London: Hogarth, 1961), 193.

67. See Taranow, *Sarah Bernhardt*, xiii, and Stokes, "Sarah Bernhardt," 32.

68. Quoted in Eric Delamarter, "Society at Bernhardt Play," *Inter Ocean*, November 1, 1910, clipping in RBML 1.20.

69. Delamarter, "Society at Bernhardt Play."

70. H. T. Parker, "A Little Study of the Incomparable Loftus," clipping in RBML 1.18.

71. For further discussions of Bernhardt's voice, see Taranow, *Sarah Bernhardt*; Stokes, "Sarah Bernhardt"; and Katherine Bergeron, *Voice Lessons: French Mélodie in the Belle Epoque* (Oxford: Oxford University Press, 2010).

72. On the perception of Bernhardt as bringing a new naturalism to acting, see, for example, "A Great French Actress. Daily Life of Sarah Bernhardt," *New York Times*, January 12, 1878, in HTC, 1870s Clippings.

73. Agate, *Madame Sarah*, 186. Alan Downer, in "Players and Painted Stage," notes that Edmund Kean similarly adopted "sudden shifts in tone, instead of the alternating waves of the classical school . . . mechanically depressing his voice, pausing suddenly then rushing on" (537).

74. Michel Georges Michel, *La France*, March 27, 1923, quoted in Horville, "The Stage Techniques of Sarah Bernhardt," 62.

75. Archie Bell, "The True Bernhardt," clipping in the Jerome Lawrence and Robert E. Lee Theatre Research Institute of the Ohio State University Libraries, Scrapbook Collection, #72.

76. Arthur Bingham Walkley, *Playhouse Impressions* (London: T. Fisher Unwin, 1892), 242.

77. James O'Donnell Bennett, "Music and the Drama," November 22, 1905, in RBML 1.5, reviewing Bernhardt in *La Sorcière*.

78. Clipping in RBML 1.20. For another description that focuses on Bernhardt's use of her fingers (in *Frou-Frou*), see Aston, *Sarah Bernhardt*, 44.

79. Bernhardt was not the only actor to use such techniques. Kean was similarly praised for his "sudden, extreme transitions between emotions" (Moody, *Illegitimate Theatre in London*, 231), and an 1883 reviewer praised Marie Prescott, the star of Oscar Wilde's early play *Vera*, as a "genius" whose "mobile face expresses the gamut of every passion." From the program for *Vera*, Union Square Theater, New York, August 25, 1883, in William Andrews Clark Memorial Library, University of California, Los Angeles, Wildeiana, Box 3, 3.10B.

80. Reynaldo Hahn, *La Grande Sarah: Souvenirs* (Paris: Hachette, 1930), 189–90.

81. For other examples of Bernhardt's use of movement, see Horville, "The Stage Techniques of Sarah Bernhardt," 51–53.

82. May Agate discusses how Bernhardt performed the second act of *Lucrèce Borgia* with her back to the audience and notes the expressiveness of Bernhardt's back, plus the effect of her face on theatergoers after she finally turned around (*Madame Sarah*, 153). On Bernhardt's willingness to turn her back to the audience, see Taranow, *Sarah Bernhardt*, 99.

83. Lemaître, "Sarah Bernhardt racontée par elle-même."

84. "Divine Sarah a Comedienne; Merveilleux!" October 31, 1910, clipping in RBML 1.20.

85. Clipping in RBML 4.

CHAPTER THREE. SAVAGERY

1. Columnist Bill Diehl used the phrase "Pelvis Presley" in an open letter to the singer quoted in "Elvis Presley-Digitation Churns Up Teen Tantrums, Scribe Raps, So-So BO," *Variety*, May 30, 1956.

2. "Virtuoso" and "blonde bombshell": Jack Gould, "TV: New Phenomenon: Elvis Presley Rises to Fame as Vocalist Who Is Virtuoso of Hootchy-Kootchy," *New York Times*, June 6, 1956; "bump-and-grind routine": Diehl quoted in "Elvis Presley-Digitation"; "odious in a man": Mac Reynolds, "Daughter Wants to See Elvis? 'Kick Her in the Teeth,'" *Sunday Sun* (Vancouver, BC), August 31, 1957, https://news.google.com/newspapers?nid=ifIdVpG6JtcC&dat=19570831&printsec=frontpage&hl=en.

3. Reynolds, "Daughter Wants to See Elvis?"

4. John Kirkwood, "Presley Fans Demented," *Vancouver Sun*, September 3, 1957, https://news.google.com/newspapers?nid=ifIdVpG6JtcC&dat=19570903&printsec=frontpage&hl=en.

5. "Elvis Presley-Digitation"; "Teeners Figure in Haley Riots on Rock 'n' Roll," *Variety*, May 30, 1956.

6. Photographer Ralph Bower, quoted in "Elvis Presley | Vancouver, Canada. Empire Stadium | August 31, 1957," ElvisPresleyPhotos.com, accessed March 18, 2018, http://www.elvispresleymusic.com.au/pictures/1957-august-31.html.

7. *Variety*, despite being a periodical devoted to promoting US show business, seemed to resent the commercial success of 1950s rock stars. "Elvis Presley-Digitation" dwelt almost maliciously on low turnout for Elvis concerts, undercutting the fact, also reported in that issue, that two of his songs, "Heartbreak Hotel" and "Blue Suede Shoes," were in that week's jukebox top ten. That hostility might be explained by another article that same week, which observed that the "free spending" of the "overwhelmingly teenage" audiences for rock and roll concerts posed a "headache for the town's motion picture exhibitors, whose biz is off from last year." "Haley 16G, San Antonio," *Variety*, May 30, 1956.

8. The gushing quotation is from "Divine Sarah as She Really Is in Spare Moments." *New York Herald*, February 15, 1891; the disdainful commentary on it can be found in a bulletin on the second page of the *Duluth Evening Herald*, February 20, 1891.

9. See Robert Justin Goldstein, "Censorship of Caricature in France, 1815–1914," *French History* 3, no. 1 (1989): 74.

10. Jacques Lethève, *La Caricature et la presse sous la IIIᵉ République* (Paris: Max Leclerc, 1961), 37. Lethève notes the increase in the sheer number of caricatures published by newspapers after 1881 (45) and discusses the 1880s uptick in anti-Semitic cartoons even in moderately progressive publications affiliated with the Third Republic, including *Le Grelot* (102–103).

11. "Yankees": Victor Fournel, "Les Oeuvres et les hommes," *Le Correspondant*, May 10, 1880; "art," "curiosity": Victor Fournel, "Les Oeuvres et les hommes," *Le Correspondant*, July 25, 1879. Here and below, unless otherwise noted, all translations from the French are my own.

12. "Scenery by the Ton," review of *Cleopatra* at the Tremont Theater, clipping in the Harvard Theatre Collection at Houghton Library, Harvard University (hereafter HTC), Sarah Bernhardt (hereafter SB), Plays P–Z, Box 2 of 3.

13. "Getting Up the Ladder," 1879, in HTC, SB 1880s Clippings.

14. "Acrobatic line": "Fortunes of the Famous," *New York Times*, July 15, 1879; "microscopic artist": "Courrier des Théâtres," *Le Globe*, April 24, 1880.

15. "Ajax": "News of the Theatres: Bernhardt, Redivivus, Triumphs Anew," December 6, 1910 clipping in Oliver Sayler scrapbook, vol. 21, 1910–11, Columbia Rare Book and Manuscript Library, Columbia University.

16. *Le Figaro* remarked sarcastically that the actress was supposedly so gifted with "universal genius" that if she wanted to, "she could start swallowing swords tomorrow," June 18, 1879. *Le Grelot* imagined Bernhardt jealous of Joan of Arc's press coverage and grumbling, "Joan of Arc never tamed Yankees and tigers!" Front cover, *Le Grelot*, August 21, 1887, in Bibliothèque nationale de France, Département des Arts du spectacle (hereafter BnF-DAS), Gr Fol-Ico-Per, SB.

17. "Bernhardt Loses Years During American Tour," June 12, 1906, in HTC, SB Mounted Clippings-Misc, Box 3 of 3.

18. A. Toxen Worm, quoted in Brooks McNamara, *The Shuberts of Broadway: A History Drawn from the Collections of the Shubert Archive* (New York: Oxford University Press, 1990), 66.

19. For a sample of box office figures that allows us to compare sales of tickets to Bernhardt performances in 1916 to those of other stage performers that year, see the ledgers for the Great Southern Theater in Columbus, Ohio, held by the Jerome Lawrence and Robert E. Lee Theatre Research Institute of the Ohio State University Libraries (hereafter TRI).

20. George Bernard Shaw, "Sardoodledom," *Saturday Review*, June 1, 1895.

21. J. Brander Matthews, *The Theatres of Paris* (New York: Scribner's, 1880), 99.

22. Marie Colombier, *Les Mémoires de Sarah Barnum* (Paris: Chez tous les libraires, 1884), 17.

23. On the knowingness involved in Barnum's acts, and the "operational aesthetic" within which his audience enjoyed analyzing how they were being tricked, see Neil Harris, *Humbug: The Art of P. T. Barnum* (Chicago: University of Chicago Press, 1981). On Barnum's exhibition of Native Americans and the association of indigenous peoples with savagery and bestiality in US freak shows, see Linda Frost, *Never One Nation: Freaks, Savages, and Whiteness in U.S. Popular Culture, 1850–1877* (Minneapolis: University of Minnesota Press, 2005), 3–6, and Bonnie Carr O'Neill, *Literary Celebrity and Public Life in the Nineteenth-Century United States* (Athens: University of Georgia Press, 2017), 36–42.

24. On the rise of anti-Semitic discourse in 1880s France, see Marc Angenot, *Ce qu'on dit des juifs en 1889. Antisémitisme et discours social* (Vincennes: Presses Universitaires de Vincennes, 1989). For a detailed account of positive French responses to Jewish difference as compatible with French universalism, see Maurice Samuels, *The Right to Difference: French Universalism and the Jews* (Chicago: University of Chicago Press, 2016).

25. Colombier, *Sarah Barnum*. "La Juive": 92 and passim; "commercial": 27; "dirty": 66.

26. "Great show woman": James Agate, "Sarah Bernhardt: The Secret of Her Greatness," *South Wales News*, March 27, 1923, SB Scrapbook, vol. 1, Theatre and Performance Collections, Victoria and Albert Theatre Museum. For the Disraeli joke, see

"A Bernhardt Task," *Funny Folks*, July 26, 1879. For another example of the British press equating Bernhardt's love of money with her Jewishness, see "At the Play," *Sporting Gazette*, July 12, 1879.

27. Newspaper clipping, ca. 1899, in BnF-DAS, Ico-Fol-Per, vol. 1, SB.

28. See the testimonies to Bernhardt provided by multiple authors in "Supplément Littéraire," *Le Figaro*, March 31, 1923, in BnF-DAS, Gr Fol-Ico-Per. Those cited include Francis de Croisset, Romain Coolus, Paul Souday, Fernand Gregh, Catulle Mendès, and André Theuriet.

29. A. L. Renner, *Sarah Bernhardt, Artist and Woman* (New York: A. Blanck, 1896), n.p.

30. Matthew Arnold, "The French Play in London," *Nineteenth Century*, July 1879. Arnold's larger point was that the English needed to draw a lesson about public policy from their infatuation with the French players and help to establish a nationally subsidized and supervised British theater along the lines of the visiting Théâtre-Français.

31. For early references to a Bernhardt craze, see Patricia Marks, *Sarah Bernhardt's First Theatrical Tour* (Jefferson, NC: McFarland, 2003), 159, 165.

32. J. A. Simpson, and E. S. C. Weiner, "Fan." *Oxford English Dictionary*, 2nd ed. (Oxford: Oxford University Press, 1989), 711. For an example of "fan" being placed in quotation marks by a magazine, see an image preserved in TRI #1, whose caption refers to a prize awarded to the "fans" of actor Francis X. Bushman. Jennifer Robertson notes that by the 1910s, "fan" as a term for actors' admirers had become a popular loanword in Japan; *Takarazuka: Sexual Politics and Popular Culture in Modern Japan* (1998; repr., Berkeley: University of California Press, 2001), 139.

33. The vision of illegitimate democracy traced here has affinities with what Nancy Ruttenburg has called "democratic personality," which thrives on unruly, uncanny, and theatrical powers of voice and speech whose effects are uncontainable, supernatural, and supraindividual. Nancy Ruttenburg, *Democratic Personality: Popular Voice and the Trial of American Authorship* (Stanford, CA: Stanford University Press, 1998), 11. One significant difference between the two concepts, however, is that in Ruttenburg's account, democratic personality presents itself as innocent and utterly lacking in agency, while accounts of illegitimate democracy exaggerate the agency of its actors. Democratic personality is an alibi, illegitimate democracy an allegation.

34. Harry Furniss, *The Confessions of a Caricaturist*, vol. 1 (New York: Harper & Brothers, 1902), 163, 133.

35. Patricia Mainardi, "*Dupinade*, French caricature, 1831," in *Getting the Picture: The Visual Culture of the News*, ed. Jason Hill and Vanessa R. Schwartz (London: Bloomsbury Academic, 2015), 16.

36. Information about the artist, publication, and date from Carol Ockman and Kenneth E. Silver, *Sarah Bernhardt: The Art of High Drama* (New Haven, CT: Yale University Press, published in association with the Jewish Museum, New York, 2005), 111.

37. For reprints of other images of Bernhardt with Jewish stars in the background, see Henry Lapauze, "Étude biographique: Madame Sarah Bernhardt," *Revue encyclopédique*, December 15, 1893. Jacques Lethève notes the anti-Semitic bent of *Le Grelot* in the 1880s in *La Caricature et la presse sous la IIIe République* (Paris: Max Leclerc, 1961), 102, as well as the genre's affinity for antagonism (94), and for chauvinistic stereotypes (112).

38. On the limits of nineteenth-century French democracy, see Joan Wallach Scott, *Gender and the Politics of History* (New York: Columbia University Press, 1988), and *Only Paradoxes to Offer: French Feminists and the Rights of Man* (Cambridge, MA: Harvard University Press, 1996). On French media coverage of feminism in general and Sarah Bernhardt in particular, see Mary Louise Roberts, *Disruptive Acts: The New Woman in Fin-de-siècle France* (Chicago: University of Chicago Press, 2002).

On the masculinist politics of Third Republic France, see Judith Surkis, *Sexing the Citizen: Morality and Masculinity in France, 1870–1920* (Ithaca, NY: Cornell University Press, 2006). On racism and French imperialism, see Edward Said, *Orientalism* (New York: Pantheon, 1978), and Patricia Lorcin, *Imperial Identities: Stereotyping, Prejudice and Race in Colonial Algeria* (London: I. B. Tauris, 1995). On French colonization's link to masculinist ideologies, see Jennifer Sessions, *By Sword and Plow: France and the Conquest of Algeria* (Ithaca, NY: Cornell University Press, 2011).

39. *La Caricature*, August 20, 1881.

40. "Aventures et mésaventures de Séraphiska," *La Caricature*, May 15, 1880.

41. On the representation of Native Americans ca. 1880, and the tendency to depict them as violent, savage, and uncivilized, see Kirsten Pai Buick, *Child of the Fire: Mary Edmonia Lewis and the Problem of Art History's Black and Indian Subject* (Durham, NC: Duke University Press, 2009); Kate Flint, *The Transatlantic Indian, 1776–1930* (Princeton, NJ: Princeton University Press, 2009); and John M. Coward, *The Newspaper Indian: Native American Identity in the Press, 1820–90* (Urbana: University of Illinois Press, 1999). Stereotypes of Indians scalping whites and engaging in cannibalism were familiar to French artists from various Romantic ballets and popular translations of James Fenimore Cooper novels; see Joellen A. Meglin, "'Sauvages, Sex Roles, and Semiotics': Representations of Native Americans in the French Ballet, 1736–1837; Part Two: The Nineteenth Century," *Dance Chronicle* 23, no. 3 (2000).

42. Homi Bhabha, "Of Mimicry and Man: The Ambivalence of Colonial Discourse," *October* 28 (Spring 1984): 132.

43. The wax museum's 1892 exhibit of human sacrifice in Dahomey is discussed and illustrated in Vanessa R. Schwartz, *Spectacular Realities: Early Mass Culture in Fin-de-Siècle Paris* (Berkeley: University of California Press, 1999), 137. For a detailed study of British imperialism and exhibition culture, see Sadiah Qureshi, *Peoples on Parade: Exhibitions, Empire, and Anthropology in Nineteenth-Century Britain* (Chicago: University of Chicago Press, 2001). On the association of black bodies with grotesque imagery of orality and eating, and the frequent depiction of African Americans in nineteenth-century imagery as waiters, caterers, and cooks, see Kyla Wazana Tompkins, *Racial Indigestion: Eating Bodies in the Nineteenth Century* (New York: New York University Press, 2012), 171.

44. The same article reported that the police made many arrests and also guarded houses and patrolled neighborhoods known to be inhabited by Jews. "A Dramatic Episode," *Bangor Daily Whig & Courier*, January 5, 1882.

45. TRI Spec. Playbills 440, for example, has this information appended to the playbill advertising Charlotte Cushman's 1858 performance at the Boston Theatre: "A box in the Second Tier has been assigned for the use of Colored Persons, who can only be admitted to that part of the Theatre." On discrimination against African American theatergoers in the United States, see Susan Curtis, *The First Black Actors on the Great White Way* (Columbia: University of Missouri Press, 1998), 53.

CHAPTER FOUR. INTIMACY

1. Alice Ross and agencies, "Andy Murray Says He Was Stalked around Europe by a Hotel Maid," *The Guardian*, October 4, 2016, https://www.theguardian.com/sport/2016/oct/04/andy-murray-stalked-hotel-maid-fan. Alina Simone, *Madonnaland: And Other Detours into Fame and Fandom* (Austin: University of Texas Press, 2016), describes a man who got himself tattooed with several of Madonna's album and

single covers (50) as well as two other men who have shrines to Madonna in their homes (50–51, 65). I explore in depth the fan's desire to collapse the distance between celebrities and their followers in two previously published articles: Sharon Marcus, "Salomé!! Sarah Bernhardt, Oscar Wilde, and the Drama of Celebrity," *PMLA* 126, no. 4 (October 2011), and "Celebrity 2.0: The Case of Marina Abramović," *Public Culture* 27, no. 1 (January 2015).

2. Henry Jenkins, *Textual Poachers: Television Fans and Participatory Culture* (New York: Routledge, 1992). Jenkins argues that stereotypes about fans unable to distinguish between reality and fantasy stem from "a projection of anxieties about the violation of dominant cultural hierarchies" (17), which fans muddy by giving popular cultural artifacts the same attention as critics give to elite ones. In *Regarding Frank Capra: Audience, Celebrity, and American Film Studies, 1930–1960* (Durham, NC: Duke University Press, 2004), Eric Smoodin traces the fear of the passive, uncritical fan at least as far back as the 1930s, when studies undertaken by the Payne Fund expressed concern about "childhood and adolescent spectatorial passivity" (94) and "a mass audience that because of its immaturity could generate little resistance to that which they saw on the screen" (94). Smoodin astutely points out that active fans could also be worrisome, since sometimes they aimed to reenact, uncritically but vigorously, exactly what they thought a film enjoined them to do, as was the case with some of the John Doe clubs that formed in response to Frank Capra's 1941 film *Meet John Doe*.

3. Jenkins writes that "fans assert their own right to form interpretations, to offer evaluations, and to construct cultural canons. Undaunted by traditional conceptions of literary and intellectual property, fans raid mass culture, claiming its materials for their own use, reworking them as the basis for their own cultural creations and social interactions" (18). Further on, he elaborates: "this book perceives fans as active producers and manipulators of meaning" (23); the fan's response "typically involves not simply fascination or adoration but also frustration and antagonism" (23), a valid point but one that discounts adoration as far less interesting than antagonism, which better allows fans to "actively assert their mastery over the mass-produced texts which provide the raw materials for their own cultural productions" (23). The term "adversarial" comes from Henry Jenkins, *Convergence Culture: Where Old and New Media Collide* (New York: New York University Press, 2006), 43, a book that remains committed to the binary model of consumers versus corporations (see, e.g., 175).

4. Jenkins, *Textual Poachers*, 45. Jenkins himself notes that "active media fans represent a small and insignificant segment of the audience required to sustain a network television series or to support a blockbuster movie" but nonetheless takes the active media fan as the paradigm for his theory.

5. Ibid., 26.

6. See Clare Pettitt, "Topos, Taxonomy, and Travel in Nineteenth-Century Women's Scrapbooks," in *Travel Writing, Visual Culture and Form, 1760–1900*, ed. Mary Henes and Brian H. Murray (Houndmills: Palgrave Macmillan, 2016), 21–41. Writing about the Sir Harry Page collection of albums and commonplace books in the Manchester Metropolitan University Special Collections, Pettitt explores how these albums, often manifestly the work of talented amateur artists, attest to the interplay of manuscript and print, personal and mass-manufactured, consumption and creation (33). As Pettitt points out, the pleasure such albums afford derives from their very ephemerality (25).

7. When she surveyed women who had been avid moviegoers in the 1940s, Jackie Stacey found that many female filmgoers remarked on the gulf between themselves and the

"unattainable" glamor of their favorite icons, so much so that she develops a concept she calls "identification based on difference." *Star Gazing: Hollywood Cinema and Female Spectatorship* (London: Routledge, 1994), 66, 171.

8. For a more in-depth discussion of this genre, see Sharon Marcus, "The Theatrical Scrapbook," *Theatre Survey* 54, no. 2 (May 2013).

9. The Leffingwell albums are housed in the Jerome Lawrence and Robert E. Lee Theatre Research Institute of the Ohio State University Libraries, Scrapbook Collection (hereafter TRI) and include #1–16, 21, 22, 29, 30, 31, 33.

10. TRI #162.

11. TRI #37.

12. There were exceptions; as Eric Smoodin has shown, the fan mail received by director Frank Capra shows how successfully he occupied the position of celebrity director, convincing audiences to view him as the author of his films and the chief person responsible for his actors' excellent performances.

13. TRI #144, compiled 1904–1916.

14. TRI #144.

15. TRI #111. Hannah had an aunt who acted in the Grace Hayward Stock Co. of Oak Park, Illinois.

16. TRI #111.

17. TRI #111. See also TRI #162, the 1904–5 scrapbook compiled by Helen Henderson, in which she similarly arranged two separate images to align the actors' sight lines, so that they appear to be looking at each other.

18. TRI #2.

19. TRI #111.

20. TRI #3.

21. TRI #78.

22. Kay Turner, ed., *I Dream of Madonna: Women's Dreams of the Goddess of Pop* (San Francisco: Collins, 1993).

23. For an early study linking film and dreams, see Hugo Munsterberg, *The Photoplay: A Psychological Study* (New York: Appleton, 1916).

24. William Allingham, *A Diary*, ed. H. Allingham and D. Radford (London: Macmillan, 1907), 41.

25. For a detailed account of Queen Victoria's relationship to photography, see Anne M. Lyden, *A Royal Passion: Queen Victoria and Photography* (Los Angeles: J. Paul Getty Museum, 2014).

26. Max Beerbohm, "Sarah" (1904), in *Around Theatres*, vol. 2 (New York: Knopf, 1930), 425. On nineteenth-century celebrity sightings, see Nicholas Dames, "Brushes with Fame: Thackeray and the Work of Celebrity," *Nineteenth-Century Literature* 56, no. 1 (June 2001).

27. E. C. F. Collier, ed., *A Victorian Diarist: Extracts from the Journals of Mary, Lady Monkswell, 1875–1895* (London: John Murray, 1944), 266.

28. Mrs. Patrick Campbell, *My Life and Some Letters*, 2nd ed. (London: Hutchinson, 1922), 81, 84, 82.

29. David Haven Blake has written compellingly about the erotic "mutuality" that obtained between Walt Whitman and his public, but often the feelings were more one-sided and decidedly aggressive. See *Walt Whitman and the Culture of American Celebrity* (New Haven, CT: Yale University Press, 2006), 150, 168.

30. "Our Grandfathers Sent Them Roses," clipping in TRI Scrapbook #5, ca. 1916.

31. Edward John Hart, "Illustrated Interviews. No. XL—Sarah Bernhardt," *Strand Magazine*, January 1895.

32. Lois Banner, *MM – Personal: From the Private Archive of Marilyn Monroe* (New York: Abrams, 2011), reproduces two pages of the young Italian fan's album plus the fan letter he sent her (120–123). On nineteenth-century fan mail, see, for example, R. Kent Rasmussen and Mark Twain, eds., *Dear Mark Twain: Letters from His Readers* (Berkeley: University of California Press, 2013).

33. Joseph R. Winchell, "Joy Family Papers," Rare Book and Manuscript Library, Columbia University.

34. David M. Henkin, *The Postal Age: The Emergence of Modern Communications in Nineteenth-Century America* (Chicago: University of Chicago Press, 2006), 56, 168; Jill E. Anderson, "'Send Me a Nice Little Letter All to Myself': Henry Wadsworth Longfellow's Fan Mail and Antebellum Poetic Culture," *University Library Faculty Publications*, no. 111 (2007): 8, https://scholarworks.gsu.edu/univ_lib_facpub/111.

35. See ALS (Miscellaneous) to Edwin Booth, Folder 4, Hampden-Booth Theatre Library (hereafter HBTL).

36. Anderson, "Send Me a Nice Little Letter All to Myself," 8, 6, 1, 4, 7, 4, 11, 15.

37. Peter Brown, *The Cult of the Saints: Its Rise and Function in Latin Christianity* (Chicago: University of Chicago Press, 1981).

38. See Jon Kelly, "What Should Celebrities Do with Fan Mail?," *BBC News Magazine*, March 20, 2013, http://www.bbc.com/news/magazine-21835118.http://www.bbc.com/news/magazine-21835118. The article also discusses male celebrities such as Johnny Depp and Robert Pattinson, who at the height of their popularity received similar numbers and types of missives.

39. "Sarah Bernhardt's Jewels," *Birmingham Daily Post*, February 8, 1883.

40. "A Chat with Sarah Bernhardt," *Belfast News-Letter*, June 27, 1881, quoted the star as saying, "The women are charming. . . . the men are not so nice as the women."

41. Nathan D. Urner, "Actress and Rajpoot, or Bernhardt's Bete Noire," *New York Clipper*, May 27, 1882, in Houghton Library at Harvard University and the Harvard Theatre Collection (hereafter HTC), SB Clippings, 1880s.

42. Clipping from the *Boston Daily Advertiser*, September 12, 1895, in HTC, SB Clippings, 1890s.

43. On the equation of nineteenth-century actresses with prostitutes, see Lenard R. Berlanstein, *Daughters of Eve: A Cultural History of French Theater Women from the Old Regime to the Fin de Siècle* (Cambridge, MA: Harvard University Press, 2001); Tracy C. Davis, *Actresses as Working Women: Their Social Identity in Victorian Culture* (London: Routledge, 1991); Kirsten Pullen, *Actresses and Whores: On Stage and in Society* (Cambridge: Cambridge University Press, 2005). Berlanstein also documents the exception made for Bernhardt.

44. Pierre Loüys, *Journal intime: 1882–1891* (Paris: Éditions Montaigne, 1929), 164. Here and below, unless otherwise noted, all translations from the French are my own.

45. See TRI #79 for album containing images of Sarah Bernhardt; for Ada Rehan and Henrietta Crosman, TRI #84.

46. Image is from TRI #79.

47. TRI #82.

48. TRI #86.

49. The reference to "ain't-she sweet" girls comes from TRI #85. For examples of clippings in these albums that report female stars marrying wealthy men, see TRI #83, which reports that actress Della Fox married diamond broker John Levy, and TRI #86, which reported that the far more established performer Julia Arthur had become the "wife of Millionaire Cheney." Arthur performed Shakespearian roles, including Hamlet, and performed with Henry Irving's British theater company.

50. Sarah Bernhardt obituary, *London Sunday Times*, 1923, in HTC, SB Clippings, Obits.

51. "Miscellaneous News," *Atchison Globe*, January 14, 1882.

52. "Our Extra-Special on the Comédie Française," *Fun*, June 25, 1879. The article noted that Bernhardt appealed to "belles" as well as "swells."

53. "Sarah as William," *Fun*, July 16, 1879; "postal service": "The Comedie's Coming," *Funny Folks*, June 7, 1879. An 1881 article about Bernhardt's first US tour similarly joked that she had "received over 300 offers of marriage, including one each from General Garfield and Sarony, besides half-a-dozen from Utah!" "More (Bern)hart-Rending Accounts from America," *Moonshine*, January 1, 1881.

54. "Before the Footlights," *Moonshine*, July 5, 1879.

55. "Bone of my bone": "Sarah Bernhardt-Achings," *Funny Folks*, August 2, 1879.

56. "Sarah Bernhardt on the Brain," *Funny Folks*, June 14, 1879.

57. "Punch at the French Play," *Punch*, June 14, 1879.

58. *Sporting Times*, June 18, 1881.

59. For more detailed discussions of London men as sexual consumers, see Peter Bailey, *Popular Culture and Performance in the Victorian City* (Cambridge: Cambridge University Press, 1998), and Judith R. Walkowitz, *City of Dreadful Delight: Narratives of Sexual Danger in Late-Victorian London* (Chicago: University of Chicago Press, 1992).

60. *Le Figaro*, June 18, 1879. Less salaciously, *La Presse*, May 22, 1876, reported that Bernhardt's sculpture *Après la tempête* attracted crowds because it piqued the public's curiosity.

61. "Seeing Sarah," *Funny Folks*, June 28, 1879.

62. "Sarah Bernhardt's Coffin Portraits," *The Era*, February 25, 1882. The article uses this phrase to describe photos Bernhardt had kept off the market but that the reporter speculates would have inspired a fight among Paris stationers had they been released.

63. "The Turf Market," *Sporting Times*, March 26, 1881.

64. TRI Spec.Playbills.341.

65. On Taglioni, see Molly Engelhardt, "Marie Taglioni, Ballerina Extraordinaire: In the Company of Women," *Nineteenth-Century Gender Studies* 6, no. 3 (Winter 2010). On Cushman, see Lisa Merrill, *When Romeo Was a Woman: Charlotte Cushman and Her Circle of Female Spectators* (Ann Arbor: University of Michigan Press, 2000).

66. For examples, see HBTL, ALS Miscellaneous letters to Edwin Booth, Folder 1.

67. Ibid.

68. HBTL, ALS Fan Letters & Misc., Edwin Booth, Folder 3.

69. Josephine Meighan, "Elsie Janis: The Girl Who Sees Fun in Everyone," *The Globe*, ca. 1905, clipping in TRI Elsie Janis Scrapbook.

70. "Wind her way": James Agate, "Sarah Bernhardt: The Secret of Her Greatness," *South Wales News*, March 27, 1923, SB Scrapbook, vol. 1, Theatre and Performance Collections, Victoria and Albert Museum (hereafter V&A); "young and spectacled": *The Era*, June 22, 1879, quoted in Elaine Aston, *Sarah Bernhardt: A French Actress on the English Stage* (Oxford: Berg, 1989), 31.

71. When traveling to Dover on November 10, 1900, diarist R. D. Blumenfeld met Lady de Grey "going to Paris to see Bernhardt in *L'Aiglon*," *R. D. B's Diary, 1887–1914* (London: Heinemann, 1930), 138. On steamy letters, see Marguerite Moreno, *Souvenirs de ma vie* (Paris: Éditions de Flore, 1948), 141; the original French is "des lettres brûlantes."

72. Julian Eltinge, "The Troubles of a Man Who Wears Skirts," *Green Book Magazine*, January 1915, clipping in TRI #2.

73. Louise Landis, "Bernhardt's Ageless Art Wins for Her New Laurels," clipping in TRI #21b, ca. 1916.

74. See "Passing of Sarah Bernhardt," *Daily Graphic*, March 27, 1923, V&A.

75. "Bernhardt Mobbed by Cheering Women at the Pier," *New York American*, November 20, 1905, in Bibliothèque nationale de France, Département des Arts du spectacle, Gr Fol-Ico-Per.

76. Jules Huret, *Sarah Bernhardt*, trans. G A. Raper (London: Chapman & Hall, 1899), 95.

77. "Edwin Booth," *Chicago Times*, February 14, 1874, in Booth Death Album, HBTL.

78. Blumenfeld, *R. D. B.'s Diary*. The quote about matinee girls is from an article in the George Backus scrapbook, TRI #110. For a scholarly study of the matinee girl, see Marlis Schweitzer, *When Broadway Was the Runway: Theater, Fashion, and American Culture* (Philadelphia: University of Pennsylvania Press, 2009).

79. "Sarah's Young Man," in HTC, SB Clippings-Misc.

80. "La Tournée de Sarah Bernhardt: Frou-Frou et Adrienne Lecouvreur," cover drawing by H. Scott and G. Clairin, *La Vie moderne*, September 18, 1880.

81. Le Souffleur, "Carnet du Souffleur," *La Vie moderne*, September 18, 1880.

82. Jennifer Robertson, *Takarazuka: Sexual Politics and Popular Culture in Modern Japan* (1998; repr., Berkeley: University of California Press, 2001), 146.

83. "Edwin Booth," *Chicago Times*, February 14, 1874, in Booth Death Album, HBTL.

84. *Georgia Weekly Telegraph*, March 10, 1882.

85. "Sarah Bernhardt's Rehearsals," *Sporting Times*, December 18, 1880.

86. Campbell, *My Life and Some Letters*, 180.

87. May Agate, *Madame Sarah* (London: Home and Van Thal, 1946), 33.

88. Alexandre Parodi, *Rome vaincue* (Paris: E. Dentu, 1876), 126.

89. "La Soirée théâtrale," *Le Figaro*, September 28, 1876. The article called her "transformation" in the role the "clou" (key moment) of the play.

90. "Notes," *The Nation*, November 16, 1876. The periodical does not identify James as the author.

91. "Variorum Notes," *The Examiner*, June 10, 1876.

92. "Notes," *The Nation*.

93. "Our Paris Letter of Gossip and Fashion," *Illustrated Household Journal and English-woman's Domestic Magazine*, May 22, 1880, 327. *La Presse*, reporting in its issue of June 17, 1880, on that year's Paris Salon, also deemed the painting strange (2).

94. Paul Fresnay, "Sarah Bernhardt's Coffin," *Georgia Weekly Telegraph*, March 17, 1882.

CHAPTER FIVE. MULTIPLICATION

1. See, for example, P. David Marshall on cinematic celebrity in *Celebrity and Power: Fame in Contemporary Culture* (Minneapolis: University of Minnesota Press, 1997), and Joseph Roach, *It* (Ann Arbor: University of Michigan Press, 2007).

2. See Lois Banner, *MM – Personal: From the Private Archive of Marilyn Monroe* (New York: Abrams, 2011), 39, 38. Banner breaks new ground in documenting Monroe's drive to direct her own career, noting that Monroe's press agent "stated that her quips and 'newsmaking frivolities' were her own ideas, not his or any other studio publicists. 'She was a literate, perceptive gal,' said Craft" (61). When Monroe married Joe DiMaggio and later when she announced her separation from him, she asked Fox publicists to help guarantee that reporters would be present at her press conference (62).

3. Clare Pettitt, "Livingstone: From Fame to Celebrity," in *David Livingstone: Man, Myth and Legacy*, ed. Sarah Worden (Edinburgh: National Museums of Scotland, 2012), 83–89.

4. On celebrity and citation, see Karen Tongson, "Empty Orchestra: The Karaoke Standard and Pop Celebrity," *Public Culture* 27, no. 1 (2015).

5. S. Paige Baty, *American Monroe: The Making of a Body Politic* (Berkeley: University of California Press, 1995), 72.

6. For examples of these regularly recurring features, see "Trend Report," *People*, May 9, 2016; "Red Carpet: Cardinal Rulers," *US Weekly*, May 9, 2016, which shows a series of female stars all dressed in "shades of sizzling scarlet" (8–9); and, in the same issue of *US Weekly*, an instance of "Who Wore It Best?" that presents the results of polling one hundred people about three pairs of women wearing the same outfits (10).

7. "'Margery Deane's' Visit to Wagner Last Summer," clipping in the Jerome Lawrence and Robert E. Lee Theatre Research Institute of the Ohio State University Libraries, Scrapbook Collection (hereafter TRI) #39, p. 19 of album, ca. 1880. According to the article, Cosima Wagner "looks a little like a Jewess, and is a woman who pays the greatest attention to her toilets. She writes very cleverly, and has a remarkable mind."

8. For an article on Bara's sculpture, see TRI #9, which notes that she played Camille and Cleopatra. Bara also played Salome on film, a role associated with Bernhardt because she had been slated to perform it in Oscar Wilde's play; see TRI #8 for an image of Bara as Salome.

9. TRI #5. Bernhardt is playing Queen Elizabeth I; Bara appears in her best-known incarnation, as a "vamp."

10. The Bernhardt image is from TRI #21; the Suratt images are from TRI #3. On Bernhardt arriving in the US in 1916 wearing "a sable gown covered with a leopard skin pelisse trimmed with sable," see "Mme. Bernhardt Arrives," clipping of October 21, 1916, in TRI #4.

11. On James Dean's path to celebrity, see Michael DeAngelis, *Gay Fandom and Crossover Stardom: James Dean, Mel Gibson, and Keanu Reeves* (Durham, NC: Duke University Press, 2001). In "That's Hollywood for You," *Photoplay*, April 1955, Sidney Skolsky wrote: "Most young actresses trying to crash the movies act as if they're Marilyn Monroe or Audrey Hepburn. All young actors trying to get into pictures act as if they're Marlon Brando" (8).

12. Max Horkheimer and Theodor W. Adorno, *Dialectic of Enlightenment*, trans. John Cumming (New York: Continuum, 1972), 154. In *Society of the Spectacle*, trans. Fredy Perlman et al. (Detroit: Black & Red, 1970), Guy Debord similarly wrote, in section 61, "The agent of the spectacle placed on stage as a star is the opposite of the individual, the enemy of the individual in himself as well as in others."

13. Walter Benjamin, "The Work of Art in the Age of Mechanical Reproduction," in *Illuminations*, ed. Hannah Arendt, trans. Harry Zohn (New York: Schocken Books, 1969), 231, 229.

14. E.g., New York Daly Theatre, which in 1898 advertised a gallery of over sixty objects displaying images of theatrical stars living and dead: a copy of Joshua Reynold's portrait of David Garrick, a bust of the 1860s star Clara Morris, numerous images of Ada Rehan (Daly's lead performer at the time), and representations of dozens of other nineteenth-century actors, including Sarah Bernhardt, Edwin Booth, and Henry Irving. See TRI #48.

15. "Cabinet photographs of the principals will be presented as souvenirs of the performance to every lady attending the Saturday matinées. One picture will be given each week . . . until the list is completed." Quoted in "'Crusoe' Is a Success," *Chicago Daily Tribune*, June 23, 1895.

16. Mary C. Henderson, *Broadway Ballyhoo: The American Theater Seen in Posters, Photographs, Magazines, Caricatures, and Programs* (New York: Abrams, 1989), 69–70.

17. Viv Gardner, "Gertie Millar and the 'Rules for Actresses and Vicars' Wives,'" in *Extraordinary Actors: Studies in Honour of Peter Thomson*, ed. Jane Milling and Martin Banham (Exeter: University of Exeter Press, 2004), 103–4.

18. Jennifer Roberts, *Transporting Visions: The Movement of Images in Early America* (Berkeley: University of California Press, 2014).

19. For discussions of how print and visual culture sought to bring publics closer to theatrical and literary figures, see Lenard Berlanstein, *Daughters of Eve: A Cultural History of French Theater Women from the Old Regime to the Fin de Siècle* (Cambridge, MA: Harvard University Press, 2001); Felicity Nussbaum, *Rival Queens: Actresses, Performance, and the Eighteenth-Century British Theater* (Philadelphia: University of Pennsylvania Press, 2010); Robyn Asleson, ed., *A Passion for Performance: Sarah Siddons and Her Portraitists* (Los Angeles: Getty Publications, 1999); and Deidre Lynch, *Loving Literature: A Cultural History* (Chicago: University of Chicago Press, 2014).

20. The Victoria and Albert Museum has several examples of porcelain figurines depicting the most famous actors of the late eighteenth and early nineteenth centuries. For images of actors on the heads of walking sticks, see Aparna Gollapudi, "Selling Celebrity: Actors' Portraits in *Bell's Shakespeare* and *Bell's British Theatre*," *Eighteenth-Century Life* 36, no. 1 (Winter 2012): 73. For mentions of other objects, see Gill Perry, with Joseph Roach and Shearer West, *The First Actresses: Nell Gwyn to Sarah Siddons* (Ann Arbor: University of Michigan Press, 2011): for fans, screens, and snuffboxes, see 16; playing cards, 80; decorative tiles, 16, 19; enamel miniatures, 43; and figurines, 16, 19, 80. To get a sense of the variety of artifacts depicting Sarah Siddons, one of the late eighteenth and early nineteenth century's most important British performers, see Asleson, *A Passion for Performance*.

21. The first woodblock illustrations of kabuki performers date to 1675; on the books, albums, playbills, signboards, broadsheets, and even paper dolls that illustrated and advertised plays and players, see Howard Link, *The Theatrical Prints of the Torii Masters* (Tokyo: Tuttle, 1977).

22. Gollapudi, "Selling Celebrity," 59–60, citing Arthur M. Hind, *A History of Engraving and Etching from the Fifteenth Century to the Year 1914* (New York: Dover, 1963), 15.

23. On print prices, see Gollapudi, "Selling Celebrity," 56.

24. In "Selling Celebrity," Gollapudi reports that Bell created two editions: a smaller volume priced at sixpence and a more luxurious one priced at a shilling, or twelve-pence (63).

25. Robin and Carol Wichard, *Victorian Cartes-de-Visite* (Princes Risborough: Shire Publications, 1999), 35, 34.

26. Henderson, *Broadway Ballyhoo*, 57. Sarony often photographed actors and other celebrities and paid Bernhardt a large fee in exchange for copyright in the resulting photographs (60); less eminent actors often sat for photographs for free and saw little if any of the money made from their sale (49).

27. Ibid., 70.

28. Robert Darnton, "Five Myths about the 'Information Age,'" *Chronicle Review*, April 17, 2011, https://www.chronicle.com/article/5-Myths-About-the-Information/127105.

29. Henderson, *Broadway Ballyhoo*, 19.

30. On Brady and Lind, see ibid., 49–50.

31. Ibid., 56.

32. By 1870, George Rockwood had devised a method for transferring photographs to printing plates and patented a photoengraving process that captured shades as well as lines (ibid., 54), but halftone images did not come into widespread use until much later.

33. See, for example, Charles F. Chandler and Arthur H. Elliott, eds., *Anthony's Photographic Bulletin* 17 (1886).

34. Henderson, *Broadway Ballyhoo*, 69.
35. See Nigel Gosling, *Nadar* (New York: Knopf, 1976), 10 and passim.
36. Jane Carlyle to Thomas Carlyle, July 30, 1865, *Letters and Memorials of Jane Welsh Carlyle*, ed. James Anthony Froude, vol. 2 (New York: Charles Scribner's Sons, 1894), 345.
37. Chandler and Elliott, *Anthony's Photographic Bulletin*. The column's author notes that Comanche John was the son of "old Blue Ruifa" and identifies the sender of the photographs as A. F. Randall of Wilcox, Arizona.
38. Henderson, *Broadway Ballyhoo*, 49.
39. *Le Figaro*, January 28, 1873. See also *La Presse*, July 4, 1879, which remarked that Bernhardt "s'est multipliée" in London. See Carol Ockman and Kenneth E. Silver, *Sarah Bernhardt: The Art of High Drama* (New Haven, CT: Yale University Press, published in association with the Jewish Museum, New York, 2005), 24–26, on how mechanical reproduction was central to Sarah Bernhardt's success and to her uniqueness. On Bernhardt as an "expert manipulator of new media," see ibid., 14. Here and below, unless otherwise noted, all translations from the French are my own.
40. Of her stop in Toulouse, *Le Figaro* wrote, "En tous lieux . . . il n'est question que d'elle" ("Sarah Bernhardt à Toulouse," September 20, 1880). The quote about her photographs is from "'Adrienne Lecouvreur' à Marseille," *Le Figaro*, September 25, 1880, which noted that Bernhardt was also dominating the newspapers.
41. Émile de Girardin and Moïse Millaud were among the habitués of Bernhardt's salon, and she knew Girardin well enough to sculpt his bust in 1878; when Paris's Grévin wax museum created a Bernhardt installation depicting her sculpting studio, they included the Girardin bust. See Miranda Eve Mason, "Making Love/Making Work: The Sculpture Practice of Sarah Bernhardt" (PhD diss., University of Leeds, 2007).
42. On Monroe, see Banner, *MM – Personal*, 61.
43. On Bernhardt and film, see David W. Menefee, *Sarah Bernhardt in the Theatre of Films and Sound Recordings* (Jefferson, NC: McFarland, 2003), and Victoria Duckett, *Seeing Sarah Bernhardt: Performance and Silent Film* (Urbana: University of Illinois Press, 2015).
44. George Luks (illustrator), "The Great Bernhardt in Her Robe and Roles," clipping from the *New York World*, May 24, 1896. Houghton Library at Harvard University and the Harvard Theatre Collection, Sarah Bernhardt (hereafter SB) Box 2 of 3, Clippings Plays P–Z.
45. TRI #3.
46. "Elsie Janis Tells Herself a Story," *World Magazine*, October 29, 1905, TRI, Elsie Janis Scrapbook.
47. "Little Elsie Janis," clipping, TRI, Elsie Janis Scrapbook.
48. Margaret D. Stetz notes that one reaction to the mass production of images was a "cult of individuality" that valorized the ability to read volumes into small differences in facial expression. *Facing the Victorians: Portraits of Writers and Artists from the Mark Samuels Lasner Collection* (Newark, DE: University of Delaware Press, 2007), 5.
49. For examples, see Gosling, *Nadar*, 30–31, 34.
50. See *Ballyhoo*, 61.
51. For a historical survey of turn-of-the-century scrapbooks, see Sharon Marcus, "The Theatrical Scrapbook," *Theatre Survey* 54, no. 2 (May 2013).
52. TRI #21.
53. On actors as types, see Stanley Cavell, *The World Viewed: Reflections on the Ontology of Film*, enl. ed. (1971; repr., Cambridge, MA: Harvard University Press, 1995),

29, 33–37; Foster Hirsch, *Acting Hollywood Style* (New York: Abrams, 1991), 15; and Pam Robertson Wojcik, "Typecasting," *Criticism* 45, no. 2 (Spring 2003), 234. On Victorian theater as itself organized around types and genres recognizable enough that entire plays could parody them, see Carolyn Williams, *Gilbert and Sullivan: Gender, Genre, Parody* (New York: Columbia University Press, 2011).

54. From clipping in TRI #21B.

55. Columbia Rare Book and Manuscript Library, Columbia University, Scrapbook 1.5.

56. In *Facing the Victorians*, Stetz discusses how common such variations in scale were; the same celebrity image could circulate in larger-than-life poster size or as a miniature stamp or bookplate (72).

57. May Agate, *Madame Sarah* (London: Home and Van Thal, 1946), 29–30.

58. "No one": "The Idol-Woman and The Other," *London Times*, March 28, 1923, SB Biographical Files, Scrapbook, vol. 1, Victoria and Albert Theatre Collection (hereafter V&A). Twain quoted in Menefee, *Sarah Bernhardt in the Theatre of Films and Sound Recordings*, 6.

59. Henri Degron, "La Princesse Lointaine," *La Plume*, December 1, 1900, in V&A, SB Personal Box 8.

60. Quoted in Claudette Joannis, *Sarah Bernhardt* (Paris: Payot, 2011), 76–77.

61. Alphonse Daudet, *Pages inédites de critique dramatique: 1874–1880* (Paris: Librairie de France, 1930), 70.

62. Virginia Woolf, "The Memoirs of Sarah Bernhardt," in *Books and Portraits: Some Further Selections from the Literary and Biographical Writings of Virginia Woolf*, ed. Mary Lyon (New York: Harcourt Brace Jovanovich, 1977), 206.

63. *New York Times*, September 26, 1871, clipping in Hampden-Booth Theatre Library (hereafter HBTL), Edwin Booth album, 1871–73.

64. For an example of Réjane looking directly at the camera, see Richard Bonynge, *A Collector's Guide to Theatrical Postcards* (1988; repr., London: Grange Books, 1993), 79; for Elliott, ibid., 87.

65. Souvenir program, HBTL.

66. Held at TRI.

67. In another exception that proves the rule, an image in Bonynge, *Theatrical Postcards*, shows Bernhardt looking at herself in a small handheld mirror (79), but again does not show her reflection, thus avoiding the doubling typical of most examples of the mirror pose.

CHAPTER SIX. IMITATION

1. Marlis Schweitzer, *When Broadway Was the Runway: Theater, Fashion, and American Culture* (Philadelphia: University of Pennsylvania Press, 2009), 170, 166.

2. Jennifer Robertson, *Takarazuka: Sexual Politics and Popular Culture in Modern Japan* (1998; repr., Berkeley: University of California Press, 2001), 6, citing an article that appeared in a 1935 Japanese magazine about the fans collecting around the all-female Takarazuka troupe, in which women played both male and female roles.

3. Timothy Green, "They Crown Their Country with a Bowl-Shaped Hairdo," *Life*, January 31, 1964.

4. "Lesbians Who Look Like Justin Bieber," accessed April 26, 2017, https://lesbianswho looklikejustinbieber.tumblr.com/.

5. Theodor W. Adorno, "The Schema of Mass Culture," in *The Culture Industry: Selected Essays on Mass Culture*, ed. J. M. Bernstein (London: Routledge Classics, 2001), 95. In a related vein, sociologist Edgar Morin wrote that imitating celebrities leads to

no real insight into either social structures or the human condition. Edgar Morin, *Les Stars* (Paris: Éditions du Seuil, 1957), 164.

6. Quoted in Margaret D. Stetz, *Facing the Late Victorians: Portraits of Writers and Artists from the Mark Samuels Lasner Collection* (Newark, DE: University of Delaware Press, 2007), 12.

7. See Jackie Stacey, *Star Gazing: Hollywood Cinema and Female Spectatorship* (London: Routledge, 1994), 201–3, 68, 169, 200; see also 216. Shelley Stamp and Hilary Hallett have documented how American women in the 1910s and 1920s identified with high-earning, physically daring, and sexually assertive movie stars such as Mary Pickford, Pearl White, and Gloria Swanson. See Stamp, *Movie-Struck Girls: Women and Motion Picture Culture after the Nickelodeon* (Princeton, NJ: Princeton University Press, 2000), and Hallett, *Go West, Young Women! The Rise of Early Hollywood* (Berkeley: University of California Press, 2013). More recently, Kim Allen has argued that fantasies of celebrity, often scorned or discouraged by middle-class pundits, help working-class girls to express ambition. "Girls Imagining Careers in the Limelight: Social Class, Gender and Fantasies of 'Success,'" in *In the Limelight and Under the Microscope: Forms and Functions of Female Celebrity*, ed. Su Holmes and Diane Negra (New York: Continuum, 2011), 149–173. Henry Jenkins, in *Textual Poachers: Television Fans and Participatory Culture* (1992; repr., New York: Routledge, 2013), has studied the contemporary communities formed around role-playing conventions. Michael Meeuwis, in "Everyone's Theater: Literary Culture and Daily Life in England, 1860–1914" (PhD diss., University of Chicago, 2011), documents how extensively amateurs emulated professional theater stars in Victorian England.

8. Robert Turnock, *Interpreting Diana: Television Audiences and the Death of a Princess* (London: British Film Institute, 2000), 53.

9. Kerry Ferris, *Stargazing: Celebrity, Fame, and Social Interaction* (New York: Routledge, 2011), 87–100.

10. See Richard Salmon, *Henry James and the Culture of Publicity* (Cambridge: Cambridge University Press, 1997), and Anne Diebel, who complicates the widely held notion that James simply rejected publicity, in "'The Dreary Duty': Henry James, *The Yellow Book*, and Literary Personality," in *Henry James Review* 32, no. 1 (Winter 2011).

11. Henry James, "The Comédie-Française in London," *The Nation*, July 31, 1879. James was one of the earliest writers to use the word "celebrity" in a pejorative sense, but he indicates his awareness of the more positive usage still prevalent in the 1870s when he immediately qualifies that point by writing that "Sarah Bernhardt is not, to my sense, a celebrity, because she is an artist." By stipulating that this particular figure did not owe her celebrity to her artistry, James acknowledged that other celebrities might have better claims to fame. On the nineteenth-century association of the term "celebrity" with worthy artistic achievement, see "Judgment."

12. Eve Adam, ed., *Mrs. J. Comyns Carr's Reminiscences*, 2nd ed. (London: Hutchinson, 1926), 83. Carr created the famous dress that Ellen Terry wore as Lady Macbeth. She and her husband often hosted private theatricals where amateurs imitated professional actors who were themselves in the audience (see 249–50). Ronald Gower similarly recorded being present at private theatricals in which a man imitated Bernhardt, Terry, and Irving in *Old Diaries, 1881–1901* (London: John Murray, 1902), 285.

13. Henry James, "The Art of Fiction," *Longman's Magazine* 4 (September 1884).

14. Nicola J. Watson, in "Fandom Mapped: Rousseau, Scott, and Byron on the Itinerary of Lady Frances Shelley," lists the many extant images of Rousseau available in the late eighteenth and early nineteenth centuries. "Romantic Fandom," ed. Eric Eisner, a volume of *Romantic Circles Praxis Series* (April 2011), https://www.rc.umd .edu/praxis/fandom/praxis.fandom.2010.watson.html. On the ways that Rousseau's

distinctive clothing made him easy to recognize in person during his visit to London in 1766, see Claire Brock, *The Feminization of Fame, 1750–1830* (New York: Palgrave Macmillan, 2006), 30. On Rousseau's celebrity, see Antoine Lilti, *Figures publiques: L'invention de la célébrité, 1750–1850* (Paris: Fayard, 2014), 153–209. Lilti mentions the London press reporting in 1766 on Rousseau's Armenian fur hat (156), and the spread, especially after 1762, of portraits depicting Rousseau, including ones advertised for sale in newspapers (210–13). On Byron's celebrity, see Tom Mole, *Byron's Romantic Celebrity: Industrial Culture and the Hermeneutic of Intimacy* (London: Palgrave Macmillan, 2007), and Clara Tuite, *Lord Byron and Scandalous Celebrity* (Cambridge: Cambridge University Press, 2014).

15. On Byron, see Katharine Harris Bradley diary, British Library Add. Mss. 46776, 1868–9, 5. On Wilde, see article in *The Court Journal*, July 7, 1883, in Wildeiana Box 10.11, William Andrews Clark Memorial Library, University of California, Los Angeles (hereafter WAC).

16. Michael Anton Budd, *The Sculpture Machine: Physical Culture and Body Politics in the Age of Empire* (New York: New York University Press, 1997).

17. Dani Busson, *Sarah-Bernhardt* (Paris: Willy Fischer, 1912), 25. Here and below, unless otherwise noted, all translations from the French are my own.

18. See 1916–1917 souvenir program of Bernhardt's last visit to America; copy in Rare Book and Manuscript Library, Columbia University (hereafter RBML), Brander Matthews Dramatic Museum Subject File, Bernhardt (hereafter SB). The same program appears in the Jerome Lawrence and Robert E. Lee Theatre Research Institute of the Ohio State University Libraries, Scrapbook Collection (hereafter TRI) #21b.

19. Matthew Arnold, "The French Play in London," *Nineteenth Century*, July 1879.

20. For Bernhardt wagons, surreys, and phaetons, see Nathan Cord's advertisement in the *St. Louis Globe-Democrat*, May 15, 1883. For the Sarah Bernhardt hair curler, see the back of a clipping of a program advertising Bernhardt and Coquelin in *Hamlet*, in the SB New York Playbills folder, THE bpf TCS 72, Box 47, Bates-Bernhardt, "Playbills and programs concerning female 'stars' ca. 1700–1930," Houghton Library at Harvard University and the Harvard Theatre Collection (hereafter HTC). For the Sarah Bernhardt pelargonium at the South Kensington Rose Show, see "The Garden," *Sporting Gazette*, July 12, 1879.

21. On Forrest, see William Rounseville Alger, *Life of Edwin Forrest, the American Tragedian* (Philadelphia: J. B. Lippincott, 1877), 2:585, and Bruce McConachie, *Melodramatic Formations: American Theatre and Society, 1820–1870* (Iowa City: University of Iowa Press, 1992), 48, 70–71. On Modjeska, see Beth Holmgren, *Starring Madame Modjeska: On Tour in Poland and America* (Bloomington: Indiana University Press, 2012), 313.

22. "London Coliseum Theater Program," 1911, SB Personal Box 8, Victoria and Albert Theatre Collection.

23. Advertisement, *Modern Screen*, April 10, 1939.

24. In *When Broadway Was the Runway*, Marlis Schweitzer establishes the many links between the theater press and the fashion press, as well as between theatrical producers and department stores.

25. Fourcaud, "Le Théâtre: La comédienne et le comédien," *La Vie moderne*, November 11, 1882.

26. For "lectrices," see "Sarah Bernhardt en province," *Le Figaro*, September 2, 1880; "dreaming": Victor Capoul, "Sarah Bernhardt à Toulouse," *Le Figaro*, September 20, 1880.

27. "Description of Our Engravings," *Myra's Journal of Dress and Fashion*, March 1, 1878, featured an illustration of "The Sarah Bernhardt Costume" on sale at a French

dressmaker's in Covent Garden. For bodice, see "The Latest Fashions from Paris," *Myra's Journal of Dress and Fashion*, April 1, 1875. For gloves, see advertisement in Sarah Bernhardt souvenir program, 1880, Brander Matthews Dramatic Library, RBML. For bonnet, see "Our Paris Letter of Fashions and Gossip," *Englishwoman's Domestic Magazine*, May 1, 1878. For ruffles, see "Our Paris Letter," *Ladies' Monthly Magazine*, December 1, 1880. For dresses, see "Spinnings in Town," *Englishwoman's Domestic Magazine*, July 1, 1874. For corsages, see "The Full-Size Patterns," *Ladies' Monthly Magazine*, June 1, 1879. For blouses, see "Description of the Plates of Costumes," *Ladies' Monthly Magazine*, September 1, 1879. For perfume, see "Advertisement for Rimmel's Specialties," *Myra's Journal of Dress and Fashion*, July 1, 1880. For hairstyle, see "More (Bern)hart-Rending Accounts from America," *Moonshine*, January 1, 1881. For hair dye, see "Parisian Gossip," *Ladies' Monthly Magazine*, July 1, 1880. Bernhardt was far from the only actress to have items of clothing named after her; for one of many examples, see the Croizette capote mentioned in "Our Paris Letter of Fashions and Gossip." Art historian and Bernhardt scholar Carol Ockman notes that Bernhardt's "unique style made her a trendsetter both on the stage and off." Carol Ockman and Kenneth E. Silver, *Sarah Bernhardt: The Art of High Drama* (New Haven, CT: Yale University Press, published in association with the Jewish Museum, 2005), 39.

28. "Copy": see "Dress," *Myra's Journal of Dress and Fashion*, March 1, 1878. Many other articles catered to readers' desires to imitate Bernhardt's onstage costumes. See, for example, "Spinnings in Town"; "The Latest Fashions from Paris," *Myra's Journal of Dress and Fashion,* April 1, 1875. For the instructions on how to make a Sarah Bernhardt ruffle, see "Our Paris Letter," *Ladies' Monthly Magazine*, December 1, 1880, which referred back to a figure in a previous issue.

29. Henry Bauer, "Sarah Bernhardt," *L'Echo de Paris*, 1896, in Bibliothèque nationale de France, Département des Arts du spectacle (hereafter BnF-DAS), Fol-Ico-Per.

30. See advertisement in Sarah Bernhardt souvenir program, 1880, Brander Matthews Dramatic Library, RBML.

31. "Our Paris Letter of Gossip and Fashion," *Illustrated Household Journal and Englishwoman's Domestic Magazine*, October 1, 1881.

32. Robin Kelsey, *Photography and the Art of Chance* (Cambridge, MA: Belknap Press of Harvard University Press, 2015), 255.

33. "Sarah Bernhardt on the Brain," *Funny Folks*, June 14, 1879.

34. Schweitzer, *When Broadway Was the Runway,* notes that in the 1890s, producer Charles Frohman paid for his female performers' gowns but let them select their stage clothes themselves (65–66). She also cites several articles in which actresses discussed designing their own gowns (118) and documents women asking their dressmakers to copy costumes seen onstage (162–77).

35. "Our Paris Letter of Gossip and Fashion," *Illustrated Household Journal and Englishwoman's Domestic Magazine*, October 1, 1881. The assignment of creativity in costume design was not unique to assessments of Bernhardt; when Lillie Langtry took to the stage, the originality and individuality of her costumes garnered more praise than her acting. See Catherine Hindson, " 'Mrs. Langtry Seems to Be on the Way to a Fortune': The Jersey Lily and Models of Late Nineteenth-Century Fame," in Holmes and Negra, *In the Limelight and Under the Microscope*, 26. Holmgren, *Starring Madame Modjeska*, similarly notes that Modjeska described herself as sewing some of her most important costumes (260) and that the only time the actress did not control costume and set design was when she toured with fellow actor Edwin Booth—and then he did (190).

36. Miss Murray Hill, "Wear for New York Women. Individuality in the Costumes of Mme. Bernhardt," April 4, 1887, in HTC, SB 1880s Clippings.

37. A reporter describing Bernhardt's costume in *L'Etrangère* noted, unsarcastically, "One can see that Mlle Bernhardt is cultivating the fine arts." Review of *L'Etrangère* in *Le Figaro*, February 15, 1876.

38. On the Romantic notion of authorship, see Martha Woodmansee, *The Author, Art, and the Market: Rereading the History of Aesthetics* (New York: Columbia University Press, 1994).

39. "As all the world knows": from "Our Paris Letter of Gossip and Fashion," October 1, 1881. On Bernhardt's fabric designs, see Bauer, "Sarah Bernhardt." For "departed," see "Bernhardt in 'Salome': Gorgeous Costumes She Will Wear in Oscar Wilde's One-Act Play," *Chicago Daily Tribune*, August 28, 1892.

40. Clipping in RBML 1.20. Another French star, Réjane, when asked about her genius for dress, similarly explained that she herself designed her costumes; see interview in RBML 1.2.

41. Oscar Wilde to Bernulf Clegg, 1891, Morgan Library and Museum, http://www.themorgan.org/collection/oscar-wilde/manuscripts-letters/36. See also Rupert Hart-Davis and Merlin Holland, eds., *The Complete Letters of Oscar Wilde* (New York: Henry Holt, 2000), 478. On dandyism, see Ellen Moers, *The Dandy: Brummell to Beerbohm* (1960; repr., Lincoln: University of Nebraska Press, 1978); Domna C. Stanton, *The Aristocrat as Art: A Study of the Honnête Homme and the Dandy in Seventeenth- and Nineteenth-Century French Literature* (New York: Columbia University Press, 1980); Rhonda K. Garelick, *Rising Star: Dandyism, Gender, and Performance in the Fin de Siècle* (Princeton, NJ: Princeton University Press, 1998); and Monica L. Miller, *Slaves to Fashion: Black Dandyism and the Styling of Black Diasporic Identity* (Durham, NC: Duke University Press, 2009).

42. "Our Captious Critic. 'Cleopatra,'" *Illustrated Sporting and Dramatic News*, June 18, 1892.

43. "The One Thing Needful," *Funny Folks*, August 4, 1883.

44. "Sarah Bernhardt's Newest Gloves," *Rocky Mountain News*, September 2, 1883.

45. James von Geldern and Louise McReynolds, eds., *Entertaining Tsarist Russia: Tales, Songs, Plays, Movies, Jokes, Ads, and Images from Russian Urban Life, 1779–1917* (Bloomington: Indiana University Press, 1998), 195, 193, 188, 189, 195.

46. Newspaper clipping, n.d., in BnF-DAS, Ico-Fol-Per, vol. 1. "Nègre" had pejorative connotations.

47. On the association of contorted gestures with people of African origin, understood as lesser, more primitive races, see Rae Beth Gordon, *Dances with Darwin, 1875–1910: Vernacular Modernity in France* (Farnham: Ashgate, 2009), 2–6, 169. Gordon notes the regular presence of blackface performers in France starting in the 1870s (147).

48. In *New World Drama: The Performative Commons in the Atlantic World* (Durham, NC: Duke University Press, 2014), Elizabeth Maddock Dillon demonstrates the links between nineteenth-century charges that African Americans were "essentially imitative" and the belief that they were uncivilized and incapable of exercising political freedom (226). See also Jason Richards, *Imitation Nation: Red, White, and Blackface in Early and Antebellum US Literature* (Charlottesville: University of Virginia Press, 2017), 9–27.

49. On the value that African Americans placed on using dress to distinguish between enslavement and liberty, see Miller, *Slaves to Fashion*, 5.

50. E. B. Duval, caricatures of Oscar Wilde in ethnic dress, ca. 1882, in WAC, Wildeiana, Box 21, Folder 3.

51. On the ways that Wilde's "American and English detractors" equated his Irishness with a racialized primitivism, and for other examples of caricatures that "linked Wilde with black Americans" as admirers and imitators, as well as Native and Chinese Americans, see Curtis Marez, "The Other Addict: Reflections on Colonialism and Oscar Wilde's Opium Smoke Screen," *ELH* 64, no. 1 (Spring 1997), who writes: "To many observers Wilde remained an Irishman trying to ape his betters" (274). Marez also explores Wilde's own investment, as an Aesthete, in British imperial views of non-Western culture.

52. "Oscar Wilde—Very Wild," in *Moonshine*, n.d., in WAC, Box 10, Oscar Wilde in America, clippings.

53. Currier and Ives, "The Aesthetic Craze," ca. 1882, in WAC, Wildeiana, Box 18, Folder 9.

54. Miller, *Slaves to Fashion*, 104. Miller argues that for Americans and Britons of African origin, black dandyism was a freedom dream, "a comment on mainstream style rather than an impersonation of it" (14), and a way of navigating between self-fashioning and stereotypes (191).

55. "Copies and originals": Eric Lott, *Love and Theft: Blackface Minstrelsy and the American Working Class* (1993; repr., New York: Oxford University Press, 2013), 40; on cartoonists and minstrels, see Lott, "Blackface and Blackness: The Minstrel Show in American Culture," in *Inside the Minstrel Mask: Readings in Nineteenth-Century Blackface Minstrelsy*, ed. Annemarie Bean, James Vernon Hatch, and Brooks McNamara (Hanover, NH: Wesleyan University Press, 1996), 92.

56. On the "ridicule" and "loathing" to which minstrel shows subjected the black dandy, see Miller, *Slaves to Fashion*, 98, and "Images of Gender and Class: Daddy Blue," in Bean, Hatch, and McNamara, *Inside the Minstrel Mask*, 265.

57. For Salvini imitators, see George C. D. Odell, *Annals of the New York Stage: 1879–1882*, vol. 11 (New York: Columbia University Press, 1939), 363. For Lind imitators, see Robert B. Winans, "Early Minstrel Music, 1843–1852," in Bean, Hatch, and McNamara, *Inside the Minstrel Mask*, 161. In *Behind the Burnt Cork Mask: Early Blackface Minstrelsy and Antebellum American Popular Culture* (Urbana: University of Illinois Press, 1999), William J. Mahar notes how often minstrel troupes burlesqued high opera (104). F. Michael Moore, in *Drag! Male and Female Impersonators on Stage, Screen and Television: An Illustrated World History* (Jefferson, NC: McFarland, 1994), notes that William Henry Rice parodied opera singer Adelina Patti as well as Bernhardt in *Camille* (64).

58. See Annemarie Bean, "Transgressing the Gender Divide: The Female Impersonator in Nineteenth-Century Blackface Minstrelsy," in Bean, Hatch, and McNamara, *Inside the Minstrel Mask*, 245.

59. For an image of Leon as Bernhardt, see Ockman and Silver, *Sarah Bernhardt*, 66. On Leon's Wilde act, and for a list of minstrel acts involving female impersonation, see Moore, *Drag!*, 56–68.

60. "Awkwardly aping": Laurence Senelick, *The Changing Room: Sex, Drag and Theatre* (London: Routledge, 2000), 297, which discusses the distinction between the two types of minstrel female impersonation (296–302). See also Robert C. Toll, *Blacking Up: The Minstrel Show in Nineteenth-Century America* (New York: Oxford University Press, 1974), 139–145. Both types of female impersonation were called "wench" performances despite the very different kinds of femininity involved. For an example of the "grotesquerie" and "draconian punitiveness" involved in the song lyrics typical of the second type of performance, see Lott, *Love and Theft*, 14. For an overview of female impersonation in minstrelsy, see Annemarie Bean, "Black Minstrelsy and Double Inversion, Circa 1890," in *African American Performance and Theater History:*

A Critical Reader, ed. Harry J. Elam Jr. and David Krasner (New York: Oxford University Press, 2001), 171–191. Bean notes that by the 1890s white women fully participated in minstrel troupes, but the minstrel versions of Bernhardt continued to be played by men. Derek Scott, "Sounds of the Metropolis," *Oxford Scholarship Online* (September 2008), notes that some minstrel songs mocked female fashions (18), while in *Behind the Burnt Cork Mask*, Mahar notes that many antebellum acts involving female impersonation parodied feminist reformers agitating for women's rights (59). Mahar also notes that white male Americans were not so amused when British comedian Charles Mathews caricatured their own linguistic oddities and threatened him with riot on his second tour of the US (61).

61. See advertisements in TRI #61.
62. "Sara Sees Heartburn," *Colorado Springs Weekly Gazette*, January 22, 1881.
63. "Grand Opening," *Hamilton Daily Democrat*, October 20, 1887.
64. For "Clam Eel," see ad for Dumont's Minstrels at the Eleventh Street Opera House in the *Philadelphia Inquirer*, March 3, 1896. Ads for performances of "Sarah Heartburn" in England, the US, and Ireland appeared in newspapers throughout the 1880s. On March 3, 1881, the *Boston Daily Globe* reported that the act had been signed to perform in Paris ("Sarah Heartburn in Paris"). For the 1906 ad, see the ad for Dumont's Minstrels at the Eleventh Street Opera House in the *Philadelphia Inquirer* "Amusements" section, January 29, 1906. The ad for "The Fate of a Chicken Croquette" appeared in the same paper on February 5, 1911.
65. Moore, *Drag!*, notes that one troupe, the Backus Minstrels, which mounted one of the first Bernhardt burlesques, in November 1880, toured Australia, India, Egypt, and China (63); for an advertisement for a Backus performance of *Sarah Heartburn*, see "Amusements," *New York Times*, November 16, 1880. On the international tours of minstrel acts, which took them to European capitals and provincial cities, as well as to Australia, New Zealand, India, and South Africa, see Richard Waterhouse, "The Internationalisation of American Popular Culture in the Nineteenth Century: The Case of the Minstrel Show," *Australasian Journal of American Studies* 4, no. 1 (July 1985). Waterhouse argues that minstrelsy represented the Americanization of global culture long before Hollywood. See also Michael Pickering, "White Skin, Black Masks: 'Nigger' Minstrelsy in Victorian England," in *Music Hall: Performance and Style*, ed. J. S. Bratton (Milton Keynes: Open University Press, 1986), and Robert Nowatzki, *Representing African Americans in Transatlantic Abolitionism and Blackface Minstrelsy* (Baton Rouge: Louisiana State University Press, 2010).
66. "Sarah Heartburn," *The Era*, June 25, 1881. The anonymous reviewer noted that others had "enthusiastically praised" the burlesque "as an imitation of the famous French actress."
67. Ibid.
68. On inversion as the principle governing minstrel acts, see William J. Mahar, "Ethiopian Skits and Sketches: Contents and Contexts of Blackface Minstrelsy, 1840–1890," in Bean, Hatch, and McNamara, *Inside the Minstrel Mask*, 198, which notes that acts often featured a servant in blackface becoming a master in ways that ridiculed both. In *Acts of Supremacy: The British Empire and the Stage, 1790–1930* (Manchester: Manchester University Press, 1991), Michael Pickering notes that minstrelsy depicted black women as the "reverse image of genteel white femininity," 198.
69. "A Surp-rice-ing Performance," *Funny Folks*, July 9, 1881, 211. On the ability to experience pain as the key differentiator between how Stowe's novel and its most popular nineteenth-century dramatizations depicted Topsy, see Robin Bernstein, *Racial Innocence: Performing American Childhood from Slavery to Civil Rights* (New York: New York University Press, 2011), 43–52.

70. Edw[ard] Le Roy Rice, *Monarchs of Minstrelsy, from "Daddy" Rice to Date* (New York: Kenny Publishing Company, 1911), 166.

CHAPTER SEVEN. JUDGMENT

1. Elizabeth Maddock Dillon, in *New World Drama: The Performative Commons in the Atlantic World, 1649–1849* (Durham, NC: Duke University Press, 2014), presents the mid-nineteenth century as a period that "saw the enclosure of the theatrical commons as the audience itself was subject to segmentation and privatization" (29). At the same time, Dillon, drawing on the theories of Jacques Rancière, emphasizes the importance of the theater as a "scene of collective embodiment" (59) in which publics could exercise sovereignty (10–11, 45, 62).

2. See Richard Dyer, *Stars* (London: British Film Institute, 1979); Jackie Stacey, *Star Gazing: Hollywood Cinema and Female Spectatorship* (London: Routledge, 1994); Joshua Gamson, *Claims to Fame: Celebrity in Contemporary America* (Berkeley: University of California Press, 1994); and, more recently, Eric Smoodin, *Regarding Frank Capra: Audience, Celebrity, and American Film Studies, 1930–1960* (Durham, NC: Duke University Press, 2004), whose introduction provides a magisterial analysis of the turn to reception in studies of film and popular culture.

3. Henry Jenkins, *Textual Poachers: Television Fans and Participatory Culture* (1992; repr., New York: Routledge, 2013).

4. "I'm Professor Sharon Marcus, from Columbia University, and I study celebrity culture in the past and in the present, AMA!," Reddit, March 17, 2015, https://www.reddit.com/r/science/comments/2zca5c/science_ama_series_im_professor_sharon_marcus/.

5. See Michael Falcone, "Obama Gets Celebrity Treatment in New McCain Ad," *New York Times*, July 30, 2008. http://thecaucus.blogs.nytimes.com/2008/07/30/obama-gets-celebrity-treatment-in-new-mccain-ad/.

6. "Cap and Gown," *New York Times,* May 22, 2015, http://www.nytimes.com/interactive/2015/05/22/us/23commencement.html?_r=0.

7. On the matinee girl, see Marlis Schweitzer, *When Broadway Was the Runway: Theater, Fashion, and American Culture* (Philadelphia: University of Pennsylvania Press, 2009). On Valentino's female fans, see Miriam Hansen, *Babel and Babylon: Spectatorship in American Silent Film* (Cambridge, MA: Harvard University Press, 1991). For a brief item that identifies one of the young Frank Sinatra's skills in "the art of how to make girls faint," see "Sinatra at White House; He Talks to President at Tea About Making Girls Swoon," *New York Times*, September 29, 1944. In *At the Picture Show: Small-Town Audiences and the Creation of Movie Fan Culture* (Washington, DC: Smithsonian Institution Press, 1996), Kathryn H. Fuller notes that although early moviegoers in the US were seen as male, early *fans*, often characterized as hysterical and lacking in judgment, were portrayed as female (116).

8. "Hysterical squeals": Jack Gould, "TV: It's the Beatles (Yeah, Yeah, Yeah)," *New York Times*, January 4, 1964; "tall youth," "gaggle," and "dissenters": Thomas Buckley, "Beatles Prepare for Their Debut," *New York Times*, February 9, 1964; "look what America's coming to": Richard F. Shepard, "Stokowski Talks of Something Called Beatles," *New York Times*, February 15, 1964.

9. Gould, "TV: It's the Beatles," reviewing the Beatles' first US television appearance, described their music as undistinguished and predicted that English Beatlemania would not take hold in the United States.

10. For a reproduction of the Nadar image, see https://upload.wikimedia.org/wikipedia/commons/9/95/Nadar%27s_Pantheon%2C_1854.jpg.

11. See Roger Bellet, *Presse et journalisme sous le Second Empire* (Paris: Armand Colin, 1967), 92.

12. William Bell Sprague, *Visits to European Celebrities* (Boston: Gould and Lincoln, 1855), v. For an example that placed illustrious living figures such as jurist Oliver Wendell Holmes and composer Giuseppe Verdi alongside long-dead immortals such as Homer, Dante, and Leonardo da Vinci, see Charles F. Horne, ed., *Great Men and Famous Women*, vol. 4 (New York: Selmar Hess, 1894).

13. William and Daniel Downey, *The Cabinet Portrait Gallery*, First Series (London: Cassell, 1890). The volume was an extension of the Downeys' photography studio, which sold large numbers of freestanding celebrity photographs.

14. Michael Bennett Leavitt, *Fifty Years in Theatrical Management, 1859–1909* (New York: Broadway Publishing, 1912), 8.

15. The distaste that writers of serious literature expressed for celebrities and celebrity culture confirms Pierre Bourdieu's insight that nineteenth-century male artists acquired cultural capital by positioning themselves against the marketplace; see Bourdieu, *The Rules of Art: Genesis and Structure of the Literary Field*, trans. Susan Emanuel (Stanford, CA: Stanford University Press, 2006).

16. On Henry James's hostility to celebrity culture, see Richard Salmon, *Henry James and the Culture of Publicity* (Cambridge: Cambridge University Press, 1997). On Whitman's own celebrity and his embrace of celebrities and fandom, see David Haven Blake, *Walt Whitman and the Culture of American Celebrity* (New Haven, CT: Yale University Press, 2006), and Bonnie Carr O'Neill, "The Personal Public Sphere of Whitman's 1840s Journalism," *PMLA* 126, no. 4 (2011).

17. Lloyd Charles Sanders, *Celebrities of the Century: Being a Dictionary of Men and Women of the Nineteenth Century* (London: Cassell, 1890).

18. See the 1888 description of a woman's album in A. Tilney Bassett, ed., *A Victorian Vintage: Being a Selection of the Best Stories from the Diaries of the Right Hon. Sir M. E. G. Duff* (London: Methuen, 1930), 100.

19. For an example of an album that unites Roosevelt, Pavlova, and the Stock Exchange, see the Jerome Lawrence and Robert E. Lee Theatre Research Institute of the Ohio State University Libraries, Scrapbook Collection (hereafter TRI) #2, compiled by Burton Leffingwell, covering the years 1915–16.

20. George Bernard Shaw, "Duse and Bernhardt," *Dramatic Opinions and Essays*, vol. 1 (1895; repr., New York: Brentano's, 1909).

21. Downey and Downey, *Cabinet Portrait Gallery*, 5. An 1886 article similarly observed, "Not a little of Sarah Bernhardt's prodigious success is due to her surpassing cleverness in persuading the world to accept her at her own valuation." "The Apotheosis of Sarah," December 11, 1896, Sarah Bernhardt (hereafter SB) Clippings–Plays P–Z, Houghton Library at Harvard University and the Harvard Theatre Collection (hereafter HTC). On the late nineteenth- and early twentieth-century tendency to see Bernhardt as the active agent of her own self-promotion, see Susan A. Glenn, *Female Spectacle: The Theatrical Roots of Modern Feminism* (Cambridge, MA: Harvard University Press, 2002), 29.

22. "Sarah Barnum," *Fun*, December 26, 1883; "intelligence": J. Comyns Carr, "An Appreciation," *Daily Telegraph*, March 27, 1923, SB Biographical Files, Scrapbook, vol. 1, Theatre and Performance Collections, Victoria and Albert Museum; on "energy," see clipping in TRI #4. For one of many other examples that attributed a sound basis to Bernhardt's fame, see Henry Bauer, "Sarah Bernhardt," *L'Echo de Paris*, 1896, in Bibliothèque nationale de France, Département des Arts du spectacle (hereafter BnF-DAS), Fol-Ico-Per. Most critics described Bernhardt as a great actress even when they disapproved of her defiant persona, but a vocal handful had a lower evaluation of her skills. An undated newspaper clipping in BnF-DAS, Ico-Fol-Per, vol. 1, for

example, dismissed Bernhardt as a "magician" who "would excel at conferring value on what lacks it." An article on "Les Oeuvres" in *Le Correspondant* (Paris), November 25, 1896, similarly faulted Bernhardt for "running around the world in pursuit of dollars" and performing in shoddy plays. Here and below, unless otherwise noted, all translations from the French are my own.

23. The few other women to appear included Charlotte Corday, Marie Antoinette, and Mme Récamier. See Alfred Stevens and Henri Gervex, "Paris Panorama of the Nineteenth Century," *The Century*, December 1889.

24. Jonas A. Barish, *The Antitheatrical Prejudice* (1981; repr., Berkeley: University of California Press, 1985), 502.

25. On collectivity, see David Kurnick, *Empty Houses: Theatrical Failure and the Novel* (Princeton, NJ: Princeton University Press, 2011). On fluidity, see Nina Auerbach, *Private Theatricals: The Lives of the Victorians* (Cambridge, MA: Harvard University Press, 1990). On commercial success, see Emily Allen, *Theater Figures: The Production of the Nineteenth-Century British Novel* (Columbus: Ohio State University Press, 2003). On self-fashioning, see Lynn M. Voskuil, *Acting Naturally: Victorian Theatricality and Authenticity* (Charlottesville: University of Virginia Press, 2004). On oratory, see Michael Meeuwis, "Everyone's Theater: Literary Culture and Daily Life in England, 1860–1914" (PhD diss., University of Chicago, 2011). On physical expressiveness, see Jane Moody, *Illegitimate Theatre in London, 1770–1840* (Cambridge: Cambridge University Press, 2000).

26. Rare Book and Manuscript Library, Columbia University (hereafter RBML) #4, 1823 article. On amateur theatricals, see Michael Meeuwis, " 'The Theatre Royal Back Drawing-Room': Professionalizing Domestic Entertainment in Victorian Acting Manuals," *Victorian Studies* 54, no. 3 (Spring 2012).

27. "The Season, by a Saunterer," *County Gentleman*, June 5, 1880.

28. Sarah Flower, *Great Aunt Sarah's Diary* (Privately printed, 1964).

29. Frank Lockwood (1846–1897), in Downey and Downey, *Cabinet Portrait Gallery*, 43. Lockwood is now best remembered for successfully prosecuting Oscar Wilde for gross indecency in 1895.

30. See TRI #47.

31. Lady Emma Ribblesdale, *Letters and Diaries* (London: Chiswick Press, 1930), 200.

32. "Arrival of Rachel," *New York Times*, August 23, 1855, refers to the gift of a bracelet in 1841. On Victoria's gift to Lind, see W. Porter Ware and Thaddeus C. Lockard Jr., *P. T. Barnum Presents Jenny Lind: The American Tour of the Swedish Nightingale* (Baton Rouge: Louisiana State University Press, 1980), 7.

33. Courtalin, "Théâtres," *Le Globe*, August 29, 1880.

34. For the French Drama Society, see TRI Correspondence K–L, Theatre-related, Box 1, Folder 1; for the "city's second oldest club" (Harmonie Club) reception, see the same collection, Box 1, Folder 16. My thanks to Elisabeth Maurer for bringing these items to my attention.

35. Beth Holmgren, *Starring Madame Modjeska: On Tour in Poland and America* (Bloomington: Indiana University Press, 2012), 301.

36. For the eighteenth-century roots of this phenomenon in England, see Felicity Nussbaum, *Rival Queens: Actresses, Performance, and the Eighteenth-Century British Theater* (Philadelphia: University of Pennsylvania Press, 2010).

37. Story cited in David Grimsted, *Melodrama Unveiled: American Theater and Culture, 1800–1850* (1968; repr., Berkeley: University of California Press, 1987), 57.

38. Ware and Lockard, *P. T. Barnum Presents Jenny Lind*, note that men outnumbered women at Lind's New York concerts (33).

39. Ibid., 35, 52.

40. On the objectification of actresses, see Lenard R. Berlanstein, *Daughters of Eve: A Cultural History of French Theater Women from the Old Regime to the Fin de Siècle* (Cambridge, MA: Harvard University Press, 2001); Tracy C. Davis, *Actresses as Working Women: Their Social Identity in Victorian Culture* (London: Routledge, 1991); and Kirsten Pullen, *Actresses and Whores: On Stage and in Society* (Cambridge: Cambridge University Press, 2005).
41. Downey and Downey, *Cabinet Portrait Gallery*, 24.
42. Terry was performing Marguerite in *Faust* in New York City. RBML, Theater Scrapbooks (Gift of MCNY), Ms. #1767, Scrapbook 5.8.
43. Gustavus Stadler, *Troubling Minds: The Cultural Politics of Genius in the United States, 1840–1890* (Minneapolis: University of Minnesota Press, 2006). See also Andrew Elfenbein, *Romantic Genius: The Prehistory of a Homosexual Role* (New York: Columbia University Press, 1999).
44. David Belasco, "Beginner on the Stage," *Saturday Evening Post*, August 30, 1919, in TRI #9. His list included Nell Gwyn, Elizabeth Barry, Nance Oldfield, Kitty Clive, Mrs. Siddons, Rachel, Charlotte Cushman, Sarah Bernhardt, Adelaide Neilson, Ellen Terry, Ada Rehan, Julia Marlowe, and Mrs. Fiske.
45. "Arrival of Rachel." For a reference to Rachel as "a woman of genius, of the highest order of genius," see George W. Smalley, "Anglo-American Memories," *New York Tribune*, May 22, 1910.
46. Benjamin Karr, "The Stage Road for Women," ca. 1923, clipping in TRI #72.
47. A. L. Renner, *Sarah Bernhardt, Artist and Woman* (New York: A. Blanck, 1896), 42.
48. E. C. F. Collier, ed., *A Victorian Diarist: Extracts from the Journals of Mary, Lady Monkswell, 1875–1895* (London: John Murray, 1944), 43, after seeing Bernhardt in *Adrienne Lecouvreur*. See also Clement Scott, "Sarah Bernhardt: 1899," in *Some Notable Hamlets of the Present Time* (London: Greening, 1900), 50. French critics similarly praised her as an "actress of genius"; see, for two of many examples, Félicien Champsaur, "Sarah Bernhardt," *Les Hommes d'aujourd'hui*, October 25, 1878, BnF-DAS clipping, and Antoine Laporte, *Beranger, Sarah Bernhardt, Bertall: Étude bibliographique* (Paris: A. Laporte, 1884): "ce regard chargé du coup de foudre du génie" (9).
49. Glenn Frank, "At Bernhardt's Grave," August 31, 1926, clipping in TRI #75.
50. See Jürgen Habermas, *The Structural Transformation of the Public Sphere: An Inquiry into a Category of Bourgeois Society*, trans. Thomas Burger, with the assistance of Frederick Lawrence (Cambridge, MA: MIT Press, 1989); Sarah Maza, *Private Lives and Public Affairs: The Causes Célèbres of Prerevolutionary France* (Berkeley: University of California Press, 1993), 11.
51. On the pleasure of judging celebrities, see Nicholas Dames, "Brushes with Fame: Thackeray and the Work of Celebrity," *Nineteenth-Century Literature* 56, no. 1 (June 2001). Writing of more recent developments in celebrity culture, Henry Jenkins has emphasized the active, creative, and participatory nature of many fan cultures; see *Fans, Bloggers, and Gamers: Exploring Participatory Culture* (New York: New York University Press, 2006). On theatergoing as direct democracy, see Jacques Rancière, "The Emancipated Spectator," in *The Emancipated Spectator*, trans. Gregory Elliot (New York: Verso, 2009); Vanessa R. Schwartz, *Spectacular Realities: Early Mass Culture in Fin-de-Siècle Paris* (Berkeley: University of California Press, 1999); and Susan Maslan, *Revolutionary Acts: Theater, Democracy, and the French Revolution* (Baltimore: Johns Hopkins University Press, 2005). On consumer culture, see Erika Diane Rappaport, *Shopping for Pleasure: Women in the Making of London's West End* (Princeton, NJ: Princeton University Press, 2001).
52. For overviews of nineteenth-century audience behavior in the US, see Lawrence W. Levine, *Highbrow, Lowbrow: The Emergence of Cultural Hierarchy in America*

(Cambridge, MA: Harvard University Press, 1990), and Daniel Cavicchi, *Listening and Longing: Music Lovers in the Age of Barnum* (Middletown, CT: Wesleyan University Press, 2011). On France, see James H. Johnson, *Listening in Paris: A Cultural History* (Berkeley: University of California Press, 1996). On England, see Jim Davis and Victor Emeljanow, *Reflecting the Audience: London Theatregoing, 1840–1880* (Iowa City: University of Iowa Press, 2001).

53. See, for example, Cavicchi, *Listening and Longing*. On the fan letters sent by Japanese audience members to the Takarazuka acting troupe over the course of the twentieth century, which similarly included critiques of performances and advice about how to publicize actors, design posters, record performances, and select scripts, see Jennifer Robertson, *Takarazuka: Sexual Politics and Popular Culture in Modern Japan* (1998; repr., Berkeley: University of California Press, 2001), 180–82.

54. Downey and Downey, *Cabinet Portrait Gallery*, 3.

55. Hampden-Booth Theatre Library (hereafter HBTL) ALS Miscellaneous to Edwin Booth, Folder 3. Richelieu letter from Joseph Jardine, March 8, 1866.

56. HBTL ALS Miscellaneous to Edwin Booth, Folder 4.

57. HBTL ALS Anonymous letters to Edwin Booth, Folder 1, letter of December 21, 1866.

58. HBTL ALS Anonymous letters to Edwin Booth, Folder 1.

59. HBTL ALS Anonymous letters to Edwin Booth, Folder 1, letter from Detroit, February 12, 1874.

60. HBTL ALS Fan Letters & Misc. to Edwin Booth, Folder 1, Winslow Purchase, December 14, no year.

61. HBTL ALS Anonymous letters to Edwin Booth, Folder 1, letter from New York, dated January 1, 1867.

62. J. G. Fay, Mount Vernon, New York, February 19, 1866. HBTL ALS Fan letters to Edwin Booth, Folder 2.

63. HBTL ALS Miscellaneous to Edwin Booth, Folder 3.

64. Mary Isabella Stone, letter to Edwin Booth, 1883, in HTC, THE BMS Thr 32.

65. Annotated copy of *The Prompt-Book: Shakespeare's Tragedy of Hamlet as Presented by Edwin Booth* (New York: Francis Hart, 1881), in HTC, THE Ms Thr 219. In *The Sarah Siddons Audio Files* (Ann Arbor: University of Michigan Press, 2013), Judith Pascoe notes that early nineteenth-century theatergoers in London similarly had their attentions trained by witnessing repeat performances of the same role (101).

66. HBTL ALS Anonymous letters to Edwin Booth, Folder 1.

67. Lent reference in letter from February 25, 1866, in HBTL ALS Miscellaneous to Edwin Booth, Folder 1. April 21, 1868; letter re Jewish Sabbath in HBTL ALS Anonymous to Edwin Booth, Folder 2.

68. The drive to criticize every aspect of a performance was not unique to the nineteenth century; in *Takarazuka*, Jennifer Robertson cites a fan of the Japanese Takarazuka theater troupe who published a 1991 essay that ranged from criticizing the overly heavy stage makeup in which actors appeared in posters to complaining about the difficulty of obtaining tickets and suggesting that the troupe inaugurate a prize for best script, open to the general public (181–82).

69. Pauline Viardot fan mail, in HTC bMs Mus 264, letter of April 21, 1860, Folder 14.

70. Ibid., Folder 23.

71. Ibid., Folder 32, letter dated December 1859.

72. Ibid., Folder 36, Paris, January 7, 1860. For other mentions of Gluck's approval, see Folders 35 and 59.

73. For the Cushman poster, see TRI Spec. Playbills.218; for the Modjeska playbill, see TRI Spec. Playbills.571.c2; for Bernhardt, see TRI #2.

74. "Star cast": TRI #110, program for *Love and Law*, at the People's Theater in Columbus, Ohio.
75. TRI Spec. Playbills.440.
76. See clipping in TRI #142.
77. RBML Oliver Sayler Scrapbooks.
78. Both images from TRI #1.
79. See Western Reserve Historical Society, Cleveland (hereafter WRHS) #1.
80. TRI Spec. TRI LMK.34.44, folder containing Elsie Janis ephemera.
81. RBML, Theater Scrapbooks (Gift of MCNY), Ms. #1767, Scrapbook 5.8.
82. WRHS Scrapbook 139.
83. RBML, Theater Scrapbooks (Gift of MCNY), Ms. #1767, Scrapbook 5.8.
84. WRHS Scrapbook #1.
85. RBML, Theater Scrapbooks (Gift of MCNY), Ms. #1767, Scrapbooks 1.7 and 1.2.
86. TRI #37.
87. RBML Scrapbooks 1–13.
88. RBML, Theater Scrapbooks (Gift of MCNY), Ms. #1767, Scrapbook 7.4.
89. TRI #144.
90. TRI #157.
91. TRI #51.
92. John A. Stevenson, Philadelphia Theater Scrapbook, 1882–90, MS 32, Brander Matthews Dramatic Library, RBML.
93. On repeat performances, see TRI #43.
94. WRHS #139.
95. This understanding has become global. In 2016, for example, Hasan Zaidi, a Pakistani media critic, described a young female murder victim as someone whose "celebrity had nothing to do with any achievement beyond her provocative presence on social media." Quoted in Salman Masood, "Pakistani Internet Celebrity Strangled, Police Say," *New York Times*, July 16, 2016, https://www.nytimes.com/2016/07/17/world/asia/qandeel-baloch-pakistan-internet-celebrity-killed.html.
96. Downey and Downey, *Cabinet Portrait Gallery*, 3.

CHAPTER EIGHT. MERIT

1. *Some Letters from a Man of No Importance: 1895–1914* (London: Jonathan Cape, 1928), 208.
2. J. Ranken Towse, "Mary Anderson," *The American Theatre as Seen by Its Critics*, ed. Montrose J. Moses and John Mason Brown (New York: W. W. Norton, 1934), 105–106.
3. Tom Robertson's *Caste*, for example, which premiered in 1867, appears in the Jerome Lawrence and Robert E. Lee Theatre Research Institute of the Ohio State University Libraries, Scrapbook Collection (hereafter TRI), #143, from 1902 and 1903, and in TRI #3, from 1910, which suggests that the play was still being performed and still drawing crowds. The compiler of TRI #3 also recorded performances of *Richelieu* (1839), in 1909, and *Lights o' London* (1881), in 1911.
4. "Music and the Drama," *Chicago Daily Tribune*, March 21, 1901.
5. For 1883, see TRI Spec.Playbills.367; for 1888, see TRI #61.
6. Richard Neville, "Plays and Players," *Los Angeles Times*, May 5, 1901.
7. In France, where the Théâtre-Français kept plays by Racine, Corneille, and Molière in permanent repertory, playwright Ernest Legouvé could compare how two different actors performing fifty years apart recited an identical passage from *Le Misanthrope*. Ernest Legouvé, *Soixante ans de souvenirs*, vol. 2 (Paris: J. Hetzel, 1887), 72–73.

8. *Press* (New York), "The Lyceum," November 13, 1881, in Hampden-Booth Theatre Library, New York (hereafter HBTL), Booth Tour Scrapbook, 1881–82.

9. HBTL ALS Fan Letters and Misc. to Edwin Booth, Folder 3.

10. Letter of December 24, 1880, HBTL ALS Fan Letters and Misc. to Edwin Booth, Folder 3.

11. "Mme Bernhardt," *Boston Daily Globe*, January 24, 1906.

12. Franklin Fyles, "Hot Nights in the Tenderloin," *Washington Post*, July 16, 1905. Although the anonymous author of *Some Letters from a Man of No Importance: 1895–1914* thought Bernhardt rose to greater heights, he noted that "many people prefer [Mrs. Patrick Campbell's] treatment of the first two acts of Magda as being quieter and more truly bourgeois" (106–7).

13. "Little Elsie Janis," clipped article in TRI 1905 Elsie Janis Scrapbook.

14. Max Beerbohm, "Hamlet, Princess of Denmark" (1899), in *Around Theatres*, vol. 1 (New York: Knopf, 1930), 46.

15. May 27, 1906, interview with the *Cleveland Plain Dealer*, in Rare Book and Manuscript Library, Columbia University (hereafter RBML) 1.8.

16. Julia Arthur played Hamlet in the US around the same time, between 1898 and 1901; see TRI #86. Jules Huret, *Sarah Bernhardt*, trans. G A. Raper (London: Chapman & Hall, 1899), notes that two French actresses, Mme Judith and Mme Lerou, performed Hamlet before Bernhardt did (179–80).

17. See Joseph R. Roach, *Cities of the Dead: Circum-Atlantic Performance* (New York: Columbia University Press, 1996), 2.

18. "Victor Hugo on Art and Peace," *Aberdeen Weekly Journal*, December 15, 1877. Bernhardt had already emulated Mars by playing trouser roles early in her career, just as the older actress had in her own youth. On Mars's trouser roles, see Patrick Berthier, *Le Théâtre Au XIXᵉ Siècle* (Paris: Presses Universitaires de France, 1986), 15. An article on Bernhardt in the August 1, 1879, theater column *Baldwin's Monthly* asserted that she "established a right to be ranked on the same level" as the greatest six French actresses of the previous two centuries. In adopting trouser roles early in her career, Bernhardt also invited comparison with renowned actress Virginie Déjazet (1798–1875), who had specialized in androgynous, puckish roles and often wore men's clothes onstage. Bernhardt's early career coincided with Déjazet's last years on the Parisian stage (she retired in 1868). During the 1870s, the older actress remained a reference point for Parisians and Londoners judging Bernhardt's performances. On Déjazet's trouser roles, see Gerda Taranow, *Sarah Bernhardt: The Art within the Legend* (Princeton, NJ: Princeton University Press, 1972), 211–14. Taranow also cites comparisons between Bernhardt and another notable predecessor whom Hugo mentions, Marie Dorval (139–40). For an overview of other performers to whom Bernhardt was compared, see Elaine Aston, *Sarah Bernhardt: A French Actress on the English Stage* (Oxford: Berg, 1989), 93–111.

19. "Our Paris Letter of Fashions and Gossip," *Englishwoman's Domestic Magazine*, January 1, 1878.

20. Hugo's original French is quoted in the account of the same event given in "Variorum Notes," *The Examiner*, December 15, 1877. Because the Théâtre-Français kept plays in repertory for decades, audiences could compare Bernhardt to Mlle Mars in other roles as well, such as the eponymous Mlle de Belle-Isle, created by Mars and reprised by the younger actress in her first performance after she returned to the Comédie-Française in 1872. Here and below, unless otherwise noted, all translations from the French are my own.

21. Legouvé, *Soixante ans de souvenirs*, 90.

22. Thomas Sadler, ed., *Diary, Reminiscences and Correspondence of Henry Crabb Robinson*, vol. 3 (London: Macmillan, 1869), 365.

23. Quoted in *The Argonaut*, July 19, 1879, https://archive.org/stream/argonaut51879sanf/argonaut51879sanf_djvu.txt.

24. *New York Times*, 1879, article in Houghton Library at Harvard University and the Harvard Theatre Collection (hereafter HTC), Sarah Bernhardt (hereafter SB) Box 2 of 3, 1870s Clippings.

25. In choosing to perform Cleopatra in 1890, Bernhardt tackled another role identified with Rachel, but used a different script. Commenting on this choice, drama critic Albert Wolff wrote that "Rachel['s] . . . fame still excites Mme Sarah Bernhardt to greater efforts even in the hour of her greatest triumphs." Quoted in Huret, *Sarah Bernhardt*, 120.

26. "At the Play," *Sporting Gazette*, June 7, 1879.

27. "London Gossip of the Day," *New York Times*, June 30, 1879.

28. Mrs. Humphrey Ward, *A Writer's Recollections*, vol. 1 (New York: Harper & Brothers, 1918), 210–11.

29. "Outre-Mer. XII. Sarah Bernhardt," *Boston Home Journal*, March 21, 1891, in HTC, SB Plays O–Z.

30. *La Presse* (Paris), January 9, 1880.

31. Impresario Schürmann, *Les étoiles en voyage. La Patti—Sarah Bernhardt—Coquelin* (Paris: Tresse and Stock, 1893), noted the 1881 rumors that Bernhardt was afraid to compete in the role of Phèdre with "Madame Walter, the Austrian Rachel" (112). For an example of Yacco being called the "Bernhardt of Japan," see the *Star*, June 5, 1901, quoted in Aston, *Sarah Bernhardt*, 111 (Aston spells the surname using the variant "Yocco"). For a reference to Mrs. Leslie Carter as the "American Sarah Bernhardt," see TRI #2.

32. Clipping in RBML 1.8.

33. "Bernhardt's 'L'Aiglon,'" *Washington Post*, December 2, 1900.

34. Beth Holmgren, *Starring Madame Modjeska: On Tour in Poland and America* (Bloomington: Indiana University Press, 2012), 283. Holmgren offers numerous other examples of reviewers and Modjeska herself fostering comparison to other actresses; see, for example, 3, 9, 12, 76, 132, 151, 157, 292.

35. James O'Donnell Bennett, "Sarah Bernhardt," November 25, 1905, review of her performance in *Sapho*; clipping in RBML 1.5. On Hading, see Aston, *Sarah Bernhardt*, 102.

36. Fred. F. Schraeder, "Bernhardt as Marguerite," *Washington Post*, January 3, 1906.

37. Pathé ad quoted in Victoria Duckett, *Seeing Sarah Bernhardt: Performance and Silent Film* (Urbana: University of Illinois Press, 2015), 41.

38. William Winter, "Mme. Bernhardt at the Lyric: Camille," *New York Tribune*, December 13, 1905.

39. May 27, 1906, interview with the *Cleveland Plain Dealer*, in RBML 1.8. On other occasions, Bernhardt resented comparison; George W. Smalley recalled her saying of herself and Modjeska, "We are two different actresses and two different women. Why should you compare us?" "Anglo-American Memories," *New York Tribune*, May 22, 1901.

40. On critical and audience interest in comparing Bernhardt to Clara Morris, Rachel, and Modjeska on the occasion of her New York debut, see George Clinton Densmore Odell, *Annals of the New York Stage*, vol. 11, *1879–1882* (New York: AMS Press, 1970), 239–40.

41. For "The Only Camille," see TRI Spec. Playbills.571.c2; for "animal and Frenchy style," see "Players of the Day, No. VIII: Sarah Bernhardt," *The Owl*, July 7, 1882.

42. "Mdlle. Bernhardt has made a success in La Dame aux Camelias," *Moonshine*, June 25, 1881. The role of Frou-Frou offers another interesting example of historical competition combined with shadow repertory. In 1880, Bernhardt decided to tackle the role, strongly associated with Aimée Desclée, who had died at a prematurely young age,

in 1874. In 1882, Modjeska, having seen Bernhardt follow her as Camille, raised the competitive stakes by adding Frou-Frou to her repertory just after Bernhardt's critical success in the role. Critics seized the occasion to compare the two actresses; one found both lacking relative to Desclée ("At the Play," *The Observer*, June 19, 1881); another deemed Modjeska "not as good as Madame Bernhardt" in the "early scenes" ("The Only Jones," *Judy*, June 15, 1881); and a third noted that Bernhardt was being "followed by Madame Modjeska in similar parts and with almost equal triumph" ("Players of the Day, No. VIII"). Later in Modjeska's career, the Polish actress avoided shadowing Bernhardt's repertory, focusing instead on roles such as Portia, a popular role for Ellen Terry, and one that highlighted the fact that Modjeska, unlike Bernhardt, could perform in English. (Bernhardt did, however, play both Portia *and* Shylock, in French, during her final 1916 tour of the US.) Late in the century, newcomers such as Rose Stahl often chose to perform Frou-Frou, selecting as a test of their abilities a role freighted with prestige after having been performed globally by both Modjeska and Bernhardt.

43. Victoria Duckett, *Seeing Sarah Bernhardt*, 78–79. Duckett also discusses Bernhardt's decision to play Queen Elizabeth in a major film of the same name as part of a move to "seek . . . comparison" with Adelaide Ristori, who had played the role onstage (104).

44. March 22, 1906, Cleveland newspaper clipping in RBML 1.8.

45. René Jeanne, "Garbo sera-t-elle Sarah Bernhardt?" *L'Écran français*, January 14, 1947. My thanks to Eric Smoodin for generously bringing this article to my attention.

46. Patricia Marks, *Sarah Bernhardt's First Theatrical Tour* (Jefferson, NC: McFarland, 2003), 148.

47. Alexis Soloski, "Laura Linney and Cynthia Nixon, Swapping Parts in 'The Little Foxes,'" April 19, 2017, https://www.nytimes.com/2017/04/19/theater/little-foxes-review-cynthia-nixon-laura-linney.html.

48. "Gaiety Theatre—French Plays," *The Times*, July 10, 1883.

49. TRI Spec.Playbill 531.

50. For details on Davenport's performances during Bernhardt's first North American tour, see Marks, *Sarah Bernhardt's First Theatrical Tour*, 148–49. For an image of one of Davenport's Sardou tours, see the Ohio Theater program in TRI #106, ca. 1895.

51. On "matchless," see the Grand Opera House program for January 21, 1884, TRI Spec. Playbills.332; on "incomparable," see Western Reserve Historical Society, Cleveland (hereafter WRHS) #1, 1887.

52. Clipping in WRHS #127. Photo is from the TRI Pfening Collection FP2.3.17, Fanny Davenport as Cleopatra, photographed by Sarony in 1891.

53. Richard F. Maynard Correspondence, Box 1, 1895–98, Folder for February–May 1896, letter dated April 7, 1896, Harvard University Archives, HUD 896.53. My thanks to Elisabeth Maurer for bringing this source to my attention.

54. WRHS 139.

55. TRI #61.

56. "One View of the Eaglets," *Washington Post*, December 16, 1900; "comparison," "futile": "Eaglet of Bernhardt," *Washington Post*, January 15, 1901.

57. "Maude Adams as the Stricken Eaglet," *New York Times*, October 23, 1900; "Bernhardt's 'L'Aiglon,'" *Washington Post*, December 2, 1900, citing William Winter.

58. WRHS #127.

59. "One View of the Eaglets," 31.

60. WRHS #127.

61. Ibid.

62. Ibid.

63. Performances of *L'Aiglon* continued to proliferate, with Marie Dressler performing a burlesque version in New York around 1900, "with apologies to Mme. Bernhardt and

Miss Adams," indicating that both actresses were identified with the role; see TRI #104. In 1934, a young Eva Le Gallienne made a bid to be included in this venerable performance genealogy when she appeared in the Rostand play.

64. "Adelaide Ristori," *New York Times*, October 10, 1906.
65. The article deems the presence of the French stars in the US "valuable for the simple reason that they afford comparison"; clipping in WRHS #127.
66. "The Lyceum," *The Mercury*, November 13, 1881.
67. November 8, 1880, article in HBTL, Booth album 1881.
68. Rastignac, "Sarah Bernhardt," *Le Soleil*, Bibliothèque nationale de France, Départe-ment des Arts du spectacle (hereafter BnF-DAS), Gr Fol-Ico-Per, clipping, ca. 1905.
69. For Irving and Terry in Philadelphia in 1894 and 1887, see TRI #61; in St. Louis on January 11, 1902, see TRI #167. On transatlantic performance networks, see Marlis Schweitzer, *Transatlantic Broadway: The Infrastructural Politics of Global Perfor-mance* (Houndmills: Palgrave Macmillan, 2015).
70. Oscar Wilde, "Literary and Other Notes III," in *Selected Journalism*, ed. Anya Clay-worth (Oxford: Oxford University Press, 2004), 111. In 1875, Ristori undertook a world tour that took her everywhere except India, according to a clipping in RBML 1.10.
71. See Rimli Bhattacharya, "Promiscuous Spaces and Economies of Entertainment: Soldiers, Actresses and Hybrid Genres in Colonial India," *Nineteenth Century The-atre and Film* 41, no. 2 (Winter 2014), and Justin A. Blum, "The Lyceum Theatre and Its Double: Richard Mansfield's Visit to the Greenwich Meridian of Late-Victorian Theatre," *Nineteenth Century Theatre and Film* 41, no. 2 (Winter 2014).
72. Lawrence Vassault, "Sarah Bernhardt," *The Cosmopolitan*, April 1901.
73. *New York Times*, 1879, article in HTC, SB 1870s Clippings; Frohman in RBML 1.29. Several obituaries made a similar point. For one example of many, Sir Sidney Low, in the "Passing of Sarah Bernhardt," *Sunday Pictorial*, April 1, 1923, called her "Not merely a wonderful actress, but a great world figure"; in Theatre and Performance Collections, Victoria and Albert Museum (hereafter V&A), SB Biographical Files, Scrapbook, vol. 2. See also "The Idol-Woman and The Other," *London Times*, March 28, 1923, V&A, SB Biographical Files, Scrapbook, vol. 1, which called Bernhardt's "prestige . . . world-wide."
74. A cartoon entitled "Reading a Play to Sarah," *Funny Folks*, August 19, 1882.
75. May Agate, *Madame Sarah* (London: Home and Van Thal, 1946), 201.
76. Edmond Haraucourt, "Sarah Bernhardt est morte," *Comoedia*, March 27, 1923, in V&A, SB Biographical Files, Scrapbook, vol. 2. In the "Passing of Sarah Bernhardt," *Daily Graphic*, March 27, 1923, Sir Sidney Low suggested that because Bernhardt trav-eled "more widely" and "constantly" than other famous actresses, she became "the world's idol, and the peculiar flavour of her art . . . triumphed over differences of race, temperament, and language." Clipping in V&A, SB Biographical Files, Scrapbook, vol. 2.
77. For a definitive discussion of Bernhardt as a representative of France, see Kenneth E. Silver, "Sarah Bernhardt and the Theatrics of French Nationalism: From Roland's Daughter to Napoleon's Son," in *Sarah Bernhardt: The Art of High Drama*, ed. Carol Ockman and Kenneth E. Silver, 75–97 (New Haven, CT: Yale University Press, pub-lished in association with the Jewish Museum, New York, 2005). A clipping in TRI #68 noted that Bernhardt's staging of *Cleopatra* in Philadelphia would "be produced with the Original Scenery and Costumes from the Porte St. Martin Theatre, Paris."
78. Rastignac, "Sarah Bernhardt." On Amsterdam musicians, see "Voyage triomphal de Mlle Sarah Bernhardt en Hollande," *La Presse*, April 1, 1880.
79. On Melbourne, see Edward John Hart, "Illustrated Interviews. No. XL—Sarah Bern-hardt," *Strand Magazine*, 531. Schürmann, *Les Étoiles en voyage*, similarly reported that in Poland a Bernhardt performance became a pro-France demonstration.

80. "Bernhardt, France's 'Greatest Missionary,'" in *Letters and Art, Literary Digest*, April 14, 1923, clipping in TRI #21b. The same phrase appears in a much earlier article, "A Great French Actress. Daily Life of Sarah Bernhardt," *New York Times*, January 12, 1878, in HTC, SB 1870s Clippings.

81. *Le Globe*, July 3, 1879.

82. *Le Globe*, August 3, 1879.

83. Clipping in RBML 1.5.

84. Robert de Beauplan, "Sarah Bernhardt," *L'Illustration*, March 31, 1923, in BnF-DAS, Fol-Ico-Per. For another Napoleon comparison, see Edmond Haraucourt, "Sarah Bernhardt est morte." For another instance of journalists attributing to the actress an "influence on the relations" between France and England "in its way quite as direct and powerful as that of any ambassador or diplomatic agent," see "The Idol-Woman and The Other." A US obituary saw her as doing more to "bind Franco-American and Franco-British relations" than any politician: "Paris Will Bury Sarah Bernhardt," March 28, 1923, HTC, SB Box 3, Obituaries folder.

85. Program for the Gala for the Sarah Bernhardt Centenary, 1944, in BnF-DAS, Fol-Ico-Per.

86. "London Gossip of the Day," *New York Times*, June 30, 1879.

87. An 1887 ad for Bernhardt's Philadelphia performance of *La Dame aux camélias*, for example, announced that it was "her first appearance in the United States, after a triumphal tour in South America" (TRI #61). Michelle Clayton, in "Modernism's Moving Bodies," *Modernist Cultures* 9, no. 1 (May 2014), similarly discusses how Latin American audiences valued the international reputations of visiting performers, whose appearances allowed them to assert parity with other world regions while also insisting on their differences from them (31, 35).

88. Clipping in RBML 1.5.

89. "At the Play," *Sporting Gazette*, June 7, 1879.

90. See Marks, *Sarah Bernhardt's First Theatrical Tour*, 68.

91. See clippings in RBML 1.6.

92. James O'Donnell Bennett, "Bernhardt Echoes," December 5, 1905, in RBML 1.5.

93. "Booth's Welcome," in the *Memphis Daily Appeal*, January 21, 1882, clipping in HBTL, Edwin Booth 1881–82 Season Scrapbook.

94. From the *St. Louis Republican*, February 19, 1882, clipping in HBTL, Edwin Booth 1881–82 Season Scrapbook.

95. Bernhardt boasted of the range of her US travels in Charles Henry Meltzer, "Mme. Bernhardt's Message to America," June 17, 1906, in RBML 1.9. For lists of her stops on the 1905–6 tour, see programs archived in BnF-DAS, Gr Fol-Ico-Per.

96. In *Sarah Bernhardt's First Theatrical Tour*, Patricia Marks quotes people complimenting themselves for seeing Bernhardt in 1880–81 (128).

97. "Bernhardt in the Corn Belt," *Inter Ocean*, March 25, 1906, in RBML 1.9.

CONCLUSION

1. "Vermin": *Narrative of the Life of David Crockett, of the State of Tennessee* (Philadelphia: E. L. Carey and A. Hart, 1834), 5, 8; "lapses": ibid., 8–9; "bragged": see Frederick S. Voss, "Portraying an American Original: The Likenesses of Davy Crockett," *Southwestern Historical Quarterly* 91, no. 4 (April 1988): 464, and Paul Andrew Hutton, "'Going to Congress and Making Allmynacks Is My Trade': Davy Crockett, His Almanacs, and the Evolution of a Frontier Legend," *Journal of the West* 37, no. 2 (April 1998): 17; "spite": *Narrative*, 167; "admitting": ibid., 139; "knack":

ibid., 142, and Voss, "Portraying an American Original," 463; "votes": *Narrative*, 143; "popular": Voss, "Portraying an American Original," 461. Crockett became a byword for racism and misogyny through the many almanacs published under his name; see, for example, *The Crockett Almanac: Containing Sprees and Scrapes in the West* (Boston: J. Fisher, 1841). On Crockett's celebrity status during and after his lifetime, see also Paul Andrew Hutton, "Davy Crockett, Still King of the Wild Frontier," *Texas Monthly*, November 1, 1986, https://www.texasmonthly.com/articles/davy-crockett-still-king-of-the-wild-frontier/.

2. See Voss, "Portraying an American Original," 464, and Alexander Saxton, *The Rise and Fall of the White Republic: Class Politics and Mass Culture in Nineteenth-Century America* (1990; repr. London: Verso, 2003), 94–99.
3. See William Rounseville Alger, *Life of Edwin Forrest, the American Tragedian* (Philadelphia: J. B. Lippincott, 1877), 2:455.
4. See Emily Carman, *Independent Stardom: Freelance Women in the Hollywood Studio System* (Austin: University of Texas Press, 2016), 105, 109.
5. Alex Ross, "The Frankfurt School Knew Trump Was Coming," *New Yorker*, December 5, 2016, https://www.newyorker.com/culture/cultural-comment/the-frankfurt-school-knew-trump-was-coming.

BIBLIOGRAPHY

KEY TO ARCHIVES

BnF-DAS   Bibliothèque nationale de France, Département des Arts du spectacle
HBTL   Hampden-Booth Theatre Library, New York
HTC   Harvard Theatre Collection at Houghton Library, Harvard University
RBML   Rare Book and Manuscript Library, Columbia University
TRI   Jerome Lawrence and Robert E. Lee Theater Research Institute of the Ohio State University Libraries
V&A   Theatre and Performance Collections, Victoria and Albert Museum
WAC   William Andrews Clark Memorial Library, University of California, Los Angeles
WRHS   Western Reserve Historical Society, Cleveland
SB   Sarah Bernhardt (in references to related material across archives)

REFERENCES

Aberdeen Weekly Journal. "Victor Hugo on Art and Peace." December 15, 1877.

Abraham, Émile. "Revue des théâtres." *Le Petit journal*, August 19, 1877. Gallica.

Adam, Eve, ed. *Mrs. J. Comyns Carr's Reminiscences.* 2nd ed. London: Hutchinson, 1926.

Adler, Moshe. "Stardom and Talent." In *Handbook of the Economics of Art and Culture*, vol. 1, edited by Victor A. Ginsburgh and David Throsby, 895–906. Amsterdam: North-Holland, 2006.

Adorno, Theodor W. *The Culture Industry: Selected Essays on Mass Culture.* Edited by J. M. Bernstein. London: Routledge Classics, 2001.

Agate, James. "Sarah Bernhardt: The Secret of Her Greatness." *South Wales News*, March 27, 1923. SB Scrapbook, vol. 1. V&A.

Agate, May. *Madame Sarah.* London: Home and Van Thal, 1946.

Alger, William Rounseville. *Life of Edwin Forrest, the American Tragedian.* 2 vols. Philadelphia: J. B. Lippincott, 1877.

Allan, Maud. *My Life and Dancing.* London: Everett, 1908.

Allen, Emily. *Theater Figures: The Production of the Nineteenth-Century British Novel.* Columbus: Ohio State University Press, 2003.

Allen, Kim. "Girls Imagining Careers in the Limelight: Social Class, Gender and Fantasies of 'Success.'" In *In the Limelight and Under the Microscope: Forms and Functions of Female Celebrity*, edited by Su Holmes and Diane Negra, 149–73. New York: Continuum, 2011.

Allingham, William. *A Diary.* Edited by H. Allingham and D. Radford. London: Macmillan, 1907.

Anderson, Amanda. *The Way We Argue Now: A Study in the Cultures of Theory*. Princeton, NJ: Princeton University Press, 2006.

Anderson, Jill E. "'Send Me a Nice Little Letter All to Myself': Henry Wadsworth Longfellow's Fan Mail and Antebellum Poetic Culture." *University Library Faculty Publications*, no. 111 (2007).

Andrews, Robert. *The Columbia Dictionary of Quotations*. New York: Columbia University Press, 1993.

Angenot, Marc. *Ce qu'on dit des juifs en 1889. Antisémitisme et discours social*. Vincennes: Presses Universitaires de Vincennes, 1989.

Arnold, Matthew. "The French Play in London." *Nineteenth Century*, July 1879.

Asleson, Robyn, ed. *A Passion for Performance: Sarah Siddons and Her Portraitists*. Los Angeles: Getty Publications, 1999.

Aston, Elaine. *Sarah Bernhardt: A French Actress on the English Stage*. Oxford: Berg, 1989.

Atchison Globe. "Miscellaneous News." January 14, 1882.

Auerbach, Nina. *Private Theatricals: The Lives of the Victorians*. Cambridge, MA: Harvard University Press, 1990.

Autrand, Michel. *Le Théâtre en France de 1870 à 1914*. Paris: Honoré Champion, 2006.

Bailey, Peter. *Popular Culture and Performance in the Victorian City*. Cambridge: Cambridge University Press, 1998.

Baldasty, Gerald J. *The Commercialization of News in the Nineteenth Century*. Madison: University of Wisconsin Press, 1992.

Bangor Daily Whig & Courier. "A Dramatic Episode." January 5, 1882.

Banner, Lois W. *MM – Personal: From the Private Archive of Marilyn Monroe*. New York: Abrams, 2011.

Barish, Jonas A. *The Antitheatrical Prejudice*. Berkeley: University of California Press, 1985. First published 1981.

Barthes, Roland. *What Is Sport?* Translated by Richard Howard. New Haven, CT: Yale University Press, 2007.

Bassett, A. Tilney, ed. *A Victorian Vintage: Being a Selection of the Best Stories from the Diaries of the Right Hon. Sir M. E. G. Duff*. London: Methuen, 1930.

Baty, S. Paige. *American Monroe: The Making of a Body Politic*. Berkeley: University of California Press, 1995.

Bauer, Henry. "Sarah Bernhardt." *L'Echo de Paris*, 1896. Fol-Ico-Per. BnF-DAS.

Bean, Annemarie. "Black Minstrelsy and Double Inversion, Circa 1890." In *African American Performance and Theater History: A Critical Reader*, edited by Harry J. Elam and David Krasner. New York: Oxford University Press, 2001.

———. "Transgressing the Gender Divide: The Female Impersonator in Nineteenth-Century Blackface Minstrelsy." In Bean, Hatch, and McNamara, *Inside the Minstrel Mask*, 245–56.

Bean, Annemarie, James Vernon Hatch, and Brooks McNamara, eds. *Inside the Minstrel Mask: Readings in Nineteenth-Century Blackface Minstrelsy*. Hanover, NH: Wesleyan University Press, 1996.

Beauplan, Robert de. "Sarah Bernhardt." *L'Illustration*, March 31, 1923. Fol-Ico-Per. BnF-DAS.

Becker, Karin E. "Photojournalism and the Tabloid Press." In *Journalism and Popular Culture*, edited by Peter Dahlgren and Colin Sparks, 130–52. London: Sage Publications, 1992.

Beerbohm, Max. *Around Theatres*. 2 vols. New York: Knopf, 1930.

———. "Hamlet, Princess of Denmark" (1899). In *Around Theatres*, 1:46–49.

———. "Sarah" (1904). In *Around Theatres*, 2: 424–27.

Belasco, David. "Beginner on the Stage." *Saturday Evening Post*, August 30, 1919. TRI #9.

Belfast News-Letter. "A Chat with Sarah Bernhardt." June 27, 1881.

Bellanger, Claude, Jacques Godechot, Pierre Guiral, and Fernand Terrou, eds. *Histoire générale de la presse française.* 5 vols. Paris: Presses universitaires de France, 1969–76.

Bellet, Roger. *Presse et journalisme sous le Second Empire.* Paris: Armand Colin, 1967.

Benjamin, Walter. "The Work of Art in the Age of Mechanical Reproduction." In *Illuminations,* edited by Hannah Arendt and translated by Harry Zohn, 217–51. New York: Schocken Books, 1969.

Bennett, James O'Donnell. "Bernhardt Echoes." December 5, 1905. Scrapbook 1.5. RBML.

———. "Review of 'La Sorcière.'" November 22, 1905. Scrapbook 1.5. RBML.

———. "Review of Sudermann's 'Magda.'" April 19, 1906. Scrapbook 1.9. RBML.

———. "Review of 'Tosca.'" April 18, 1906. Scrapbook 1.9. RBML.

———. "Sarah Bernhardt." November 25, 1905. 1.5. RBML.

Bergeron, Katherine. *Voice Lessons: French Mélodie in the Belle Epoque.* Oxford: Oxford University Press, 2010.

Berlanstein, Lenard R. *Daughters of Eve: A Cultural History of French Theater Women from the Old Regime to the Fin de Siècle.* Cambridge, MA: Harvard University Press, 2001.

Bernhardt, Sarah. *Dans les nuages: Impressions d'une chaise.* Paris: G. Charpentier, 1878.

Bernstein, Robin. *Racial Innocence: Performing American Childhood from Slavery to Civil Rights.* New York: New York University Press, 2011.

Berthier, Patrick. *Le Théâtre au XIXe siècle.* Paris: Presses Universitaires de France, 1986.

Berton, Claude. "La Grande Sarah." *La Revue mondiale,* April 15, 1923. BnF-DAS.

Bhabha, Homi. "Of Mimicry and Man: The Ambivalence of Colonial Discourse." *October* 28 (Spring 1984): 125–33.

Bhattacharya, Rimli. "Promiscuous Spaces and Economies of Entertainment: Soldiers, Actresses and Hybrid Genres in Colonial India." In Biers and Marcus, "World Literature and Global Performance," 50–75.

Biers, Katherine, and Sharon Marcus, ed. "World Literature and Global Performance." Special issue, *Nineteenth Century Theatre and Film* 41, no. 2 (Winter 2014).

Birmingham Daily Post. "Sarah Bernhardt's Jewels." February 8, 1883.

Blake, David Haven. *Walt Whitman and the Culture of American Celebrity.* New Haven, CT: Yale University Press, 2006.

Blanchard, Edward L. *The Life and Reminiscences of E. L. Blanchard.* London: Hutchinson, 1891.

Blondheim, Menahem. *News over the Wires: The Telegraph and the Flow of Public Information in America, 1844–1897.* Cambridge, MA: Harvard University Press, 1994.

Blum, Justin A. "The Lyceum Theatre and Its Double: Richard Mansfield's Visit to the Greenwich Meridian of Late-Victorian Theatre." In Biers and Marcus, "World Literature and Global Performance," 102–121.

Blumenfeld, R. D. *R. D. B.'s Diary, 1887–1914.* London: Heinemann, 1930.

Bonynge, Richard. *A Collector's Guide to Theatrical Postcards.* London: Grange Books, 1993. First published 1988.

Boorstin, Daniel. *The Image: A Guide to Pseudo-Events in America.* New York: Knopf, 2012. First published 1961.

Booth, Michael R. *Victorian Spectacular Theatre, 1850–1910.* Boston: Routledge & Kegan Paul, 1981.

Booth, Michael R., Richard Southern, Frederick and Lise-Lone Marker, and Robertson Davies, eds. *The Revels History of Drama in English.* Vol. 6, 1750–1880. London: Methuen, 1975.

Boston Daily. "The Seductive Sarah." October 31, 1880.

Boston Daily Globe. "Mme Bernhardt." January 24, 1906.

———. "Sarah Heartburn in Paris." March 3, 1881.

———. "Two Plays." January 21, 1906.

Boston Herald. "Sarah Sees a Prize Fight." April 28, 1891. SB Box 3, Clippings–Obits Folder. HTC.

Boston Home Journal. "Harlequin." February 28, 1891. SB Box 2, 1890s Clippings. HTC.

Bourdieu, Pierre. *The Rules of Art: Genesis and Structure of the Literary Field.* Translated by Susan Emanuel. Stanford, CA: Stanford University Press, 2006.

Bratton, J. S., et al. *Acts of Supremacy: The British Empire and the Stage, 1790–1930.* Manchester: Manchester University Press, 1991.

———, ed. *Music Hall: Performance and Style.* Milton Keynes: Open University Press, 1986.

Braudy, Leo. *The Frenzy of Renown: Fame and its History.* Vintage Books: New York, 1986.

Brooklyn Eagle. "Charles Frohman Ingenuously Defends the 'Star System': Insists That Public and Not the Managers Create Theatrical Luminaries." November 19, 1911. Scrapbook 1.24. RBML Dramatic Museum Scrapbooks Collection.

Brock, Claire. *The Feminization of Fame, 1750–1830.* New York: Palgrave Macmillan, 2006.

Brown, Peter. *The Cult of the Saints: Its Rise and Function in Latin Christianity.* Chicago: University of Chicago Press, 1981.

Brown, Tina. *The Diana Chronicles.* New York: Broadway Books, 2007.

Brownstein, Rachel. *Tragic Muse: Rachel of the Comédie-Française.* New York: Knopf, 1993.

Buckley, Thomas. "Beatles Prepare for Their Debut." *New York Times,* February 9, 1964.

Budd, Michael Anton. *The Sculpture Machine: Physical Culture and Body Politics in the Age of Empire.* New York: New York University Press, 1997.

Buick, Kirsten Pai. *Child of the Fire: Mary Edmonia Lewis and the Problem of Art History's Black and Indian Subject.* Durham, NC: Duke University Press, 2009.

Busson, Dani. *Sarah-Bernhardt.* Paris: Willy Fischer, 1912.

Butler, Elizabeth. *An Autobiography.* London: Constable, 1922.

Campbell, Mrs. Patrick. *My Life and Some Letters.* 2nd ed. London: Hutchinson, 1922.

Capoul, Victor. "Sarah Bernhardt à Toulouse." *Le Figaro,* September 20, 1880.

Carlson, Marvin. *The French Stage in the Nineteenth Century.* Metuchen, NJ: Scarecrow Press, 1972.

Carlyle, Jane. Jane Carlyle to Thomas Carlyle, July 30, 1865. In *Letters and Memorials of Jane Welsh Carlyle,* vol. 2, edited by James Anthony Froude. New York: Charles Scribner's Sons, 1894.

Carman, Emily. *Independent Stardom: Freelance Women in the Hollywood Studio System.* Austin: University of Texas Press, 2016.

Carr, J. Comyns. "An Appreciation." *Daily Telegraph,* March 27, 1923. SB Biographical Files, Scrapbook, vol. 1. V&A.

Cavell, Stanley. *The World Viewed: Reflections on the Ontology of Film.* Enl. ed. Cambridge, MA: Harvard University Press, 1995. First published 1971.

Cavicchi, Daniel. *Listening and Longing: Music Lovers in the Age of Barnum.* Middletown, CT: Wesleyan University Press, 2011.

Champsaur, Félicien. "Sarah Bernhardt." *Les Hommes d'aujourd'hui,* October 25, 1878. BnF-DAS.

Chandler, Charles F., and Arthur H. Elliott, eds. *Anthony's Photographic Bulletin* 17 (1886). New York: E. & H. T. Anthony.

Charle, Christophe. *Le Siècle de la presse, 1830–1939.* Paris: Seuil, 2004.

Chicago Daily Tribune. "Bernhardt Appears in 'Gismonda.'" June 2, 1895.

———. "Bernhardt in 'Salome': Gorgeous Costumes She Will Wear in Oscar Wilde's One-Act Play." August 28, 1892.

———. "'Crusoe' Is a Success." June 23, 1895.

———. "Music and the Drama." March 21, 1901.

Chicago Times. "Edwin Booth." February 14, 1894. Edwin Booth Death Album. HBTL.

Christensen, Jerome. *Lord Byron's Strength: Romantic Writing and Commercial Society.* Baltimore: Johns Hopkins University Press, 1993.

Clayton, Michelle. "Modernism's Moving Bodies." *Modernist Cultures* 9, no. 1 (May 2014): 27–45.

Cleave, Maureen. "How Does a Beatle Live? John Lennon Lives like This." *London Evening Standard*, March 4, 1966.

Cliff, Aimee. "How Rihanna Maintains Control." *Fader*, April 28, 2016. http://www .thefader.com/2016/04/28/rihanna-needed-me-video-nipples-objectification-control.

Cohen, Margaret. *The Novel and the Sea.* Princeton, NJ: Princeton University Press, 2010.

Collier, E. C. F., ed. *A Victorian Diarist: Extracts from the Journals of Mary, Lady Monkswell, 1875–1895.* London: John Murray, 1944.

Colombier, Marie. *Les Mémoires de Sarah Barnum.* 2nd ed. Paris: Chez tous les libraires, 1884.

Colorado Springs Weekly Gazette. "Sara Sees Heartburn." January 22, 1881.

Cosnier, Colette. *Le Silence des filles: De l'aiguille à la plume.* Paris: Fayard, 2001.

County Gentleman. "The Season, by a Saunterer." June 5, 1880.

Courtalin. "Théâtres." *Le Globe* (Paris), August 29, 1880.

Court Journal. July 7, 1883. Wildeiana Box 10.11. WAC.

Cowan, Brian. "News, Biography, and Eighteenth-Century Celebrity." *Oxford Handbooks Online*, September 2016. http://doi.org/crzx.

Coward, John M. *The Newspaper Indian: Native American Identity in the Press, 1820–90.* Urbana: University of Illinois Press, 1999.

Cowen, Ruth. *Relish: The Extraordinary Life of Alexis Soyer, Victorian Celebrity Chef.* London: Weidenfeld & Nicolson, 2006.

Crockett, Davy. *The Crockett Almanac: Containing Sprees and Scrapes in the West.* Boston: Turner & Fisher, 1841.

Crowther, Bosley. "Lower and Lower." *New York Times.* January 22, 1944.

Currier and Ives. "The Aesthetic Craze." Ca. 1882. Wildeiana Box 18, Folder 9. WAC.

Curtis, Susan. *The First Black Actors on the Great White Way.* Columbia: University of Missouri Press, 1998.

Daily Beast. "Beliebers Revolt Against Their Deity, Justin Bieber, Over New Girlfriend Sofia Richie." August 14, 2016. https://www.thedailybeast.com/beliebers -revolt-against-their-deity-justin-bieber-over-new-girlfriend-sofia-richie.

Daily Graphic. "Passing of Sarah Bernhardt." March 27, 1923. V&A.

Daily Sketch. "The Unconventional Sarah: Why She Was the World's Great Bohemian." March 28, 1923.

Daily Telegraph. "Madame Sarah Bernhardt. 'L'Aiglon' at the Coliseum." September 20, 1910. SB Personal Box 8. V&A.

Dames, Nicholas. "Brushes with Fame: Thackeray and the Work of Celebrity." *Nineteenth-Century Literature* 56, no. 1 (June 2001): 23–51.

Dana, Charles A. *The Art of Newspaper Making.* New York: D. Appleton, 1895.

Danner, Chas. "Muhammad Ali's Life in Poetry, Activism, and Trash Talk." Daily Intelligencer (blog), *New York*, June 4, 2016. http://nymag.com/daily/intelligencer/2016/06 /muhammad-alis-poetry-activism-and-trash-talk.html.

Darnton, Robert. "Five Myths about the 'Information Age.'" *Chronicle of Higher Education*, April 17, 2011, sec. Chronicle Review. https://www.chronicle.com/article /5-Myths-About-the-Information/127105.

Daudet, Alphonse. *Pages inédites de critique dramatique: 1874–1880.* Paris: Librairie de France, 1930.

Davis, Jim, and Victor Emeljanow. *Reflecting the Audience: London Theatregoing, 1840–1880*. Iowa City: University of Iowa Press, 2001.

Davis, Tracy C. *Actresses as Working Women: Their Social Identity in Victorian Culture*. London: Routledge, 1991.

———. *The Economics of the British Stage, 1800–1914*. Cambridge: Cambridge University Press, 2000.

———. "The Sociable Playwright and Representative Citizen." In *Women and Playwriting in Nineteenth-Century Britain*, edited by Tracy C. Davis and Ellen Donkin, 15–34. Cambridge: Cambridge University Press, 1999.

Davis, Tracy C., and Peter Holland. *The Performing Century: Nineteenth-Century Theatre's History*. Basingstoke: Palgrave Macmillan, 2007.

DeAngelis, Michael. *Gay Fandom and Crossover Stardom: James Dean, Mel Gibson, and Keanu Reeves*. Durham, NC: Duke University Press, 2001.

Debord, Guy. *Society of the Spectacle*. Translated by Fredy Perlman et al. Detroit: Black & Red, 1970.

deCordova, Richard. *Picture Personalities: The Emergence of the Star System in America*. Urbana: University of Illinois Press, 1990.

Degron, Henri. "La Princesse lointaine." *La Plume*, December 1, 1900. SB Personal Box 8. V&A.

Delamarter, Eric. "Society at Bernhardt Play." *Inter Ocean*, November 1, 1910. Scrapbook 1.20. RBML.

de Mille, Agnes. *Dance to the Piper*. New York: New York Review Books, 2015. First published 1951.

de Mortemar, Julie. "A Queen of Diamonds." In *Folly's Queens; or, Women Whose Loves Have Ruled the World: Life Sketches of the Most Famous Belles of Cupid's Court for Two Centuries*, 35–41. New York: Richard K. Fox, 1882.

Desjardins, Mary R. *Recycled Stars: Female Stardom in the Age of Television and Video*. Durham, NC: Duke University Press, 2015.

d'Heyli, Georges [Antoine Edmund Poinsot]. *La Comedie-Francaise à Londres (1871–1879). Journal inédit de E. Got—Journal de F. Sarcey*. Paris: Ollendorf, 1880.

Diebel, Anne. " 'The Dreary Duty': Henry James, *The Yellow Book*, and Literary Personality." *Henry James Review* 32, no. 1 (Winter 2011): 45–59.

Dillon, Elizabeth Maddock. *New World Drama: The Performative Commons in the Atlantic World, 1649–1849*. Durham, NC: Duke University Press, 2014.

Donohue, Joseph W. *Dramatic Character in the English Romantic Age*. Princeton, NJ: Princeton University Press, 1970.

Downer, Alan S. "Players and Painted Stage: Nineteenth Century Acting." *PMLA* 61, no. 2 (June 1946): 522–76.

Downey, William, and Daniel Downey. *The Cabinet Portrait Gallery*. First Series. London: Cassell, 1890.

Doyle, Sady. *Trainwreck: The Women We Love to Hate, Mock, and Fear . . . and Why*. Brooklyn: Melville House, 2016.

Drew, Mary. *Mrs. Gladstone: Her Diaries and Letters*. Edited by Lucy Masterman. London: Methuen, 1930.

Duckett, Victoria. *Seeing Sarah Bernhardt: Performance and Silent Film*. Urbana: University of Illinois Press, 2015.

Dufief, Anne-Simone. *Le Théâtre au XIXᵉ siècle*. Paris: Bréat, 2001.

Duval, E. B. *Caricatures of Oscar Wilde in Ethnic Dress*. Ca. 1882. Box 21, Folder 3. WAC.

Dyer, Richard. *Stars*. London: British Film Institute, 1979.

Eimelle. "Marie Dorval Kitty Bell Chatterton Vigny Drame Romantique." *Les carnets d'Eimelle*, December 5, 2012. http://lecture-spectacle.blogspot.com/2012/12/marie-dorval-kitty-bell-chatterton.html.

Elfenbein, Andrew. *Romantic Genius: The Prehistory of a Homosexual Role*. New York: Columbia University Press, 1999.

Eltinge, Julian. "The Troubles of a Man Who Wears Skirts." *Green Book Magazine*, January 1915. TRI #2.

ElvisPresleyPhotos.com. "Elvis Presley | Vancouver, Canada. Empire Stadium | August 31, 1957." Accessed March 18, 2018. http://www.elvispresleymusic.com.au/pictures/1957-august-31.html.

Emeljanow, Victor. *Victorian Popular Dramatists*. Boston: Twayne, 1987.

Emerson, Ralph Waldo. "Self-Reliance." In *Ralph Waldo Emerson: Essays and Lectures*, edited by Joel Porte. New York: Library of America, 1983.

Engelhardt, Molly. "Marie Taglioni, Ballerina Extraordinaire: In the Company of Women." *Nineteenth-Century Gender Studies* 6, no. 3 (Winter 2010): 1–29.

Englishwoman's Domestic Magazine. "Our Paris Letter of Fashions and Gossip." January 1, 1878.

———. "Our Paris Letter of Fashions and Gossip." May 1, 1878.

———. "Spinnings in Town." July 1, 1874.

The Era. "Sarah Bernhardt and Daria in Brussels." May 20, 1882.

———. "Sarah Bernhardt's Coffin Portraits." February 25, 1882.

———. "Sarah Heartburn." June 25, 1881.

Erdman, Andrew L. *Blue Vaudeville: Sex, Morals, and the Mass Marketing of Amusement, 1895–1915*. Jefferson, NC: McFarland, 2004.

Evans Asbury, Edith. "Time Inc. to Revive *Life* as a Monthly." *New York Times*. April 25, 1978.

Evening World. "Bernhardt in 'Ashes.' " December 7, 1916.

Eveno, Patrick. *Histoire de la presse française: De Théophraste Renaudot à la révolution numérique*. Paris: Flammarion, 2012.

———. *L'Argent de la presse française des années 1820 à nos jours*. Éditions du CTHS, 2003.

The Examiner. "French Players: Mlle. Sarah Bernhardt." March 18, 1876.

———. "Variorum Notes." June 10, 1876.

———. "Variorum Notes." December 15, 1877.

Falcone, Michael. "Obama Gets Celebrity Treatment in New McCain Ad." *New York Times*, July 30, 2008. http://thecaucus.blogs.nytimes.com/2008/07/30/obama-gets-celebrity-treatment-in-new-mccain-ad/.

Fawcett, Julia H. *Spectacular Disappearances: Celebrity and Privacy, 1696–1801*. Ann Arbor: University of Michigan Press, 2016.

Ferris, Kerry. *Stargazing: Celebrity, Fame, and Social Interaction*. New York: Routledge, 2011.

Fishing Gazette. "Sarah Bernhardt." August 21, 1880.

Flint, Kate. *The Transatlantic Indian, 1776–1930*. Princeton, NJ: Princeton University Press, 2009.

Flower, Sarah. *Great Aunt Sarah's Diary*. Privately Printed, 1964.

Fouquier, Henry. "Bernhardt and Coquelin." *Harper's Magazine*, December 1900.

Fourcaud. "Le Théâtre: La comédienne et le comédien." *La Vie moderne* (Paris), November 11, 1882.

Fournel, Victor. "Les Oeuvres et les hommes." *Le Correspondant* (Paris), July 25, 1879. Salle 10. BnF-DAS.

———. "Les Oeuvres et les hommes." *Le Correspondant* (Paris), May 10, 1880.

Fox, Celina. *Graphic Journalism in England during the 1830s and 1840s*. New York: Garland Publishing, 1988.

Frank, Glenn. "At Bernhardt's Grave," August 31, 1926. TRI #75.

Frédérix, Pierre *Un Siècle de chasse aux nouvelles: De l'agence d'information Havas à l'agence France-Presse, 1835–1957*. Paris: Flammarion, 1959.

Fresnay, Paul. "Sarah Bernhardt's Coffin." *Georgia Weekly Telegraph*, March 17, 1882.

Freud, Sigmund. *Letters of Sigmund Freud: 1873–1939*. Edited by Ernst L. Freud. Translated by Tania Stern and James Stern. London: Hogarth, 1961.

Frost, Linda. *Never One Nation: Freaks, Savages, and Whiteness in U.S. Popular Culture, 1850–1877*. Minneapolis: University of Minnesota Press, 2005.

Fuller, Kathryn H. *At the Picture Show: Small-Town Audiences and the Creation of Movie Fan Culture*. Washington, DC: Smithsonian Institution Press, 1996.

Fun. "Our Extra-Special on the Comedie Francaise [*sic*]." June 25, 1879.

———. "Sarah as William." July 16, 1879.

———. "Sarah Barnum." December 26, 1883.

Funny Folks. "A Bernhardt Task." July 26, 1879.

———. "A 'Bony' Contention." August 16, 1879.

———. "The Comedie's Coming." June 7, 1879.

———. "The One Thing Needful." August 4, 1883.

———. "Reading a Play to Sarah." August 19, 1882.

———. "Sarah Bernhardt-Achings." August 2, 1879.

———. "Sarah Bernhardt on the Brain." June 14, 1879.

———. "Sarah's Future." May 8, 1880.

———. "Seeing Sarah." June 28, 1879.

———. "A Surp-Rice-Ing Performance." July 9, 1881.

Furniss, Harry. *The Confessions of a Caricaturist*. Vol. 1. New York: Harper & Brothers, 1902.

Fyles, Franklin. "Hot Nights in the Tenderloin." *Washington Post*, July 16, 1905.

Gabler, Neal. *Barbra Streisand: Redefining Beauty, Femininity, and Power*. New Haven, CT: Yale University Press, 2016.

Gamson, Joshua. *Claims to Fame: Celebrity in Contemporary America*. Berkeley: University of California Press, 1994.

Ganderax, Étienne. "Sarah Bernhardt et la Comédie-Française." *La Revue de Paris*, June 1, 1930.

Gardner, Viv. "Gertie Millar and the 'Rules for Actresses and Vicars' Wives.'" In *Extraordinary Actors: Studies in Honour of Peter Thomson*, edited by Jane Milling and Martin Banham, 97–112. Exeter: University of Exeter Press, 2004.

Garelick, Rhonda K. *Rising Star: Dandyism, Gender, and Performance in the Fin de Siècle*. Princeton, NJ: Princeton University Press, 1998.

Gielgud, John. *Early Stages*. New York: Macmillan, 1939.

Gledhill, Christine. "Signs of Melodrama." In *Stardom: Industry of Desire*, 207–29. London: Routledge, 1991.

Glenn, Susan A. *Female Spectacle: The Theatrical Roots of Modern Feminism*. Cambridge, MA: Harvard University Press, 2002.

Globe. "Paris Gossip." April 6, 1882. SB Personal Box 7. V&A.

Gobert, R. Darren. *The Mind-Body Stage: Passion and Interaction in the Cartesian Theatre*. Stanford, CA: Stanford University Press, 2013.

Goffman, Erving. *Asylums: Essays on the Condition of the Social Situation of Mental Patients and Other Inmates*. New York: Anchor Books, 1961.

———. *Interaction Ritual: Essays on Face-to-Face Behavior*. New York: Anchor Books, 1967.

Goldstein, Robert Justin. "Censorship of Caricature in France, 1815–1914." *French History* 3, no. 1 (1989): 71–107.

Gollapudi, Aparna. "Selling Celebrity: Actors' Portraits in *Bell's Shakespeare* and *Bell's British Theatre*." *Eighteenth-Century Life* 36, no. 1 (Winter 2012): 54–81.

Gordon, Eleanor, and Gwyneth Nair. *Murder and Morality in Victorian Britain: The Story of Madeleine Smith*. Manchester: Manchester University Press, 2009.

Gordon, Rae Beth. *Dances with Darwin, 1875–1910: Vernacular Modernity in France*. Farnham: Ashgate, 2009.

Gosling, Nigel. *Nadar*. New York: Knopf, 1976.

Gould, Jack. "TV: It's the Beatles (Yeah, Yeah, Yeah)." *New York Times*, January 4, 1964.

———. "TV: New Phenomenon: Elvis Presley Rises to Fame as Vocalist Who Is Virtuoso of Hootchy-Kootchy." *New York Times*, June 6, 1956.

Gourevitch, Philip. "Mr. Brown." *New Yorker*, July 29, 2002. https://www.newyorker.com/magazine/2002/07/29/mr-brown.

Gower, Ronald. *Old Diaries, 1881–1901*. London: John Murray, 1902.

Green, Timothy. "They Crown Their Country with a Bowl-Shaped Hairdo." *Life*, January 31, 1964.

Grimsted, David. *Melodrama Unveiled: American Theater and Culture, 1800–1850*. Berkeley: University of California Press, 1987. First published 1968.

Gubar, Marah. "Peter Pan as Children's Theatre: The Issue of Audience." In *The Oxford Handbook of Children's Literature*, edited by Julia Mickenberg and Lynne Vallone, 475–95. New York: Oxford University Press, 2011.

Guénoun, Denis. *Actions et acteurs: Raisons du drame sur scène*. Paris: Belin, 2005.

Guex, Jules. *Le Théâtre et la société française de 1815 à 1848*. Geneva: Slatkine Reprints, 1973.

Guibert, Noëlle. *Portrait(s) de Sarah Bernhardt*. Paris: Bibliothèque nationale de France, 2000.

Habermas, Jürgen. *The Structural Transformation of the Public Sphere: An Inquiry into a Category of Bourgeois Society*. Translated by Thomas Burger, with the assistance of Frederick Lawrence. Cambridge, MA: MIT Press, 1989. Originally published, in German, in 1962.

Hadley, Elaine. *Living Liberalism: Practical Citizenship in Mid-Victorian Britain*. Chicago: University of Chicago Press, 2010.

Hahn, Reynaldo. *La Grande Sarah: Souvenirs*. Paris: Hachette, 1930.

Hallett, Hilary. *Go West, Young Women! The Rise of Early Hollywood*. Berkeley: University of California Press, 2013.

Hamilton Daily Democrat. "Grand Opening." October 20, 1887.

Hampf, M. Michaela, and Simone Müller-Pohl, eds. *Global Communication Electric: Business, News, and Politics in the World of Telegraphy*. Frankfurt: Campus Verlag, 2013.

Hampshire Telegraph and Sussex Chronicle. "Things Theatrical." December 8, 1880.

Hansen, Miriam. *Babel and Babylon: Spectatorship in American Silent Film*. Cambridge, MA: Harvard University Press, 1991.

Haraucourt, Edmond. "Sarah Bernhardt est morte." *Comoedia*, March 27, 1923. SB Biographical Files, Scrapbook, vol. 2. V&A.

Harradence Diary, entry for May 7, 1895. WRHS.

Harris, Neil. *Humbug: The Art of P. T. Barnum*. Chicago: University of Chicago Press, 1981.

Harris Bradley, Katharine. "Katharine Harris Bradley Diary," 1868–9. Add. Mss. 46776. British Library.

Hart, Edward John. "Illustrated Interviews. No. XL: Sarah Bernhardt." *Strand Magazine*, January 1895.

Hattenstone, Simon. "Lena Dunham: 'People Called Me Fat and Hideous, and I Lived.'" *The Guardian*. January 11, 2014. https://www.theguardian.com/culture/2014/jan/11/lena-dunham-called-fat-hideous-and-i-lived.

Hauser, Thomas. *The Lost Legacy of Muhammad Ali*. Wilmington, DE: SPORTClassic Books, 2005.

Hazlitt, William. *The Spirit of the Age*. London: Henry Colburn, 1825.

Heffernan, Thomas J. *Sacred Biography: Saints and Their Biographers in the Middle Ages*. Oxford: Oxford University Press, 1992.

Henderson, Mary C. *Broadway Ballyhoo: The American Theater Seen in Posters, Photographs, Magazines, Caricatures, and Programs.* New York: Abrams, 1989.

Hengstler-Castor, T., and Max Nordau. "Outre-Mer. XII. Sarah Bernhardt." *Boston Home Journal*, March 21, 1891. Plays O–Z. HTC.

Henkin, David M. *The Postal Age: The Emergence of Modern Communications in Nineteenth-Century America.* Chicago: University of Chicago Press, 2006.

Hichens, R. S. *The Green Carnation.* New York: Mitchell Kennerley, 1894.

Hill, Jason, and Vanessa R. Schwartz, eds. *Getting the Picture: The Visual Culture of the News.* London: Bloomsbury Academic, 2015.

Hill, Miss Murray. "Wear for New York Women. Individuality in the Costumes of Mme. Bernhardt," April 4, 1887. SB Clippings, 1880s. HTC.

Hillyard, Kim. "Taylor Swift Writes Open Letter to Apple Music: 'We Don't Ask You for Free iPhones.'" *New Musical Express*, June 21, 2015. https://www.nme.com/news/music/taylor-swift-134-1225572.

Hindson, Catherine. "'Mrs. Langtry Seems to Be on the Way to a Fortune': The Jersey Lily and Models of Late Nineteenth-Century Fame." In Holmes and Negra, *In the Limelight and Under the Microscope*, 17–36.

Hirsch, Foster. *Acting Hollywood Style: With Photographs from the Kobal Collection.* New York: Abrams, 1991.

Holmes, Su, and Diane Negra, eds. *In the Limelight and Under the Microscope: Forms and Functions of Female Celebrity.* New York: Continuum, 2011.

Holmgren, Beth. *Starring Madame Modjeska: On Tour in Poland and America.* Bloomington: Indiana University Press, 2012.

Homans, Margaret. *Royal Representations: Queen Victoria and British Culture, 1837–1876.* Chicago: University of Chicago Press, 1998.

Horkheimer, Max, and Theodor W. Adorno. *Dialectic of Enlightenment.* Translated by John Cumming. New York: Continuum, 1972. Originally published, in German, in 1944.

Horne, Charles F., ed. *Great Men and Famous Women.* Vol. 4. New York: Selmar Hess, 1894.

Horville, Robert. "The Stage Techniques of Sarah Bernhardt." In *Bernhardt and the Theater of Her Time*, 35–65. Westport, CT: Greenwood Press, 1984.

Huret, Jules. *Sarah Bernhardt.* Translated by G. A Raper. London: Chapman & Hall, 1899. Originally published as *Sarah Bernhardt* (Paris: F. Juven, 1899).

Hutchens, John K. "Visit to the Shrine: Notes on an Evening Among Mr. Sinatra's Admirers at the Saturday 'Hit Parade.'" *New York Times.* November 7, 1943.

Hutton, Paul Andrew. "Davy Crockett, Still King of the Wild Frontier." *Texas Monthly*, November 1, 1986. https://www.texasmonthly.com/articles/davy-crockett-still-king-of-the-wild-frontier/.

———. "'Going to Congress and Making Allmynacks Is My Trade': Davy Crockett, His Almanacs, and the Evolution of a Frontier Legend." *Journal of the West* 37, no. 2 (April 1998): 10–22.

Illustrated Life of Sarah Bernhardt. New York: A. J. Fisher, 1880.

Illustrated Household Journal and Englishwoman's Domestic Magazine. "Our Paris Letter of Gossip and Fashion." May 22, 1880.

———. "Our Paris Letter of Gossip and Fashion." October 1, 1881.

Illustrated Sporting and Dramatic News. "Our Captious Critic. 'Cleopatra.'" June 18, 1892.

Inter Ocean. "Amusements. Columbia." April 26, 1887. SB Clippings-Misc. HTC.

———. "Amusements. Dramatic. Bernhardt." May 1, 1887. SB Box 2, 1890s Clippings. HTC.

———. "Amusements. Dramatic. Bernhardt's Return." October 4, 1891. SB Box 2, 1890s Clippings. HTC.

———. "Bernhardt in the Corn Belt." March 25, 1906. RBML 1.9.

James, Henry. "Coquelin." In *The Scenic Art*, 198–218.

———. "George Sand." In *French Poets and Novelists*, 149–63. London: Macmillan, 1893. First published 1878.

———. "The Art of Fiction." *Longman's Magazine*, September 1884.

———. "The Comédie-Française in London." *The Nation*, July 31, 1879.

———. *The Scenic Art: Notes on Acting and The Drama: 1872–1901*. Edited by Alan Wade. New Brunswick, NJ: Rutgers University Press, 1948.

———. "The Théâtre Français." In *The Scenic Art*, 68–92.

Jeanne, René. "Garbo sera-t-elle Sarah Bernhardt?" *L'Écran français*, January 14, 1947.

Jenkins, Henry. *Convergence Culture: Where Old and New Media Collide*. New York: New York University Press, 2006.

———. *Fans, Bloggers, and Gamers: Exploring Participatory Culture*. New York: New York University Press, 2006.

———. *Textual Poachers: Television Fans and Participatory Culture*. New York: Routledge, 2013. First published 1992.

Joannis, Claudette. *Sarah Bernhardt*. Paris: Payot, 2011.

Johnson, James H. *Listening in Paris: A Cultural History*. Berkeley: University of California Press, 1996.

Jordan, Matthew. "In a Post-Truth Election, Clicks Trump Facts." *The Conversation*, October 25, 2016. https://theconversation.com/in-a-post-truth-election -clicks-trump-facts-67274.

Judy. "Our Weekly One." September 8, 1880.

———. "The Only Jones." June 15, 1881.

Kalifa, Dominique, ed. *La Civilisation du journal: Histoire culturelle et littéraire de la presse française au XIXe siècle*. Paris: Éditions Nouveau Monde, 2011.

Karr, Benjamin. "The Stage Road for Women." Ca. 1923. TRI #72.

Keeley, James. "Newspaper Work: An Address Delivered before the Students in the Course of Journalism at Notre Dame University, November 26, 1912." Pamphlet in the library of the Chicago Historical Society.

Kelly, Jon. "What Should Celebrities Do with Fan Mail?" *BBC News Magazine*, March 20, 2013. http://www.bbc.com/news/magazine-21835118.

Kelsey, Robin. *Photography and the Art of Chance*. Cambridge, MA: The Belknap Press of Harvard University Press, 2015.

Kember, Joe. *Marketing Modernity: Victorian Popular Shows and Early Cinema*. Exeter: University of Exeter Press, 2009.

King, Andrew, and John Plunkett, eds. *Victorian Print Media: A Reader*. Oxford: Oxford University Press, 2005.

Kirkwood, John. "Presley Fans Demented." *Vancouver Sun*, September 3, 1957.

Krauss, Bob. "Hipster Hexes Hysterical Hepsters." *Honolulu Advertiser*, November 11, 1957.

Kurnick, David. *Empty Houses: Theatrical Failure and the Novel*. Princeton, NJ: Princeton University Press, 2011.

La Caricature (Paris). "Aventures et mésaventures de Séraphiska." May 15, 1880.

Ladies' Monthly Magazine. "Our Paris Letter." December 1, 1880.

———. "Parisian Gossip." July 1, 1880.

———. "The Full-Size Patterns." June 1, 1879.

Lancaster, Albert Edmund. "All Hail, Bernhardt!" *New York Mirror*. SB Box 2, 1890s Clippings. HTC.

Landis, Louise. "Bernhardt's Ageless Art Wins for Her New Laurels." Ca. 1916. TRI #21b.

Lapauze, Henry. "Étude biographique: Madame Sarah Bernhardt." *Revue encyclopédique*, December 15, 1893.

Laporte, Antoine. *Beranger, Sarah Bernhardt, Bertall: Étude bibliographique*. Paris: A. Laporte, 1884.

La Presse (Paris). "Courrier de Paris." July 4, 1879.

———. "Une Nouvelle Jeanne d'Arc." August 26, 1880.

———. "Voyage Triomphal de Mlle Sarah Bernhardt en Hollande." April 1, 1880.

Leavitt, Michael Bennett. *Fifty Years in Theatrical Management, 1859–1909*. New York: Broadway Publishing, 1912.

Le Correspondant (Paris). "Les Oeuvres." November 25, 1896.

Le Figaro. "'Adrienne Lecouvreur' à Marseille." September 25, 1880.

———. "Echos de Paris." May 6, 1870.

———. "La Fuite de Mlle Sarah Bernhardt." April 21, 1880.

———. "La Soirée théâtrale." September 28, 1876.

———. "Sarah Bernhardt en province." September 2, 1880.

———. "Supplement Litteraire." March 31, 1923. Gr Fol-Ico-Per. BnF-DAS.

———. "Une lettre de Sarah Bernhardt." April 26, 1880.

———. Unsigned review of *L'Etrangère*. February 15, 1876.

Le Souffleur. "Carnet du Souffleur." *La Vie moderne* (Paris), September 18, 1880.

Le Globe (Paris). "Courrier des Théâtres." April 24, 1880.

Legouvé, Ernest. *Soixante ans de souvenirs*. Vol. 2. Paris: J. Hetzel, 1887.

Lemaître, Jules. "Sarah Bernhardt racontée par elle-même—Opinions." *Revue encyclo-pédique*, December 15, 1893.

"Lesbians Who Look Like Justin Bieber." Accessed April 26, 2017. https://lesbianswholooklikejustinbieber.tumblr.com/.

Lethève, Jacques. *La Caricature et la presse sous la IIIᵉ République*. Paris: Max Leclerc, 1961.

Letters and Art, Literary Digest. "Bernhardt, France's 'Greatest Missionary.'" April 14, 1923. TRI #21b.

Levine, Lawrence W. *Highbrow, Lowbrow: The Emergence of Cultural Hierarchy in America*. Cambridge, MA: Harvard University Press, 1990.

Lewes, George Henry. *On Actors and the Art of Acting*. London: Smith, Elder, 1875.

Lilti, Antoine. *Figures publiques: L'invention de la célébrité, 1750–1850*. Paris: Fayard, 2014.

Link, Howard. *The Theatrical Prints of the Torii Masters*. Tokyo: Tuttle, 1977.

Lipsyte, Robert. "Muhammad Ali Dies at 74: Titan of Boxing and the 20th Century." *New York Times*, June 4, 2016. https://www.nytimes.com/2016/06/04/sports/muhammad-ali-dies.html.

Livois, René de. *Histoire de la presse française*. Vol. 1. Paris: Les Temps de la presse, 1965.

London Era. "Letter." December 15, 1880. SB Box 2, Folder: 1880s Clippings. HTC.

London Sunday Times. Sarah Bernhardt obituary. 1923. SB Clippings, Obits. HTC.

London Times. "Sarah Bernhardt." March 27, 1923.

———. "The Idol-Woman and The Other." March 28, 1923. SB Biographical Files, Scrapbook, vol. 1. V&A.

Lorcin, Patricia M. E. *Imperial Identities: Stereotyping, Prejudice and Race in Colonial Algeria*. London: I. B. Tauris, 1995.

Lott, Eric. *Love and Theft: Blackface Minstrelsy and the American Working Class*. New York: Oxford University Press, 2013. First published 1993.

Louys, Pierre. *Journal intime: 1882–1891*. Paris: Éditions Montaigne, 1929.

Low, Sir Sidney. "Passing of Sarah Bernhardt." *Sunday Pictorial*, April 1, 1923. SB Biographical Files, Scrapbook, vol. 2. V&A.

Lowenthal, Leo. "The Triumph of Mass Idols." In *Literature, Popular Culture, and Society*, 109–40. Palo Alto: Pacific Books, 1968. First published 1944.

Luckhurst, Mary, and Jane Moody, eds. *Theatre and Celebrity in Britain, 1660–2000*. Basingstoke: Palgrave Macmillan, 2005.

Lyden, Anne M. *A Royal Passion: Queen Victoria and Photography*. Los Angeles: J. Paul Getty Museum, 2014.

Lynch, Deidre Shauna. *Loving Literature: A Cultural History*. Chicago: University of Chicago Press, 2015.

Mahar, William J. *Behind the Burnt Cork Mask: Early Blackface Minstrelsy and Antebellum American Popular Culture*. Urbana: University of Illinois Press, 1999.

———. "Ethiopian Skits and Sketches: Contents and Contexts of Blackface Minstrelsy, 1840–1890," in Bean, Hatch, and McNamara, *Inside the Minstrel Mask*, 179–222.

Malin, Brenton J. *Feeling Mediated: A History of Media Technology and Emotion in America*. New York: New York University Press, 2014.

Marcus, Sharon. "Celebrity 2.0: The Case of Marina Abramović." *Public Culture* 27, no. 1 (January 2015): 21–52.

———. "I'm Professor Sharon Marcus, from Columbia University, and I Study Celebrity Culture in the Past and in the Present, AMA!" Reddit, March 17, 2015. https://www.reddit.com/r/science/comments/2zca5c/science_ama_series_im_professor_sharon_marcus/.

———. "Salome!! Sarah Bernhardt, Oscar Wilde, and the Drama of Celebrity." *PMLA* 126, no. 4 (October 2011): 999–1021. https://doi.org/10.1632/pmla.2011.126.4.999.

———. "The Theater of Comparative Literature." In *A Companion to Comparative Literature*, edited by Ali Behdad and Dominic Thomas, 136–154. Chichester: John Wiley & Sons, 2011.

———. "The Theatrical Scrapbook." *Theatre Survey* 54, no. 2 (May 2013): 283–307.

Marez, Curtis. "The Other Addict: Reflections on Colonialism and Oscar Wilde's Opium Smoke Screen." *ELH* 64, no. 1 (Spring 1997): 257–87.

Marker, Frederick and Lise-Lone. "Actors and their Repertory." In Booth et al., *The Revels History of Drama in English*, 6:95–143.

Marks, Patricia. *Sarah Bernhardt's First Theatrical Tour*. Jefferson, NC: McFarland, 2003.

Marra, Kim. *Strange Duets: Impresarios and Actresses in the American Theatre, 1865–1914*. Iowa City: University of Iowa, 2006.

Marshall, P. David. *Celebrity and Power: Fame in Contemporary Culture*. Minneapolis: University of Minnesota Press, 1997.

Martin-Fugier, Anne. *La Vie elégante ou la formation du Tout-Paris, 1815–1848*. Paris: Fayard, 1990.

Maslan, Susan. *Revolutionary Acts: Theater, Democracy, and the French Revolution*. Baltimore: Johns Hopkins University Press, 2005.

Mason, Miranda Eve. "Making Love/Making Work: The Sculpture Practice of Sarah Bernhardt." PhD diss., University of Leeds, 2007.

Masood, Salman. "Pakistani Internet Celebrity Strangled, Police Say." *New York Times*, July 16, 2016. https://www.nytimes.com/2016/07/17/world/asia/qandeel-baloch-pakistan-internet-celebrity-killed.html.

Matthews, J. Brander. *The Theatres of Paris*. New York: Scribner's, 1880.

Mayer, David. *Stagestruck Filmmaker: D. W. Griffith and the American Theatre*. Iowa City: University of Iowa Press, 2009.

Maza, Sarah. *Private Lives and Public Affairs: The Causes Célèbres of Prerevolutionary France*. Berkeley: University of California Press, 1993.

McArthur, Benjamin. *Actors and American Culture, 1880–1920*. Iowa City: University of Iowa Press, 1984.

McConachie, Bruce. *Melodramatic Formations: American Theatre and Society, 1820–1870*. Iowa City: University of Iowa Press, 1992.

McLean, Adrienne L. *Being Rita Hayworth: Labor, Identity, and Hollywood Stardom*. New Brunswick, NJ: Rutgers University Press, 2004.

McNamara, Brooks. *The Shuberts of Broadway: A History Drawn from the Collections of the Shubert Archive*. New York: Oxford University Press, 1990.

Mead, Rebecca. "Downtown's Daughter." *New Yorker*, November 15, 2010. https://www.newyorker.com/magazine/2010/11/15/downtowns-daughter.

Meglin, Joellen A. "'Sauvages, Sex Roles, and Semiotics': Representations of Native Americans in the French Ballet, 1736–1837; Part Two: The Nineteenth Century." *Dance Chronicle* 23, no. 3 (2000): 275–320.

Meighan, Josephine. "Elsie Janis: The Girl Who Sees Fun in Everyone." *The Globe*, ca. 1905. Elsie Janis Scrapbook. TRI.

Memphis Daily Appeal. "Booth's Welcome." January 21, 1882. Edwin Booth 1881–82 Season Scrapbook. HBTL.

Menefee, David W. *Sarah Bernhardt in the Theatre of Films and Sound Recordings*. Jefferson, NC: McFarland, 2003.

Meeuf, Russell. *Rebellious Bodies: Stardom, Citizenship, and the New Body Politics*. Austin: University of Texas Press, 2017.

Meeuwis, Michael. "Everyone's Theater: Literary Culture and Daily Life in England, 1860–1914." PhD diss., University of Chicago, 2011.

———. "'The Theatre Royal Back Drawing-Room': Professionalizing Domestic Entertainment in Victorian Acting Manuals." *Victorian Studies* 54, no. 3 (Spring 2012): 427–37.

The Mercury. "The Lyceum." November 13, 1881.

Merrill, Lisa. *When Romeo Was a Woman: Charlotte Cushman and Her Circle of Female Spectators*. Ann Arbor: University of Michigan Press, 2000.

Mikhail, E. H., ed. *Oscar Wilde: Interviews and Recollections*. Vol. 1. London: Macmillan Press, 1979.

Mill, John Stuart. *On Liberty*. Edited by Currin V. Shields. Indianapolis: Bobbs-Merrill Company, 1956. First published 1859.

Miller, Monica L. *Slaves to Fashion: Black Dandyism and the Styling of Black Diasporic Identity*. Durham, NC: Duke University Press, 2009.

Milne, Esther. *Letters, Postcards, Email: Technologies of Presence*. New York: Routledge, 2010.

Modern Screen. "Success—The Hard Way." April 1939.

Moers, Ellen. *The Dandy: Brummell to Beerbohm*. Lincoln: University of Nebraska Press, 1978. First published 1960.

Mole, Tom. *Byron's Romantic Celebrity*. London: Palgrave Macmillan, 2007.

Moonshine. "Before the Footlights." July 5, 1879.

———. "More (Bern)hart-Rending Accounts from America." January 1, 1881.

———. "Mdlle. Bernhardt Has Made a Success in 'La Dame aux Camelias.'" June 25, 1881.

———. "Oscar Wilde—Very Wild." n.d. Box 10, Oscar Wilde in America, Clippings. WAC.

Moody, Jane. *Illegitimate Theatre in London, 1770–1840*. Cambridge: Cambridge University Press, 2000.

Moore, F. Michael. *Drag! Male and Female Impersonators on Stage, Screen and Television: An Illustrated World History*. Jefferson, NC: McFarland, 1994.

Moreno, Marguerite. *Souvenirs de ma vie*. Paris: Éditions de Flore, 1948.

Morin, Edgar. *Les Stars*. Paris: Éditions du Seuil, 1957.

Morris, Clara. *Life on the Stage*. Cabin John, MD: Wildside Press, 1977. First published 1901.

Müller, Simone M. *Wiring the World: The Social and Cultural Creation of Global Telegraph Networks*. New York: Columbia University Press, 2016.

Munsterberg, Hugo. *The Photoplay: A Psychological Study*. New York: Appleton, 1916.

Murray, Susan. *Hitch Your Antenna to the Stars: Early Television and Broadcast Stardom*. New York: Routledge, 2005.

———. "Trump's 'Fake News Awards' and the Danger of a Reality TV Presidency." *Newsweek*, January 16, 2018. http://www.newsweek.com/trump-fake-news-awards-danger-reality-tv-presidency-782586.

Myra's Journal of Dress and Fashion. "Description of Our Engravings." March 1, 1878.
———. "Dress." March 1, 1878.
———. "The Latest Fashions from Paris." April 1, 1875.
The Nation. "Notes." November 16, 1876.
Naugrette, Florence. *Le Théâtre romantique: Histoire, écriture, mise en scène*. Paris: Éditions du Seuil, 2001.
Naugrette-Christophe, Catherine. *Paris sous le second empire: Le théâtre et la ville*. Paris: Librairie théâtrale, 1998.
Neville, Richard. "Plays and Players." *Los Angeles Times*, May 5, 1901.
Newbury, Michael. "Celebrity Watching." *American Literary History* 12, no. 1&2 (Spring/Summer 2000): 272–83.
Newton, Lord. *Retrospection*. London: John Murray, 1941.
New York American. "Bernhardt Mobbed by Cheering Women at the Pier." November 20, 1905. Gr Fol-Ico-Per. BnF-DAS.
New York Herald. "'Adrienne Lecouvreur' at Booth's Theatre." November 9, 1880.
———. "The Scene at Booth's." November 10, 1880. SB Box 2, 1880s Clippings. HTC.
New York Times. "Adelaide Ristori." October 10, 1906.
———. "A Great French Actress. Daily Life of Sarah Bernhardt." January 12, 1878. SB 1870s Clippings. HTC.
———. "Amusements." November 16, 1880.
———. "Arrival of Rachel." August 23, 1855.
———. "Cap and Gown." May 22, 2015. http://www.nytimes.com/interactive/2015/05/22/us/23commencement.html?_r=0.
———. "Fortunes of the Famous: Instances of Unstable Glory." July 15, 1879.
———. "London Gossip of the Day." June 30, 1879.
———. "Maude Adams as the Stricken Eaglet." October 23, 1900.
———. "Sinatra at White House; He Talks to President at Tea About Making Girls Swoon." September 29, 1944.
———. "Sinatra Fans Pose Two Police Problems and Not the Less Serious Involves Truancy." October 13, 1944.
———. "My Impressions of Sarah Bernhardt. By Her American Manager." October 1915. Mounted Clippings—SB Box 3. HTC.
Ng, Alfred. "Rihanna Slams Snapchat over Controversial Ad: 'Shame on You.'" CNET, March 15, 2018. https://www.cnet.com/news/rihanna-slams-snapchat-over-controversial-ad-shame-on-you/.
Nolletti Jr., Arthur. "Classical Hollywood, 1928–1946." In *Acting*, edited by Claudia Springer and Julie Levinson, 49–73. New Brunswick, NJ: Rutgers University Press, 2015.
Nord, David Paul. *Communities of Journalism: A History of American Newspapers and Their Readers*. Urbana: University of Illinois Press, 2001.
Nowatzki, Robert. *Representing African Americans in Transatlantic Abolitionism and Blackface Minstrelsy*. Baton Rouge: Louisiana State University Press, 2010.
Nussbaum, Felicity. *Rival Queens: Actresses, Performance, and the Eighteenth-Century British Theater*. Philadelphia: University of Pennsylvania Press, 2010.
The Observer. "At the Play." June 19, 1881.
Ockman, Carol, and Kenneth E. Silver. *Sarah Bernhardt: The Art of High Drama*. New Haven, CT: Yale University Press, published in association with the Jewish Museum, New York, 2005.
Odell, George Clinton Densmore. *Annals of the New York Stage*. Vol. 11, *1879–1882*. New York: AMS Press, 1970.
O'Neill, Bonnie Carr. *Literary Celebrity and Public Life in the Nineteenth-Century United States*. Athens: University of Georgia Press, 2017.

———. "The Personal Public Sphere of Whitman's 1840s Journalism." *PMLA* 126, no. 4 (October 2011): 983–98.

Otis, Laura. *Networking: Communicating with Bodies and Machines in the Nineteenth Century*. Ann Arbor: University of Michigan Press, 2011.

The Owl. "Players of the Day, No. VIII: Sarah Bernhardt." July 7, 1882.

Pall Mall Gazette. "Letter from Paris." December 19, 1873.

Parodi, Alexandre. *Rome vaincue*. Paris: E. Dentu, 1876.

Pascoe, Judith. *The Sarah Siddons Audio Files*. Ann Arbor: University of Michigan Press, 2013.

Pearl, Sharrona, and Dana Polan. "Bodies of Digital Celebrity." *Public Culture* 27, no. 1 (January 2015): 185–92.

Pellegrini, Ann. *Performance Anxieties: Staging Psychoanalysis, Staging Race*. New York: Routledge, 1997.

People. "Trend Report." May 9, 2016.

Perry, Gill, Joseph Roach, and Shearer West. *The First Actresses: Nell Gwyn to Sarah Siddons*. Ann Arbor: University of Michigan Press, 2011.

Petersen, Anne Helen. *Too Fat, Too Slutty, Too Loud: The Rise and Reign of the Unruly Woman*. New York: Plume, 2017.

Pettitt, Clare. *"Dr. Livingstone, I Presume?": Missionaries, Journalists, Explorers and Empire*. Cambridge, MA: Harvard University Press, 2007.

———. "Livingstone: From Fame to Celebrity." In *David Livingstone: Man, Myth and Legacy*, edited by Sarah Worden, 83–99. Edinburgh: National Museums of Scotland, 2012.

———. "Topos, Taxonomy, and Travel in Nineteenth-Century Women's Scrapbooks." In *Travel Writing, Visual Culture and Form, 1760–1900*, edited by Mary Henes and Brian H. Murray, 21–41. Houndmills: Palgrave Macmillan, 2016.

Philadelphia Inquirer. "The Fate of a Chicken Croquette." February 5, 1911.

Pickering, Michael. "White Skin, Black Masks: 'Nigger' Minstrelsy in Victorian England." In *Music Hall: Performance and Style*, edited by J. S. Bratton. Milton Keynes: Open University Press, 1986.

Press (New York). "The Lyceum." November 13, 1881. Booth Tour Scrapbook, 1881–82. HBTL.

The Prompt-Book: Shakespeare's Tragedy of Hamlet as Presented by Edwin Booth. New York: Francis Hart, 1881.

Pullen, Kirsten. *Actresses and Whores: On Stage and in Society*. Cambridge: Cambridge University Press, 2005.

Punch. "Punch at the French Play." June 14, 1879.

Qureshi, Sadiah. *Peoples on Parade: Exhibitions, Empire, and Anthropology in Nineteenth-Century Britain*. Chicago: University of Chicago Press, 2001.

Rancière, Jacques. "The Emancipated Spectator." In *The Emancipated Spectator*. Translated by Gregory Elliot. New York: Verso, 2009. Originally published as *Le spectateur emancipé* (Paris: Éditions La Fabrique, 2008).

Rappaport, Erika Diane. *Shopping for Pleasure: Women in the Making of London's West End*. Princeton, NJ: Princeton University Press, 2001.

Rasmussen, R. Kent, ed. *Dear Mark Twain: Letters from His Readers*. Berkeley: University of California Press, 2013.

Rastignac. "Sarah Bernhardt." *Le Soleil*. Ca. 1905. Gr Fol-Ico-Per, clipping. BnF-DAS.

Rebhorn, Matthew. *Pioneer Performances: Staging the Frontier*. Oxford: Oxford University Press, 2012.

Redmond, Sean. "Introduction to Part Two." In *A Companion to Celebrity*, edited by P. David Marshall and Sean Redmond. Chichester, UK: Wiley Blackwell, 2016.

Ribblesdale, Lady Emma. *Letters and Diaries*. London: Chiswick Press, 1930.

Richards, Jason. *Imitation Nation: Red, White, and Blackface in Early and Antebellum US Literature*. Charlottesville: University of Virginia Press, 2017.

Reed Jr., Isaac. *Too Thin, or Skeleton Sara*. New York: Evans & Kelly, 1880.

Remnick, David. "The Outsized Life of Mumammad Ali." *New Yorker*, June 4, 2016. http://www.newyorker.com/news/news-desk/the-outsized-life-of-muhammad-ali.

Renner, A. L. *Sarah Bernhardt, Artist and Woman*. New York: A. Blanck, 1896.

Reynolds, Mac. "Daughter Wants to See Elvis? 'Kick Her in the Teeth!'" *Vancouver Sun*, August 31, 1957.

Rice, Edw[ard] Le Roy, *Monarchs of Minstrelsy, from "Daddy" Rice to Date* (New York: Kenny Publishing Company, 1911).

Roach, Joseph R. *Cities of the Dead: Circum-Atlantic Performance*. New York: Columbia University Press, 1996.

———. *It*. Ann Arbor: University of Michigan Press, 2007.

———. *The Player's Passion: Studies in the Science of Acting*. Ann Arbor: University of Michigan Press, 1993.

Roberts, Jennifer L. *Transporting Visions: The Movement of Images in Early America*. Berkeley: University of California Press, 2014.

Roberts, Mary Louise. *Disruptive Acts: The New Woman in Fin-de-Siècle France*. Chicago: University of Chicago Press, 2002.

Robertson, Jennifer Ellen. *Takarazuka: Sexual Politics and Popular Culture in Modern Japan*. Berkeley: University of California Press, 2001. First published 1998.

Robertson Wojcik, Pam. "Typecasting." *Criticism* 45, no. 2 (Spring 2003): 223–50.

Rocky Mountain News. "Sarah Bernhardt's Newest Gloves." September 2, 1883.

Rojek, Chris. *Celebrity*. London: Reaktion Books, 2001.

Rolling Stone. "Madonna Fights Back: Inside Rolling Stone's New Issue." February 25, 2015. https://www.rollingstone.com/music/news/madonna-fights-back-inside-rolling-stones-new-issue-20150225.

Ross, Alex. "The Frankfurt School Knew Trump Was Coming." *New Yorker*, December 5, 2016. https://www.newyorker.com/culture/cultural-comment/the-frankfurt-school-knew-trump-was-coming.

Ross, Alice, and agencies. "Andy Murray Says He Was Stalked around Europe by a Hotel Maid." *The Guardian*, October 4, 2016. https://www.theguardian.com/sport/2016/oct/04/andy-murray-stalked-hotel-maid-fan.

Ruttenburg, Nancy. *Democratic Personality: Popular Voice and the Trial of American Authorship*. Stanford, CA: Stanford University Press, 1998.

Sadler, Thomas, ed. *Diary, Reminiscences and Correspondence of Henry Crabb Robinson*. Vol. 3. London: Macmillan, 1869.

Said, Edward. *Orientalism*. New York: Pantheon, 1978.

Salmon, Eric. "Introduction." In *Bernhardt and the Theater of Her Time*, edited by Eric Salmon, 3–12. Westport, CT: Greenwood Press, 1984.

Salmon, Richard. *Henry James and the Culture of Publicity*. Cambridge: Cambridge University Press, 1997.

Samuels, Maurice. *The Right to Difference: French Universalism and the Jews*. Chicago: University of Chicago Press, 2016.

Sanborn, Geoffrey. *Plagiarama!: William Wells Brown and the Aesthetic of Attractions*. New York: Columbia University Press, 2015.

Sanders, Lloyd Charles. *Celebrities of the Century: Being a Dictionary of Men and Women of the Nineteenth Century*. London: Cassell, 1890.

San Francisco Examiner. "How Bernhardt Dresses." May 24, 1891.

Sarah Bernhardt: Paris Sketches. Boston: Moore, 1880. FL 398.7.25. HTC.

Saxton, Alexander. *The Rise and Fall of the White Republic: Class Politics and Mass Culture in Nineteenth-Century America*. London: Verso, 2003. First published 1990.

Schickel, Richard. *Intimate Strangers: The Culture of Celebrity*. Garden City, NY: Doubleday, 1985.

Schraeder, Fred. F. "Bernhardt as Marguerite." *Washington Post*, January 3, 1906.

Schudson, Michael. *Discovering the News: A Social History of American Newspapers*. New York: Basic Books, 1978.

Schurmann, Impresario. *Les Étoiles en voyage. La Patti—Sarah Bernhardt—Coquelin*. Paris: Tresse & Stock, 1893.

Schwartz, Vanessa R. *Spectacular Realities: Early Mass Culture in Fin-de-Siècle Paris*. Berkeley: University of California Press, 1999.

Schweitzer, Marlis. *Transatlantic Broadway: The Infrastructural Politics of Global Performance*. Houndmills: Palgrave Macmillan, 2015.

——. *When Broadway Was the Runway: Theater, Fashion, and American Culture*. Philadelphia: University of Pennsylvania Press, 2009.

Scott, Clement. *Some Notable Hamlets of the Present Time*. London: Greening, 1900.

——. "The Playhouses." June 18, 1892. Clippings–Misc. HTC.

Scott, Derek B. *Sounds of the Metropolis: The 19th-Century Popular Music Revolution in London, New York, Paris and Vienna*. New York: Oxford University Press, 2008. https://doi.org/10.1093/acprof:oso/9780195309461.001.0001.

Scott, Joan Wallach. *Gender and the Politics of History*. New York: Columbia University Press, 1988.

——. *Only Paradoxes to Offer: French Feminists and the Rights of Man*. Cambridge, MA: Harvard University Press, 1996.

Seitz, Don C. *The James Gordon Bennetts: Father and Son, Proprietors of the* New York Herald. Indianapolis: Bobbs-Merrill, 1928.

Senelick, Laurence. *The Changing Room: Sex, Drag and Theatre*. London: Routledge, 2000.

Sessions, Jennifer E. *By Sword and Plow: France and the Conquest of Algeria*. Ithaca, NY: Cornell University Press, 2011.

Shapiro, Janice. "Crushable: John Lennon." In *Crush: Writers Reflect on Love, Longing, and the Lasting Power of Their First Celebrity Crush*, edited by Cathy Alter and Dave Singleton, 61–71. New York: HarperCollins, 2016.

Shaw, George Bernard. "Duse and Bernhardt." In *Dramatic Opinions and Essays*, vol. 1, 134–42. New York: Brentano's, 1909. First published 1895.

——. "Sardoodledom." *Saturday Review*, June 1, 1895.

Shepard, Richard F. "Stokowski Talks of Something Called Beatles." *New York Times*, February 15, 1964.

Sherman, Stuart. "Garrick among Media: The 'Now' Performer Navigates the News." *PMLA* 126, no. 4 (October 2011): 966–82.

Silver, Kenneth E. "Sarah Bernhardt and the Theatrics of French Nationalism: From Roland's Daughter to Napoleon's Son." In Ockman and Silver, *Sarah Bernhardt*, 75–97.

Simone, Alina. *Madonnaland: And Other Detours into Fame and Fandom*. Austin: University of Texas Press, 2016.

Simpson, J. A., and E. S. C. Weiner. "Fan." *Oxford English Dictionary*, 2nd ed. Oxford: Oxford University Press, 1989.

Sinnema, Peter W. *The Wake of Wellington: Englishness in 1852*. Athens: Ohio University Press, 2006.

Skolsky, Sidney. "That's Hollywood for You." *Photoplay*, April 1955.

Smalley, George W. "Anglo-American Memories." *New York Tribune*, May 22, 1910.

Smith, Matthew Wilson. *The Nervous Stage: Nineteenth-Century Neuroscience and the Birth of Modern Theater*. New York: Oxford University Press, 2018.

Smoodin, Eric Loren. *Regarding Frank Capra: Audience, Celebrity, and American Film Studies, 1930–1960*. Durham, NC: Duke University Press, 2004.

Soloski, Alexis. "Laura Linney and Cynthia Nixon, Swapping Parts in 'The Little Foxes.'" *New York Times*, April 19, 2017. https://www.nytimes.com/2017/04/19/theater/little -foxes-review-cynthia-nixon-laura-linney.html.

Some Letters from a Man of No Importance: 1895–1914. London: Jonathan Cape, 1928.

Sporting Gazette. "At the Play." June 7, 1879.

———. "At the Play." July 12, 1879.

———. "The Garden." July 12, 1879.

———. "Sarah Bernhardt's Rehearsals." December 18, 1880.

———. "The Turf Market." March 26, 1881.

Sprague, William Bell. *Visits to European Celebrities*. Boston: Gould and Lincoln, 1855.

Stacey, Jackie. *Star Gazing: Hollywood Cinema and Female Spectatorship*. London: Routledge, 1994.

Stadler, Gustavus. *Troubling Minds: The Cultural Politics of Genius in the United States, 1840–1890*. Minneapolis: University of Minnesota Press, 2006.

Stamp, Shelley. *Movie-Struck Girls: Women and Motion Picture Culture after the Nickelodeon*. Princeton, NJ: Princeton University Press, 2000.

Stanton, Domna C. *The Aristocrat as Art: A Study of the Honnête Homme and the Dandy in Seventeenth- and Nineteenth-Century French Literature*. New York: Columbia University Press, 1980.

Sternheimer, Karen. *Celebrity Culture and the American Dream: Stardom and Social Mobility*. New York: Routledge, 2011.

Stetz, Margaret D. *Facing the Victorians: Portraits of Writers and Artists from the Mark Samuels Lasner Collection*. Newark, DE: University of Delaware Press, 2007.

Stevens, Alfred, and Henry Gervex. "Paris Panorama of the Nineteenth Century." *The Century*, December 1889.

Stokes, John, Michael R. Booth, and Susan Bassnett. *Bernhardt, Terry, Duse: The Actress in Her Time*. Cambridge: Cambridge University Press, 1988.

Stoneman, Patsy. *Jane Eyre on Stage, 1848–1898*. Aldershot: Ashgate, 2007.

Stowe, Harriet Beecher. "Sojourner Truth, the Libyan Sibyl." *The Atlantic*, April 1863.

Strachey, Lytton. "Sarah Bernhardt." *Nation and Athenaeum*, May 5, 1923. SB Mounted Clippings—Scrapbook. HTC.

Surkis, Judith. *Sexing the Citizen: Morality and Masculinity in France, 1870–1920*. Ithaca, NY: Cornell University Press, 2006.

Susman, Warren. *Culture as History: The Transformation of American Society in the Twentieth Century*. New York: Pantheon, 1984.

Symons, Arthur. "Drama. Sarah Bernhardt." *The Academy*, June 21, 1902.

Taranow, Gerda. *Sarah Bernhardt: The Art within the Legend*. Princeton, NJ: Princeton University Press, 1972.

Terdiman, Richard. *Discourse/Counter-Discourse: The Theory and Practice of Symbolic Resistance in Nineteenth-Century France*. Ithaca, NY: Cornell University Press, 1989.

The Times. "Gaiety Theatre—French Plays." July 10, 1883.

Tocqueville, Alexis de. *Democracy in America: And Two Essays on America*. Translated by Gerald E. Bevan. London: Penguin, 2003. Originally published, in French, in 1835.

Toll, Robert C. *Blacking Up: The Minstrel Show in Nineteenth-Century America*. New York: Oxford University Press, 1974.

Tompkins, Kyla Wazana. *Racial Indigestion: Eating Bodies in the Nineteenth Century*. New York: New York University Press, 2012.

Tongson, Karen. "Empty Orchestra: The Karaoke Standard and Pop Celebrity." *Public Culture* 27, no. 1 (January 2015): 85–108.

Townshend, Chauncy Hare. *Facts in Mesmerism, with Reasons for a Dispassionate Inquiry into It*. New York: Harper & Brothers, 1843. First published 1840.

Towse, J. Ranken. "Mary Anderson." In *The American Theatre as Seen by Its Critics*, edited by Montrose J. Moses and John Mason Brown. New York: W. W. Norton, 1934.

Tucker, Jennifer. *Nature Exposed: Photography as Eyewitness in Victorian Science*. Baltimore: Johns Hopkins University Press, 2005.

———. "Voyages of Discovery on Oceans of Air: Scientific Observation and the Image of Science in the Age of 'Balloonacy.' " *Osiris*, 2nd ser., 11, Science in the Field (1996): 144–76.

Tuite, Clara. *Lord Byron and Scandalous Celebrity*. Cambridge: Cambridge University Press, 2014.

Tur, Katy. *Unbelievable: My Front-Row Seat to the Craziest Campaign in American History*. New York: Dey Street Books, 2017.

Turner, Kay, ed. *I Dream of Madonna: Women's Dreams of the Goddess of Pop*. San Francisco: Collins, 1993.

Turner, Victor. *Dramas, Fields, and Metaphors: Symbolic Action in Human Society*. Ithaca, NY: Cornell University Press, 1974.

Turnock, Robert. *Interpreting Diana: Television Audiences and the Death of a Princess*. London: British Film Institute, 2000.

Urner, Nathan D. "Actress and Rajpoot, or Bernhardt's Bete Noire." *New York Clipper*, May 27, 1882. SB Clippings, 1880s. HTC.

US Weekly. "Red Carpet: Cardinal Rulers." May 9, 2016.

———. "Who Wore It Best?" May 9, 2016.

Variety. "Elvis Presley-Digitation Churns Up Teen Tantrums, Scribe Raps, So-So B.O." May 30, 1956.

———. "Haley 16G, San Antonio." May 30, 1956.

———. "Marilyn Wins Concessions in Return to 20th." January 5, 1956.

———. "Teeners Figure in Haley Riots on Rock 'n' Roll." May 30, 1956.

Vassault, Lawrence. "Sarah Bernhardt." *The Cosmopolitan*, April 1901.

Verneuil, Louis. *La Vie merveilleuse de Sarah Bernhardt*. Paris: Brentano's, 1942.

Vlock, Deborah. *Dickens, Novel Reading, and the Victorian Popular Theatre*. Cambridge: Cambridge University Press, 1998.

von Geldern, James, and Louise McReynolds, eds. *Entertaining Tsarist Russia: Tales, Songs, Plays, Movies, Jokes, Ads, and Images from Russian Urban Life, 1779–1917*. Bloomington: Indiana University Press, 1998.

Voskuil, Lynn M. *Acting Naturally: Victorian Theatricality and Authenticity*. Charlottesville: University of Virginia Press, 2004.

Voss, Frederick S. "Portraying an American Original: The Likenesses of Davy Crockett." *Southwestern Historical Quarterly* 91, no. 4 (April 1988): 457–82.

Walkley, Arthur Bingham. *Playhouse Impressions*. London: T. Fisher Unwin, 1892.

Walkowitz, Judith R. *City of Dreadful Delight: Narratives of Sexual Danger in Late-Victorian London*. Chicago: University of Chicago Press, 1992.

Wanko, Cheryl. *Roles of Authority: Thespian Biography and Celebrity in Eighteenth-Century Britain*. Lubbock: Texas Tech University Press, 2003.

Ward, Mrs. Humphrey. *A Writer's Recollections*. Vol. 1. New York: Harper & Brothers, 1918.

Ware, W. Porter, and Thaddeus C. Lockard Jr. *P. T. Barnum Presents Jenny Lind: The American Tour of the Swedish Nightingale*. Baton Rouge: Louisiana State University Press, 1980.

Warner, Michael. *Publics and Counterpublics*. New York: Zone Books, 2002.

Washington Post. "Bernhardt's 'L'Aiglon.' " December 2, 1900.

———. "Eaglet of Bernhardt." January 15, 1901.

———. "One View of the Eaglets." December 16, 1900.

Waterhouse, Richard. "The Internationalisation of American Popular Culture in the Nineteenth Century: The Case of the Minstrel Show." *Australasian Journal of American Studies* 4, no. 1 (July 1985): 1–11.

Watson, Nicola J. "Fandom Mapped: Rousseau, Scott, and Byron on the Itinerary of Lady Frances Shelley." "Romantic Fandom," ed. Eric Eisner, a volume of *Romantic Circles Praxis Series* (April 2011). https://www.rc.umd.edu/praxis/fandom/praxis.fandom.2010.watson.html.

Watts, Duncan J. *Everything Is Obvious: Once You Know the Answer.* New York: Crown Business, 2011.

West, Rebecca. *Ending in Earnest: A Literary Log.* Freeport, NY: Books for Libraries Press, 1967. First published 1931.

Wichard, Robin, and Carol Wichard. *Victorian Cartes-de-Visite.* Princes Risborough: Shire Publications, 1999.

Wilde, Oscar. "Literary and Other Notes III." In *Selected Journalism*, edited by Anya Clayworth, 107–111. Oxford: Oxford University Press, 2004.

———. Oscar Wilde to Bernulf Clegg, 1891. Morgan Library and Museum. https://www.themorgan.org/collection/oscar-wilde/manuscripts-letters/36.

———. *The Complete Letters of Oscar Wilde.* Edited by Rupert Hart-Davis and Merlin Holland. New York: Henry Holt, 2000.

Williams, Carolyn. *Gilbert and Sullivan: Gender, Genre, Parody.* New York: Columbia University Press, 2011.

———. "Melodrama." In *The Cambridge History of Victorian Literature.* Edited by Kate Flint. Cambridge: Cambridge University Press, 2012.

Williams, Henry L. *All About Sarah "Barnum" Bernhardt, Her Loveys, Her Doveys, Her Capers, and Her Funniments.* London: International Publishing Offices, 1884.

Wilson, Garff B. *A History of American Acting.* Bloomington: Indiana University Press, 1966.

Wilson, John S. "2,900-Voice Chorus Joins the Beatles." *New York Times.* February 13, 1964.

Winans, Robert B., "Early Minstrel Music, 1843–1852," in Bean, Hatch, and McNamara, *Inside the Minstrel Mask*, 141–62.

Winchell, Joseph R. "Joy Family Papers," October 1, 1851. Joy Family Papers. RBML.

Winter, William. "Mme. Bernhardt at the Lyric: Camille." *New York Tribune*, December 13, 1905.

Woodmansee, Martha. *The Author, Art, and the Market: Rereading the History of Aesthetics.* New York: Columbia University Press, 1994.

Woolf, Virginia. "The Memoirs of Sarah Bernhardt." In *Books and Portraits: Some Further Selections from the Literary and Biographical Writings of Virginia Woolf*, edited by Mary Lyon, 201–7. New York: Harcourt Brace Jovanovich, 1977.

World Magazine, "Elsie Janis Tells Herself a Story." October 29, 1905. Elsie Janis Scrapbook. TRI.

Worthen, William B. *The Idea of the Actor.* Princeton, NJ: Princeton University Press, 1984.

Zi-Zim. "Sarah Bernhardt." *Les Femmes du jour*, April 3, 1886. 4* Fol-Ico-Per, clipping. BnF-DAS.

ILLUSTRATION CREDITS

Figures 7.6 and 8.3: Western Reserve Historical Society (WRHS).

Figure 7.8: Theater Scrapbooks (Gift of Museum of the City of New York), Ms. #1767. Rare Book and Manuscript Library, Columbia University Libraries (RBML).

Figures 8.1 and 8.2: AF archive/Alamy Stock Photo.

INDEX

Note: SB in subheadings refers to Sarah Bernhardt. Illustrations are indicated with **bold** font.